NEW DIRECTIONS IN CHILDREN'S AND ADOLESCENTS' INFORMATION BEHAVIOR RESEARCH

LIBRARY AND INFORMATION SCIENCE

Series Editor: **Jens-Erik Mai**

Recent and Forthcoming Volumes

Christine Bruce, Kate Davis, Hilary Hughes, Helen Partridge, and Ian Stoodley
Information Experience: Approaches to Theory and Practice

Mark Hepworth and Geoff Walton
Developing People's Information Capabilities: Fostering Information Literacy in Educational, Workplace and Community Contexts

Jung-Ran Park and Lynne C. Howarth
New Directions in Information Organization

Amanda Spink and Jannica Heinström
Trends and Research: Europe

Gunilla Widén and Kim Holmberg
Social Information Research

Dirk Lewandowski
Web Search Engine Research

Donald Case
Looking for Information, Third Edition

Amanda Spink and Diljit Singh
Trends and Research: Asia-Oceania

Amanda Spink and Jannica Heinström
New Directions in Information Behaviour

Eileen G. Abels and Deborah P. Klein
Business Information: Needs and Strategies

Leo Egghe
Power Laws in the Information Production Process: Lotkaian Informetrics

Mike Thelwall
Link Analysis: An Information Science Approach

Matthew Locke Saxton and John V. Richardson
Understanding Reference Transactions: Transforming an Art into a Science

Robert M. Hayes
Models for Library Management, Decision-Making, and Planning

Charles T. Meadow, Bert R. Boyce, and Donald H. Kraft
Text Information Retrieval Systems, Second Edition

A. J. Meadows
Communicating Research

V. Frants, J. Shiparo, and V. Votskunskii
Automated Information Retrieval: Theory and Methods

LIBRARY AND INFORMATION SCIENCE

NEW DIRECTIONS IN CHILDREN'S AND ADOLESCENTS' INFORMATION BEHAVIOR RESEARCH

EDITED BY

DANIA BILAL
School of Information Sciences, University of Tennessee, Knoxville, TN, USA

and

JAMSHID BEHESHTI
School of Information Studies, McGill University, Montreal, Quebec, Canada

Series Editor: Jens-Erik Mai

Emerald

United Kingdom • North America • Japan
India • Malaysia • China

Emerald Group Publishing Limited
Howard House, Wagon Lane, Bingley BD16 1WA, UK

First edition 2014

British Library Cataloguing in Publication Data
A catalogue record for this book is available from the British Library

ISBN: 978-1-78350-813-6
ISSN: 1876-0562 (Series)

Contents

SECTION II: SPECIAL POPULATION

SECTION III: DESIGNING SYSTEMS

List of Reviewers

June Abbas
College of Arts and Sciences, School of Library and Information Studies, University of Oklahoma, Norman, OK, USA

Eliza Dresang
Information School, University of Washington, Mary Gates Hall, Seattle, WA, USA

Jannica Heinström
Information Studies, School of Business and Economics, Abo Akademi University, Turku, Finland

Heidi Julien
Department of Library and Information Studies, University at Buffalo, State University of New York, Buffalo, NY, USA

Ya-Ling Lu
Department of Library & Information Science, School of Communication and Information, Rutgers University, New Brunswick, NJ, USA

A. D. Madden
Learning and Teaching Services, University of Sheffield, Sheffield, UK

Lynne McKechnie
Faculty of Information & Media Studies, University of Western Ontario, London, ON, Canada

Ross Todd
Department of Library & Information Science, School of Communication and Information, Rutgers University, New Brunswick, NJ, USA

List of Contributors

Dhary Abuhimed	School of Information Studies, McGill University, Montreal, Quebec, Canada
Naresh Kumar Agarwal	Graduate School of Library and Information Science, Simmons College, Boston, MA, USA
Mohammed J. AlGhamdi	School of Information Studies, McGill University, Montreal, Quebec, Canada
Jamshid Beheshti	School of Information Studies, McGill University, Montreal, Quebec, Canada
Dania Bilal	School of Information Sciences, College of Communication and Information, University of Tennessee, Knoxville, TN, USA
Ann Peterson Bishop	Graduate School of Library and Information Science, University of Illinois, USA
Charles Cole	School of Information Studies, McGill University, Montreal, Quebec, Canada
Stacy Creel	School of Library and Information Science, The University of Southern Mississippi, Hattiesburg, MS, USA
Philip Fawcett	Microsoft Research, Redmond, WA, USA; University of Washington Information School, Seattle, WA, USA
Karen E. Fisher	Information School, Communication, University of Washington, Seattle, WA, USA
Valerie Jopeck	School of Information Sciences, College of Communication and Information, University of Tennessee, Knoxville, TN, USA

Isabelle Lamoureux	School of Information Studies, McGill University, Montreal, Quebec, Canada
Audrey Laplante	École de bibliothéconomie et des sciences de l'information, Université de Montréal, Montréal, Québec, Canada
Spencer C. Lilley	Te Pūtahi a Toi: School of Māori Art, Knowledge and Education, Massey University, New Zealand
Lassana Magassa	University of Washington Information School, Seattle, WA, USA
Marcia A. Mardis	School of Library and Information Studies, Florida State University, Tallahassee, FL, USA
Bharat Mehra	School of Information Sciences, College of Communication and Information, University of Tennessee, Knoxville, TN, USA
Valerie Nesset	Graduate School of Education, State University of New York at Buffalo, Buffalo, NY, USA
Laura I. Spears	School of Library and Information Studies, Florida State University, Tallahassee, FL, USA

Editorial Advisory Board

Introduction

"Children are our future" goes a famous song. Children and adolescents are the future professionals, doctors, lawyers, engineers, trades people, and researchers. They are growing up in an era that has provided them with the Web, mobile technologies, text messaging, social networks, and virtual reality gaming worlds. Many of these digital natives, Millennials, or the Google generation have not in all likelihood used a traditional hardcopy encyclopedia or a library card catalog to find a book in the library. They are, however, versed in using the new information and communication technologies to multitask, collaborate, produce, and consume terabytes of information. Their information behavior is being transformed through a paradigm shift, from the physical libraries to virtual libraries, from printed text to multimedia websites, and from traditional reference tools to online forums and blogs.

During the past three decades, an increasing number of scholars have engaged in research on the information behavior of children and youth. The culmination of this research has shown that children and adolescents encounter challenges and obstacles in searching for information, retrieving relevant results for specific tasks, as well as experience difficulty comprehending and interpreting results in various information environments. The new generation tends to skim and surf for information, is constantly multitasking, engages in collaborative behavior, and creates and shares information on social networks.

The *Library and Information Science* series, the *New Directions in Children's and Adolescents' Information Behavior Research* comprises contributions from scholars, who have ventured beyond the traditional research on the children's and youth's information behavior to respond to the 21st century challenges. This book presents innovative research in three primary sections. Section I: Through the Ages; Section II: Special Population; and Section III: Designing Systems.

Section I consists of three contributed chapters on the information behavior of youth covering toddlers to adolescents. It begins with a chapter by

Naresh Kumar Agarwal titled, "Use of Touch Devices by Toddlers or Preschoolers: Observations and Findings from a Single-Case Study." Agarwal provides observational accounts of a child's use of and interaction with the iPhone and iPad as the child moves from being a toddler to a preschooler. The child's interaction with the physical environment does not deter her from engaging with the physical environment or from activities centered on creativity and interpersonal engagement. Supported by her parents, the child is able to move seamlessly between the digital and physical environments showing how and why she uses and engages with digital devices and physical objects. Agarwal provides a framework for a child's effective engagement with touch-based devices while ensuring all-round development. The framework includes four phases: point of engagement, sustained engagement, disengagement, and reengagement alongside the tasks performed and apps the child uses. Agarwal indicates that while the design of the touch-based devices influenced the child's engagement and interaction, the child experiences information overload and distraction. Parental intervention was necessary to reduce the overload, support the child's information discovery, and ensure access to appropriate content. Studies of toddlers and preschoolers information behavior and interaction with digital devices (i.e., iPhone and iPad) and physical environments are scarce. Agarwal's chapter will contribute to our understanding of what makes a digital native as young as two years old attracted to using touch-based devices and how the child engages with and disengages from these devices in favor of using the surrounding physical environment.

The second chapter in Section I by Valerie Nesset presents a model (Beginning, Acting, Telling (BAT)) in her chapter titled, "Depicting the Intersection between Information-Seeking Behavior and Information Literacy in the Research Process: A Model" for elementary school classroom. The BAT model is informed by empirical studies that Nesset conducted in previous research including a doctoral dissertation (2009). It has recently been successfully pilot-tested in two third-grade classrooms. In this chapter, Nesset provides an overview of research in which information-seeking behavior and information literacy models have intersected. The BAT model is the first model integrating features inherent in both information-seeking behavior and information literacy, which uses imagery and mnemonic to teach the research process to students, beginning in the earliest grades of elementary school. The BAT model has three stages: the beginning and telling stages which form the "wings," and the acting stage which forms the head of the bat (the animal). Using the bat as analogy, the wings, body, and head form a whole, giving equal importance to each stage of the information-seeking process. Nesset describes the key actions associated with each phase. The model integrates cognitive (Thinking and Reflection), affective behaviors (Feelings), and Things that Matter, associated with each stage. It depicts the three stages — Beginning, Acting, and Telling as fluid, iterative, and constantly in motion, depicting of the information-seeking process very differently from previously published models. Use of imagery, visual cues, and mnemonic provides unique and relevant representation of the process to which elementary school students relate. The model has implications for theory and practice. By using the BAT model as an instructional tool, teachers and librarians can instill use of images and mnemonic to help students in elementary school classroom environment to easily recognize, remember, and internalize the research process and build a foundation for life-long learning.

Use of resources in one's social network to seek help for schoolwork has hardly been investigated in the literature. In the third chapter of Section I, Audrey Laplante explores use of resources embedded in late adolescents' social networks to obtain help in completing assignments for schoolwork. Using in-depth interviewing, critical incident technique, and social network analysis, Laplante found that most adolescents (ages 14–17) had a solid personal social network but did not always take advantage of the resources embedded in it for schoolwork. Availability was the most important criteria for deciding who to approach for help. Social Network Services (SNSs) were often used to obtain the help they needed alongside phone calls and in-person visits. In exploring the core social network the adolescents used, Laplante found that most of them had the resources needed in their core social network to receive the help and support they needed for schoolwork. These resources consisted of strong ties with whom they had frequent in-person interactions and distant contacts. Adolescents sought different types of help (procedural, proofreading/comparing answers, factual, and executive), and preferred to seek help mostly from friends, followed by parents, classmates, and teachers. Analysis of the adolescents' sociograms show how seeking help gravitated toward specific actors and roles such as friendship ties, family ties, family and friendship ties, and others (e.g., teachers and school librarians). The findings from this study make significant contribution to our understanding of how and why late adolescents use resources in their social networks to seek help and support for schoolwork. They also have implications for services that educators and school librarians should provide to support the educational needs of these users including availability to provide help and support in-person and virtually.

Section II, Special Population, begins with a chapter authored by Dania Bilal and Valerie Jopeck titled, "Young Girls' Affective Responses to Access and Use of Information and Communication Technology (ICT) in Information-Poor Societies." The authors analyzed published literature in the fields of information science, human–computer interaction, ICT, and education technologies covering the period from early 1990s to mid-2014 to identify the status of published literature on young girls' affective responses to access and use of ICT in these countries' information-poor societies, in particular. They situated the literature review within theoretical frameworks including the affective paradigm, role of emotions in the process of information seeking. Erik Erikson's theory on meaningful technology and children's feeling of competence; gendered digital divide; Elfreda Chatman's information poverty theory, and Technology Acceptance Model (TAM). The review of research included focused areas such as young children's affective behavior in the United States, their behavior in cross-cultural environments, involvement in interface design, affective responses to access and use of ICT in the United States and developing countries, gender differences identified in work by scholars in the United States, studies on gender differences in ICT in developing countries, technology programs implemented in developing countries to narrow the digital divide in access to and use of ICT, and review of research on use of mobile technologies in developing countries. The authors found that while a large body of literature exists on ICT in developing countries, the study of user information behavior, youth information behavior, and young girls' affective information behavior in accessing and using ICT is almost non-existent. Despite the fact that many developing countries are investing in ICT to improve socioeconomic conditions, to bridge the digital divide, and to empower illiterate youth living in poor regions, there is a strong voice in the literature that is challenging disparity in access to and use of ICT. The authors noted that the fast penetration of mobile technologies in developing countries and its use by women and girls in urban and poor, rural regions, as well as the implementation of technology programs exported from the United States to these countries bring new opportunities for researchers to study user information behavior in general, and young girls' affective responses to access and use of ICT, in particular.

In the second chapter of Section II, Karen E. Fisher, Ann Peterson Bishop, Philip Fawcett, and Lassana Magassa report on a research project that explored how ethnic minority youth act as mediaries to help members of their social networks, especially elders, with everyday life situations through use of information and technology. Titled "InfoMe: A Field-Design Methodology for Research on Ethnic Minority Youth as Information Mediaries," the chapter reports on the Teen Design Days methodology the authors employed to gather information from 500 ethnic teen youth (immigrant and refugees) in six schools and multiple community partners in King County, Washington, on how this group of users engage as information mediaries in different community settings. The authors situated the understanding of InfoMe (Information Mediaries) in different contexts, including the everyday information worlds of youth, the information mediaries information behavior, and in the results of a 2010 nationwide impact study that provided evidence of ethnic minority youth as information mediaries. The focus of this chapter is on the Teen Design methodology the authors employed as a framework to gain a deeper understanding of how ethnic minority youth serve as information, technology, language, and cultural mediaries within their social networks and larger communities. Teens were involved in workshops to explore their information needs, information encountering, information creating and remixing, information management, information curation, and information sharing and giving. Youth experiences as mediaries were elicited using different innovative approaches including social mapping tools and cultural probes, which involved storytelling, images, and dramatic play, as well as design, prototyping, and programming principles. Teens used tools such as smartphones, laptops, Microsoft Surface, among others, to illustrate their InfoMe behavior. Findings showed that teens are largely unaware of their InfoMe behavior but are able to describe it with diagrams, role-playing skits, and brief written narratives. Teens served as active information mediaries for different types of people, including relatives, friends, known adults, and complete strangers. The authors noted that Teen Design Day methodology is highly helpful in understanding the social and information worlds of ethnic minority youth, as well as for developing relationships and ongoing partnerships with youth and community groups. Among the many implications the findings of this study provide is developing customized library and community services and tools that can be used in support of immigrants and other minority groups; developing software applications that employ the principles of personal information management to inform how information mediaries organize and keep track of the needs of people they are helping, and all the information they seek and share; and to develop understanding of the level of teens' information literacy that reflects their information seeking on behalf of the needs of other people.

Understanding the information behavior and needs of children with special needs (CSN) who live in impoverished areas such as the Southern and Central Appalachian region (SCA) was tackled by Bharat Mehra in his chapter, "Perspectives of Rural Librarians about the Information Behaviors of Children with Special Needs in the Southern and Central Appalachian Region: An Exploratory Study to Develop User-Centered Services." Based on interviewing and surveying 31 rural librarians, Mehra analyzed the most important information needs and wants of the CSN in the SCA rural libraries, information resources and services they seek and use, perceived need for providing effective library services, and ways that the SCA rural libraries can improve to better serve the CSN in their local communities. Emerging from the excruciating economic, social, and cultural conditions that have adversely affected library services and the population living in this region, and the lack of attention to the information needs of CSN in the SCA rural library environments, Mehra's study is grounded in theoretical frameworks of specific information behavior models and "linking theories to action." Based on analysis of qualitative and quantitative data, Mehra found that, among other things, key areas in developing and implementing improvements in user-centered effective library services for the CSN include: staff development and training, collections and services, programming and events planning, physical resources and appropriate policies and implementation, partnerships and community involvement, and alternative and creative revenue streams. Participating rural librarians suggested specific strategies for improving each of these key areas. They also indicated that a high number of CSN with different levels of special needs use the SCA rural library services. However, they did not have systematic documentation of the CSN information behaviors, or of the effectiveness of the library services they used to meet their needs. Of the key areas of library services identified, the participants commented on the need for education and training to develop better understanding of the CSN in the SCA region. Mehra's study is a first-time effort toward developing understanding of the information needs and information uses of the CSN in the SCA region through the lenses of the rural librarians that serve them. The findings challenge the notions stereotyping and marginalizing of the "South" and, especially the CSN who are well-deserving of effective services and of becoming successful information consumers and producers in the 21st century information society.

The last chapter in the special population section is written by Spencer C. Lilley who studied the information behavior of Māori secondary school students in New Zealand in the context of the social information grounds theorized by Karen Fisher and colleagues in 2005. Lilley surveyed 139 students, ages 16–18, from four diverse secondary schools. He also used six focus groups (total of 45 students) to gather and elicit information about the students' social networks. The study of indigenous people's information behavior, in general, and the behavior of Māori students, in particular, is an understudied area of research. Lilley's research addressed these two research questions: (1) Where at school do the students meet to share, exchange, and seek information and (2) What type of information do the students share, exchange, and seek. Lilley found that the students' main source of information was interpersonal interactions with friends, parents, siblings, teachers, and members of the extended family of the same indigenous group. Gathering points for the students were the school grounds, outside the attended school's convenient shop, restrooms, gymnasium, sports practice, and the smokers' hangout where students were not engaged in any formal educational practices. Students shared and exchanged different types of information in the gathered place that centered in large on social chatter, including gossip about people in the school; celebrities and family, and discussions about films, television programs, music, and schoolwork.

Although each of the schools had its unique features, the types of information grounds were very similar across the schools. Information "carriers" were the people who spread the information across groups. In sum, the findings of this study identified the importance that Māori students place on information obtained through their social networks. These networks played an instrumental role in assisting the students to understand the social and education environment in the affiliated schools. Thus, providing library services to these students should target their primary information grounds. Lilley provided suggestions for future research involving Māori students.

Section III, Designing Systems, consists of three chapters. It begins with a chapter written by Laura I. Spears and Marcia A. Mardis titled, "A Failure to Connect: The Elusive Relationship between Broadband Access and Children's Information Seeking in American Academic Research." The authors sought to identify gaps in the attention given to the role of broadband in the information-seeking environment of youth aged 5–18. The authors posited that despite the mounting broadband literature, very little focus had been given to the impact that access to and adoption of broadband had on information seeking of youth. The authors addressed four research questions in the context of an overarching question: What is the nature of academic research concerning broadband and children's information seeking in the United States? They employed a mixed method synthesis of research published in peer-reviewed journals between 1991 and 2011 that reported on the information seeking of youth. Based on specific terms the authors searched in nine online databases, 15 articles qualified for analysis. These were classified into one of Kuhlthau's Information Search Process (ISP) stages (Initiation, Selection, Exploration, Formulation, Collection, and Closure), which was used as a framework for designing, framing, and analyzing the investigation of information-seeking behavior of youth. The authors found that the ways in which broadband impacts imposed information seeking upon children in K-20 environments is not widely studied in scholarly research. Over twenty years of published research, only 15 studies considered broadband; no study included broadband until 1999. In few occurrences of published research, broadband appeared to have a minimal role in children's use of the Internet for schoolwork, especially in stage four of the ISP (Formulation). Due to the small number of qualified articles included in the study, the authors were unable to conduct the synthesis; instead, they conducted a quantitative relationship analysis and qualitative content analysis. The findings have implications for future research on youth information seeking and availability of broadband in school settings and at homes. National imperatives for ubiquitous broadband warrant its inclusion as a factor in studying youth information-seeking behavior in future research.

In the next chapter of Section III, Stacy Creel goes back in time when online catalogs were the subject of many user studies. Interest in investigating use of these tools by children has plummeted in light of the rise of web search engines. However, Creel's study of the design of three online catalogs used in public libraries reminds us of the importance of these tools for locating information in library collections. She examined the influence of system design on the searching strategies and search success of 51 children, ages 5–8. Using a quasi-experimental approach and interviews, she explored children's search strategies and success in relation to the design of the three catalogs, as well as the rationale they provided for using icons and taxonomies in the catalogs. She addressed two research questions in the context of the overarching question: Do current children's online catalog designs function in a manner that is compatible with their information-seeking behavior? She found that use of images and text were helpful in searching the catalogs. However, children misidentified interface design representations reflected in icons in all the three catalogs. While children created valid search paths, the catalogs did not produce results. Creel concluded that the design representations of the three catalogs mismatched with the children's cognitive abilities. The findings from Creel's study have implications for the interface design of today's online catalogs. Children should be involved in the design of these catalogs, Designers should consider new forms of representations such as auditory icons, verbal mouse overs, and zooms to support today's children's information-seeking behavior and success in finding information.

Jamshid Beheshti, Mohammed J. AlGhamdi, Charles Cole, Dhary Abuhimed, and Isabelle Lamoureux, in the last chapter of Section III entitled "Designing an Intervention Tool for Students with Students," describe their research project, the objective of which is to create an intervention tool for middle school students engaged in an assigned inquiry-based project. The conceptual framework for the unique four-year research project is based on Kuhlthau's ISP Model and the Zone of Intervention. In this chapter, two research questions are addressed: What are the major challenges students face when they engage in an inquiry-based project? What type of intervention tool may be designed to assist the students in completing their projects? In the first phase of the study, the authors observed 44 grade eight students engaged in an inquiry-based history project over a twelve-week period. The results of the first phase of the study demonstrated a need for an intervention tool to reduce the time required to choose a topic for the assigned project, and to reduce the amount of consultation that students felt they needed to overcome their uncertainties. During the second phase of the study, a low-tech proof-of-concept intervention tool, the Guide, was designed by an intergenerational team comprising grade nine students and researchers using the Bonded Design methodology. The responses to a survey on the usefulness of the Guide by grade eight students after completing their history projects showed that overall the Guide was helpful to them. In the third phase of the study, the Guide was transformed to a high-tech Web Guide with input from grade nine students participating in focus groups. Again, a survey was distributed among grade eight students during and after completion of their history projects. The results of the survey showed the Web Guide was beneficial for students. The implications of the research are twofold: An intervention tool based on the ISP Model can assist students overcome their uncertainties during an inquiry-based project, and such a tool may be designed by an intergenerational team using Bonded Design or similar participatory methodologies.

The research presented in this book poses a snapshot of diversity of theories, conceptual frameworks, and methodologies, upon which scholars rely to contextualize their work, conduct their studies, and advance the knowledge base in information behavior of children and adolescents. Agarwal in studying a very young child's use of mobile technology demonstrates how she engages and disengages effortlessly with physical world and the digital world. Nesset, focusing on elementary school students, proposes a model consisting of imagery and mnemonic to bridge the gap between information behavior and information literacy for this age group. Laplante illustrates adolescents' reliance on their social circles, including friends, family, and teachers, to gather information in different contexts. Bilal and Jopeck examine the literature for trends in affective responses of girls in developing countries to ICT, and conclude that a research gap exists in this area. Fisher and her colleagues investigate the role of teens as information intermediaries in minority communities and deduce that tools should be available to this group to assist them with their intermediation. Mehra explores information needs of children with special needs in impoverished areas to make recommendations, one of which is education and training of information professionals to sensitize them to the needs of this special group. Lilley investigates trends and patterns in the information behavior of Māori high school students and finds that physical social networks play an important role in everyday information gathering of these students. Spears and Mardis examine the role of broadband in the literature on information behavior and discover a gap in the research on this topic. In experimenting with online catalogs, Creel concludes that disparities exist between young children's cognitive abilities and the features presented by catalogs. Beheshti and his colleagues report on their research in designing an intervention tool for high school students engaged in inquiry-based projects. They find it is feasible to create such a tool using participatory methodologies.

In this book, we have invited scholars from diverse backgrounds, institutions, and locales to report on their current research in an attempt to investigate new research directions in the information behavior of children and adolescents. The multiplicity of theoretical and methodological approaches attest to the complexity of the challenges, problems, and obstacles faced by these researchers. A common thread that emerges from these studies is the enormous impact of the fast-pace technological evolution on the information behavior of the new generation. From the very young to teenagers, their information behavior has changed dramatically in the past decade or so; toddlers who seamlessly move between physical and digital worlds, young girls in developing countries attempting to cope with the new technologies, and youngsters who act as information intermediaries. Many more questions that are beyond the scope of this book remain unanswered requiring in-depth investigation and research, the outcome of which will determine the shape of future technologies that empower the new generation to become more effective and efficient information users and producers. Here, we have attempted to provide only a glimpse in the new directions of research in information behavior of children and adolescents.

Dania Bilal
Jamshid Beheshti
Editors

SECTION I

THROUGH THE AGES

Chapter 1

Use of Touch Devices by Toddlers or Preschoolers: Observations and Findings from a Single-Case Study

Naresh Kumar Agarwal

Abstract

Purpose – Through observing the use of iPhone and iPad by a child between the ages of two and four years and a half, this study presents accounts on the child's use of and interaction with these devices, as well as her interaction with the physical environment.

Design/methodology/approach – Unstructured, naturalistic observation was employed in this study. The study is grounded in theories of user engagement with digital and physical objects.

Findings – A child's interaction with touch-based devices does not deter the child from engaging effectively with the physical environment or from activities centered on creativity and interpersonal engagement. A child is able to move back and forth seamlessly between the physical and digital environments.

Practical implications – Findings from this study could help parents, educators, and system designers understand why and how toddlers and preschoolers use and engage with touch-based devices, as well as the kind of tasks they perform.

Originality/value – Studies of toddlers' or preschoolers' information behavior and interaction with touch-based devices are scarce. Children born toward the end of the first decade of the twenty-first

New Directions in Children's and Adolescents' Information Behavior Research
Library and Information Science, Volume 10, 3–37

ISSN: 1876-0562/doi:10.1108/S1876-056220140000010045

century are growing up with a propensity to using touch-based devices. This study provides a framework for effective usage of such devices while ensuring all-round cognitive and physical development of the child.

Keywords: Information behavior; interaction with technology; toddlers or preschoolers; touch-based devices; iPad; iPhone

1.1. Introduction

Most studies on information behavior have focused on adults, largely in task-based environments (see, e.g., Agarwal, Xu, & Poo, 2011, 2009; Case, 2012) or everyday life (Savolainen, 1995). Few studies on children's information behavior have examined the way youngsters adopt, interact, and engage with technology (Beheshti & Large, 2013; Bilal & Sarangthem, 2008; Druin, 2009; Graves, n.d.; Huang, Kinshuk, & Spector, 2013; Marsh et al., 2005; Nesset, 2013; Nesset & Large, 2004; Rideout & Hamel, 2006; Spink & Heinstrom, 2011).

Toddlers and preschoolers are a new generation of users of touch-based devices such as iPhones and iPads, which only became popular in the last 3–4 years. Children born in 2008 onward are growing up with a natural propensity to using these devices. According to Merriam-Webster Dictionary (Merriam-Webster, n.d.), a *toddler* is a young child who is just learning to walk (anywhere between one and three years old). A *preschooler* is a child who can talk and walk but is too young to go to school (typically between the ages of two and five).

Studies of toddlers' or preschoolers' information behavior and interaction with touch-based devices are scarce. This chapter reports on a case study of the use of iPhone and iPad by a child between the ages of two and five and describes changes in the behavior and interaction as the child's transitions from being a toddler to a preschooler (the terms toddlers and preschoolers are used interchangeably in this chapter). This study provides a framework for effective use of such devices while ensuring all-round cognitive and physical development of toddlers and preschoolers.

Insights gained from the study will shed light on the information behavior and interaction of very young children with touch-based mobile devices. They will provide understanding of a relatively new phenomenon that has not been widely explored in the literature. Findings from this study have implications for parents, educators, and interface designers.

1.1.1. Research Questions

Three overarching research questions were investigated in the study:

RQ-1: Why do toddlers or preschoolers use touch-based devices (iPad and iPhone)?

a. What's the difference between engaging with touch-based devices versus engaging with objects in the physical environment?

RQ-2: What are the enabling factors for using the iPad and iPhone by a toddler or preschooler?

a. What sets of tasks are performed?
b. What change occurs in usage of touch-based devices over time?
c. How does the time spent on using the iPad and iPhone relate to time spent interacting with the physical environment?

RQ-3: How should a child effectively engage with touch-based devices while ensuring all-round cognitive and physical developments?

1.2. Literature Review

The literature relevant to this study includes children's information behavior and children's interaction and engagement with technology.

1.2.1. Children's Information Behavior

The field of human information behavior can be understood as the ways and means by which people go about looking for information when faced with an information need and the contextual factors that shape this process. In the Sense-Making methodology, Dervin, Foreman-Wernet, and Lauterbach (2003) sought to set the assumptions about humans (pretty much all of us) who engage in the information seeking and communication processes (see Agarwal, 2012 for an introduction to Sense-Making). Dervin et al. (2003) write that "humans always are potentially changing, or becoming, and that movement through time-space is an irreducible aspect of the human condition" (p. 8). This process of changing and becoming, and the movement through time-space is even more rapid in studying the information behavior and interaction with technology of very young people, especially, toddlers and preschoolers.

Walter (1994) in her interview of adults on the information needs of children identified that the potential sources for information (and sometimes, misinformation) were parents, teachers, peers, and media. These needs continue to be the same in today's environment. Todd (2003) concludes that children and adolescents are an understudied group considering their numbers and importance. However, since that time, a number of studies have examined adolescents' information seeking in the digital environment. Alexandersson's and Limberg's (2003) ethnographic study of how 11-year-olds construct meaning from books, digital information and pictures found that they adopted a fact-finding approach, frequently used pictures in information sources and that their learning process was oriented toward procedure rather than content. Bilal and Sarangthem (2008) presented task-based models relating to the information behavior of children aged 6–10 when using a digital library. The models consisted of seven modes of behavior (starting, recognizing, browsing, differentiating, reading, exploring, and finishing) and a range of moves associated with each mode. They found that children's behavior was iterative and non-linear, and influenced by the tasks they performed. Apart from these, there are other studies on children's information behavior cited by Graves (n.d.), who provides a bibliography of 16 studies between 1997 and 2008 focusing on children's use of electronic resources, and by Case (2012, pp. 349–355) who reviewed 15 studies where age was a factor, and cited other relevant works. However, most of these studies involved children above the age of five. Most recently, Spink and Heinstrom (2011) explored the information behavior development in early childhood, especially in children ages three to five. Their study of the connection between general cognitive development and information behavior is relevant to the study presented in this chapter. Spink (2010) proposed two new dimensions to information behavior: (1) that information behavior is shaped by both instinctive and environmental dimensions, and (2) that information behavior emerges in early childhood and develops over a lifetime. She noted that the human cognitive and social behavior level includes the dimensions of information intelligence, biological secondary ability, multitasking, and coordinating, which develop in infancy and childhood; and the dimensions of socio-cognitive ability, environment, affective traits, and information processing, which continue to develop through adulthood.

While researchers have looked at children as library users (e.g., Cooper, 2002; Larkin-Lieffers, 2002; Todd, 2003), others have examined the everyday life information behavior of young people. Abbas and Agosto (2013), for example, conclude that while we might view young people as digital natives, they face the same issues that children always have faced, but with access to more information sources.

In their recent book, Beheshti and Large (2013) bring together authors from various disciplines discussing the information behavior of children and teens in the twenty-first century. In investigating whether the information behavior of children and youth has changed significantly over the last two decades, Beheshti and Large (2013) characterized the new behavior by increased skimming and multitasking, more creating and producing content as opposed to only consuming it, and much more social collaboration influenced by social media.

Information behavior may be understood as a person's interaction with information both from the perspective of the physical environment (people, books, etc.), and with technology (Agarwal et al., 2011). In the next section, selected work on children's use of and interaction with technology is reviewed.

1.2.2. Children's Interaction with Technology

A number of studies have examined the use of technology by children and adolescents in varied digital environments — ranging from searching the web (Bilal, 2000, 2001, 2002; Bilal & Kirby, 2002; Kafai & Bates, 1997; Lazonder, Biemans, & Wopereis, 2000) to library catalogues (Hirsh, 1997, 1999) to digital libraries (Bilal & Bachir, 2007a, 2007b; Bilal, Sarangthem, & Bachir, 2008; Druin, 2005; Reuter & Druin, 2004) to mobile technologies (Druin, 2009).

1.2.2.1. Searching the web Children and youth will increasingly turn to the World Wide Web (hereafter web) for reading, and for answers to their questions (Case, 2012). During early development of the web, Kafai and Bates (1997) investigated how elementary school children interact with the Internet by asking them to build an annotated directory of web sites for other children. Children were lost in navigating the web and experienced difficulty finding information. Using loosely structured interviews, Watson (1998) explored the feelings of nine eighth grade students in using technology and found that they were highly motivated and perceived themselves successful in using the web. In a study of high school students using observation, think aloud, and interviews, Fidel et al. (1999) found that students enjoyed searching, and that they were satisfied with their searches and results, but impatient with slow response from the search engines used. Bilal (2000, 2001, 2003) found that use of search engines designed specifically for middle schoolers (i.e., Yahooligans!; now defunct) is intellectually challenging, gratifying, and motivating, but frustrating.

One of the very few studies that involved very young children is by Spink, Danby, Mallan, and Butler (2010). The authors examined the search behaviors of children between the ages of five and six in the preparatory year before compulsory schooling. They found that children engaged in complex web search behaviors, including keyword searching and browsing, query formulation and reformulation, relevance judgments, successive searches, multitasking, and collaborative behaviors. It appears that children at a very young age are adept to interacting with the web. More recently, Nesset (2013) developed the BAT model based on young children's information literacy skills and information seeking.

Limited research has explored children's involvement in the design of search engines. For example, Bilal (2003) worked with eleven middle schoolers who designed web search engine interfaces that meet their needs. Children's involvement in search engine design process is covered thoroughly in research by Large, Bowler, Beheshti, and Nesset (2007); Bowler, Large, Beheshti, and Nesset (2005); and Nesset and Large (2004) who developed History Trek search engine that focuses on Canadian history.

1.2.2.2. Library catalogues Using interviews, observations, and card sorting, Hirsh (1997) studied the search behavior of 64 fifth grade children in using a Science Library catalogue. The study found that task complexity and children's prior knowledge on the topic influenced search success. Akin (1998) investigated the experience and feelings of 177 fourth graders, and 88 eighth graders when experiencing information overload, taking children's information-fatigue-syndrome into account. Using interviews, observations, and think aloud techniques, Hirsh (1999) studied search strategies employed by high school children when finding information related to a class assignment from an on-line catalogue, an electronic encyclopedia, an electronic magazine index, and the web. Students spent a large amount of their time finding pictures, identified sources found interesting, but did not question the authority of these sources. Todd (2003) found similar results, and concluded that besides insecurity and uncertainty when searching, children's inability to judge the quality of search results surfaced as barriers. He stressed the need to develop the intellectual scaffolds for children to appropriately engage with information.

1.2.2.3. Digital libraries Studies on children's use of the International Children's Digital Library (ICDL) (see, e.g., Bilal & Bachir, 2007a, 2007b; Druin, 2005; Reuter & Druin, 2004) found that children experienced difficulty in using the ICDL, although the Library was specifically designed for their age levels. "Inadequate design of the interfaces, age, and insufficient level of knowledge in how to use the interfaces" surfaced as problems (Bilal, 2007, p. 40). Bilal et al. (2008) suggested a model of children's use of digital libraries that could be employed by information professionals to train these young users in effective use of the ICDL. New studies of children's interaction with the ICDL are needed especially since the design of its interfaces have changed since these studies were published.

1.2.2.4. Mobile technologies The changing nature of the technology landscape has a significant impact on the way children are growing up in the digital environments. A recent report indicates that the number of mobile-cellular subscriptions worldwide (6.8 billion) is approaching the number of people in the world (7.1 billion), and is expected to exceed the number of people by the end of 2014 (ITU, 2013). Mobile broadband subscriptions have climbed from 268 million in 2007 to 2.1 billion in 2013, with an annual growth rate of 40%. Soloway et al. (2001) make a case for children whipping out "handheld devices from their backpacks and desks instead of pencils and paper" (p. 20). Today, use of mobile devices has become ubiquitous among children of various age and intellectual levels. Devices harnessed for children and youth with special needs are evidenced in the number and variety of iPad-compatible apps available for people with special needs, including but not limited to, children on the Autism Spectrum Disorder (ASD). The Autism Spectrum Disorder Foundation (ASDF) has implemented a program that donates iPads to "individuals and special education classrooms to help nonverbal autistic children with communication and learning ..." (ASDF, 2012a). These devices offer much flexibility than laptops or desktop computers. Touchscreen makes the iPad more accessible "for children who have learning or coordination difficulties." In addition, "tapping and sliding motions are much easier than typing. iPads can also go wherever the child goes, which means they have ways to calm, focus, and learn while on-the-go" (ASDF, 2012b).

Druin (2009) "presents a compelling picture of the need, opportunity, and potential impact of mobile technology solutions for children" and calls "for action to promote mobile technology development for child development" (p. x). While children are growing up valuing the ownership of mobile devices (Guernsey, 2009), parents are concerned about creating a healthy balance between the use of these devices with outdoor play and reading books.

These concerns were also echoed in previous studies by Marsh et al. (2005) and Rideout and Hamel (2006) who studied children under the age of 5 (i.e., toddlers and preschoolers). In a survey of 1852 parents and caregivers of children in England, Marsh et al. (2005) found that young children (from birth to six years old) are immersed in practices relating to new technologies and are growing up in a digital world. Parents and other family members scaffold this learning. They also found that parents are generally very positive about the role of media in their young children's social, emotional, linguistic, and cognitive development. However, early childhood practitioners had concerns about the perceived amount of time children spend engaging with technology. In a survey of 1051 parents with children age six months to six years old using a series of focus groups across the United States, Rideout and Hamel (2006) found that while parents appreciated the educational benefits of technology and related content for kids, their focus was on the "safety" activities their children could engage in, among other things.

Use of technology can also create barriers to children's success in finding information. Based on their review of published studies, Lingnau, Ruthven, and Landoni (2011) identified three problems children faced: (1) dealing with the complexity of searching, including formulating search queries; (2) complex displays in the search system, leading to information overload (also identified by Akin, 1998); and (3) search behavior characterized by identifying interesting information, as opposed to relevant information. The authors suggested a system-design solution for children between the ages of six and nine, whereby the child shows an object to the system, and the system responds by telling the child something about the object. In many ways, the app-based interfaces in iPhones and iPads are in line with what the authors advocated, especially in relation to the *show* and *tell* approach. These interfaces were the tools use by the child who is the subject of study in this chapter.

1.3. Theoretical Perspectives

This study is grounded in specific theoretical perspectives relating to children's interaction, use, and engagement with technology and the physical environment (i.e., the overall information behavior of children). These theoretical perspectives and prior research in this area have guided the research questions and will provide a framework for answering them.

RQ-1: *Why do toddlers or preschoolers use touch-based devices (iPad and iPhone)?*

Decision to adopt/point of engagement. Shneiderman (2002) writes that the "old computing was about what computers could do; the new computing is about what users can do" (p. 2). Goodhue and Thompson's (1995) Task-Technology Fit (TTF) theory holds that a piece of technology is more likely to have a positive impact on individual performance and be used if the capabilities of the technology match the tasks that the user must perform. Children's information needs vary from those of adults (Bilal, 2007; Walter, 1994). Thus, iPhones and the iPads should be designed based on the information needs of children, as well as on the tasks and activities they perform. The Technology Acceptance Model (TAM) by Davis (1989) suggests that when presented with a new technology, a number of external variables influence its perceived ease of use (PEoU) and perceived usefulness (PU). These include, but are not limited to, the touch-screen feature, size and weight, number of applications, as well as adoption by parents. TAM and TTF have been validated in hundreds of studies on technology adoption in a variety of contexts (Davis, 1989; Goodhue & Thompson, 1995).

Sustained engagement. The use of the iPhone and iPad in this study covers early adoption (as is explained by the TAM model) to sustained engagement over time. To develop understanding of why toddlers or preschoolers choose to engage with touch-based devices over a sustained period of time, three communication approaches grounded in Dervin's Sense-Making Methodology (Dervin et al., 2003) are used: (1) it is possible to design and implement communication systems and practices that are responsive to human needs; (2) it is possible for humans to enlarge their communication repertoires to pursue this vision and to discipline their communicating to achieve these possibilities; and (3) achieving these outcomes requires the development of communication-based methodological approaches. These approaches address weaknesses in conceptualization and study of users and, at the same time, provide a systematic approach that can be used both qualitatively and quantitatively in developing critical practice for the design of responsive systems (Agarwal, 2012).

A part of sustained engagement is the *aesthetic experience*. Looking at technology as experience, and building on the works of John Dewey and Mikhail Bakhtin, McCarthy and Wright (2004) explore people's interaction with technology in terms of *aesthetic* engagement, situated creativity, centers of value, and sense-making. Building on Dewey's work, they argue against conceptions of technology that separate it from people's experience, and note that we should approach technology as part of ordinary, everyday lived experience. Following Bakhtin, they emphasize the particularity and feltness of this technology as experience. They show technology to be deeply embedded in everyday experience, in ways that are aesthetic, ethical, and functional. The *aesthetic experience* is an important part of why the iPhone and the iPad are sources of sustained engagement by toddlers and preschoolers. Apart from their functional utility for entertainment and education, children at this stage of development engage in interacting with these devices to develop their basic, discovery skills. To be effective, the *aesthetic experience* should be built around (1) a holistic approach wherein the person with feelings, emotions, and thoughts is the focus of design; (2) a constructivist stance in which self is seen as continuously engaged and constituted in making sense of experience; and (3) a dialogical ontology in which self, others, and technology are constructed as multiple centers of value (Wright, Wallace, & McCarthy, 2008).

Another theory related to engagement is *Radical Change*. Dresang's (1999) radical change theory sees digital books and hypertext formats as bringing about a positive shift in reading interaction for children based on three digital-age principles — interactivity, connectivity, and access. Dresang (1999, 2013) lists four fundamental assumptions: (1) children are capable and seeking connections; (2) the digital environment nurtures children's capabilities; (3) hand-held books (in iPhones and iPads) offer digital-age connections; and (4) adults and youth including toddlers and preschoolers are partners in the digital world. These four assumptions largely apply in the present study.

A number of studies that have examined user engagement with technology (see, e.g., Desmet, Porcelijn, & van Dijk, 2007; O'Brien & Toms, 2008, 2010). Desmet et al. (2007) discuss a design approach that focuses on the emotions that constitute a *wow-experience* — pleasant surprise, fascination, and desire, and applied it to the design of a mobile telephone prototype. O'Brien and Toms (2008, 2010) found that engagement is a process comprising four distinct stages: point of engagement, period of sustained engagement, disengagement, and reengagement. This process is characterized by attributes of engagement that pertain to the user, the system, and user–system interaction. They define engagement as "the quality of user experience characterized by attributes of challenge, positive affect, endurability, aesthetic and sensory appeal, attention, feedback, variety/novelty, interactivity, and perceived user control" (p. 938). In relation to toddlers and preschoolers, the point of engagement with the iPhone and iPad are explored in the findings.

The reviewed literature shows that there is very little research work on toddlers' and preschoolers' interaction with and use of touch-based devices. This study is a first attempt toward filling this gap.

1.4. Methodology

This study employs the case study approach of the use of iPhone and iPad by a child (toddler/preschooler) between the ages of two and four years and a half. The term *case study* can be used to describe a unit of analysis (a single child's interaction with touch-based devices) or a research method. According to Yin (2014), the distinctive need for case study research arises out of the desire to understand complex social phenomena. It allows investigators to focus on a "case" and retain a holistic and real-world perspective. Qualitative case study research can be approached from multiple philosophical perspectives (Myers, 1997) — positivist (Yin, 2014), interpretive (Agarwal, Poo, & Tan, 2007; Klein & Myers, 1999; Pan & Tan, 2011), or critical (Carr & Kemmis, 1986). The present study was approached from an interpretive perspective. With its philosophical base as hermeneutics and phenomenology, interpretive research starts with the assumption that access to reality is only through social constructions such as language, consciousness, and shared meanings (Myers, 1997) and focuses on the full complexity of human sense-making as the situation emerges (Kaplan & Maxwell, 1994).

Data was gathered through observation, which is a natural way to see how people behave in their "real world" settings. As opposed to questionnaire survey or interviews, "observation is a more reliable indicator of how people really conduct themselves in a given situation" (Beck & Manuel, 2008, p. 109). In this case, since the observation was of a toddler's/preschooler's use of an iPad (primarily) and iPhone over a span of 2–3 years, a naturalistic observation was the best suited approach. The phenomenon of interest was observing the process and behavior in the child's interaction and engagement with the devices. Beck and Manuel (2008) note that young children can be participants in an observation study "who might prove impossible to interview because they are unable to express themselves, but their actions can be observed" (p. 110).

In this naturalistic observation, the child is studied in a natural setting without the participants' awareness of the observation, over an extended period of time (Beck & Manuel, 2008). Most of the observation was unstructured, though periods of structured observation were carried out on specific days to note: (1) the participant's behavior/interaction when using the iPad, and (2) the sequence of steps when performing different tasks on the iPad. Unstructured observation allows observing an activity without a limited predetermined list of behaviors (Larkin-Lieffers, 2002; Zweizig, Johnson, Robbins, & Besant, 1996) or assumptions or expectations.

Unstructured naturalistic observation was also utilized due to the limitations imposed by Apple, Inc. on running multiple applications on the iPhone and iPad at the same time. These applications running simultaneously would be needed for usability testing — to record the screen and to share/display the screen, while the child is using the device. It is only recently that some workarounds may have been found (Krug, 2013). Even with these workarounds, recording and interpreting behavior is more difficult in the absence of a mouse cursor (Krug, 2013).

In the continuum of research (Cole, 2013, p. 5), this study would be on the exploratory-descriptive end. The study can also be classified as an ethnographic study where the researcher was immersed in the learning environment of the child, as well as her engagement with the iPhone and the iPad. This is in line with the principle of interaction between the researchers and the subjects (Klein & Myers, 1999), where immersion implies that the researcher is not fully separated from the environment of the subject. Pacey (1999) as well as McCarthy and Wright (2004) note that we do not just use or admire technology; we live with it, and make the case for academic and professional comment on technology to not resist discussion of personal experience. "It is only by seeing technology as participating in felt experience that we understand the fullness of its potential" (McCarthy & Wright, 2004, p. x). In the present study, the relationship between the researcher and the child and other matters related to the child's involvement in this study is kept confidential to protect her identity and her parents' privacy.

1.4.1. Data Collection

The researcher relied on note taking during observation. The presence of particular apps (photo, video, phone, YouTube, Safari, and those for interactive games) and pictures taken by the child (Ella, name changed) also served as a record of the tasks performed. The photo and video apps stored the images and video captured by the child. The phone history showed the numbers dialed, those that were not dialed by her parents. The YouTube history showed the list of videos watched. The Safari browser history showed the list of sites visited or the last search done. The app for games recorded the progress made on particular levels. Unstructured notes were written on paper based on Ella's commonly used apps, the sequence of steps performed, the help she sought when using them, the sets of tasks performed, the difficulties she countered when doing those tasks, how she got over the difficulties, as well as the change in her device preference and app usage over time. This data was organized, coded, and analyzed.

1.4.2. The Case of One Child Participant

While the study is limited to one child, it does provide valuable insights on the wide range of engagements in a variety of tasks over two years and six months. Even in usability testing, small sample sizes of five or eight (Nielsen, 2000) or even three (Krug, 2009) are generally considered enough, even though cases have been made for larger sample sizes (Faulkner, 2003). Tomlin (2010) makes the case for usability testing, even if it is with one participant. He cites the successful usability testing of the site (http://heardable.com) using only one participant. On usability testing with one person, Tomlin quotes Nielsen (2000), "As soon as you collect data from a single test user, your insights shoot up and you have already learned almost a third of all there is to know about the usability of the design. The difference between zero and even a little bit of data is astounding." While this study focused more on observation than usability (even though both are related), the case for using a single subject as a starting point should still hold especially because this is an exploratory study, qualitative in nature, and does not seek to generalize the findings. Insights gained from this study should provide basis for further lines of inquiry in a research area that is understudied.

1.4.3. Ella: The Child Participant

Bilal (2007) cites a number of studies examining children's interactions with electronic interfaces that suggest "that system developers build interfaces that support children's developmental levels, affective states, and information seeking behaviors" (p. 40). Bilal also cites Erikson, who believed that technology "must reach meaningfully into [a child's] life, supporting in every child a feeling of competence — that is, the free exercise of dexterity and intelligence in the completion of serious tasks unimpaired by an infantile sense of inferiority" (Erikson, 1968, p. 126). With this in mind, the iPhone and iPad have turned out to be incredibly popular with children.

Among the generation of children that grew up naturally with touchscreen devices is Ella, the subject in the case study reported in this paper. Ella was born after two versions of the iPhone were released. In July 2009, her parents decided to get smartphones with unlimited 3G data connectivity. They bought two of the latest iPhone 4S for themselves, a month after it had been released. Ella was not even one-year old at that time. This decision was to shape the way Ella was to grow up — in the company of Apple's iOS (the operating system supporting iPhones and iPads) devices as her parents, as well as day care and preschool friends.

Along with some of her toys that had battery-powered musical notes, the earliest exposure of Ella to technology was watching nursery rhymes videos on YouTube on a desktop computer. Perched on her high chair with baby food and fruits before her, Ella would watch the videos play continuously based on a playlist created by her parents. This would keep her entertained at least for 30 minutes.

By the time Ella was two years old, she had started using one of her parents' two smartphones. Initial attempts to dissuade Ella from using the iPhone (by setting a screen-lock password) failed. Ella would enter numbers by random, and after a number of unsuccessful attempts, this would lead to lock of the phone by Apple for long periods of time. Ultimately, to preserve access to their phones, Ella's parents had to disable the screen-lock feature. In her journey so far from 2 years to 4 years and six months, Ella has been a regular user of touch-based interfaces. Sometime in mid-2011, her father purchased an iPad 2 for himself, but it was soon to be taken over by Ella who instantly took to the bigger screen of the iPad. By the time her parents upgraded to the iPhone 4S and iPhone 5, Ella was juggling between the iPhone 4S, iPhone 5, and the iPad — choosing any one based on nearest access, and switching to the other when one would run out of charge. While she used these devices at home, her time in day care or preschool (8 hours a day, 5 days a week) was totally away from these devices (individual and group activity centered around learning and face-to-face interaction, creative works such as building or painting, playing in the park, and visits to the library).

1.4.4. Mobile Devices

In the Macworld convention in January 2007, Steve Jobs announced the iPhone — a cell phone, iPod and a mini-computer all in one device, with touch-screen features (Mather, 2007). In June 2007, the first iPhone was released in the United States, and Apple announced support for third-party applications (apps) to run on the new phone. The iPhone 5 was released in September 2012. In November 2012, Apple released the 4th generation iPad, as well as the iPad mini, a smaller, 7.9 inch version of the iPad (Apple, 2013a; Associated Press, 2012). Vincenti notes that "although we have always worked with applications or computer programs designed to carry out particular tasks, 'Apps' have gained a significant popularity since portable computing has reached such high peaks" (2013, p. 160). As of April 2013, Apple claims that its app store has more than 800,000 apps (Apple, 2013b).

1.4.5. Data Coding

The collected data consisted of the child's information behavior and interaction with the devices during the duration of the study. The data was coded using open, axial, and selective coding (Corbin & Strauss, 1990). To account for limitations imposed by a single coder, the results of the coding were ascertained by consulting a parent of the child participant. Open coding included an initial pass through the data (recorded on the devices, and notes taken on paper) to come up with candidate concepts for categories. These include the tasks and apps mentioned above, the time spent on each, use and the interaction process in performing these tasks in the iPhone and iPad. After an initial level of analysis, categories were combined into major categories (axial coding). Finally, the focus shifted to core categories (selective coding), those that emerged from open and axial coding as the most important. These included enabling factors, tasks, barriers and ways to overcome, change with time, interaction with physical environment, and safety precautions. These core categories related to the processes with which the child used the devices, and gave rise to the second set of research questions (RQ-2, listed under Section 1.1, and addressed under Section 1.5).

1.5. Analysis and Findings

In this section, Ella's interaction with the iPhone, iPad and her surrounding environment is described and answers to the rest of the research questions (including sub-questions) are provided. It is noteworthy that the answers to the first research question, RQ-1: *Why do toddlers or preschoolers use touch-based devices (iPad and iPhone)?* were grounded in the theoretical perspectives discussed earlier in this chapter. The findings for the corresponding sub-question (RQ-1a), and for the other research questions follow.

RQ-1a. *What's the difference between engaging with touch-based devices versus engaging with objects in the physical environment?*

Disengagement with technology and engagement with other physical objects and activities is an important part in the day of toddlers and preschoolers who use touch-based devices.

In a recent study, Weigle (2013) defined physical objects as those that may be touched, grasped, moved, positioned, stroked, held, and manipulated by hand. In the case of physical objects, Weigle found that aesthetic and sensory appeal, attention, pleasure, interactivity, as well as numinous qualities of unity of moment, imaginative empathy, and inquisitive thinking are characteristics of user engagement. Her definition of user engagement with physical objects is one that is characterized by attributes of aesthetic and sensory appeal, variety and novelty, curiosity and inquisitive of mind, emotional connection and numinous qualities such as empathy and reverence, memory of place and time, affect and interest.

"User engagement with physical objects is immediate because there are no barriers between the user and the artefact" (Weigle, 2013, p. 5). Having the ability to handle objects is not only enjoyable, but also enriches the learning experience (Overbeeke, Djajadiningrat, Hummels, Wensveen, & Frens, 2003). Lapetino (2012) notes that holding an object is a kind of connection and experience that can be difficult to replicate on the digital environment and human–computer interaction. On the contrary, an iPad or iPhone is unique because in itself is a physical portable object with digital content that a child can carry around the living and playing spaces. These mobile devices have embodiment characteristics — the interactions that happen in the physical and social worlds and provide meaning (Dourish, 2001; Druin, 2009; Marshall & Rogers; 2009; Price, Roussos, Pontual Falcão, & Sheridan, 2009).

RQ-2: *What are the enabling factors for using the iPad and iPhone by a toddler or preschooler?*

An important factor in Ella's journey toward becoming a digital native is the availability of multiple mobile devices that she had access to in her parents' home. The enabling factors for Ella's use of the iPad and iPhone included the following:

Access and connectivity. The adoption of the devices by Ella's parents was a conduit for Ella's access to the iPad and iPhone. High-speed wireless connectivity at home was also important for accessing many of the apps and videos that relied on Internet connectivity. Presence of a desktop and laptops at home and the parents' "encouragement" of Ella to use the mobile devices (as appropriate) have endorsed Ella's constant demand for these devices. For example, when the power on the iPad or one of the two iPhones would run out, Ella would quickly win over the mild protests of a parent in using his or her iPhone. She would ask: "Can I use your phone? I think, yours [phone] is green [has power or charged]." However, as a young child, Ella was not aware that use of the iPhone is not allowed on the plane. Therefore, during air travel the parents did not allow Ella to use the iPhone despite her persistence; instead, they would give her crayons and a drawing pad instead and divert her attention to the scenes around her (e.g., other youngsters playing with toys or other objects).

Parental awareness and support. Parental support for allowing Ella to use the mobile devices is necessary at a number of levels:

a. *Awareness of tablets and their use for education*: Ella's parents were both working professionals. They largely have accepted their child's interaction with the iPhone and iPad as a phenomenon of the times, and were often surprised at the ease and speed with which Ella picked up the steps of using a new game or language app or a feature on the devices.
b. *Degree of parental comfort with time spent*: Many parents are concerned with the amount of time their child spends using the devices and try to mandate fixed times for such use. There are varying degrees of parental success in doing so. In Ella's case, her parents did not try to control her iPhone and iPad usage. She was free to use these, as well as her other toys and outdoor play when she wanted. However, besides travel, other times Ella was discouraged to use the devices was when eating,

when the parents needed to make calls, and when the volume of any video Ella was watching was very high. In the latter case, Ella was asked to lower the volume and she would oblige by bringing it down a few levels. The positive aspect of this "free to use" rule had given Ella a sense of assurance that the devices would not be taken away from her arbitrarily. Thus, on her own accord, Ella made time to put down these devices and engage with other toys, books, and indoor and outdoor activities.

c. *Providing scaffolds for the child to learn*: Ella was found to learn something new first, by carefully observing, and then trying it out on her own. With her keen sense of observation, she would ask a parent to show her how to do something once (when engaging with a new gaming app such as Cut the Rope, Fruit Ninja or LestTans Cls, a jigsaw app such as Puzzle Map, a drawing app such as Paper, or a Math app such as Toddler Math) and then want to try it herself. She would then spend a lot of time practicing on her own. At age 3, when Ella got stuck at a certain level, she came to a parent and asked for help by saying: "Can you show me how to do this? It is too difficult"; or at times, she would ask: "Can you do this? Try it! You can do it!" Ella took back the device from the parent as soon as she realized that she could do the difficult task on her own.

Shared devices with parents. Ella shared use of the devices with her parents. While each parent had an iPhone, Ella had no preference as to which one to use as long as she was able to use one. She would ask a parent for sharing his or her phone by saying: "Can you share this one [pointing to the phone], because I don't have a phone?" As to the iPad, Ella considered it her own especially since there were many apps on it were for her. These were categorized under Books, Math, Drawing, Language, Music, and Games. The parents also had their own apps on this device including Email and Dropbox, as well as other ones categorized under Work and Useful.

RQ-2a. *What sets of tasks does a toddler or preschooler perform in the mobile devices?*

The tasks that Ella chose to perform on the iPhone and iPad were structured by the default apps in Apples iOS operating system, as well as the educational apps installed for her by her parents. As the devices were shared, there were specific folders created for use of Ella, as well as for her parents. While Ella browsed and went through most available apps, she was drawn to a small set of apps at any given time.

Tasks/apps used. By the time she was three, Ella was *clicking photos* using the iPhone — using both the front and back facing cameras. The initial photos (and videos sometimes) were often blurred and not composed well. By the time she was four, Ella was clicking relatively well-composed photos. She would also scroll through and see the photos clicked by others, as well as by herself. By identifying the initial letters in the list of contacts, Ella also learned to *dial the phone* of a parent. Based on the photo or image displayed on the phone or Skype, she could identify the person calling. One of the major problems in letting Ella use the iPhone at age two was dialing the numbers of the top-listed contacts stored on one of the parent's devices. At times, this led to incurring international call charges. The issue was then resolved by storing different numbers at the top of the list and removing country codes from international numbers. Apart from these, one of the most heavily used parts of the iPhone and the iPad by Ella was the *video/ YouTube* application. When Ella was two years old, her parents ran a play-list of nursery rhymes for her. As she became older, she started watching videos of cartoon characters such as Mickey Mouse, Dora, Barney, Pocoyo, Calliou, SpongeBob, Tro, Tom and Jerry, and Little Einsteins. It was difficult to measure the time spent watching videos. The time certain videos were "on" and playing was different from the time Ella actually watched them. Many times, the videos were *used like a television* that was switched on, while she would engage in other tasks such as drawing and painting, cutting paper, eating, or playing in her sandbox.

Keyword search. To limit her video watching, her parents used the 'Restrictions' setting on the devices to hide the YouTube icon at times. Ella would then request a parent to search for a video on the Safari browser. This was also the time when she was beginning to learn to spell certain words (at 3 years six months to 4 years of age). Based on the *recent searches* stored by Safari, Ella could pull out her desired videos (see Figure 1.1), which shows a portion of the sequence of steps she used in getting access to Pocoyo. Ella did so by (1) clicking on the Safari icon; (2) clicking on the Google top right search bar; (3) typing "po" [pocoyo gets displayed from recent searches]; (4) clicking on "pocoyo"; (5) scrolling down to the resulting list of videos; and (6) watching the desired video.

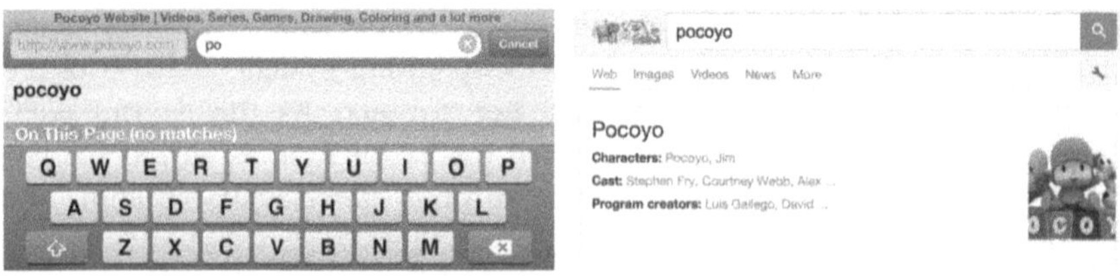

Figure 1.1: Sequence of steps for keyword search for videos. *Source*: pocoyo.com.

Other tasks/apps used: Apart from these, there has been a wide variety of apps Ella used. These included jigsaw puzzles, reading interactive books, shapes and colors, drawing and coloring, alphabet and words, math, being exposed to a second language through language apps and memory or goal-based games. Ella also became amused in seeing content featuring herself — photos of herself, photos taken by her, videos of her, or a video of her and a parent reading books so that Ella could watch later on her own. At age of four, Ella started discovering new applications on her own and asked a parent to download them. The choice of apps was often based on color, as well as the look-and-feel of and familiarity with the icons. For example, she would download apps featuring Hello Kitty or SpongeBob SquarePants, or those in bright colors (such as Paint & Create), or those with smiley emoticons.

Device handling: Ella dropped a parent's iPhone in water when she was 2 years old; she also threw away the phone from a window out onto the street. When the power in one of the devices Ella was using ran out, she often turned to a device held by another parent and asked to use it. At times when both devices were being charged, Ella was impatient and unplugged one of them within one to two minutes so that she could use it.

Along with the length of time spent on watching videos, a big issue was of *appropriateness of video content*. Google does provide a safety mode when logged in using a parent's account. While it might block pornography, the mode did not block content the parents judged as inappropriate due to violence. An example of this content is Dora Gets Shot, and Marshmallow Murder (Figure 1.2).

RQ-2b. *What change occurs in a toddler's or preschooler's usage of touch-based devices over time?*

It was not until Ella was nearly two years old that her parents noticed a heightened interest in the iPad, which had become her favorite toy later on. During this period, Ella had already learned how to use the touch-based and sliding features of the iPhone (with her forefinger to slide the phone open and close). The earliest applications were either watching a video on the phone, pressing and dialing numbers or putting a string of characters as updates on a parent's Facebook account.

In terms of *videos*, her early exposure was to nursery rhymes that she used to sing along with. As she grew older, she had a favorite cartoon character at different points in time. She grew from clicking on the YouTube icon to doing a keyword search for her favorite video by the time she was four. The *types of apps* she liked also changed, based on what she was learning at home and school (e.g., word formation, Math, drawing or a language skill).

Figure 1.2: Inappropriate videos on YouTube. *Source*: YouTube.com.

As Ella reached age four and six months, her *device size preference also changed*, from using the iPad most of the time to using one of the iPhones. There could be a few reasons for this change: (1) the iPhone was easily accessible, (2) it was smaller and easier to handle, and (3) there were too many apps on the iPad. When asked why she wanted to use the iPhone and not the iPad, Ella said, "Because there is too much." While the apps downloaded by a parent were organized into folders, the newer apps she would download would often not be organized. Also, not all the downloaded apps (either by a parent or by herself) were of interest to Ella. She often reverted to familiar apps such as YouTube or video search using the Safari browser.

RQ-2c. *How does the time a toddler or a preschooler spent on using the iPad and iPhone relate to the time spent interacting with the physical environment?*

While Ella actively engages with the iPad, this has not stopped her from engaging equally well with the physical environment. Jones (2009) describes three broad categories of activity spaces for children that are outside formal learning contexts, with many activities falling in more than one category. These are: (1) play; (2) interests, hobbies, causes; and (3) communication, self-expression, identity. Ella's activities were analyzed in the context of these categories.

(1) *Play*: Many of the interactions Ella made with the iPhone and iPad were seamless with the real world. For example, when she sees and an image of the moon on the iPad or in a book, she remarked it looking at the moon in the evening and comments on its shape (is a semi-circle or a circle). She also practices with various shapes available on the iPhone and iPad, cut them out on paper, and connects them to real objects in her environment. She would learn a new word or identify a fruit in one or her books or devices, and remember it upon seeing it around the house or outside. Ella would as easily play with jigsaw puzzles on the iPad as with real ones. There is also the simultaneous merging of the physical and digital contexts at times. Time solving a jigsaw puzzle on the carpet or cutting a heart shape out of paper may be also when the iPad is on with a Calliou video playing on it … or solving the puzzle with a parent, or sitting on a parent's lap and engaging with her iPhone. All of these activities were when Ella was between the ages of three years and six months and four years and six months.

(2) *Interests, hobbies, causes.* Around the same age, Ella was using drawing and coloring apps on the iPhone and iPad, as well as performing these activities using paper and color crayons, Ella's parents spent time with her as she painted on full-sized canvas(es) using a brush with child-safe paint. The comfort with iPhone and iPad did not take away from her interest in dealing with paint and paper or canvas and switching from digital colors to physical pigments, or from physical colors to digital ones. While both are colors, both are seen as different and unique. At the earliest opportunity to go out and play, Ella easily put down her iPad or iPhone and went out cycling or playing with a ball or helping in the yard or using the slides or the swing. She was equally interested in helping around the house — whether unloading spoons from the dishwasher or in sorting laundry after a wash. Along with the camera on the iPhone, Ella used a Digital SLR camera and engaged in viewing photos stored on these devices as well as hard copy photos organized in albums.

(3) *Communication, self-expression, and identity*: Also around three and four years of age, Ella interacted with her virtual friends — Calliou, Dora, and Mickey Mouse, played with her schoolmates or neighbors or cousins, and interacted with parents and other adults. For language learning, alphabet and word formation, Ella used the apps in the devices, played with physical flashcards, and practiced writing both in digital and physical workbooks. Her engagement with read-aloud interactive e-books was interspersed with requests to read aloud to her from a physical book.

Ella's interaction with the iPad and iPhone is with a physical object such as a toy that she can hold and carry (as opposed to sitting in front of a computer), and one which has digital content within it. Ella can carry around and situate the iPad/iPhone in the larger context of her other physical activities, such as keeping them next to her when making a sand castle, for example, or when sitting on a parent's lap.

RQ-3: *How should a toddler or preschooler effectively engage with touch-based devices while ensuring all-round development?*

Table 1.1 describes the framework that reflects on Ella's engagement with the iPad or iPhone. While in the process of developing her personality, understanding herself and the world around her, she is able to ensure continuity of experience in her transition between the digital activities on her iPad/iPhone and other physical activities during her day. The first row in the table discusses reasons for Ella's use of the devices, for sustained periods of engagement, for disengagement with the devices (and reengagement with the physical world), and when she gets back to using the devices. The second row summarizes the tasks or apps she uses for short periods versus during periods of sustained engagement. The third row summarizes the precautions her parents take for proper device use and to ensure Ella's overall development.

1.6. Discussion and Implications

Ella's ability to use the iPhone and iPad since she was two years old is in line with the findings by Revelle and Strommen (1990) who noted that it was somewhere around 2–3 years of age when children become able to manipulate a joystick, mouse, trackball and interact with touch-based interfaces. The aesthetic appeal and touch-based interactive features of the iPhone and iPad ensured that Ella could spend countless hours over time on these devices without getting bored. In addition, the large number and wide variety of apps kept Ella tuned to different things to do. The fact that she could hold these devices in her hands (as opposed to using a laptop or a desktop computer) meant that she could situate the devices as one of her toys in her larger environment — when playing, sitting, or reading. "Portability is the 'special sauce'" (Guernsey, 2009, p. 262) in this case. These features, coupled with ease of use (e.g., by tapping onto specific icons to access apps) meant that she could experience these technology tools. Based on observing Ella, aesthetics, interactivity, and portability supported her engagement with the devices as they became embodied in her everyday environment. In fact, Ella was able to interact with and move seamlessly and back and forth between the mobile devices and the physical objects in her environment.

Along with access (Agarwal et al., 2011), interactivity and connectivity (Dresang, 1999, 2013), the degree and type of *parental awareness and support* have enabled Ella to freely use the mobile devices. Rideout and Hamel (2006) noted that parents' beliefs and levels of comfort with technology are strongly related to the amount of time or pattern of technology used by children. Indeed, Ella's parents placed minimal restrictions on her use of the iPad and iPhone, and were also heavy users of these devices themselves. In addition, Ella was not intimidated by the problems she experienced with the devices. Instead, she sought her parents' help whenever she felt "stuck" using a particular app. The help seeking and guidance in solving problems Ella received from her parents is what Vygotsky (1978) refer to as the Zone of Proximal Development (ZPD). He specifically defined ZDP as "the distance between the actual development level as determined by independent problem solving and the level of potential development as determined through problem solving under adult guidance or in collaboration with more capable peers" (p. 86).

Ella shared the mobile devices with her parents. Having *devices shared* between the child and parents or siblings has multiple benefits, including but not limited to, parental awareness of the installed apps on the iPhone and iPad has allowed them to monitor Ella's behavior, block inappropriate apps, teach her about collaboration and sharing, and encourage her to seek help whenever needed. The fact that Ella's parents were comfortable using different technology tools and, specifically, the two mobile devices in everyday life, have also supported Ella's interactions with the devices.

The *tasks/apps* Ella spent most of her time performing/using (sustained engagement) included watching videos (many of which feature educational and lifestyle content for preschoolers), jigsaw puzzles, drawing and coloring, educational tools (shapes, colors, alphabet, words, math), and games. She spent some time looking at different folders (belonging to her parents). In analyzing the implications of Piaget's four stages of cognitive development of children, Bilal (2007) writes that children "are different from adults due to their cognitive developmental abilities. Accordingly, *tasks and other learning activities* designed for children should be developmentally appropriate and challenging but not beyond the children's abilities to achieve them" (p. 45). Ella often did well, and engaged better with the apps designed for toddlers and preschoolers, though, by the time she was four, she did very well using more complex jigsaw puzzles and tangram puzzles such as LestTans Cls. The app-based structure of the iOS allowed Ella to pick and choose the apps she liked without having to go through a traditional browser all the time.

Along with change in the types of apps, the biggest change over time for Ella was a *decrease in interest* in the iPad and iPhone and an *increase in interest* in the surrounding environment and outdoor games such as running and using the swing or cycling. With the assurance that the devices were always there, Ella spent time engaging in activities with her parents such as drawing and cutting paper and with outdoor activities. As she was drawn to new activities in her environment and as use of the iPad became "common" (Jones, 2009), Ella's "disengagement" with the iPad increased. This behavior is not surprising, as it was confirmed in previous studies by O'Brien and Toms (2008) and Weigle (2013), among others.

Druin (2009) cites a number of researchers who have suggested that we are entering a new era of technology-enhanced learning, characterized as mobile learning (e.g., Sharples, Taylor, & Vavoula, 2005; Tatar, Roschelle, Vahey, & Penuel, 2003), seamless learning (Chan et al., 2006), and ubiquitous learning (Rogers et al., 2005). Druin (2009) notes that "central to these notions is the idea that mobile technologies can be designed to enable children to move in and out of overlapping physical, digital, and communicative spaces" (pp. 4–5). This is in line with the idea of embodiment as expressed by Marshall and Rogers (2009), Price et al. (2009), and Dourish (2001), and possibly multitasking (Beheshti & Large, 2013). As to Ella, she would take the device and situate herself in various physical environments ranging from eating to playing in a sandbox to sitting with a parent, to drawing/coloring on paper or cutting and gluing paper while watching a video, thus experiencing "continuity across various learning experiences" (Druin, 2009, p. 5). Ella was also able to make a connection between the digital and physical worlds. For example, when she looked for shapes in the iPad (e.g., sky, clouds, and stars), she contemplated the clouds in the sky later in the evening. She never tried to swipe through physical photos as she did on the touch-based devices. This ability to distinguish between the two worlds is likely because of the adequate time spent by Ella in physical play and activities apart from her use of the touch devices.

While like Ella, children at very young age become motivated to use mobile devices, parents should be able to monitor use of these devices to ensure that the children are not disconnected from their physical environments. Deciding on access (e.g., limited or timed), preventing undesired use on shared devices (such as dialing a number or posting on Facebook), protecting the devices from damage, and guarding against hefty bills by disabling in-app purchases, and blocking inappropriate contents (e.g., violent cartoon videos) are examples of precautions that parents should take. Parents can also customize content by creating a list of videos that are appropriate for youngsters to watch. Use of apps such as those provided by *PBS Kids Education* will provide young users with age-appropriate content. However, it may prevent them from experimenting with searching by keyword at an early age.

Of importance is ensuring that young children are not absorbed by the digital world. Rosen (2013) recommends that children up to 4–5 years of age use technology at a ratio of 1 to 5, whereby 30 minutes of iPad usage is followed by 150 minutes spent doing something else including, but not limited to, talking to people, interacting with toys that promote creativity (and mind wandering), and doing activities that calm the brains. He cautions that children's overuse of technology can result in three primary issues: (1) a lack of time for essential personal interactions in the real world, (2) lack of time for creative thought and mind wandering (daydreaming and other non-task-oriented behaviors), and (3) lack of time for calming overactive brains (Rosen, 2012, 2013). Small and Vorgan (2008) echoed Rosen's concern. Turkle (2012) identifies the additional issue of "mind wandering," caused by a lack of time to learn about solitude and to be alone. Bilton (2013) notes that ensuring all-round child development while using technology should also include learning. Druin (2009) notes three important factors in designing effective mobile technology for children in support of learning: (1) avoid information overload; (2) prevent children from becoming too distracted by their mobile devices; and (3) constrain the design of the learning experience so that children do not work largely by themselves, if the desired goal is for them to collaborate.

Based on the findings from this study and the theoretical frameworks that guided this work, the framework shown in Table 1.1 describes Ella's engagement with the iPhone and iPad while ensuring all-round development. This framework should be validated in future research.

A child is situated in a context — home or day care or preschool, with his or her living and playing environment, and surrounded by adults. Thus, embodiment within a physical environment is a key aspect of a child's mobile interaction (Dourish, 2001; Druin, 2009; Marshall & Rogers, 2009; Price et al., 2009). Jones's (2009) three broad classes of activity spaces outside formal learning contexts can be classified under personal and shared contexts (see Agarwal et al., 2009). The attitudes and personalities of adults is part of the shared context of the child — an environment where a child communicates and expresses oneself. A child also brings in one's own personal context based on age (toddler or preschooler), personality and identity (Jones, 2009), interests and hobbies, ownership (e.g., "It's mine!") (Guernsey, 2009) and curiosity.

As per O'Brien and Toms (2008) and Weigle (2013), a child alternates between the cycles of point of engagement, sustained engagement, disengagement, and reengagement when interacting with devices such as iPads and iPhones. A series of factors affect each of these phases. In this process,

Table 1.1: Framework for effective engagement of toddlers or preschoolers with touch-based portable devices while ensuring all-round development.

Child in context	The child is situated/embodied in a physical environment; has personal unique attributes based on personality — "it's mine!", identity, interests, hobbies, causes, curiosity, age; shares context with people — plays, communicates, expresses self.			
	Moves seamlessly from physical ⇔ digital environment			
Process of device use	*Point of engagement*	*Sustained engagement*	*Disengagement*	*Reengagement*
Facilitated by	Device accessibility; ease of use; aesthetics; interactivity; portability; variety of suitable apps	Device aesthetics; interactivity; portability — embodiment, numinous qualities; variety of apps	Move to physical environment; interpersonal activity; another device; difficulty	Time alone; "It's mine!"; emotional connection; novelty/new apps; scaffolds/help from parents
Tasks — apps Based on purpose; variety; and access	Photo taking/browsing; personalization; own content; languages; finding/accessing; discovering new apps	Videos; jigsaw puzzles; drawing and coloring; educational features (shapes, colors, alphabet, words, math); games; reading		
Parental precautions	Device safety/charging; hefty bills; undesired content; limiting access	Information overload; distraction/zoning out; inappropriate content	Interpersonal interaction; creative thoughts; mind wandering	Shared usage; collaboration; attending to problems

a child also interacts with physical objects (Latham, 2009; Weigle, 2013) and moves seamlessly from the digital to the physical and back to digital or vice versa (Chan et al., 2006; Druin, 2009; Rogers et al., 2005; Sharples et al., 2005).

The factors facilitating point of engagement and sustained engagement were described under RQ-1. The child might choose to disengage with the device as she might be drawn to the physical environment (by a family member or to play), an interpersonal activity (playing, engaging in activities, talking, communicating), another device (when the charge in one device runs out) or finds difficulty with a particular app (which goes outside the ZPD (Vygotsky, 1978)). Finally, a child might want to reengage with the device either because she has time alone (after playing outside, for example), wants to assert ownership of the device and specific apps she has become attuned to, knows that new apps have been installed by the parents and wants to explore them, or because she want to retry a difficult tasks that the parents had solved (Bilal, 2007; Vygotsky, 1978). Parents should educate a child in what to watch or use, as well as in how to solve a problem in the right manner. To sustain engagement with the devices, a child's parent will need to guard against information overload (organize apps in folders; install limited apps; delete unused apps), prevent distraction, and filter inappropriate content. As to moving from the digital world to engagement the physical world, a parent will need to ensure that the child makes time for: interpersonal interaction with family and peers, creative activities, mind wandering and daydreaming (e.g., going for a walk or cycling), calming the mind (e.g., listening to music, meditating, sleeping), and learning about solitude (periods without access to devices) (Rosen, 2013; Turkle, 2012). Finally, shared usage of devices is important to ensure adequate insight into what is installed and being used by a child. A parent needs to be aware of all apps on a child accesses on a given device. In addition, the parent should support the child's seamless movement or disengagement from the digital environment and reengagement with the physical environment and vice versa.

1.7. Limitations

This study has the following limitations:

First, it observed only a single subject. Future work should include multiple subjects of various young age levels and gender to validate the framework described in this study.

Second, the observation based on which the data was collected provided insights into the child's observable behavior with the devices used, and excluded the child's thought processes and affective behaviors. To develop a better understanding of the child's holistic interaction with and use of the mobile devices, cognitive and affective behaviors should be explored, in addition to the actions made. (Bilal, 2007).

Third, the study did not assess the usability of the mobile devices the child used. Future research should examine the behaviors and interaction by a child and evaluate interface design features of the iPhone, iPad, or other mobile devices a child uses to unveil problem areas and provide suggestions for system-design improvements.

1.8. Conclusions and Future Work

This study sought to answer questions pertaining to the reasons why a toddler and preschooler child might want to use and engage with the iPad and the iPhone. It also examined the seamless relationship between the child's digital and physical worlds. Based on the findings from this study, parents should ensure a balance between a child's digital environment, social interaction, and the surrounding physical environment. This balance is essential for the child's all-round development.

A child emulates a parent's behavior. If a parent prevents the child from using digital devices that he or she is using on a regular basis, then the parent should restrict his or her own access of the devices. While technology is certainly a big part of our everyday life, there is more to parenting than the inclusion of technology. Establishing a value system and making a child feel loved and valued are among the factors that contribute to shaping the overall development of a child. Technology, while important, is just one part in a child's development, especially at a very young age.

The apps and factors leading to sustained engagement described in the Framework should be taken into consideration by parents or guardians, teachers, and school librarians to prevent overuse of the technology. As mobile devices such as the iPhone and iPad become ubiquitous among toddlers and preschoolers, system designers should provide targeted programming (e.g., reading, Math) for these young children, as well as consider the usability of the interface design of these devices.

Future work should build upon the findings of this study to examine the effect of and changes in mobile device use by children as they move from early childhood to adolescence. In addition, the Framework described in this study should be tested and validated in future research.

Acknowledgments

The author is grateful to Ella and her rich interaction with the mobile devices, which made this study possible. He thanks the anonymous reviewers of this chapter for their valuable comments and suggestions for improving it. He also thanks the editors (Dania Bilal and Jamshid Beheshti) for their thorough comments, suggestions, and editing of this chapter. He gives thanks to Joshua Jasper for suggesting edits to this chapter.

References

Abbas, J., & Agosto, D. E. (2013). Everyday life information behavior of young people. In J. Beheshti & A. Large (Eds.), *The information behavior of a new generation: Children and teens in the 21st century* (pp. 65–92). Plymouth, UK: The Scarecrow Press.

Agarwal, N. K. (2012, October 26–31). Making sense of sense-making: Tracing the history and development of Dervin's sense-making methodology. In *2012 pre-conference on the history of ASIS&T and the history of information science and technology worldwide*, Baltimore, MD.

Agarwal, N. K., Poo, D. C. C., & Tan, K. H. (2007, December 9–12). Impediments to sharing knowledge outside the school: Lessons learnt from the development of a taxonomic e-learning portal. In *Proceedings of the International Conference on Information Systems* (Paper 81, pp. 1–16), Montreal, Canada.

Agarwal, N. K., Xu, Y. (C.), & Poo, D. C. C. (2009, November 6–11). Delineating the boundary of "context" in information behavior: Towards a contextual identity framework. *ASIS&T 2009 Annual Meeting*, Vancouver, BC, Canada. Retrieved from http://www.asis.org/Conferences/AM09/open-proceedings/papers/52.xml

Agarwal, N. K., Xu, Y. (C.), & Poo, D. C. C. (2011). A context-based investigation into source use by information seekers. *Journal of the American Society for Information Science and Technology*, *62*(6), 1087–1104.

Akin, L. (1998). Information overload and children: A survey of Texas elementary school students. *School Library Media Quarterly Online*, *1*, 1–15.

Alexandersson, M., & Limberg, L. (2003). Constructing meaning through information architects. *The New Review of Information Behavior Research*, *4*(1), 17–31.

Apple. (2013a). *Identifying iPad models*. Retrieved from http://support.apple.com/kb/ht5452. Accessed on April 28, 2013.

Apple. (2013b). *iPhone*. Retrieved from http://www.apple.com/iphone/built-in-apps/. Accessed on April 28, 2013.

ASDF. (2012a). *iPad program*. Autism Spectrum Disorder Foundation. Retrieved from http://www.myasdf.org/site/our-programs/ipad-program/. Accessed on October 27, 2013.

ASDF. (2012b). *Why the iPad is such a helpful learning tool for children with autism*. Retrieved from http://www.myasdf.org/site/media-center/articles/why-the-ipad-is-such-a-helpful-learning-tool-for-children-with-autism/. Accessed on October 27, 2013.

Associated Press. (2012, September 12). *Timeline: Apple iPhone to iPhone 5*. Retrieved from http://ibnlive.in.com/news/timeline-apple-iphone-to-iphone-5/290889-11.html. Accessed on April 29, 2013.

Beck, S. E., & Manuel, K. (2008). Observation and usability. In *Practical research methods for librarians and information professionals* (pp. 109–129). New York, NY: Neal-Schuman Publishers.

Beheshti, J., & Large, A. (Eds.). (2013). *The information behavior of a new generation: Children and teens in the 21st century*. Plymouth, UK: The Scarecrow Press.

Bilal, D. (2000). Children's use of the Yahooligans! Web search engine: I. Cognitive, physical and affective behaviors on fact-based search tasks. *Journal of the American Society for Information Science and Technology*, *51*(7), 646–665.

Bilal, D. (2001). Children's use of the Yahooligans! Web search engine: II. Cognitive and physical behaviors on research tasks. *Journal of the American Society for Information Science and Technology*, *52*(2), 118–136.

Bilal, D. (2002). Children's use of the Yahooligans! Web search engine: III. Cognitive and physical behaviors on fully self-generated search tasks. *Journal of the American Society for Information Science and Technology*, *53*, 1170–1183.

Bilal, D. (2003). Draw and tell: Children as designers of web interfaces. In R. Todd (Ed.), *Humanizing information technology: From ideas to bits and back. Proceedings of the 66th ASIS&T annual meeting* (Vol. 40, pp. 135–142). Medford, NJ: Information Today.

Bilal, D. (2007). Grounding children's information behavior and system design in child development theories. In D. Nahl & D. Bilal (Eds.), *Information and emotion: The emergent affective paradigm in information behavior research and theory* (pp. 39–50). Medford, NJ: Information Today.

Bilal, D., & Bachir, I. (2007a). Children's interaction with cross-cultural and multilingual digital libraries. I. Understanding interface design representations. *Information Processing and Management*, *43*, 47–64.

Bilal, D., & Bachir, I. (2007b). Children's interaction with cross-cultural and multilingual digital libraries. II. Information seeking, success, and affective experience. *Information Processing and Management*, *43*, 65–80.

Bilal, D., & Kirby, J. (2002). Differences and similarities in information seeking: Children and adults as web users. *Information Processing and Management*, *38*, 649–670.

Bilal, D., & Sarangthem, S. (2008, August 3–7). Task-based models of children's information-seeking behavior in digital libraries. In *Proceedings of the International Association of School Librarians (IASL) Conference*, Berkeley, CA.

Bilal, D., Sarangthem, S., & Bachir, I. (2008). Toward a model of children's information seeking behavior in using digital libraries. *Proceedings of the international symposium on information interaction in context*. New York, NY: ACM.

Bilton, N. (2013). The child, the tablet and the developing mind. *The New York Times – Bits*. Retrieved from http://bits.blogs.nytimes.com/2013/03/31/disruptions-what-does-a-tablet-do-to-the-childs-mind/. Accessed on April 28, 2013.

Bowler, L., Large, A., Beheshti, J., & Nesset, V. (2005). Children and adults working together in the zone of proximal development: A theory for user-centered design. In *Proceedings of the Canadian Association for Information Science 2005 Annual Conference*, June 2-4, London, Ontario.

Carr, W., & Kemmis, S. (1986). *Becoming critical: Education, knowledge and action research*. London: Falmer Press.

Case, D. O. (2012). *Looking for information: A survey of research on information seeking, needs and behavior* (3rd ed.). Bingley, UK: Emerald Group Publishing Limited.

Chan, T. W., Roschelle, J., Hsi, S., Kinshuk, K., Sharples, M., Brown, T., ... Milrad, M. (2006). One-to-one technology-enhanced learning: An opportunity for global research collaboration. *Research and Practice in Technology Enhanced Learning*, *1*(1), 3–29.

Cole, C. (2013). Concepts, propositions, models, and theories in information behavior research. In J. Beheshti & A. Large (Eds.), *The information behavior of a new generation: Children and teens in the 21st century* (pp. 1–22). Plymouth, UK: The Scarecrow Press.

Cooper, L. Z. (2002). A case study of information-seeking behavior in 7-year-old children in a semistructured situation. *Journal of the American Society for Information Science and Technology*, *53*, 904–922.

Corbin, J., & Strauss, A. (1990). Grounded theory research: Procedures, canons, and evaluative criteria. *Qualitative Sociology*, *13*(1), 3–21.

Davis, F. D. (1989). Perceived usefulness, perceived ease of use, and user acceptance of information technology. *MIS Quarterly*, *13*(3), 319–340.

Dervin, B., Foreman-Wernet, L., & Lauterbach, E. (Eds.). (2003). *Sense-making methodology reader: Selected writings of Brenda Dervin*. Cresskill, NJ: Hampton Press.

Desmet, P. M. A., Porcelijn, R., & van Dijk, M. B. (2007). Emotional design; application of a research-based design approach. *Knowledge Technology & Policy*, *20*, 141–155.

Dourish, P. (2001). *Where the action is: The foundations of embodied interaction*. Cambridge, MA: MIT Press.

Dresang, E. T. (1999). *Radical change: Books for youth in a digital age*. New York, NY: H.W. Wilson.

Dresang, E. T. (2013). Digital age libraries and youth: Learning labs, literacy leaders, radical resources. In J. Beheshti & A. Large (Eds.), *The information behavior of a new generation: Children and teens in the 21st century* (pp. 93–116). Plymouth, UK: The Scarecrow Press.

Druin, A. (2005). What children can teach us: Developing digital libraries for children with children. *Library Quarterly*, *75*, 20–41.

Druin, A. (Ed.). (2009). *Mobile technology for children: Designing for interaction and learning*. Morgan Kaufmann Series in Interactive Technologies. Burlington, MA: Morgan Kaufmann Publishers.

Erikson, E. H. (1968). *Identity: Youth and crisis*. New York, NY: W. W. Norton & Company.

Faulkner, L. (2003). Beyond the five-user assumption: Benefits of increased sample sizes in usability testing. *Behavior Research Methods, Instruments, & Computers, 35*(3), 379–383.

Fidel, R., Davies, R. K., Douglass, M. H., Holder, J. K., Hopkins, C. J., Kushner, E. J. ... Toney, C. D. (1999). A visit to the information mall: Web searching behavior of high school students. *Journal of the American Society for Information Science and Technology, 50*(1), 24–37.

Goodhue, D. L., & Thompson, R. L. (1995). Task-technology fit and individual performance. *MIS Quarterly, 19*(2), 213–236.

Graves, A. (n.d.). *Children's information-seeking behavior: A bibliography*. Retrieved from http://www.pages.drexel.edu/~aeg46/bib.html. Accessed on February 1, 2014.

Guernsey, L. (2009). "It's mine": Kids carrying their culture wherever they go. In A. Druin (Ed.), *Mobile technology for children: Designing for interaction and learning* (pp. 245–264). Morgan Kaufmann Series in Interactive Technologies. Burlington, MA: Morgan Kaufmann Publishers.

Hirsh, S. (1997). How do children find information on different types of tasks? Children's use of the science library catalog. *Library Trends, 45*(4), 725–745.

Hirsh, S. (1999). Children's relevance criteria and information seeking on electronic resources. *Journal of the American Society for Information Science and Technology, 50*(14), 1265–1283.

Huang, R., Kinshuk, & Spector, J. M. (Eds.). (2013). *Reshaping learning: Frontiers of learning technology in a global context*. New Frontiers of Educational Research. London: Springer.

ITU. (2013, February 27). *The world in 2013: ICT facts and figures*. Geneva, Switzerland: International Telecommunication Union, ICT Data and Statistics Division, Telecommunication Development Bureau.

Jones, M. (2009). Mobile interaction design matters. In A. Druin (Ed.), *Mobile technology for children: Designing for interaction and learning* (pp. 101–124). Morgan Kaufmann Series in Interactive Technologies. Burlington, MA: Morgan Kaufmann Publishers.

Kafai, Y., & Bates, M. (1997). Internet web-searching instruction in the elementary classroom: Building a foundation for information literacy. *School Library Media Quarterly, 25*(2), 103–111.

Kaplan, B., & Maxwell, J. A. (1994). Qualitative research methods for evaluating computer information systems. In J. G. Anderson, C. E. Aydin, & S. J. Jay (Eds.), *Evaluating health care information systems: Methods and applications* (pp. 45–68). Thousand Oaks, CA: Sage.

Klein, H. K., & Myers, M. D. (1999). A set of principles for conducting and evaluating interpretive field studies in information systems. *MIS Quarterly, 23*(1), 67–94.

Krug, S. (2009). *Rocket surgery made easy: The do-it-yourself guide to finding and fixing usability problems*. Berkeley, CA: New Riders.

Krug, S. (2013, March 28). Usability: These are a | few of my | fav- or- ite | things.... *Some Slightly Irregular: Steve Krug's blog about usability (mostly)*. Retrieved from http://someslightlyirregular.com/2013/03/these-are-a-few-of-my-fav-or-ite-things/. Accessed on April 27, 2013.

Lapetino. (2012, January 21). A digital generation searching for analog experiences. *Zeroside*. Hexanine. Retrieved from http://www.hexanine.com/zeroside/a-digital-generation-searching-for-analog-experiences/. Accessed on April 28, 2013.

Large, A., Bowler, L., Beheshti, J., & Nesset, V. (2007, April 15). Creating web portals with children as designers: Bonded design and the zone of proximal development. *McGill Journal of Education*, *42*(1), 61–82.

Larkin-Lieffers, P. A. (2002). Informational picture books in the library: Do young children find them? *Public Library Quarterly*, *20*(3), 3–28.

Latham, K. F. (2009). *Numinous experiences with museum objects*. Doctoral dissertation, ProQuest Dissertations and Theses database (ATT 3357980).

Lazonder, A. W., Biemans, H. J., & Wopereis, I. (2000). Differences between novice and experienced users in searching information on the world wide web. *Journal of the American Society for Information Science and Technology*, *52*(6), 576–581.

Lingnau, A., Ruthven, I., & Landoni, M. (2011, July 28). Show and tell: Supporting children's search by interactively creating stories. In *SIGIR workshop on "Entertain me: Supporting complex search tasks"*, Beijing, China.

Marsh, J., Brooks, G., Hughes, J., Ritchie, L., Roberts, S., & Wright, K. (2005). *Digital beginnings: Young children's use of popular culture, media and new technologies*. Sheffield: Literacy Research Centre, University of Sheffield.

Marshall, P., & Rogers, Y. (2009). Embodied learning: A new approach. In Proceedings of the 13th Biennial EARLI Conference for Research on Learning and Instruction, August 25–29, Amsterdam, The Netherlands.

Mather, J. (2007, February 19). iMania. *The Ryerson Review of Journalism*. Retrieved from http://www.rrj.ca/m4058/. Accessed on April 29, 2013.

McCarthy, J., & Wright, P. (2004). *Technology as experience*. Cambridge, MA: The MIT Press.

Merriam-Webster. (n.d.). *Merriam-Webster.com*. Retrieved from http://www.merriam-webster.com/dictionary. Accessed on February 1, 2014.

Myers, M. D. (1997, June). Qualitative research in information systems. *MIS Quarterly*, *21*(2), 241–242. MISQ Discovery archival version. Retrieved from http://www.qual.auckland.ac.nz/. Accessed on October 27, 2013.

Nesset, V. (2013, April). Two representations of the research process: The preparing, searching, and using (PSU) and the beginning, acting and telling (BAT) models. *Library & Information Science Research*, *35*(2), 97–106.

Nesset, V., & Large, A. (2004). Children in the information technology design process: A review of theories and their applications. *Library and Information Science Research*, *26*(2), 140–161.

Nielsen, J. (2000, March 19). Why you only need to test with 5 users. In *Jacob Neilsen's Alertbox*. Fremont, CA: Nielsen Norman Group. Retrieved from http://www.nngroup.com/articles/why-you-only-need-to-test-with-5-users/. Accessed on April 27, 2013.

O'Brien, H. L., & Toms, E. G. (2008). What is user engagement? A conceptual framework for defining user engagement with technology. *Journal of the American Society for Information Science and Technology*, *59*(6), 938–955.

O'Brien, H. L., & Toms, E. G. (2010). The development and evaluation of a survey to measure user engagement. *Journal of the American Society for Information Science and Technology*, *61*(1), 50–69.

Overbeeke, K., Djajadiningrat, T., Hummels, C., Wensveen, S., & Frens, J. (2003). Let's make things engaging. In M. A. Blythe, K. Overbeeke, A. F. Monk, & P. C. Wright (Eds.), *Funology: From usability to enjoyment* (pp. 7–17). Dordrecht, The Netherlands: Kluwer Academic Press.

Pacey, A. (1999). *Meaning in technology*. Cambridge, MA: The MIT Press.

Pan, S. L., & Tan, B. (2011). Demystifying case research: A structured–pragmatic–situational (SPS) approach to conducting case studies. *Information and Organization*, *21*(3), 161–176.

Price, S., Roussos, G., Pontual Falcão, T., & Sheridan, J. (2009). Embodiment: The body, knowledge, creativity and communication. *Review for beyond current horizons*. Bristol: DCSF.

Reuter, K., & Druin, A. (2004). Bringing together children and books: An initial descriptive study of children's book searching and selection behavior in a digital library. *Proceedings of the American Society for Information Science and Technology Annual Meeting*, *41*, 339–348.

Revelle, G. L., & Strommen, E. F. (1990). The effects of practice and input device used on young children's computer control. *Collegiate Microcomputer*, *8*(4), 33–41.

Rideout, V., & Hamel, E. (2006). *The media family: Electronic media in the lives of infants, toddlers preschoolers and their parents*. Menlo Park, CA: The Henry J. Kaiser Family Foundation.

Rogers, Y., Price, S., Randell, C., Stanton-Fraser, D., Weal, M., & Fitzpatrick, G. (2005). Ubi-learning: Integrating outdoor and indoor learning experiences. *Communications of the ACM*, *48*(1), 55–59.

Rosen, L. (2013, April 24). How much technology should you let your child use? *Huff Post ScreenSense*. Retrieved from http://www.huffingtonpost.com/dr-larry-rosen/how-much-technology-shoul_b_3142227.html. Accessed on April 28, 2013.

Rosen, L. D. (2012). *iDisorder: Understanding our obsession with technology and overcoming its hold on us*. New York, NY: Palgrave Macmillan.

Savolainen, R. (1995, Summer). Everyday life information seeking: Approaching information seeking in the context of "way of life". *Library & Information Science Research*, *17*(3), 259–294.

Sharples, M., Taylor, J., & Vavoula, G. (2005). Toward a theory of mobile learning. *Proceedings of mLearn 2005 conference*, Cape Town.

Shneiderman, B. (2002). *Leonardo's laptop*. Cambridge, MA: The MIT Press.

Small, G., & Vorgan, G. (2008). *iBrain: Surviving the technological alteration of the modern mind* (1st ed.). New York, NY: Collins Living.

Soloway, E., Norris, C., Blumenfeld, P., Fishman, B., Krajcik, J., & Marx, R. (2001, June). Handheld devices are ready-at-hand. Log on education. *Communications of the ACM*, *44*(6), 15–20.

Spink, A. (2010). *Information behavior: An evolutionary instinct* (Vol. 16). Information Science and Knowledge Management. Heidelberg, Germany: Springer.

Spink, A., Danby, S., Mallan, K., & Butler, C. (2010). Exploring young children's web searching and technoliteracy. *Journal of Documentation*, *66*(2), 191–206.

Spink, A., & Heinström, J. (2011). Information behavior development in early childhood. In A. Spink & J. Heinström (Eds.), *New directions in information behaviour* (pp. 245–256). Bingley, UK: Emerald Group Publishing Limited.

Tatar, D., Roschelle, J., Vahey, P., & Penuel, W. (2003, September). Handhelds go to school: Lessons learned. *Computer, IEEE Computer Society*, *9*, 30–37.

Todd, R. J. (2003). Adolescents of the information age: Patterns of information seeking and use, and implications for information professionals. *School Libraries Worldwide*, *9*(2), 27–46.

Tomlin, W. C. (2010, February 18). Heardable and usability testing with 1 person. *Useful Usability*. Retrieved from http://www.usefulusability.com/heardable-and-usability-testing-with-1-person/. Accessed on April 25, 2013.

Turkle, S. (2012). *Alone together: Why we expect more from technology and less from each other* (First Trade Paper Edition). New York, NY: Basic Books.

Vincenti, G. (2013). Gaming and virtual environments. In J. Beheshti & A. Large (Eds.), *The information behavior of a new generation: Children and teens in the 21st century* (pp. 143–166). Plymouth, UK: The Scarecrow Press.

Vygotsky, L. (1978). *Mind in society: The development of higher psychological processes*. Cambridge, MA: Harvard University Press.

Walter, V. A. (1994). The information needs of children. In I. Godden (Ed.), *Advances in librarianship* (Vol. 18, pp. 111–129). San Diego, CA: Academic Press.

Watson, J. S. (1998). If you don't have it, you can't find it: A close look at students' perceptions of using technology. *Journal of the American Society for Information Science and Technology*, *49*(11), 1024–1036.

Weigle, A. (2013). *User engagement with physical objects: An investigation on the multi-dimensional experience of archival users*. Unpublished manuscript, Simmons College, Boston, MA.

Wright, P., Wallace, J., & McCarthy, J. (2008). Aesthetics and experience-centered design. *ACM Transactions on Computer-Human Interaction*, *15*(4), 1–18, 21.

Yin, R. K. (2014). *Case study research: Design and methods* (5th ed.). Thousand Oaks, CA: Sage.

Zweizig, D., Johnson, D., Robbins, J., & Besant, M. (1996). *The tell it! Manual: The complete program for evaluating library performance*. Chicago, IL: American Library Association.

Chapter 2

Depicting the Intersection between Information-Seeking Behavior and Information Literacy in the Research Process: A Model

Valerie Nesset

Abstract

Purpose – The purpose of this chapter is to present a model (Beginning, Acting, Telling (BAT) model) developed for the elementary-school classroom that integrates features identified by research into information-seeking behavior and information literacy.

Methodology/approach – The chapter provides an overview of research in the areas of information-seeking behavior and information literacy and models in which they have intersected (namely, the Information Search Process (ISP) model) to provide a theoretical framework in which to situate the BAT model. Examples from previous empirical studies conducted by the author that informed the model are provided.

Findings – A preliminary iteration of the BAT model has successfully been piloted in two third-grade classrooms in Buffalo, New York. Plans are underway to introduce the model to a wider audience.

Practical implications – The BAT model with its use of image and mnemonic cues can be used to teach the research process to students, beginning in the earliest grades of elementary school.

New Directions in Children's and Adolescents' Information Behavior Research
Library and Information Science, Volume 10, 39–66

ISSN: 1876-0562/doi:10.1108/S1876-056220140000010017

Originality/value of chapter – This chapter is the first time the final iteration of the BAT model has been presented. It is the first model integrating features inherent in information-seeking behavior and information literacy that also makes use of imagery and mnemonic.

Keywords: Information-seeking behavior; information literacy; children; elementary school; research process; Beginning, Acting, Telling (BAT) model

2.1. Introduction

For the past several decades, information-seeking behavior has been recognized as an important research area within the discipline of library and information science (LIS). Similarly, literacy and reading have been key components of research both in LIS and in education, most recently coming to the fore in LIS with the advent of the Internet and other information technologies. While the two disciplines share an interest in literacy, investigation of the literature into information-seeking behavior and information literacy shows a sharp divide. LIS research concentrates mainly on information-seeking behavior; that is, on the users and how they search for, locate, retrieve, and use information. Furthermore, this research has tended to concentrate on older adolescents (high school), undergraduate and graduate students; little research has been done with younger children. Conversely, while the educational literature is rich with research studies in the K-12 milieu that investigate what in LIS is termed, "information literacy," educational studies tend to focus on instructional methods and the efficacy of these methods in terms of student achievement; there is little mention of what behaviors the students are exhibiting. Indeed, the term, "information-seeking behavior" is not even seen in the educational literature unless the research is related in some way to librarianship (e.g., research conducted in school library media centers).

This chapter presents a model of the research process that was developed for elementary school students for use inside and outside the classroom. This three-stage model integrates aspects culled from research into information-seeking behavior (e.g., modeling, stages of process, identification of cognitive and affective behaviors) with those from information literacy instruction (e.g., preparation of the student through instruction, information use) and evidence gathered during a study of the information-seeking behavior of third-grade students (Nesset, 2007, 2009, 2013). The model makes use of a visual (a bat; the word "bat" is an acronym for "beginning, acting, telling") and mnemonic the labels for each of the stages to help students, especially younger ones, readily learn, remember, and internalize the research process. To set the framework for the model, it is necessary to investigate the relevant research both in information-seeking behavior and information literacy instruction.

2.2. Models of Information-Seeking Behavior

Information-seeking behavior has been defined as "a process that includes multiple stages of question asking and refining, information gathering and evaluating ... synthesis and use of information" (Wallace, Kupperman, Krajcik, & Soloway, 2000, p. 97) as well as "a process in which humans purposefully engage in order to change their state of knowledge" (Marchionini, 1995, p. 5). Several studies of children (mainly older elementary school students and adolescents) have shown that children's information needs and search methods differ from those of adults, especially in the digital environment (Bilal, 2012; Bilal & Kirby, 2002; Cooper, 2002a; Revelle et al., 2002; Shenton & Dixon, 2003a; Walter, 1994) and that a relationship exists between children's information needs and their search methods (Bilal, 2000, 2001, 2002, 2012; Kuhlthau, 1988b). Furthermore, research has identified a number of children's characteristics and external factors that influence information seeking: a lack of strategic thinking and planning when seeking the information needed to complete an assigned task (Cooper, 2002a; Hirsh, 1997; Kuhlthau, 1988b, 1991; Large & Beheshti, 2000; Moore, 2000; Schacter, Chung, & Dorr, 1998); information-seeking behavior can vary depending on the level of domain knowledge (Bilal, 2000; Hirsh, 1996, 1997; Lawless, Mills, & Brown, 2002) and the amount of prior searching experience (Slone, 2003); and finally, affective behaviors often play as large a role as cognition in children's information-seeking behavior — much more so than they do in adults (Cooper, 2002a, 2002b; Kuhlthau, 1988a).

In addition to the characteristics listed above, there are external factors that can impact information-seeking processes and outcomes: project/assignment design (Curtis, 2002; Kuhlthau, 1988b; Shenton & Fitzgibbons, 2010); web-related features such as the design of search engines and websites (Bilal, 2000, 2001, 2002, 2012; Borgman, Hirsh, Walter, & Gallagher, 1995); the efficacy of filtering systems (Bruce, 1999; Wolinsky, 2001); resource currency, appropriateness of content (especially on the Web), and readability levels (Bowler, Nesset, Large, & Beheshti, 2004); and the design and complexity of metadata (e.g., indexes, tables of contents, and subject directories) and classification schemes (Joyce & Joyce, 1970; Laverty, 2002; Shenton & Dixon, 2003c).

Typically, the main goal of studies investigating information-seeking behavior is to produce models that can be used to predict and/or modify behavior of different user groups. Models differ from theories in that models focus on more specific or limited problems (Case, 2012). Although both models and theories present simplified versions of reality, models do so in a more concrete and visual manner, usually through the use of diagrams. Both models and theories identify and describe relationships between concepts but models are linked more to the real world (Case, 2012) and can be used as "framework[s] for thinking about a problem … they are statements, often in the form of diagrams, that attempt to describe an information-seeking activity, the causes and consequences of that activity, or the relationships among stages in information-seeking behaviour" (Wilson, 1999b, p. 250). Thus, most if not all of these models focus on process. The efficacy of such models can be asserted by their proliferation. Since the early 1980s, many models of information-seeking behavior have been developed (see, e.g., Case, 2012; Fisher, Erdelez, & McKechnie, 2005) to identify and explain the information-seeking behavior of many different user groups. Yet, despite this proliferation, existing models concentrate mainly on the search task and they often assume fairly advanced research, reading, and writing skills and/or are based on research with older adolescents or adults. The few models that have been developed using empirical evidence from studies of young people (e.g., Agosto, 2002; Kuhlthau, 1988a, 1991, 2004; Shenton & Dixon, 2003b; Shenton & Hay-Gibson, 2011b) while they begin to address the research process more holistically, still tend to focus heavily on the search task.

As representative models of information-seeking behavior, although often developed through empirical research with different user groups, the above models share two critical elements: they are at least partially diagrammatic and they focus on process (mainly that of searching).

2.3. Models of Information Literacy

Although information literacy has been defined in many different ways within different contexts, it is generally seen as a process involving learning, reasoning/problem-solving, experience, interaction, and reflection; furthermore, historically it often emphasized adherence to a set of established standards and/or skills (Bruce, 2000a, 2000b; Eisenberg & Berkowitz, 1990; Herring, 2009; Kuhlthau, 2004; Marland, 1981; Moore, 1995, 2000). It should be noted, however, that some scholars have called for recognition of the roles that such things as context (Lloyd, 2005, 2010), uncertainty (Kuhlthau, 1988c, 1999, 2004; Wilson, 1999a), and curiosity (Bowler, 2010) play.

Information literacy models tend to differ from information-seeking models both in their intended audience (usually children and educators, including both teachers and information professionals, in the K-12 system) and in the way they are presented. Unlike models of information-seeking behavior which are most often visual and diagrammatic in nature and attempt to identify and explain patterns of behavior to inform such areas as information system design, information literacy models are most often used for instructional purposes. They do not necessarily identify actual behaviors and/or processes but instead typically present an idealized, prescriptive set of steps (often written in the form of questions) to provide a framework for the teacher/librarian and to encourage metacognition on the part of the student. As with the Information Power (American Association of School Librarians & Association for Educational Communications and Technology, 1998) and the most recent "Standards for the 21st Century Learner in Action" (American Association of School Librarians [AASL], 2009) approach, they may rely on a set of skills and/or standards and often emphasize the experience. Bruce (2000a) identifies seven "faces" or experiences of information literacy (p. 216): The IT experience, the information sources experience, the information-process experience, the information control experience, the knowledge construction experience, the knowledge extension experience, and the wisdom experience. Each experience builds upon the others to produce an information product and/or increase the individual's knowledge base so that s/he can apply it to later situations. Even the most cursory search of the literature in both Education and LIS reveals numerous models of information literacy — so many, in fact, it is only possible to provide a small sample of those that focus on process and have been used in the K-12 environment: the Big6 (Eisenberg & Berkowitz, 1990), the Purpose, Location, Use, Self-Evaluation (PLUS) model (Herring, 1996), and the Extending Interactions with Text (EXIT) model (Wray & Lewis, 1995).

The Big6 (Eisenberg & Berkowitz, 1990) is a skill-based model comprised of six steps that encourage students to engage in metacognitive practices by helping to make them aware of necessary steps in the information-seeking process. The six steps are: (1) Task Definition: What needs to be done? (2) Information-Seeking Strategies: What resources can I use? (3) Location and Access: Where can I find these resources? (4) Use of Information: What can I use from these resources? (5) Synthesis: What can I make to finish the job? (6) Evaluation: How will I know I did my job well? (Choi, Wheelehan, & Beers, 2001). Based on the Big6, Eisenberg and Robinson (2007) introduced Super3 specifically for younger children (grades K-2). Comprised of three simple steps, "1) Plan 2) Do 3) Review," presented in a "logical" sequence, the Super3 was designed to be broad enough to encompass different activities in a different order, while also being simple to remember and learn (Eisenberg & Robinson, 2007; Robinson, 2008). The Big6 has been validated in several studies (e.g., Eisenberg, 2003; Wolf, Brush, & Saye, 2003) and the Super3 has been validated in studies such as that done by Chen and Chen (2013) with second-grade students.

While the Big6 model has been and continues to be used extensively in K-12 classrooms throughout North America and beyond (e.g., Chang et al., 2012), its several steps, rather sophisticated vocabulary, and lack of a visual component and/or mnemonic can make it harder for students to remember on their own. Similarly, its offshoot, the Super3 while easier to remember, is very broad, which may make it very difficult for young students to be able to use independently. Indeed, one of the findings of the study done by Chen and Chen (2013) was that the second-grade students performed well only in the Plan phase; they needed the teachers' help to pose inquiry questions. It would seem that both models require significant adult guidance and intervention to be successful.

The EXIT (EXtending Interactions with Text) model (Wray & Lewis, 1995), built upon the work of Marland (1981) and developed in the United Kingdom for elementary school students, is based on the idea that "any model aiming to describe the process of interacting with expository texts must account for its transactional nature and build in a strong element of the reader contributing to the constructed meaning" (p. 3). The model also emphasizes the importance of learning material by making connections with prior knowledge; "Learning which does not make connections with our prior knowledge is learning at the level of rote only, and is soon forgotten once deliberate attempts to remember it have stopped" (Wray & Lewis, 1995, p. 4) as well as connecting a learning activity (e.g., learning how to use an index to locate information) "within the context of actually doing it, usually as part of an investigative project" (p. 5). The EXIT model comprises 10 metacognitive questions: the first two questions concentrate on thinking about how to go about looking for information, the next seven focus on actions associated with information seeking; and the last (tenth) question deals with the presentation of the information. As with the Big6, so many sequential questions or steps may be difficult to remember, especially for younger children and the mnemonic is not useful for this purpose. The EXIT model also assumes knowledge of at least basic reading, writing, and research skills, some of which younger students may not yet possess.

The PLUS (Purpose, Location, Use, Self-Evaluation) model was developed in the United Kingdom for use with secondary school students (Herring, 1996). Similar to the Big6, the PLUS model does not assume prior domain knowledge and research skills and it advocates the preparation of students before they begin to search for information. The model was validated in a study of 112 seventh-grade students (aged 11–12 years) who were studying physics (Herring, Tarter, & Naylor, 2002). It was found that "... most of them [students] found using the model generally beneficial, as it helped them to plan their work, to be more organized, and to reflect on the different stages of the information skills process" (p. 19). While the model was successful in the subsequent study, provides an engaging mnemonic, and makes many suggestions for guiding the students through the information research process (e.g., concept mapping, using indexes and subject directories, brainstorming, communicating information, self-evaluating), it does not provide the opportunity to see the entire process at once; instead, it relies on a fairly lengthy description of the four stages to communicate its point.

All of these information literacy models share three common features: they rely on metacognitive questions or steps to convey their ideas; they outline a best-practice scenario, and they are more conceptual in nature with few empirical studies that provide evidence indicating they are effective in helping young students navigate and master the various elements inherent in information literacy. Furthermore, only the EXIT model explicitly mentions information behavior, and it does so only peripherally in the context of some of its questions.

2.4. The Intersection of Information-Seeking Behavior and Information Literacy

As noted above, the main differences between models of information-seeking behavior and information literacy instruction are the fact that the former are almost always visualized in some way and focus on behavior and process, while the latter are not visualized and rely on metacognitive steps and/or questions to aid instruction. While there are these main differences, there are similarities as well. Both make use of models to present best practice (although information literacy models are not usually diagrammatic), and both can be used to modify and/or predict behavior. Carrying this even further, models for information literacy instruction could be made more holistic and comprehensive with the inclusion of behaviors, models of information-seeking behavior could be enhanced with the addition of metacognitive elements, and both areas could benefit from the fact that all of the steps and associated elements are visible at the same time. Many researchers (e.g., Julien & Williamson, 2010; Limberg & Sundin, 2006) have conducted and/or discussed research integrating information-seeking behavior and information literacy and have even proposed models (e.g., Shenton & Hay-Gibson, 2011a) but to date it would appear that only the Information Search Process (ISP) model developed by

Kuhlthau (1988a, 1988b, 1988c, 1991, 1993b, 2004, 2010) has been empirically proven to have successfully integrated research into information-seeking behavior and information literacy.

Over almost three decades the ISP has proven itself to be a comprehensive and holistic model successful not only within the school environment (Kuhlthau, 1988a, 1988b, 1988c, 1991, 1993b, 2004; Kuhlthau, Heinström, & Todd, 2008; Kuhlthau, Maniotes, & Caspari, 2007; Kuhlthau, Turock, George, & Belvin, 1990) but also in higher education (Kracker, 2002; Kuhlthau, 1988c, 2004) and in the workplace (Kuhlthau, 1999, 2004; Kuhlthau & Tama, 2001). Thus, the model has been used not only "to examine theoretical concepts within librarianship and information science … [but also] to develop practice in diverse contexts including education, work and every-day life information seeking" (Kuhlthau et al., 2008, p. 3). The ISP consists of six steps: task initiation, selection, exploration, formulation, collection, and presentation which are presented within the three dimensions of behavior: feelings (affective), thoughts (cognitive), and actions (physical). In so doing, the ISP situates itself squarely in the intersection between information-seeking behavior and information literacy. More recently, the ISP has been used to support an approach to learning Kuhlthau terms, "guided inquiry" (Kuhlthau, 2010; Kuhlthau et al., 2007). Indeed, Kuhlthau (2010) describes guided inquiry as one of the results of the natural progression of school librarianship over the past three decades, "school librarianship has evolved from emphasis on library skills to information skills in the 1980s, to information literacy in the 1990s, to inquiry as a way of learning in the first decade of the 21st century" (p. 19).

While the ISP integrates elements from research into the areas of information-seeking behavior and information literacy and in its depiction of a process approach to research has proven to be a useful tool regardless of context, it does not make use of visual imagery and/or mnemonic. Research into children's intellectual development has demonstrated that children often rely on visual cues when learning new concepts (Ginsburg & Opper, 1988; Kail, 2004; Piaget & Inhelder, 1969; Siegler, 1998). In the area of language acquisition, specifically vocabulary, the use of mnemonic as a memory aid has been shown to be efficacious (Amiriyousefi & Ketabi, 2011; Fontana, Scruggs, & Mastropieri, 2007; Levin, McCormick, Miller, Berry, & Pressley, 1982; McCormick & Levin, 1984).

As the ISP has proven, a process approach to research can be used over a wide spectrum of grade levels and contexts especially when such research occurs over a long period of time (e.g., over an entire semester). Indeed, Marland (1981) argues "that from primary school project to PhD thesis the questions and the processes are fundamentally the same" (p. 14). It would follow, then, that a process model that integrates visuals (characteristic of many models of information-seeking behavior) along with a mnemonic (characteristic of many models for information literacy instruction), could be more easily learned, assimilated, and remembered by younger students. The Beginning, Acting, Telling (BAT) model strives to combine all of these features into one visual model to facilitate recognition, learning, and retention of the research process. Furthermore, like the ISP, the BAT can be applied to any subject area although it is designed specifically for the elementary-school environment. In addition to the use of visual imagery and mnemonic, the BAT significantly differs from the ISP in its inclusion of the "beginning" stage. This stage, equal in emphasis to the others, and recognizing the importance of preparing students (literacy instruction) before they begin to search and use information, does not appear with the same emphasis in the ISP or other models of information-seeking behavior. In these models, if there is a beginning stage, it relates much more to the actual task at hand than to the general preparation of the student.

Originally, the BAT model was embedded into another model, the Preparing, Searching, Using (PSU) model (Nesset, 2013) which arose from empirical evidence gathered as part of a dissertation study on the information-seeking behavior of third-grade students in a suburb of Montreal, Quebec, Canada (see Figure 2.1) and was informed by the work of researchers investigating information-seeking behavior (Bates, 1989; Gross, 1995; Kuhlthau, 1988a, 1991, 2004; Shenton & Dixon, 2003b; Taylor, 1968; Wilson, 1999a, 1999b) and information literacy (Bruce, 2000a, 2000b; Eisenberg & Berkowitz, 1990; Herring, 1996; Wray & Lewis, 1995). In spring of 2012, a pilot study was conducted in two third-grade classes to investigate the efficacy of the more simplified representation of the PSU, the BAT model.

2.5. Pilot Study: The First Iteration of the BAT Model in Operation

The pilot study investigating the efficacy of the first iteration of the BAT model (Figure 2.2) as an aid in teaching the research process to younger elementary school students was conducted in spring 2012 in two third-grade classrooms (one class comprising 27 students, the other, 28) in an elementary school in Buffalo, New York. Each class chose a different theme (one class chose countries, the other, biospheres) to investigate. At the beginning of the research, a pre-questionnaire was administered to provide a baseline for later comparison.

The first few classes were devoted to introducing and explaining how the BAT model could be used to help the students with their individual projects. Then, the classroom teacher embarked on the beginning stage which is heavily instructional. It was not until several classes later that the students struck out on their own (the acting and telling stages), using the BAT

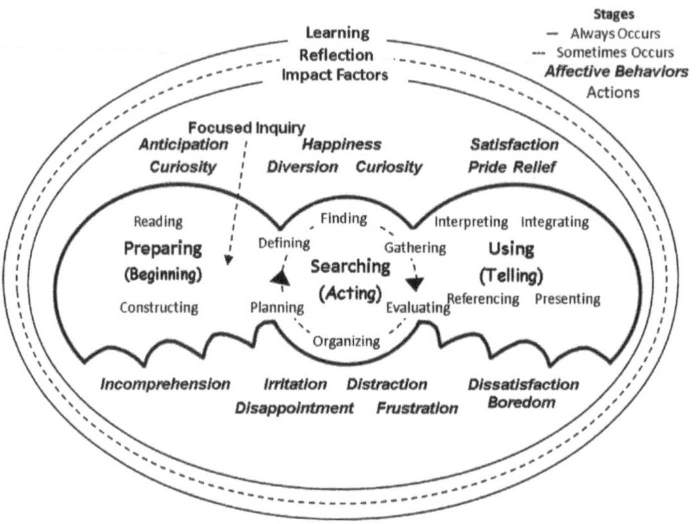

Figure 2.1: Preparing, Searching, Using (PSU) model with embedded Beginning, Acting, Telling (BAT) model. *Source*: © Valerie Nesset.

Figure 2.2: Beginning, Acting, Telling (BAT) model: First iteration. *Source*: © Valerie Nesset.

as a guide. Throughout the duration of the study (approximately three months), the students were observed and their actions and comments documented through field notes and audiotape for further analysis. At the end of the project, a questionnaire (consisting mainly of multiple-choice questions) to solicit their opinions on using the BAT was administered. When asked how the BAT helped them with their projects (several choices were given), of the 37 students who replied, 30 indicated that it helped them to remember the steps in the research process, and/or it helped them realize when they were missing information, and/or it helped them understand the research process. Seven students replied that it did not help them and when asked if they would use the BAT in the future, of those who provided feedback, the most typical answer was that it sometimes confused them. Typical of the responses were stated by a boy, "I would not use Bat [sic] again because I thought it was complicated"; and a girl, "No, because I don't understand the words on there. Maybe when I get older I'll understand."

Although seven students did experience difficulties using the BAT model, the overwhelming majority found it to be an efficacious tool for helping them to identify and remember the steps inherent in the research process. The students' responses indicated that it was the simplicity of the model that appealed to them. This finding initiated a review of the more complex PSU and the BAT representations, with the result that the elements unique to the PSU model were incorporated into the BAT (Figure 2.3).

The BAT is divided into three stages: the beginning and telling stages which form the wings, and the acting stage which forms the head of the bat; the thought being that the beginning (preparation) stage and the telling (using) stage are governed by the acting (searching) stage. Yet, no one stage is more important than the other; as the bat (the animal) requires the wings, body, and head to form a whole, in the same way all three stages are necessary to represent a holistic process. Within each stage, the associated actions are identified and discussed; however, it is understood that they can appear in other stages as well. To keep the model simple and child-friendly, specific affective behaviors associated with each stage have been omitted from the main image, they are now listed at the bottom, so that the teacher

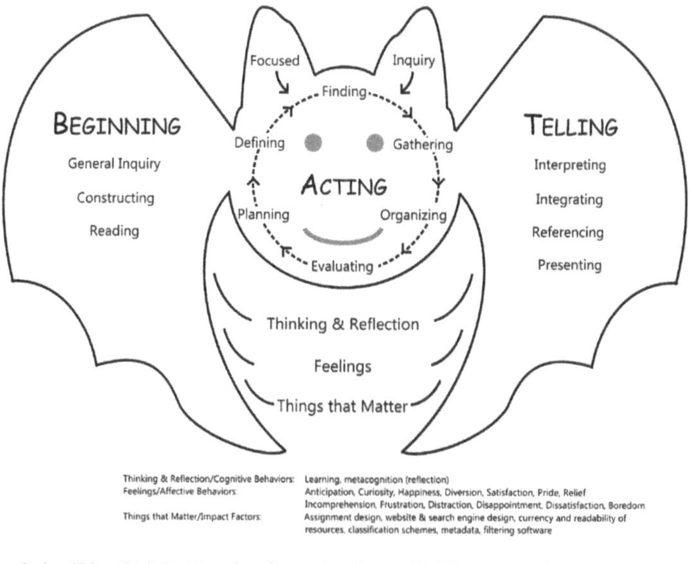

Figure 2.3: The BAT (Beginning, Acting, Telling) model: Final iteration. *Source*: © Valerie Nesset.

or librarian is aware of them and can then help encourage the more positive behaviors and mitigate or eliminate the more negative ones. Also, some specific activities associated with each stage as observed in the dissertation study are described — out of description grows prescription. The following section describes the BAT model.

2.5.1. The Beginning Stage

This preliminary stage is quite broad; that is, it is a general form of inquiry, and is highly instructional. In this stage, it is important to create activities that help to prepare the students to search for information on their own during the more focused inquiry. For the sake of brevity, these activities have been categorized and presented in the model as "Reading" and "Constructing."

- *Reading (silently or aloud)*. The specific activities grouped here help students to become familiar with the terminology associated with the subject under study and improve their reading skills in general. This improves students' ability to formulate search queries, use indexes and/or tables of contents as well as reading comprehension which is essential in the successful navigation of the information search process as a whole. Such activities can include:
  - *Reading aloud and vocabulary lessons* (e.g., spelling and grammar instruction). These activities expose the students to new terminology (potential search terms) and more complex sentence structure while at the same time introduce new concepts related to the subject matter;
  - *Silent reading*. Allowing time for silent reading of material that interests each student (fiction or nonfiction) promotes the importance of reading while also making it fun;
  - *Creative storytelling and writing*. Activities focusing on these concepts encourage children to think critically and to exercise their imaginations.
- *Constructing*. As with reading, activities associated with constructing should help the students to acquire the knowledge necessary to successfully navigate the acting and telling stages (both of which are centered on the focused inquiry). Activities concentrating on vocabulary, comprehension, evaluation, and interpretation should be encouraged.
  - *Concept mapping* helps students to plan their work by manipulating concepts and corresponding terms (which can later be used to create search queries) in order to visually represent relationships between these concepts (see also Gallenstein, 2005; Glynn, 1997; Leide, Large, Beheshti, Brooks, & Cole, 2003);

- *Guest speakers* provide the children with another important research source, the significant adult (Shenton & Dixon, 2003d; Wray & Lewis, 1995);
- *Group presentations* help the students to develop their social and public speaking skills.

As part of the bat's ears, the concept of the "focused inquiry" is introduced. The focused inquiry, reminiscent of Gross' imposed query (Gross, 1995), Kuhlthau's focus formulation stage (Kuhlthau, 1991, 2004) and guided inquiry (Kuhlthau, 2010; Kuhlthau et al., 2007) and usually occurring toward the end of the beginning stage, could take the form of a specific project or assignment that will serve as the focal point of the acting and telling stages. By introducing a focused inquiry, the teacher/librarian roots the process in reality and prevents it from becoming too abstract. This is especially important for the concrete-operational thinker (Ginsburg & Opper, 1988; Piaget & Inhelder, 1969; Siegler, 1998). Furthermore, the focused inquiry can serve as the medium for assessing students' progress. The reason it is contained within the bat's ears is to encourage the metaphor of listening to inform practice. By listening to the teacher's/librarian's instructions on what form the focused inquiry (assignment) will take (e.g., pictorial, text-based, multi-media), the students can adapt accordingly their actions within the acting and telling stages.

2.5.2. *The Acting Stage*

While this stage (involving primarily searching for information) comprises a main focus in the LIS literature, it is largely ignored in the educational literature, especially in the early grades. This provides an excellent example of where the research on information-seeking behavior can and should be integrated into research on various types of literacy. For example, the teacher in the dissertation study (Nesset, 2009, 2013) appeared typical in her view that the actual searching for identification and retrieval of relevant information was not important and considered these steps as merely a means for the students to have some information with which to work; she was more interested in how they used information than how they searched for it. Thus, she, like many other teachers, lost an opportunity to show the students how the activities from the beginning stage can be used to enhance searching (e.g., referring to the vocabulary exercises to help develop potential search terms). This low priority given to the acting stage is unfortunate because this stage is crucial to the overall research process and the reason it forms the head of the bat in the model. Many, if not all, of the actions take place not only in this stage, but in the two other stages as well.

Furthermore, this stage tends to be the one that is frequently revisited throughout the process, and it is in this stage that the students mainly rely on their own initiative rather than on the teacher's instruction (in other words, they *act* on their own). In both print and on the Web, it is the student that is in charge of the search.

Some key actions associated with the acting stage are:

- *Planning* should occur at the beginning of each stage and of certain actions when appropriate (e.g., presenting — even though this is the last action in the process, it needs to be planned in advance). In this stage, planning refers specifically to the search. Activities can include referring to concept maps to find possible search terms, deciding which search engine to use, etc.
- *Defining* permeates the entire research process. To facilitate student success, before any action can be performed effectively it must be defined within the context of the particular situation or task (focused inquiry). Defining an action ensures that the students understand exactly what is expected of them and helps them not only to focus their efforts on the task at hand, but also to plan for undertaking future steps in the process. In the acting stage defining may involve decisions regarding appropriate search terms, choice of an appropriate search engine and/or web portal, and deciding when a search is finished.
- *Finding* is the first step in the actual search and retrieval of information from a potentially broad range of information formats whether electronic or physical (e.g., print or a "significant adult" such as a teacher or librarian). Indeed, "finding" could be viewed as entering a search query into a search engine on the Web to generate a results list, investigating indexes in books, or asking a question of an adult. Except in the latter situation, it is often the user's first visual presentation of the surrogates or pointers to actual information items. Although the action is the most strongly associated with the acting stage, in recognition of the iterative nature of the process, it can be (and often is) present in the other stages as well (e.g., in the beginning stage when learning about indexes and search engines and/or in the telling stage when going back to investigate a source).
- *Gathering* occurs when the student interacts with an actual information item, whether it is a website or a reference book.
- *Evaluating* can occur in any stage of the process, and is likely to be used several times throughout. Evaluation can be associated with all of the actions within the three stages and should be emphasized as the crucial thread that runs through the research process. In order to teach general evaluation techniques, activities such as the following can be introduced:
  - *Source evaluation.* This can be taught at the simplest level in the print environment by teaching children the difference between a reference or

informational book and a work of fiction. On the Web, the students can be taught to recognize different domain names (e.g., commercial (".com"), government (".gov"), organization (".org"), university (".edu")) and that the information associated with each of them often differs in authority and accuracy.

- *Keywords.* Teaching students to recognize significant keywords within blocks of text can help them to more quickly and effectively identify relevant material.
- *Images.* Teaching students that the quality of an image does not necessarily translate to the quality of textual information accompanying it will go a long way to helping them become discriminating searchers.

Once the information has been retrieved, the concept of extraction as defined by Ellis (1989) is inextricably intertwined with evaluation since evaluation necessarily involves the choosing from the retrieved information discrete pieces that directly inform the final product (Bates, 1989; Ellis, 1989; Kuhlthau, 2004; Shenton & Dixon, 2003b). Due to this inextricability and the effort to keep the model as simple as possible, the two concepts are encompassed into one: evaluation. This combination of evaluative and extractive behaviors can be accomplished in many different ways; for example, by taking notes, highlighting relevant text within copies of the materials themselves, and even by drawing.

- *Organizing* is an action that is most often associated with physical materials (e.g., organizing the information that has been retrieved during a search) making it seem applicable only to the latter two stages. Organization, however, can and should be applied to more abstract entities such as thoughts. Since thinking occurs throughout the entire information-seeking process, organizing these thoughts is an action that occurs in all stages, although for some students it is a much more natural process than for others.

2.5.3. *The Telling Stage*

In the educational environment, the use of information is very important as a means to evaluate learning objectives; it requires the students to interpret (analyze), integrate, and present the information they have searched for and found, informed by all of the concepts learned earlier in the beginning and acting stages. In terms of referencing (citing) sources, although important to librarians and included in the BAT model, it may be (especially in the early grades) that teachers prefer not to place much emphasis on this; however, the actions within the telling stage are important to teachers as a concrete means of assessing the students' learning outcomes. By examining the deliverable, whatever form it may take, the teacher will be able to determine if the students have learned and understood the concepts and are able to apply them.

Thus, it is during this third and final stage that the students actually use and present the retrieved information found during the acting stage. During the telling stage, the students may feel the need to revisit one or both of the previous stages to fill in gaps, yet when they revisit one or both of the previous stages they should be much more focused as they are looking for very specific information to fill in the gaps they have identified.

The actions specifically associated with the telling stage are:

- *Interpreting*. Interpreting is accomplished by rereading and re-evaluating the information found and then rewriting it in the student's own words. The purpose of this exercise is to demonstrate to the teacher that the student is able to understand and internalize the information and make it his or her own, not always an easy task. As one young student stated, "They [authors] use all the best words" (Nesset, 2013, p. 103).
- *Integrating*. Once the students have interpreted the information found, they need to incorporate it to fit the guidelines of the assignment. Depending on the nature of the assignment and the particular student, this can be a very natural, or conversely, counterintuitive exercise.
- *Referencing*. To support accountability and academic integrity, students should reference their sources. While it may be too much to require elementary school students to master the intricacies of citation style, they are certainly capable of writing down the title and author of a book or the URL of a website where they have found their information.
- *Presenting*. Presenting can take several forms, depending on the teacher's preference. For example, the students may be required to present their assignments in physical form (e.g., essay, diorama, or poster) or orally (e.g., individual or group presentations to the class). While in the upper grades, this is probably the most important part of the process as students are usually assessed entirely on the end-product (whether oral or written) as evidence of their learning; in the lower grades the students are typically evaluated on the entire process of which the final product is but one aspect.

2.6. Affective Behaviors (Feelings)

As found in previous studies (e.g., Kuhlthau, 1988a), especially with young children (e.g., Cooper, 2002a, 2002b), affective behaviors play as important a role in information seeking as cognitive behaviors. In the dissertation study (Nesset, 2009), two categories of affective behaviors associated with each stage were identified; some more positive and others more negative. To be more child-friendly and for brevity, they are identified in the actual model as "Feelings" with the specific behaviors listed in the legend. They, like "Thinking & Reflection" (cognitive behaviors) and "Things that Matter" (impact factors), appear as part of the motion produced by the bat's wings to emphasize their importance to the entire process. Just as a bat's wings affect the direction of flight these concepts affect the direction and progress of the research process.

Three affective behaviors are associated with the beginning stage: anticipation, curiosity (more positive), and incomprehension (more negative). The first two relate to uncertainty, a concept identified and discussed by Kuhlthau (1991, 2004), Wilson (1999a), and Nahl and Bilal (2007).

- *Anticipation*. Students who demonstrate anticipation (manifested by signs of excitement and enthusiasm) are anxious to start looking for information on their own for their focused inquiry (assignment). These students seemed to be empowered by the things they learn in this stage and are motivated to take what they have learned and apply it themselves in different ways in the next stages.
- *Curiosity*. The curious student is interested and motivated to learn about different aspects of the research process and content with which they are unfamiliar. Indeed, curiosity appears to play an important role in keeping them motivated and focused on the learning activities assigned by the teacher/librarian (see also Bowler, 2010).
- *Incomprehension*. This is exhibited by students who appear not to understand why they are instructed to undertake the activities the teacher/librarian assigns and do not see any relevance between them and the next stages of the research process. At best, incomprehension can act as a demotivator for the completion of future learning activities, causing some students to become bored and/or disassociated with the process, and at worst it can prevent some of the students from learning key concepts. This highlights the importance of informing students of the purpose of assigned learning activities and how they impact on the different stages in the research process.

Seven affective behaviors are prevalent in the Acting stage. More positive ones include happiness, diversion, and curiosity; more negative ones are irritation, disappointment, distraction, and frustration.

- *Happiness*. The ability to apply on their own concepts learned in the beginning stage can empower students, helping them to feel more confident in themselves and their abilities. This in turn leads to a feeling of happiness and well-being.

- *Diversion.* Often, students find information that although not particularly relevant to their specific tasks is still interesting to them, thus diverting their attention. Providing the diversion is temporary and does not result in a loss of valuable time and/or resources (e.g., taking precious minutes away from a scheduled Internet search session) it sometimes provides serendipitous information retrieval and may broaden the students' knowledge base. Diversion does have the potential, however, to result in a lack of focus and missed opportunity.
- *Curiosity.* As in the beginning stage, curiosity also may play a part in keeping the students motivated and interested. For example, curiosity about websites and/or books that are thought to contain information related to a particular subject can often in serendipitous information retrieval. Sometimes, however, there is a downside; curiosity can lead to more negative affective behaviors as distraction, irritation, disappointment, and frustration, especially if the information first perceived to be available is actually not.
- *Irritation.* Irritation can occur when a student finds information that at first glance looks useful but upon closer scrutiny proves to be unrelated to the information need. On the Internet, this most often occurs upon scrutiny of a retrieved (most often commercial) website which may include images that look relevant but do not have any information that pertains to the actual focused inquiry (assigned task). As reading is often a slow process for many young students and they are often under fairly severe time restrictions at school, they can become irritated if they spend time examining a site that is found to be irrelevant, feeling perhaps that their time has been wasted. In the print environment, irritation sometimes occurs when searching for a term in a long list of entries in a back-of-the-book index. As reported by Shenton and Dixon (2003c) many students find this to be a tedious exercise.
- *Disappointment and frustration.* These two behaviors often occur together when little or no relevant information can be found, but unlike irritation, they occur upon reflection on the search and not during it. As discovered in the dissertation study (Nesset, 2009), when students are engrossed in the actions of searching for information, they are not likely to reflect on whether or not it will be sufficiently comprehensive. It is only when the information is being evaluated, synthesized, and integrated to satisfy the assignment instructions that gaps and/or overlaps appear and disappointment develops. Frustration in the fact that more work must be done in order to produce a satisfactory deliverable also may appear.
- *Distraction.* Becoming distracted may not be perceived as a problem by students but can be a barrier to effectively completing the task at hand.

Although it may be argued that a small difference exists between diversion and distraction, the former can be beneficial in terms of learning more about related topics but the latter may distract the students from their task and interfere with the searching process.

Five affective behaviors are associated with the telling stage. More positive ones include pride, relief, and satisfaction. More negative ones are dissatisfaction and boredom.

- *Pride.* At the end of what can be a lengthy process the students should feel proud of their accomplishments.
- *Relief.* Some students may express relief that they are finished their assignments not because they dislike the research process, but rather in the context of producing a deliverable. They may thoroughly enjoy all of the activities but nonetheless be keen to start a new topic.
- *Satisfaction.* Typically, most students at this age are satisfied with their work and are often eager to begin the process again. Some (especially those who experience incomprehension, irritation, and/or frustration), may not experience this feeling.
- *Dissatisfaction.* Students who have difficulties with comprehension, focus, and/or motivation may become dissatisfied with the research process in general and their own work in particular.
- *Boredom.* Boredom can largely depend on the assigned topic. It is therefore very important for the teacher/librarian to find a topic that will engage the majority of students while also providing the most opportunity to put the research process into action.

All of these affective behaviors manifested to varied degrees in the dissertation study (Nesset, 2009) and were also apparent in the pilot study. It is interesting to note that in the pilot study, no new affective behaviors were identified, despite the difference in location (Buffalo, New York versus Montreal, Quebec).

2.7. Cognitive Behaviors (Thinking & Reflection)

As with affective behaviors, cognition is an integral part of the entire research process, hence its position as part of the motion of the bat's wings. The learning component invokes Pitts' (1994) learning strands: subject-matter learning strand, information-seeking-and-use strand, production strand, and life-skills strand. It can be safely assumed that some learning has taken place over the duration of the process, although it may not be exactly what the teacher/librarian anticipates. For example, some students may have learned little or nothing about the subject matter, but did learn how to manage their time more effectively (life-skills strand). More specifically, including learning within the cognitive behaviors signifies that what is learned during the execution of the three stages may be re-applied to an information-seeking event in the future.

This learning is facilitated and enhanced by metacognition, or reflection. It has been shown that by reflecting on past behaviors students can recognize their mistakes and/or weaknesses and take measures to correct them (Moore, 1995). While proven to be valuable, enhancing the learning process, reflection does not always occur, especially in the case of young children whose metacognitive abilities are just starting to develop. Such abstract thought is not a characteristic of concrete-operational thinkers (Ginsburg & Opper, 1988; Piaget & Inhelder, 1969; Siegler, 1998) making it crucial for teachers/librarians to encourage and teach young students how metacognition can be used to facilitate and improve the research process.

2.8. Impact Factors (Things that Matter)

There are several factors that directly or indirectly impact upon the research process. They are identified as "Things that Matter" to encourage the student to be aware of them, and they are shown in the model as part of the motion of the bat's wings, to indicate that they affect all three stages within the process. These impact factors are often beyond the control of the student's and teacher/librarian although some can be mitigated and/or encouraged, depending on their effect. Some examples of impact factors are:

- *Currency of resources*. Depending on the subject matter under investigation, older resources could be outdated and contain obsolete and/or inaccurate information. This problem is often associated with the print milieu (e.g., an atlas published before the breakup of the former Soviet Union) but can also exist within a digital environment. For example, with many websites it is often difficult to know how long they have been available and if and when they have been updated. If the topic is fairly stable (e.g., animals), currency is not an issue, with a topic such as human health, however, the currency of available resources takes on much greater importance.
- *Classification schemes*. The choice of classification scheme can directly impact information seeking. If it is too broad, there is the risk of not

being able to find specific resources; if it is too specific, it may be difficult for young students to understand (Joyce & Joyce, 1970).

- *Search engine design.* The type of search engine used can directly affect the research process. While children's web portals such as KidzSearch (http://www.kidzsearch.com/) often search a limited inventory of pre-selected sites, general search engines such as Google do not, increasing the risk of the discovery of irrelevant and/or inappropriate content. Display options on web portals, even those developed for children may also impact the process. For example, the use of subject directories containing long alphabetical lists of terms may be difficult to navigate (Large, Beheshti, Nesset, & Bowler, 2005, 2006; Shenton & Dixon, 2003c). Furthermore, enhanced synonym control or cross-referencing may be necessary to compensate for young students' limited vocabulary.
- *Readability and content.* As discussed earlier, websites found by a general-purpose search engine such as Google are often for adults and use vocabulary and syntax which young students may find difficult to read and comprehend and/or contain inappropriate content. Furthermore, children may have difficulty differentiating between commercial and informational websites.
- *Metadata.* Types of metadata tools and how they are displayed can affect the research process. Tables of Contents can be too broad, indexes too detailed. If either contains long lists of terms, they become more difficult and time-consuming to navigate (Nesset, 2013; Shenton & Dixon, 2003c).
- *Filtering software.* Overly restrictive filtering systems, because they are unable to understand the nuances of language, often block potentially useful sites. For example, the filters block words such as "sex," meaning that a webpage about the Mar*s Ex*plorer might not be found.
- *Assignment design.* The design of the assignment may directly impact the information-seeking behavior of the students. The students may make decisions based on what they believe the teacher/librarian expects from them and/or on what they have determined to be the subject focus (Kuhlthau, 1993b; Shenton & Dixon, 2004). A good assignment would be broad enough to encourage information seeking from multiple sources and formats yet narrow enough to help channel the students' focus.

2.9. Conclusion

The purpose of the BAT model is to introduce young students to the idea of the research process as a coherent whole. Specifically, the BAT, through the use of mnemonic and a familiar visual representation depicts the elements inherent in research as belonging to three stages of a fluid, iterative process which is constantly in motion. The diagrammatic nature of the model allows presentation of the key elements of the research process within one readily-identifiable image. The model is influenced and informed by research into information-seeking behavior and the development of visual models. Implicit within the model are Taylor's (1968) levels of need, the iterative elements of Bate's (1989) evolutionary search characteristic of her Berry-picking model, the identification and recognition of the importance of process, affective behaviors, focus formulation, and guided inquiry intrinsic in the work of Kuhlthau (1988a, 1988b, 1988c, 1991, 1993b, 2004, 2010), Gross' (1995) imposed query, and the uncertainty principle as defined by Kuhlthau (1993a, 1999, 2004) and Wilson (1999a). While it is influenced also by some of the elements intrinsic in information literacy research (especially the use of mnemonic, stages, and steps) the BAT allows for easier recognition and the imposition of a lower cognitive load than a set of questions or steps, the more typical form of information literacy instruction. As students become familiar with the BAT representation and grow and mature intellectually, the more specific concepts encompassed in the terms, "Thinking & Reflection," "Feelings," and "Things that Matter" can be gradually introduced to them to help them to identify and become more aware of elements that impact on the process. In this way, the students can fully exploit all aspects of the research process largely independent of content. Furthermore, previous research has demonstrated that students can benefit from knowing about the different facets of the research process before embarking on a specific research task. In a study conducted by Kracker (2002) it was found that undergraduate students who attended a presentation explaining Kuhlthau's ISP were less anxious about performing research for a course research project than those who did not attend. Similarly, a study of eighth-grade students indicated that in the successful completion of a class project, the Big6 Information Skills model acted as a metacognitive scaffold (Wolf et al., 2003). Thus, it can be posited that by becoming aware of the affective behaviors, impact factors, and the roles that reflective practice and learning can play on the process, teachers, librarians, and students can then take measures to accentuate and exploit the positive influences and eliminate or at least mitigate the more negative ones.

The BAT has been developed to be used within the elementary-school classroom environment; its use of image and mnemonic are designed to help students more easily recognize, remember, and internalize the crucial aspects of the research process. Thus, by using the BAT model as an instructional tool, teachers and librarians can instill these aspects in their students, over time building a solid foundation upon which to continue life-long learning.

Acknowledgments

The author would like to acknowledge the wonderful third-grade students and teachers with whom she conducted the two studies. She would also like to thank Ms. Susan Janczak (former School Library Coordinator, Department of Library and Information Studies, University at Buffalo, SUNY) and Michael Cambria (Director, Buffalo School Library System), who helped refine the model to its present form.

References

Agosto, D. E. (2002). A model of young people's decision-making in using the Web. *Library and Information Science Research*, *24*, 311–341.

American Association of School Librarians. (2009). *Standards for the 21st century learner in action*. Chicago, IL: American Association of School Librarians.

American Association of School Librarians & Association for Educational Communications and Technology. (1998). *Information power: Building partnerships for learning*. Chicago, IL: ALA Editions.

Amiriyousefi, M., & Ketabi, S. (2011). Mnemonic instruction: A way to boost vocabulary learning and recall. *Journal of Language Teaching and Research*, *2*(1), 178–182.

Bates, M. J. (1989). The design of browsing and berrypicking techniques for the online search interface. *Online Review*, *13*, 407–424.

Bilal, D. (2000). Children's use of the Yahooligans! Web search engine: I. Cognitive, physical and affective behaviors on fact-based search tasks. *Journal of the American Society for Information Science and Technology*, *51*, 646–665.

Bilal, D. (2001). Children's use of the Yahooligans! Web search engine: II. Cognitive and physical behaviors on research tasks. *Journal of the American Society for Information Science and Technology*, *52*, 118–136.

Bilal, D. (2002). Children's use of the Yahooligans! Web search engine. III. Cognitive and physical behaviors on fully self-generated search tasks. *Journal of the American Society for Information Science and Technology*, *53*, 1170–1183.

Bilal, D. (2012). Ranking, relevance judgment, and precision of information retrieval on children's queries: Evaluation of Google, Yahoo!, Bing, Yahoo! Kids, and ask Kids. *Journal of the American Society for Information Science and Technology*, *63*, 1879–1896.

Bilal, D., & Kirby, J. (2002). Differences and similarities in information seeking: Children and adults as web users. *Information Processing & Management*, *38*, 649–670.

Borgman, C., Hirsh, S., Walter, V., & Gallagher, A. L. (1995). Children's searching behavior on browsing and keyword online catalogs: The science library catalog project. *Journal of the American Society for Information Science and Technology*, *46*, 663–684.

Bowler, L. (2010). The self-regulation of curiosity and interest during the information search process of adolescent students. *Journal of the American Society for Information Science and Technology*, *61*, 1332–1344.

Bowler, L., Nesset, V., Large, A., & Beheshti, J. (2004). Using the web for Canadian history projects: What will children find? *Canadian Journal of Information and Library Science*, *28*(3), 3–24.

Bruce, C. (2000a). Information literacy programs and research: An international review. *The Australian Library Journal*, *49*(3), 209–218.

Bruce, C. (2000b). Information literacy research: Dimensions of the emerging collective consciousness. *Australian Academic & Research Libraries*, *31*(2), 91–109.

Bruce, D. (1999). Filtering the Internet for young people: Products and problems. *Teacher Librarian*, *26*(5), 13–17.

Case, D. O. (2012). *Looking for information: A survey of research on information seeking, needs, and behavior* (3rd ed.). Bingley, UK: Emerald Group Publishing Limited.

Chang, Y., Zhang, Z., Mokhtar, I. A., Foo, S., Majid, S., Luyt, B., & Theng, Y. (2012). Assessing students' information literacy skills in two secondary schools in Singapore. *Journal of Information Literacy*, *6*(2), 19–34.

Chen, L. C., & Chen, Y.-P. (2013). Development of information literacy assessment and students performance: A case study on a second-grade information literacy curriculum. *Journal of Educational Media & Library Sciences*, *51*(1), 91–129.

Choi, S. M., Wheelehan, D., & Beers, P. (2001). *Where do I start? A school library handbook*. Worthington, OH: Linworth Publishing.

Cooper, L. Z. (2002a). A case study of information seeking behavior in 7-year-old children in a semistructured situation. *Journal of the American Society for Information Science and Technology*, *53*, 904–922.

Cooper, L. Z. (2002b). Methodology for a project examining cognitive categories for library information in young children. *Journal of the American Society for Information Science and Technology*, *53*, 1223–1231.

Curtis, D. (2002). The power of projects. *Educational Leadership*, *60*(1), 50–53.

Eisenberg, M. B. (2003). Implementing information skills: Lessons learned from the Big6 approach to information problem-solving. *School Libraries in Canada*, *22*(4), 20–23.

Eisenberg, M. B., & Berkowitz, R. (1990). *Information problem solving: The Big Six skills approach to library & information skills instruction*. Norwood, NJ: Ablex.

Eisenberg, M. B., & Robinson, L. E. (2007). *The Super3: Information skills for young learners*. Worthington, OH: Linworth Publishing.

Ellis, D. (1989). A behavioural approach to information retrieval system design. *Journal of Documentation*, *45*(3), 171–212.

Fisher, K. E., Erdelez, S., & McKechnie, L. (Eds.). (2005). *Theories of information behavior*. Medford, NJ: Information Today.

Fontana, J. L., Scruggs, T., & Mastropieri, M. A. (2007). Mnemonic strategy instruction in inclusive secondary social studies classes. *Remedial & Special Education*, *28*(6), 345–355.

Gallenstein, N. L. (2005). Never too young for a concept map. *Science and Children*, *43*(1), 44–47.

Ginsburg, H., & Opper, S. (1988). *Piaget's theory of intellectual development*. Upper Saddle River, NJ: Prentice Hall.

Glynn, S. M. (1997). Drawing mental models. *The Science Teacher*, *64*(1), 30–32.

Gross, M. (1995). The imposed query. *RQ*, *35*, 236–343.

Herring, J. (1996). *Teaching information skills in schools*. London: Library Association Publishing.

Herring, J. (2009). A grounded analysis of year 8 students' reflections on information literacy skills and techniques. *School Libraries Worldwide*, *15*(1), 1–13.

Herring, J., Tarter, A.-M., & Naylor, S. (2002). An evaluation of the use of the PLUS model to develop pupils' information skills in a secondary school. *School Libraries Worldwide*, *8*(1), 1–24.

Hirsh, S. G. (1996). *The effect of domain knowledge on elementary school children's information retrieval behavior on an automated library catalog*. Unpublished doctoral dissertation, University of California, Los Angeles, CA.

Hirsh, S. G. (1997). How do children find information on different types of tasks? Children's use of the science library catalog. *Library Trends*, *45*, 725–745.

Joyce, B. R., & Joyce, E. A. (1970). The creation of information systems for children. *Interchange*, *1*(2), 1–12.

Julien, H., & Williamson, K. (2010). Discourse and practice in information literacy and information seeking: Gaps and opportunities. *Information Research*, *16*(1). paper 458. Retrieved from http://InformationR.net/ir/16-1/paper458.html

Kail, R. V. (2004). *Children and their development* (3rd ed.). Upper Saddle River, NJ: Pearson Education.

Kracker, J. (2002). Research anxiety and students' perceptions of research: An experiment. Part I. Effect of teaching Kuhlthau's ISP model. *Journal of the American Society for Information Science and Technology*, *53*, 282–294.

Kuhlthau, C. C. (1988a). Developing a model of the library search process: Cognitive and affective aspects. *RQ*, *28*(2), 232–242.

Kuhlthau, C. C. (1988b). Meeting the information needs of children and young adults: Basing library media programs on developmental states. *Journal of Youth Services in Libraries*, *2*(1), 51–57.

Kuhlthau, C. C. (1988c). Perceptions of the information search process in libraries: A study of changes from high school through college. *Information Processing and Management*, *24*(4), 419–427.

Kuhlthau, C. C. (1991). Inside the search process: Information seeking from the user's perspective. *Journal of the American Society for Information Science and Technology*, *42*, 361–371.

Kuhlthau, C. C. (1993a). A principle of uncertainty for information seeking. *Journal of Documentation*, *49*, 339–355.

Kuhlthau, C. C. (1993b). Implementing a process approach to information skills: A study identifying indicators of success in library media programs. *School Library Media Quarterly*, *22*(1), 11–18.

Kuhlthau, C. C. (1999). The role of experience in the information search process of an early career information worker: Perceptions of uncertainty, complexity construction and sources. *Journal of the American Society for Information Science and Technology*, *50*(5), 399–412.

Kuhlthau, C. C. (2004). *Seeking meaning: A process approach to library and information services* (2nd ed.). Westport, CT: Libraries Unlimited.

Kuhlthau, C. C. (2010). Guided inquiry: School libraries in the 21st century. *School Libraries Worldwide*, *16*(1), 17–28.

Kuhlthau, C. C., Heinström, J., & Todd, R. J. (2008). The "information search process" revisited: Is the model still useful? *Information Research*, *13*(4) paper 355. Retrieved from http://InformationR.net/ir/13-4/paper355.html

Kuhlthau, C. C., Maniotes, L. K., & Caspari, A. K. (2007). *Guided inquiry: Learning in the 21st century*. Westport, CT: Libraries Unlimited.

Kuhlthau, C. C., & Tama, S. (2001). Information search process of lawyers: A call for "just for me" information services. *Journal of Documentation*, *57*(1), 25–43.

Kuhlthau, C. C., Turock, B., George, M., & Belvin, R. (1990). Validating a model of the search process: A comparison of academic, public and school library users. *Library and Information Science Research*, *12*(1), 5–32.

Large, A., & Beheshti, J. (2000). The Web as a classroom resource: Reactions from the users. *Journal of the American Society for Information Science and Technology*, *51*, 1069–1080.

Large, A., Beheshti, J., Nesset, V., & Bowler, L. (2005, June 2–4). Web portal characteristics: Children as designers and evaluators. In L. Vaughn (Ed.), *Data, information, and knowledge in a networked world: Proceedings of the Canadian Society for Information Science and Technology*, London.

Large, A., Beheshti, J., Nesset, V., & Bowler, L. (2006, November 3–8). Web portal design guidelines as identified by children through the processes of design and evaluation. In *Information realities: Shaping the digital future for all: Proceedings of the 69th ASIS&T annual meeting*, Austin, TX. Silver Springs, MD: American Society for Information Science and Technology.

Laverty, C. (2002). The challenge of information seeking: How children engage in library work. In L. C. Howarth, C. Cronin, & A. T. Slawek (Eds.), *Advancing knowledge: Expanding horizons for information science: Proceedings of the Canadian Association for Information Science*. Retrieved from http://www.cais-acsi.ca/proceedings/2002/Laverty_2002.pdf

Lawless, K. A., Mills, R., & Brown, S. W. (2002). Children's hypertext navigation strategies. *Journal of Research on Technology in Education*, *35*(3), 274–284.

Leide, J. E., Large, A., Beheshti, J., Brooks, M., & Cole, C. (2003). Visualization schemes for domain novices exploring a topic space: The navigation classification scheme. *Information Processing and Management*, *39*(6), 923–940.

Levin, J. L., McCormick, C. B., Miller, G. E., Berry, J. K., & Pressley, M. (1982). Mnemonic versus nonmnemonic vocabulary-learning strategies for children. *American Educational Research Journal*, *19*(1), 121–136.

Limberg, L., & Sundin, O. (2006). Teaching information seeking: Relating information literacy education to theories of information behaviour. *Information Research*, *12*(1) paper 280. Retrieved from http://informationr.net/ir/12-1/paper280.html

Lloyd, A. (2005). Information literacy: Different contexts, different concepts, different truths? *Journal of Librarianship and Information Science*, *37*(2), 82–88.

Lloyd, A. (2010). Framing information literacy as information practice: Site ontology and practice theory. *Journal of Documentation*, *66*(2), 245–258.

Marchionini, G. (1995). *Information seeking in electronic environments*. New York, NY: Cambridge University Press.

Marland, M. (Ed.). (1981). *Information skills in the secondary curriculum*. London: Methuen Educational (Schools Council Curriculum Bulletin 9).

McCormick, C. B., & Levin, J. R. (1984). A comparison of different prose-learning variations of the mnemonic keyword method. *American Educational Research Journal*, *21*(2), 379–398.

Moore, P. (1995). Information problem solving: A wider view of library skills. *Contemporary Educational Psychology*, *20*, 1–31.

Moore, P. (2000). Primary school children's interaction with library media. *Teacher Librarian*, *27*(3), 7–11.

Nahl, D., & Bilal, D. (2007). *Information and emotion: The emergent affective paradigm in information behavior research and theory*. Medford, NJ: Information Today.

Nesset, V. (2007). Grade-three students' use of print and electronic resources. In C. Arsenault & K. Dalkir (Eds.), *Information sharing in a fragmented world: Crossing boundaries: Proceedings of the Canadian Association for Information Science (CAIS)*, Montreal, QC. Retrieved from http://www.cais-acsi.ca/proceedings/2007/nesset_2007.pdf. Accessed on May 10–12, 2007.

Nesset, V. (2009). *The information-seeking behaviour of grade-three elementary school students in the context of a class project*. Unpublished doctoral dissertation, McGill University. Retrieved from ProQuest Dissertations & Theses Full Text (NR66580).

Nesset, V. (2013). Two representations of the research process: The preparing, searching, and using (PSU) and the beginning, acting and telling (BAT) models. *Library & Information Science Research*, *35*(2), 97–106.

Piaget, J., & Inhelder, B. (1969). *The psychology of the child*. New York, NY: Basic Books.

Pitts, J. M. (1994). *Personal understandings and mental models of information: A qualitative study of factors associated with the information-seeking and use of adolescents*. Unpublished doctoral dissertation, Florida State University, Tallahassee, Florida.

Revelle, G., Druin, A., Platner, M., Weng, S., Bederson, B., Hourcade, J. P., & Sherman, L. (2002). Young children's search strategies and construction of search queries. *Journal of Science Education and Technology*, *11*(1), 48–57.

Robinson, L. E. (2008). Information literacy and early learners. *Library Media Connection*, *27*(2), 10–11.

Schacter, J., Chung, G., & Dorr, A. (1998). Children's Internet searching on complex problems: Performance and process analysis. *Journal of the American Society for Information Science and Technology*, *49*, 840–849.

Shenton, A. K., & Dixon, P. (2003a). Just what do they want? What do they need? A study of the informational needs of children. *Children & Libraries*, *1*(2), 36–42.

Shenton, A. K., & Dixon, P. (2003b). Models of young people's information seeking. *Journal of Librarianship and Information Science*, *35*(1), 5–22.

Shenton, A. K., & Dixon, P. (2003c). Sequential or selective access? Young people's strategies for finding information in non-fiction books. *The New Review of Children's Literature and Librarianship*, *9*, 57–69.
Shenton, A. K., & Dixon, P. (2003d). Youngsters' use of other people as an information-seeking method. *Journal of Librarian and Information Science*, *35*(4), 219–233.
Shenton, A. K., & Dixon, P. (2004). Information needs issues emerging from school assignments. *Education Libraries Journal*, *47*(2), 21–29.
Shenton, A. K., & Fitzgibbons, M. (2010). Making information literacy relevant. *Library Review*, *59*(3), 165–174.
Shenton, A. K., & Hay-Gibson, N. V. (2011a). Information behaviour and information literacy: The ultimate in transdisciplinary phenomena? *Journal of Librarianship and Information Science*, *43*, 166–175.
Shenton, A. K., & Hay-Gibson, N. V. (2011b). Modelling the information-seeking behaviour of children and young people: Inspiration beyond LIS. *Aslib Proceedings: New Information Perspectives*, *63*(1), 57–75.
Siegler, R. S. (1998). *Children's thinking* (3rd ed.). Upper Saddle River, NJ: Prentice Hall.
Slone, D. (2003). Internet search approaches: The influence of age, search goals, and experience. *Library and Information Science Research*, *25*(4), 403–418.
Taylor, R. S. (1968). Question-negotiation and information seeking in libraries. *College and Research Libraries*, *29*, 178–194.
Wallace, R. W., Kupperman, J., Krajcik, J., & Soloway, E. (2000). Science on the Web: Students online in a sixth-grade classroom. *The Journal of the Learning Sciences*, *9*(1), 75–104.
Walter, V. A. (1994). The information needs of children. *Advances in Librarianship*, *18*, 111–129.
Wilson, T. D. (1999a). Exploring models of information behaviour: The "uncertainty" project. *Information Processing and Management*, *35*, 839–849.
Wilson, T. D. (1999b). Models in information behaviour research. *Journal of Documentation*, *55*, 249–270
Wolf, S., Brush, T., & Saye, J. (2003). The big six information skills as a metacognitive scaffold: A case study. *School Library Media Research*, *6*(1). Retrieved from http://www.ala.org/ala/mgrps/divs/aasl/aaslpubsandjournals/slmrb/slmrcontents/volume62003/bigsixinformation.cfm. Accessed in 2011.
Wolinsky, A. (2001). Mandating the wrong filters. *Teacher Librarian*, *29*(1), 26–27.
Wray, D., & Lewis, M. (1995). Extending interactions with non-fiction texts; an EXIT into understanding. *Reading*, *29*(1), 2–9.

Chapter 3

Social Capital and Academic Help Seeking: Late Adolescents' Use of People as Information Sources

Audrey Laplante

Abstract

Purpose – The study examines how late adolescents use the resources embedded in their social network to obtain the information and support they need to do their homework. A particular attention is paid to how social network sites (SNSs) are used and perceived by late adolescents for academic help seeking.

Design/methodology/approach – This qualitative study uses in-depth interviewing and critical incident technique. An egocentric approach to Social Network Analysis is also employed to examine the core social network of each participant.

Findings – Most adolescents had a solid personal social network but did not always fully take advantage of the resources embedded in it for schoolwork. Availability was the most important criteria for deciding who to approach. SNSs were often used to obtain the help they needed, although phone calls and in-person visits were considered more efficient in certain situations.

Research limitations/implications – This study draws on a small purposive sample that may limit generalization. This research contributes to our understanding of the resources late adolescents have access to within their core social network, the way they take advantage (or not) of these resources for schoolwork, and the role SNSs play in the process. Findings have implications for services that educators and

New Directions in Children's and Adolescents' Information Behavior Research
Library and Information Science, Volume 10, 67–103

ISSN: 1876-0562/doi:10.1108/S1876-056220140000010046

school librarians should provide to support the educational needs of late adolescents.

Originality/value – This study contributes more generally to our understanding of late adolescents' use of people as primary sources of information to complete school-related homework.

Keywords: Academic help seeking; adolescents; everyday-life information behavior; social network sites (SNSs); Facebook; school-related homework

3.1. Introduction

Information and communication technologies (ICT) are transforming schools. Computers, tablets, and interactive whiteboards are now commonplace in classrooms. Schools and teachers do not only have to adapt to these new technologies, but also to adapt to a new clientele who is born with the Web. Generation Y, Millenials, Net Generation, and Google Generation are some of the terms used to refer to today's adolescents and younger adults. Prensky (2001) refers to them as "digital natives," emphasizing the ease with which they use technologies. Prensky says that because they grew up with technologies, this generation "thinks and processes information fundamentally differently from their predecessors" (p. 1). Although not everyone agrees with this statement, many researchers agree on several other attributes that characterize this generation. Today's young adults are confident, strongly oriented toward teamwork, and digitally literate (Gibbons, 2007; Howe & Strauss, 2000). As students, they prefer to be actively engaged in their learning process. Learning is also a profoundly social process that involves discussing and arguing with peers (Holliday & Li, 2004; Manuel, 2002).

Considering these attributes, it is not surprising that the Pew Internet & American Life Project (Lenhart et al., 2011) showed that adolescents (12–17 years) are the age group with the highest proportion of Internet users (95%). Older adolescents (14–17 years) represent the group with the highest proportion of social media users (88%), 95% of which have a *Facebook* account. Social network sites (SNSs) provide users with a variety of tools for connecting with other members, as well as for sharing and communicating information.

Considering the importance of peer-learning for this generation and the new tools that are available to them and allow them to maintain extended social networks, it becomes important to re-examine how these adolescents use the resources in their social network to seek the help they need when they do schoolwork outside of the classroom. Despite existing research on use of SNSs by adolescents (see, e.g., Abbas & Agosto, 2013 for a literature review), adolescents' school-related information- and help-seeking behavior for homework is an understudied area of research. In particular, although people were found to play an important role in providing help and information in that context, scarce work has focused on the resources that were embedded in the social networks of adolescents. Similarly, little work has examined the criteria adolescents use in choosing the people to approach for help. Additionally, existing studies that explored the use of SNSs for school-related activities did not include an information science perspective. A few questions thus remain unanswered: Do adolescents make use of the increased social capital they have access to through these new tools? How have these tools affected students' help- and information-seeking behavior? Who do they approach for help? How do they choose who to approach? What role do SNSs play in the process? This chapter reports on a study that examined how late adolescents (ages 15–17) use the resources embedded in their social network to obtain the information and the help they need for schoolwork, and how SNSs are used for that purpose.

Findings from this study should enrich our understanding of the information- and help-seeking behavior of adolescents, ages 14–17, in the context of schoolwork. These findings have implications for educators and school librarians in providing services and support for this generation of late adolescents.

3.2. Research Questions

The study sought to answer the following questions:

1. What are the resources late adolescents have access to in their core social network?
2. Do late adolescents take full advantage of these resources when they need them for their schoolwork? If not, why?
3. Who do late adolescents approach when they need help with their schoolwork?
4. How do late adolescents use and perceive online SNSs to get the help and information they need for schoolwork?

3.3. Related Literature

3.3.1. The Importance of People as Information Sources

Research on information behavior shows that the social environment plays an important role in the acquisition of information in everyday life. For instance, the study by Julien and Michels (2000) on how people select and use help sources in various daily life situations uncovered that 57% of the time, people chose as a first step to approach other people rather than seek print or digital sources. Similarly, Savolainen's (2008) study on people's source preferences when seeking problem-specific information in everyday life found that they have a strong preference for friends, experts, colleagues; and Internet sources (e.g., email, Web) above other sources such as print (e.g., magazines, books) or organizational sources (e.g., libraries, health centers), especially in the early phases of the information-seeking process. Xie and Cool (2009) found that help seeking begins early in the information-seeking process of novice digital library users. One could invoke the Principle of Least Effort (Zipf, 1949) to explain the motivation behind turning to relatives or friends rather than use formal sources of information. However, the findings of these studies revealed that people preferred to approach friends, relatives, colleagues, or other acquaintances not only for convenience, but also for the quality of the information they receive. People were praised for their capacity to offer advice, to make knowledgeable judgments, and to filter the information to their needs (Julien & Michels, 2000; Savolainen, 2008). In adding the affective dimension, Julien and Michels (2000) found that people who provided help show empathy and give reassurance when needed. Reaching out to someone to obtain the information needed can also contribute to strengthening the relationship the information seeker maintains with that person, since the interaction is often enjoyable and the experience can allow them to get to know each other better.

People also play a primary role in the provision of information in the lives of adolescents. Agosto and Hughes-Hassell (2005, 2006) studied the everyday-life information behavior of 27 adolescents (14–17 years) from an urban community. Again, their participants showed a clear preference for human sources — more specifically for friends and relatives — over all other information sources. They also examined the nature of the information needs of their participants and uncovered that schoolwork was their principal source of information need. Similar results were found in the study of how youngsters use people as information sources (Shenton & Dixon, 2003). The authors examined this phenomenon in everyday life among children and adolescents of all ages (3–18 years) and examined who they consulted and the nature of their information needs. They found that the persons they approached to satisfy their information needs could be grouped in three different categories: people of convenience (i.e., people, mostly relatives, who are available when the need arises); people in a comparable position (i.e., people, mostly friends, who have similar needs); and experts (i.e., people who are perceived as having an expertise in relation to the subject of the need). They also identified 13 types of information needs, including "advice," "school-related subject information," and "affective support." This study encompassed all situations in which information is needed and includes young people of almost all ages.

Several researchers have examined school-related information seeking of children and adolescents. The emphasis, however, has been mostly on the use of formal information sources (e.g., printed sources, web sources, libraries). Some looked at how young people searched for and used information in relation to a particular school project (e.g., Bowler, 2011; Chung & Neuman, 2007; Large & Beheshti, 2000). Other researchers have focused on how young people used a particular type of source (search engine/directory) in a learning situation, such as Bilal (2000, 2001, 2002) who looked at how middle-school students used a web search engine designed especially for children to answer factual questions and find information for research-based tasks.

In the field of education, several studies investigated how students from primary to high school use adults and peers in their social network to overcome the difficulties they encounter when doing schoolwork. In these studies, the emphasis has been on the instrumental role of help seeking in learning. For example, Nelson-Le Gall (1985) examined how help seeking contributes to learning and understanding. Ryan and Pintrich (1997) studied how motivation affects help-seeking behavior. Newman (2000) focused on the role help seeking plays in the social and intellectual development of elementary- and middle-school children. Newman and Goldin (1990) looked at the inhibitors to academic help seeking. Most scholars from the field of education perceive academic help seeking as beneficial if not essential: it is considered one of the most important skills children should develop (Nelson-Le Gall, 1985). As summarized by Newman and Goldin (1990): "Seeking help can be more beneficial than giving up prematurely, more adaptive than waiting passively, and more efficient than persisting unsuccessfully on one's own" (p. 92). However, if help seeking has the potential of being beneficial for the student who receives help, this is not always the case. Researchers make a distinction between "instrumental help seeking" (i.e., help seeking oriented toward enhancing the student's competence) and "executive help seeking" (i.e., help seeking oriented toward avoiding the task) (Nelson-Le Gall, 1985). Very few researchers examined who youngsters prefer to approach in order to get the help they need for schoolwork. Nelson-Le Gall and Gumerman (1984) found that as they get older, children's preferences regarding the person to turn to for help gradually move, initially from parents to teachers, than from teachers to peers.

3.3.2. *Social Networks, Social Capital, and SNSs*

If social networks have drawn the attention of researchers in information science, it is probably because each person in one's network represents a potential source of information. Additionally, as mentioned before, if people show a strong penchant for humans over other information sources, it is not only for their capacity to provide the information needed, but also for the king of help, moral support, and advice they might provide. In sociology as in information science, the term "social capital" is used to refer to the resources (e.g., information, help) embedded in one's social network and to which a person has access through his or her relationships (Lin, 2009). In simpler terms, Burt writes:

> Social capital explains how people do better because they are somehow better connected with other people. Certain people are connected to certain others, trusting certain others, obligated to support certain others, dependent on exchange with certain others. (Burt, 2005, p. 4)

Hence, one's social capital is subject to the size of his/her social network: the more developed a person's social network is, the most important the resources embedded in it are. The size of a social network is not the only factor likely to influence social capital: one's social capital also depends on the resources the individuals in his/her social network have and their willingness to help him/her if needed. The "Strength of Weak Ties" theory elaborated by Granovetter (1973, 1983) allows for further refinement. According to this theory, the degree of heterogeneity of a social network affects access to resources. Strong ties (i.e., the persons with whom we maintain a close relationship or with whom we communicate frequently) and weak ties (i.e., the persons with whom we communicate less often and to which we usually refer as "acquaintances") play distinct and complementary roles. Weak ties are considered the most instrumental in getting novel information. According to Granovetter, the degree of overlap between the social network of two individuals would be directly related to the strength of their tie: the closer these individuals are, the bigger the overlap (1983). In other words, people usually have a number of close friends, who most likely know each other, as well as acquaintances, who are less likely to know each other. Therefore, weak ties play a crucial role in the flow of information: they can act as a bridge between two "closely knit" groups of friends. It is, therefore, through these weak ties that an individual can obtain information from distant groups of people, which means that individuals with a social network that is both large and heterogeneous potentially have access to more resources than someone who would have a network mostly composed of close ties. This is not to say that strong ties are not instrumental in the flow of information. Granovetter (1983) points out that they are usually more motivated to help and more easily available than weak ties. Weimann (1980, as cited in Granovetter, 1983) adds that strong ties also have more credibility, which explains why influence in mostly exerted through these ties.

From this perspective, SNSs such as *Facebook* seem well-positioned to facilitate information access since they allow people to maintain weak ties, which could have been ephemeral otherwise, with little effort (Ellison, Steinfield, & Lampe, 2007). Many users of these sites tend to integrate into their virtual social network almost every person they meet. As a result, if it were to happen that they lost touch with these people for various reasons or circumstances, there would nevertheless be a latent tie they could easily reactivate and transform into a weak tie at any time (Ellison et al., 2007). Using the tools SNSs offer, weak ties can then be maintained by sending birthday wishes, or by commenting or "liking" things (e.g., statuses, photos, videos) they publish on these platforms from time to time. Indeed, SNSs have not only changed the way people develop and maintain their own social network, but have also created new forms of interpersonal communication. They offer a variety of tools to communicate and share information with people in one's network, facilitating the exchange of information and help between people. For instance, it is not uncommon for a *Facebook* member to enlist the help of all members of his or her network to find a new apartment or a new job, simply by posting a message (or "status") on their "wall." It is certainly for these reasons that several information scientists (Donath & boyd, 2004; Ellison et al., 2007) have a positive perception of SNSs: these sites have the potential to allow their members to expand and diversify their social network, which should normally result in greater social capital. It probably also explains why scholars from the field of education have shown interest in studying use of these sites. For instance, Luckin et al. (2009) examined how adolescents (11–16 years) used and perceived Web 2.0 technologies for learning. The authors found that the participants were heavy users of SNSs but that they did not take advantage of all the Web 2.0 tools that were available, which the authors attribute to a lack of technical knowledge. The adolescents were mostly interested in using these technologies for school-related activities but were able to note the limitation of the tools when the situation called for more substantive collaboration. Greenhow and Robelia (2009) focused their attention on the use of a particular SNS — *MySpace* — by older adolescents (ages 17–19). They uncovered that they used SNSs for several purposes, including getting the support they needed for their schoolwork. The authors provided an overview of their school-related activities on the SNS. They noted:

> This took several forms, some more direct than others, such as "chatting" online to mitigate school-related stress, asking

> questions about instructions or deadlines, planning study groups, broadcasting or requesting educational resources from the network [...], gathering project materials, brainstorming ideas, sharing written work, and exchanging feedback. (Greenhow & Robelia, 2009, p. 1148)

In retrospect, SNSs are used by adolescents of different age groups to solicit various types of help, receive emotional support, and obtain information, instructions, and ideas about tasks or activities.

Considering the primary role people play in the provision of information in the lives of adolescents and the importance of their school-related needs, it seems relevant to focus on these two aspects in the present study.

3.4. Methods

3.4.1. Social Network Analysis

A qualitative approach to social network analysis (SNA) was adopted to study how late adolescents used the resources embedded in their core social network for academic help seeking. According to Wasserman and Faust (1994), SNA focuses on the "relationships among social entities, and on the patterns and implications of these relationships" (p. 3). It is used to examine the pattern of ties in a network to understand how it affects the flow of resources (e.g., information, power, good, services) between the actors (Wellman, 1983). It provides methods and theoretical concepts that are used to analyze a social network and describes the attributes of its structure, as well as the ties of which it composed. Although SNA was first developed and used in sociology, it is now utilized in several other domains, including the information science field where it has proven useful to explain information access (Haythornthwaite, 1996). In the present study, an egocentric approach to SNA was adopted, as opposed to the whole network approach. This means that social networks from the perspective of an actor in the network (the "Ego") were examined. By contrast, the whole network approach consists of examining the ties that all members of a well-delimited population (e.g., all members of a work organization) maintain with each other.

3.4.2. Participants and Setting

The study took place during the winter and spring of 2011. The participants were recruited from a public school located in the center of Montreal. According to the deprivation indicators established by the Quebec Ministry of Education, Recreation and Sports, the school is located in an underprivileged area, which is typical for Montreal public high schools. All 10th and 11th grade (15–17 years old) students were invited to participate in the study. Students were all receiving their schooling in French. The maximum variation sampling strategy was used to select the participants (Patton, 2002). However, considering the relatively small number of adolescents who volunteered to participate, not all criteria could be taken into account. Data collection continued until the saturation point had been reached, that is when the information collected during the interviews became redundant and when it was felt that no new viewpoints were expressed. All activities – from recruiting participants to data collection – took place in a room within the school that was reserved for this project.

The sample consisted of 19 participants, of which 14 were females. Twelve were in grade 10 and 7 in grade 11. One was immigrant and two were born in Canada to immigrant parents. French was the first language of all but two participants, who were nevertheless fluent in French. Since the participants were minors, the consent of both the adolescent and a parent or tutor was sought. To preserve the confidentiality of the participants, pseudonyms are used in the present chapter for the participants as well as for the persons they named during their interviews.

3.4.3. Data Collection Instruments

A pilot study was conducted with six adolescents in the summer of 2010 to test the data collection instruments. The instruments were refined based on feedback from the participants. Data was collected through in-depth, face-to-face individual interviews. To collect information about the social network of each participant, a sociogram or a social network mapping tool was employed (Carrasco, Hogan, Wellman, & Miller, 2008). Sociograms allow participants to visually represent their core or personal social network, which means that participants were only asked to include individuals they felt close or very close to (i.e., intimates) or with whom they had frequent contacts (i.e., routine ties) (Wellman, Carrington, & Hall, 1997). In SNA terms, these individuals are called alters. A sociogram consists of a set of seven concentric circles at the center of which is the participant (called "Ego"). The map is also divided into quadrants.

3.4.4. Procedures

To fill the map, participants were asked to think about how people were clustered in their life (e.g., school, family, friends from elementary school, friends from summer camp). The three most important clusters were attributed a quadrant each. The fourth quadrant was used for other significant individuals who did not belong to the other clusters. Considering the relative homogeneity of the participants, they were asked to use two quadrants for family and school. To elicit the names of the persons to be included on their map, a *name generator*, which consists of asking, for each cluster identified, the names of the people to which they felt close or very close was utilized. The participants were also asked to draw lines between people in their network who knew each other.

Participants were administered a questionnaire to collect information about each alter (e.g., age, gender, level of education) as well as about the ties they maintain with them (e.g., nature of ties, frequency of contacts, duration of relationship). When positioning alters on the sociogram, participants used the concentric circles to indicate how emotionally close they felt to them. The critical incident technique (Flanagan, 1954), whose objective is to rely on a concrete situation (i.e., the critical incident) to generate a more accurate report than hypothetical questions would was also employed. Participants were invited to recall the last time they had been stuck while doing schoolwork outside of the classroom and to provide a detailed account of the context. To help participants recall the situation, the interviewer could ask additional questions, such as "What type of homework did you have to do?," "What kind of problem did you encounter?," "What did you do?," "Why did you asked this person?," or "Why didn't you seek the help of someone?." If participants named people who were not already in their sociogram while reporting on these incidents, they were invited to add them. Additional interview questions about the participants' academic help-seeking behavior, grades, and usage of SNSs, as well as general demographic questions were included. All interviews were recorded and transcribed. The interviews lasted between 61 and 95 minutes (mean = 79 minutes).

3.5. Data Analysis

The data was analyzed inductively, using the constant comparative method (Glaser & Strauss, 1967). The software package QDA Miner by Provalis Research was utilized to assist with the coding of the data. The data collected through the questionnaire about the alters were compiled and descriptive statistics were computed.

3.6. Results

3.6.1. Adolescents Social Network Attributes

The social network mapping tool (i.e., sociogram) allowed for collecting data about the core social network of participants. Each participant placed between 7 and 33 alters on their sociogram (mean = 18.6; median = 19; standard deviation = 6.32), for a total of 349 alters for the 19 participants. Of the 349 alters, 270 (77.4%) were strong ties (mean = 14.2) and 79 (22.6%) were weak ties (mean = 4.2). Among the strong ties, 100 (37%) were very strong ties or intimates, which means that participants placed them on the first of the seven concentric circles used to represent the strength of the relationship. The sociograms were divided into quadrants: one for family ties, one for school ties, one for any other cluster of ties, and a last one for other significant people who did not belong to any of the other quadrants. Family members accounted for 35.4% of the ties while school friends and other classmates accounted for 39.9% (no teachers were included in the core social network of participants). The quadrant for the additional cluster of ties was only used by 13 participants (six did not have any other cluster of ties to report). For those who used it, it was for ties from a school they previously attended ($n = 4$), a summer camp they attended ($n = 3$), an extra-curricular activity in which they were engaged ($n = 2$), the church they were going to ($n = 1$), a community organization of which they were member ($n = 1$), or, for immigrants or children of immigrants, their home country ($n = 2$). Participants placed 11.2% of the ties in this quadrant. Ties not related to any cluster accounted for the remaining 13.8% of the ties. On average, a social network was composed of 6.6 family ties, 7.2 school ties, 2.1 ties from

Table 3.1: Strength of ties per quadrant.

Quadrant	**Strength**	***n***	**Mean**	**Median**	**% within the quadrant**	**% within the whole social network**
Family	Ties	125	6.6	7	100	35.8
	Strong ties	93	4.9	4	74.4	26.6
	Weak ties	32	1.7	2	25.6	9.2
School	Ties	137	7.2	8	100	39.3
	Strong ties	111	5.8	5	81	31.8
	Weak ties	26	1.4	1	19	7.4
Other cluster of ties	Ties	39	2.1	2	100	11.2
	Strong ties	34	1.8	1	87.2	9.7
	Weak ties	5	0.3	0	12.8	1.4
Other alters	Ties	48	2.5	2	100	13.8
	Strong ties	32	1.7	1	66.7	9.2
	Weak ties	16	0.8	0	33.3	4.6
Total	Ties	349	18.4	19		100
	Strong ties	270	14.2	12		77.4
	Weak ties	79	4.2	2		22.6

another cluster, and 2.5 ties that did not belong to any cluster. Table 3.1 provides a summary of strong and weak ties per quadrant.

Overall, the majority of adolescents who participated in this study seemed to have a good core social network, which included both friends and family ties as well as a good number of intimate ties. However, there were a few participants who were more socially isolated. One participant's social network stood out as being particularly small and dispersed: it was composed of only seven ties, none of which being very close (i.e., 1 or 2 on a 7 point scale) (see Figure 3.1(a) for a simplified version of this sociogram). At the opposite end of the spectrum, two participants seemed highly social and had a very well-populated sociogram, with 30 or more

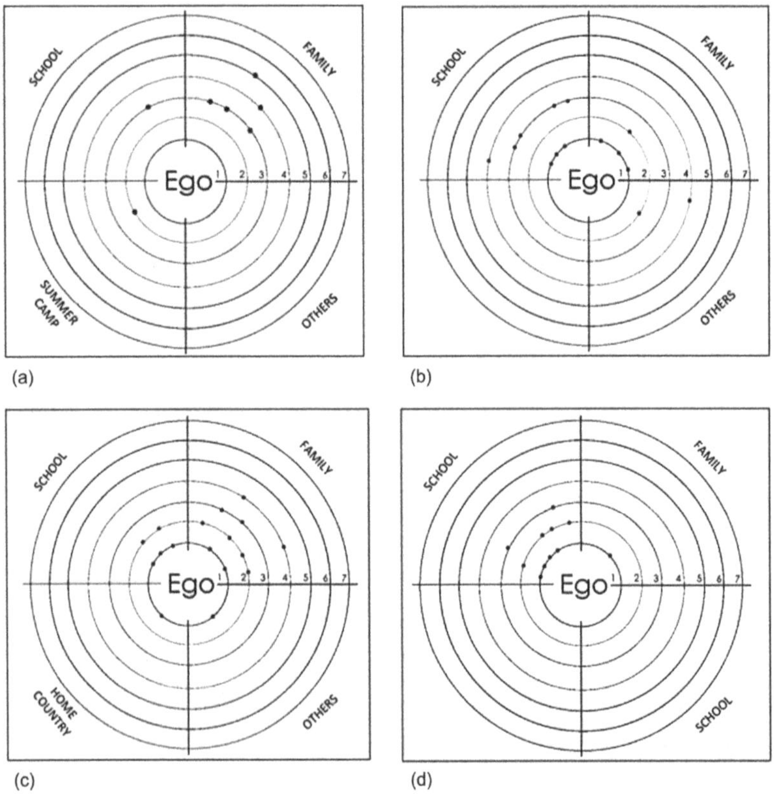

Figure 3.1: Examples of simplified versions of the participants' sociograms. (a) Example of a small and dispersed network. (b) Example of network evenly distributed between family and friendship ties. (c) Example of a network where ties gravitate toward family ties. (d) Example of a network where ties gravitate toward friends ties.

ties. Size was not the only aspect on which there were disparities. The way the ties were distributed among the quadrants also varied greatly. In several social networks ($n=5$), ties were fairly evenly distributed between family ties and school/friendship ties, which means that there was at most a difference of two ties between these two types of ties (see Figure 3.1(b) for an example of such a sociogram). In others, ties gravitated more toward family ties ($n=2$) (see Figure 3.1(c)) or toward school/friendship ties ($n=11$) (see Figure 3.1(d)). In two cases, family ties were not only scarce; they were also mostly weak, suggesting that these adolescents had conflicting relationships with their close family. Hence, even though participants were supposed to include in their sociogram people with whom they interacted often (i.e., routine ties), two participants chose not to include their mother in their sociogram although they were both living with her, and one did not include any of his parents with whom he was also living.

3.6.2. Frequency of Contact

Participants were in very frequent touch with a great portion of their network members. Face-to-face contacts were frequent, in large part because most people in their core social network were either classmates, who they see at least every weekday at school, or relatives (parents and siblings), with whom they often live. Hence, they had three or more face-to-face encounters with more than half (57.3%) of the members of their social network.

Participants reported having distant contacts with 289 of their 349 ties (82.2%). The proportion of family ties with whom they had remote contact was comparable (83.6%), whereas the proportion was slightly higher for friendship ties: they had distant contacts with 172 of the 182 friendship ties, which corresponds to 93% of these ties. There were also differences in the frequency of these distant contacts depending on the nature of the ties. They had weekly or daily mediated contacts with almost half of their friends (49.4%) compared with 20% for relatives. Having daily distant contacts seemed to be reserved to their friends: they reported interacting remotely with 22.1% of their friends several times per day, whereas only one relative (a parent) entered in this category.

Participants were asked to provide the primary medium used for distant communication with each member of their core social network. The mediums of communication most often mentioned were *Facebook*, phone calls, and SMS. *Facebook* was the principal means of communication for 112 of the 289 ties (38.8%) with which they had remote contacts. Phone calls and mobile phone text messages or SMS were the principal mediums for 71 ties

(24.6%) each. Again, the nature of the ties affected the distribution between these mediums. Among the 172 friends with whom they had distant contacts, *Facebook* was the primary means of communication with 81 (47.1%), SMS with 58 (33.7%), and phone calls with 21 (12.2%). The proportions between these mediums were quite different for relatives. Phone calls were by far the most commonly used means of communication with family members: it was the primary medium for 47 of the 89 relatives (52.8%) with whom participants had remote contacts. *Facebook* and SMS were much less popular. *Facebook* was the primary means of communication with 16 relatives (18%), and SMS with 10 relatives (11.2%) only.

3.6.3. School Achievement and Level of Education

Participants were asked to evaluate, on a 7 point scale, how each member of their core social network performed in school — or used to perform for those who were not at school anymore. Participants had between 0 and 15 very close ties (1 or 2 on the 7 point scale) who, from their perception, had or had had good or excellent grades (mean = 4.5; median = 4; standard deviation = 3.7). Only two participants did not have such ties, meaning that the vast majority had intimates that were or had been what they considered to be school achievers. Participants were also asked to provide the level of education of their network members. It is worth noting that the 32 parents that were named by the participants had a high school diploma. Thirty-one of them (96.9%) also had college education, and 22 (68.8%) had university education.[1]

3.6.4. Summary

In sum, most adolescents who participated in the study seemed to have the resources needed in their core social network to receive the help and support they needed for schoolwork. Indeed, the majority had a good size core social network that included several strong ties with whom they had frequent in-person and distant contacts. Most also had close ties who were or had been good at school and had one or two parents who had gone to college or university. According to the Strength of Weak Ties Theory (Granovetter, 1973, 1983), close ties are usually more motivated to help. Therefore, since several

1. It should be mentioned that the parents of the participants were relatively highly educated compared with national averages: according to Statistics Canada, 89% of Quebecers aged 25 to 54 have completed at least high school, 70.8% have a postsecondary diploma or higher, and 27.6% have a university degree.

of the participants' close ties appeared to have the required level of knowledge to help them with their schoolwork, it can be assumed that most participants had access to the resources they needed in their social network. It should, nevertheless, be repeated that this was not true for everyone. There were also a small number of adolescents who did not have this kind of resources in their core social network and who had few or no close ties on which they could rely when they needed help doing schoolwork.

In the following sections, the results of how and if the adolescents made use of the resources embedded in their core social network when they needed help with their schoolwork, and what they did when none of their close ties could provide the help they needed are reported.

3.7. Seeking Help

During the interviews, participants were asked to name the people from whom they usually ask for help when they are stuck doing schoolwork outside of the classroom. Most preferred to solicit the help of strong ties. Indeed, 15 of the 19 adolescents named one or both parents and 15 named one or more close friends. There were, however, a few exceptions. For example, Renaud (male, age 16) relied mostly on his teachers and his math tutor for help, none of which was strong ties. It should be noted that this is the participant who had a small and dispersed social network (see Figure 3.1 (a)). Another participant, Stéphanie (female, age 17), preferred relying on an "acquaintance" rather than on a close friend for reasons of efficiency:

> He explains it to me without bothering me. [...] He really just explains it to me, it takes two seconds; then I go back to my desk understanding everything. It's efficient. He talks like I talk. And yet, he is not my friend *at all*. It is a nice acquaintance.

The fact that Stéphanie mentioned that the person does not "bother" her suggests that it might be easier for her to receive help from someone with whom she is not emotionally involved. In the same vein, she explained that she prefers not to ask one of her close friends for help to avoid conflicts:

> But her, she truly *is* a friend of mine but, I don't know, she sort of gets on my nerves. And she never does what she needs to do, she never understands anything, you know ... I like her very much as a person but I can't work with her.

Other participants also named weak ties, although it was often presented as a "last-resort" option, when no people around them were available or able to help them. Teachers were among these weak ties. Three participants also talked about a service, *Allô prof*,[2] which offers the possibility to speak on the phone or chat with a teacher for free after school (from 5 to 8 p.m.). It can also be noted that all but two of the peers named by the adolescents were same-gender peers. To speak in social network terms, the ties were mostly homophilous with regard to gender. In the same way, 27 of the 29 peers were also classmates.

The critical incident technique elicited recent situations in which the participants felt they were stuck while doing schoolwork outside of the classroom. Two participants could not recall any incidents, maintaining that they were enrolled in the regular program — as opposed to the enriched program — and, as a result, they did not have any homework to do this year. This resulted in 17 different incidents that were recalled.

The analysis of the incidents showed that different types of help were sought. These were categorized in four different groups: procedural help, proofreading/comparing answers, factual information, and executive help (e.g., copying an assignment) (see Table 3.2). It can be noted that procedural help was by far the type of help that was the most frequently sought. This may probably be explained by the fact that procedural help often requires some time to provide; these events might have come to mind more easily than cases when factual information was sought, for example. It is

Table 3.2: Type of help sought as reported with the critical incident technique.

Type of help sought	*n*	Examples
Procedural help	11	Solving a mathematic problem Creating graphics with Excel for an assignment in economy Searching for information on the Web for an assignment in history
Proofreading/ comparing answers	3	Proofreading an essay in English Comparing answer for an assignment in history
Factual	2	Definition of a "foot" in poetry URL addresses of a reliable website for GPD data
Executive help	1	Copying a French assignment

2. http://www.alloprof.qc.ca/

also possible that participants did not feel comfortable enough to relate cases where they had copied the assignment of a classmate. Related to that, the first category — procedural help — included almost exclusively instances of instrumental seeking, that is, instances where the adolescent asked for help with the objective of acquiring autonomy or mastery. The other categories included cases of non-instrumental help seeking. Copying an assignment was an obvious example. In other cases, the context of help seeking was necessary to determine if this was instrumental or not. In some situations, for instance, the participants had made no prior efforts to solve the problem by themselves. One example is the case where the participant, Oscar (male, age 16), wanted the definition of a "foot" in poetry. Without trying to look up the word in a dictionary or on the Web, he asked "several persons" for the answer.

In two cases, the adolescent chose not to seek help and to not hand in his/her homework. In the incidents in which help was sought, participants often approached more than one person. The persons the adolescents asked for help were not always close ties: a few participants ($n=5$) sometimes simply turned to classmates who were available when they needed help. Close friends were also more represented than parents: five participants approached one or more close friends, whereas only three approached a parent. These discrepancies between the persons they say they rely on (their answers to the hypothetical question "Who do you ask for help when you are stuck?") and the persons they actually rely on (the critical incidents they reported) suggest that there might be a difference between who they thought they should be asking for help and who they approached when the need arose in reality. Teachers were solicited by two participants, one participant reported having called his personal math tutor and one called *Allô prof*, the free online tutoring service.

3.7.1. Criteria the Participants Used to Justify Who They Ask for Help

During the interviews, participants were asked who they relied on to get the help they need and to explain why they solicited the help of these individuals. The participants affirmed choosing people according to their personal qualities, pedagogical skills, and knowledge. Several reported avoiding people who were not patient and did not explain well. For example, Karine (female, age 15) justified not seeking the help of one of her close friends in the following way:

> [Esther] is really good, but sometimes she just can't explain it. If I tell her: "But why is it like that?" She replies: "BECAUSE IT'S LIKE THAT!".

Similarly, Marine (female, age 15) explained why she usually does not ask the help of her friend Iris although she has good grades:

> [Iris] is very good but .... She is so good that she goes too far when she explains. I don't know how to put it ... It is not easy for her. And she kind of loses her patience at times. [...] But [Ève], she is the one who is the most patient. I can ask her "Repeat again, repeat!" and she will go on.

Most also favored peers who worked hard, did their homework, and stayed focused in the classroom. Simone (female, age 15) justified her choice by saying that her friend "always does her homework." In the same vein, they also tended to favor those who were perceived as being smart and who scored higher than average in school. Fanny (female, age 16) said that she relied on two close friends because they were "real nerds," while Manuel (male, age 16) explained that he often turned to his father for help because he was "very good at school," adding that he had attended a renowned university.

Some participants also reported determining who they would ask for help based on the subject of their homework. While there were sometimes people around them who could help them with any subject, others were perceived has having some sort of "expertise" and were solicited only when this expertise was needed. Hence, Simone (female, 15) explained: "I often go see [Erika] for math because she understands math very well." Fanny (female, age 16) reported that her friend Émilie "helps everyone in mathematics" because it is her "area of expertise." Charlotte (female, age 16) said that she would ask her mother for help if it were for French but not for mathematics because: "I think my mother was not very good in math, but French was really *her* thing."

The analysis of the critical incidents, however, revealed that other criteria were often applied in real life. More precisely, availability and physical proximity was the most frequently mentioned reason for asking a particular person. The physical proximity of the person had been a determinant factor for 11 participants. For example, Laurier (male, age 16) justified not having sought the help of his teacher by the fact that "he is often busy doing other things and he is too far!" Feeling a little ashamed of his answer, he then commented: "This is the lazy person's answer ..." Another participant, Cynthia (female, age 16), affirmed that she simply asks the person that is "next to her" and that her choice is "truly random." Online, this translates into going on *Facebook* and soliciting the help of any classmate who would happen to be connected. Having the possibility to get an immediate answer, without too much effort, seems to prevail over other criteria such as the pedagogical skills or the expertise of the person, as illustrated by the following excerpt from the interview with Cynthia (female, age 16):

Interviewer: Do you think there would have been someone else in your social network who would have been in a better position to help you?
Cynthia: [Jasmine].
Interviewer: And why didn't you ask [Jasmine]?
Cynthia: I don't know. Well … she was not connected on *Facebook* at the time.

Similarly, Simone (female, age 15) relates that she would have liked to request the help of her teacher but, when she realized she needed help, it was too late: "I was at home. I had only started to work [on the assignment] that night and it was due the following day …"

In conclusion, although the participants claimed seeking the assistance of people who were knowledgeable and patient, the critical incidents they reported suggest that it is not always the case. Availability played a more important role than they first admitted. Lack of motivation or laziness could probably partly explain this behavior. But the fact that they often wait until the last minute to do their homework is also certainly part of the explanation. When pressed for time, these participants could not afford to wait for the right person to help them, indicating that they did not always take full advantage of the resources embedded in their social network.

3.7.2. Reasons for Not Seeking Help

The reasons for asking for help are relatively obvious: high school students have assignments to do and they are expected to do everything they can to complete them and hand them in on time. They also have strong incentives to complete these assignments: they are often graded and students who do not complete them might receive a scolding from their teacher or even from the school principal if it is not their first "offense." Why would adolescents decide not to seek help if they cannot complete an assignment by themselves?

As it was mentioned earlier, in two of the 17 critical incidents reported, the participants did not seek help and, as a result, were not able to complete the assignment. In one of these situations, the participant, Karine (female, age 15), estimated that she was ahead of her classmates in mathematics — the subject in which she had homework to do — and determined that it was not worth asking for help since, according to her, it was unlikely that her classmates would have been able to finish it. Therefore, she would not be alone in this situation and was, thus, less afraid of the potential consequences. In the other incident, the participant, Renaud (male, age 16), who had no close friends and seemed to have difficult relations with his parents, simply did not have anyone he could ask for help. He had no close friends to call, and no parents or siblings willing to help him. Since he was not a member of *Facebook*, he could not contact classmates through this medium either.

Some participants also gave other reasons for not approaching people around them that would have had the expertise to help them. Several participants mentioned being afraid of disturbing or bothering people. This sentiment seems to be stronger when they were considering soliciting the help of weak ties. For instance, Fanny (female, 16) explains:

> Seriously, [Stéphane] and [Pierre-Luc] would certainly have been in a better position to help me with this type of thing, but they have other things to do, while [Thalia]... I know she works on the same things as I do.

While Fanny feels comfortable requesting the assistance of her best friend (Thalia; strength of tie: 1), she is reluctant to ask the help of more casual friends (Stéphane and Pierre-Luc; strength of ties: 4) by fear of disturbing them. Perhaps this also explains why in all incidents where participants needed procedural help (e.g., for solving a math problem, using a computer application, searching for information), they solicited close ties. This type of help is often best provided in person and requires more time than do factual questions. They might, therefore, be more at ease to "bother" a close friend or a parent than a simple classmate.

Another reason provided by one participant was to avoid potential conflict or frustration. Samuel (male, age 16) explained that he preferred trying everything he could to find the information by himself for the following reason: "Because it is just better for the other person and for me. Sometimes, the way they explain, it is not very clear. I just don't get how they reason, so I prefer to check online." For two participants, lack of motivation or interest and perhaps laziness seemed to explain why they did not always seek help when they needed it. Oscar (male, age 16) said with the tone of someone who did not care: "If I am at home and I have an assignment to do and I don't understand, I don't do it. If I understand, I do it." Similarly, Stéphanie (female, age 17) explained: "Sometimes, the assignments are just not relevant, really. So I'm not going to put efforts into that. I'll just not do it."

Finally, a few participants expressed taking pride in finding the information by themselves, without the help of anyone. They would therefore spend a lot of time searching for information online before seeking help from someone. For example, Stéphanie reported that she was a "loner" and that she "just do[es]n't need help in life." She then added:

> I help a lot of people but I'm not able to receive help because it frustrates me. I just want to find the information myself so that I can be proud of myself because I did it.

3.8. Different Actors, Different Roles

As we saw, the analysis of the interviews demonstrated that participants preferred to seek help mostly from their friends and, to a lesser extent, from their parents, classmates, and teachers. But what role do these different actors play? These questions are answered in the next section.

3.8.1. The Role of Friendship Ties

Friends hold a special place in the lives of adolescents. Therefore, it is not surprising to note that friends also play a central role in their learning process. Participants mentioned various reasons for relying on friends for help with schoolwork. First, as was already mentioned, the friends they rely on are predominantly also classmates: they are enrolled in the same school and, most of the times, are in the same school group. As such, they have the same teachers and the same assignments, which greatly facilitates the process, as they do not have to provide detailed information about the subject and the assignment when they ask for help. Hence, Oscar (male, age 16) justified never seeking the help of his girlfriend, although he considered that she is really good at school, by the fact that "she is in advanced math, chemistry, and physics," meaning that she had chosen the *Science* option, while he was in the *Cultural, Social and Technical* option. Being enrolled in different programs, although in the same school, seemed for him to be a sufficient reason for not asking for her help. For another participant, Élodie (female, age 16), seeking the help of her friends who attended a different school did not seem natural to her since their friendship was not based on school. She said: "We don't talk a lot about that [school] and, since we are not in the same school, I don't know … It's just that in my head, I have to ask people who go to [name of her school]."

Although being in the same school group was frequently mentioned as a justification for seeking the help of a particular friend, there were a few cases where closeness seemed to be more important. One participant, Charlotte (female, age 16), reported that she prefers asking friends from outside of the school:

> I always felt that … it doesn't bother them as much or that they take more pleasure helping me. Because I have the feeling that, if I asked one of my friends from school, *maybe* they would be happy, but they would probably do that quickly, while my other friends, they will take the time to do it well.

In addition to feeling more comfortable asking her close friends from another school, Élodie seemed to consider that this was a way to strengthen her bonds with them: from her point of view, they are pleased and perhaps flattered when she seeks their help.

As already mentioned, close ties were also more often solicited when participants needed procedural help. With classmates who were not close friends, they tended to limit their requests to things that would not require too much time. They reported asking factual questions, comparing answers. A few also admitted having asked classmates if they would let them copy an assignment.

3.8.2. The Role of Family Ties

Among the family ties, parents were by far the most often solicited for help with schoolwork. Although not as important as friends, they were still a good source of help for several participants. They are usually willing to help and available when the need arises. For instance, Arielle (female, age 17) had an assignment to do for which she had to find information on the Web. Searching for information turned out to be more challenging than she had anticipated, which is why she requested the help of her mother:

> My mother helped me search on the Web because I was fed up and tired. She did some research for me, she clicked on pages to see if it could be interesting, she read … She is better than me to find interesting and relevant information in a text.

However, when talking about the potential help their parents could offer, most participants mentioned that they solicited their parents only for certain subjects. For instance, many perceived their parents as not having the necessary knowledge to help them, at least in some subjects. Many attributed this to the reform of the education system in Québec that was initiated in 2000. According to the participants, the teaching and learning methods and practice had changed so much that the participants' parents, who had done their schooling before the reform, were not always able to assist them adequately. For example, Cynthia (female, age 16) explained:

> Sometimes, my parents don't understand because of the reform. Things are explained differently. […] My mother, at one point, was looking at a problem and she could not figure out what it meant. Even after seeing the right answer the following day. She said that the question was poorly formulated. Or it was differently formulated.

Similarly, when asked why he does not seek the help of his parents in math, Laurier (male, age 16) answered:

> I think they don't remember anymore but, also, it has changed a lot. I don't think we are taught the same things as before. Sometimes, the teachers say "Before, it was called blah blah blah." Before means 10 years ago. Imagine 25 or 30 years!

The fact that most parents had completed their education many years ago also contributed to increasing the chances that they would have forgotten some notions. According to the adolescents, their parents did not always understand the material enough to help them. As Anne (female, age 16) noted: "When I was at the elementary school, I used to ask my mother for help but now, I know she does not understand more than I do!" This was particularly problematic for mathematics and sciences, which parents were more likely to have forgotten if they did not need to use this knowledge for work. Irène (female, age 15), for example, said about her parents: "Most of the time, if it's for math, they understand nothing. [...] Really, in math, they're useless!" However, in other subjects, in particular in French or history, participants reported seeking the help of their parents more frequently, as illustrated by the following quote from Arielle (female, age 17):

> If it were for French, I would be much more inclined to ask my mother. [...] We had to write several argumentative essays in the recent years. So I often went to see her to ask her: "I have to talk about this subject. What do you know about it?" And sometimes, just talking about it with her helped me. But otherwise, in math or science, my mother — or any people in my family — they really don't know what to answer if I ask their help.

A few participants admitted avoiding asking the help of one or both of their parents for reasons other than a lack of knowledge, mostly in connection with the relationship they had with their parents. Some reported having conflicting relationships with one or both of their parents. For example, Stéphanie (female, age 17) explained with obvious bitterness why she never sought the help of her parents:

> I've never needed help because I never received help. Since I was *born*. I've *never* received help with my homework. My mother *never* helped me or if she helped me, I would yell at her because I did not understand. It never worked! Besides, it was not her fault if I was yelling at her and crying. I was very touchy!

This quote illustrates how soliciting the help of a parent can contribute to increase a latent tension when there is one, thus resulting in the adolescent avoiding seeking help from that parent. But even when they maintained a close relationship with their parents, receiving help from them could nevertheless be an irritating experience. Stéphanie (female, age 17) explained that when her parents helped her with schoolwork, "it's like if they were too close to me. I lose it. So it's just better if I'm on my own." By contrast, for Eugénie (female, age 16), who maintains a strong and harmonious relationship with her mother, not seeking her help is a way to protect her and let her have some time to herself. She said: "You know, she [her mother] works very hard, so I really don't want to bother her. The only relaxing time she gets is during the evening."

Besides parents, very few family members were mentioned by the participants as providing the help they needed for their schoolwork. Indeed, only two participants reported receiving help from an older sibling but even for them, this was occasional. It is also interesting to note that in both cases, the sibling was much older and was now living on his/her own. Apart from that, one participant reported seeking the help of an aunt who frequently visited them, and one participant sought the help of her stepparents from time to time.

3.8.3. The Role of Teachers

Outside of the classroom, most participants only rarely sought the help of their teachers. Even in the classroom, peers were often consulted first, as the following quote from Éloldie (female, age 16) shows: "First of all, we all get together to try to understand and see if someone in the group understands. If nobody does, *then* we go ask the teacher." Various reasons were cited to explain this type of behavior.

Some participants mentioned the lack of availability of their teachers. Teachers are usually available at specific times, when they did not necessarily need their help. Considering that many participants admitted frequently doing their homework at the last minute, the need for help was more likely to arise at night or during the weekend, the day before the assignment is due. Therefore, asking the help of a teacher in these circumstances was not an option. Other reasons for not seeking help from teachers included fear of disturbing them. The perception of these participants was that teachers had more important things to do than to help them. For instance, to explain why he did not ask his teacher, Oscar (male, age 16) said: "The course was about to start and she was busy doing stuff." Others attributed their reluctance to seek help from their teachers to their personality or pedagogical skills. Some teachers were criticized for being intimidating or for "not explaining well." For example, Renaud (male, age 16) affirmed: "I don't feel comfortable with my math teacher. I don't like her at all." Irène (female, age 15) maintained that some teachers "explain so badly" that it is not worth seeking their help. Eugénie said that she would only seek the help of certain teachers: "It depends on the personality of the teacher. Some are not patient. Some might as well tell you 'figure it out yourself' or 'it's in your notes.' So I go see my friends in those situations." But one of the reasons mentioned the most frequently by the participants was the fear of looking dumb in front of the teacher or of being lectured by him or her for not being attentive enough in class. When asked if she sometimes sought the help of her teacher, Karine (female, age 15) gave the following answer:

> No. Before doing that, I will ask my friends, then I ask the whole group, and *then* I ask the teacher. Because I don't like to do that. I don't know ... Because sometimes, she says "Come on, I just explained it!"

This answer was representative of several of the answers the participants provided to that question. Nevertheless, there were a few participants who were less hesitant to ask their teachers for assistance. Eugénie (female, age 16), for example, praised the pedagogical skills of her teachers compared to her friends:

> I know the teacher will give me the right answer. And I understand better. He knows how to explain it to me. With my friends, if I don't understand the first time, they are not able to explain it differently. They tell me this is how they understand it and that's it.

As for Irène (female, age 15), although she affirmed she would not approach all of her teachers for help, she reports feeling comfortable seeking the assistance of her math teacher: "I go see her without any hesitation. Because she is nice, she is fun. Well, she's not *truly* nice, but I like how she works. She explains well."

Finally, it is noteworthy that teachers can sometimes partly compensate for the lack of resources in a student's social network. For Renaud (male, age 16), the participant who had an exceptionally small social network, teachers played a more important role. Renaud seemed to be highly isolated in school: he reported no friendship ties among his classmates. This certainly greatly affected his confidence. As a result, he only very rarely asked his classmates for help. Similarly, when asked if his classmates sometimes solicited his help, his answer was "I don't think so." Having teachers who were supportive and available for Renaud seemed crucial, especially since he was struggling academically. One of his teachers appeared to have noticed his need and was giving him more attention and support than to other students:

> In French, it is the teacher who comes to see me. He takes the initiative. I think he knows I'm not very good in French. It's my weak point. So most of the time, he comes to see me before I even get the chance to tell him I don't understand.

Having a private math tutor he could call for help was also a precious resource for him. Although this was fairly recent, he had already called him a few times to obtain help with math assignments.

3.9. Usage and Perception of SNSs for Help Seeking

One of the objectives of this study was to look more closely at how adolescents used SNSs in relation to academic help seeking. Participants were asked various questions regarding their use of these sites. Not surprisingly, *Facebook* was by far the most popular SNS among the participants: all but one participant were *Facebook* members. The focus of attention was therefore directed on how participants used this site to solicit and receive the help they needed for their schoolwork. It should first be mentioned that it was common for participants to have in their *Facebook* friends almost all of their classmates. As it is often said, "friendship" takes a different meaning in *Facebook*. As a result, several participants had over 500 *Facebook* friends, some even thousands of friends, so that they could use that platform not only to stay in touch with their close friends but also with acquaintances and, in this case, with their classmates.

Facebook was used in various ways by participants in the context of academic help seeking. Since they could easily contact their classmates on this site, it was not uncommon to solicit the help of one or several classmates at once, even if they were not close friends. Many seemed to be less intimidated to contact classmates through *Facebook* than to call a close friend. The tools used to make contact with their peers varied. A few reported posting their question as a status on their wall so that all their *Facebook* friends would see it. Laurier (male, age 16) explained that, when there is an assignment to hand in:

> There is almost always someone [on *Facebook*] who writes on his wall: "Is there anyone who has the answer to that question?" It's almost always like this, especially when the assignment is for all secondary 4 [grade10] students.

Therefore, when asked what he does when he needs help with a math assignment, Laurier answered: "I go check on *Facebook*. Because when there is a big assignment, or when we are preparing for an exam, there is always someone who is on *Facebook*."

Most participants, however, preferred more "private" means of communication than the wall. A few even expressed some contempt for those who used their wall to ask for help, such as Anne (female, age 16) who seems proud to say that she is not "the type of person who does that." Instead of the wall, most participants used *Facebook*'s chat service to contact their classmates. A common strategy was to go on *Facebook* to see who among their classmates were connected. They would first contact their close friends but, if they were not available, would contact any classmate that happened to be connected. For instance, Ève (female, age 16) explained that, the day before an assignment is due, "everybody is connected." When asked how she determines who she is going to contact, she said: "I ask my friends but often, when I don't understand, my friends don't understand either. Then, I ask other people. Anyone, even in other classrooms."

The interactions are indeed not necessarily limited to one person. Élodie (female, age 16) relates how she and several of her classmates had found themselves working collaboratively on an assignment on *Facebook* on a Sunday evening:

> The day before [the assignment was due], we were all on *Facebook* trying to … We just wanted to know who had the right answers. I had completed it [the assignment] so everyone was asking me: "What did you find for the GDP? Because there are a lot of different sites …" […] It was late at night and we were all still on *Facebook* working.

However, the mediums of communication available in *Facebook* limited the type of help one could receive or give. The analysis of the incidents and the description the participants gave of their use of *Facebook* for academic help seeking revealed that this platform was mostly used to compare answers, ask for URL addresses to useful websites or for missing instructions. Chatting did not seem to be the adequate means of receiving procedural help. For instance, Eugénie (female, age 16) explained that she prefers calling her friends than using *Facebook* "because it takes too much time to type, and we cannot explain well." Marine (female, 15) has a similar explanation: "I text her to say 'call me' and then she calls me. I don't use *Facebook* or texting because I don't feel like typing everything. It's really much faster orally."

Overall, most participants made use of the different tools *Facebook* offers to work collaboratively with their classmates. Having the possibility to get in touch with almost all of their classmates greatly increased the chances of finding someone who could help them when they needed that help. Nevertheless, in situations that called for more detailed explanations or procedural help, some participants felt that phone calls or face-to-face visits remained the most appropriate medium of communication.

3.10. Discussion

Although several studies have demonstrated that people played an important role in information provision in daily life and that instrumental help seeking contributes to the social and intellectual development of children and adolescents alike, our knowledge of the resources that are embedded in the adolescents' social network and the criteria they use to select the person to approach remains limited. In addition, considering that the adolescents who participated in this study belonged to the Generation Y, a generation that is known for having a distinctive — more collaborative — learning style and increased technological skills, it seems important to re-examine academic help seeking.

In the next section, the discussion of the findings is provided in the context of the research questions posed.

3.10.1. What are the Resources Late Adolescents Have Access to in Their Core Social Network?

It is difficult to assess how the core social networks of the participants in this study compare to the social networks of other adolescents. Based on the analysis of the sociograms, a vast majority of participants appeared to have a well-populated personal social network, which included several strong ties. Moreover, most counted in their close ties friends who were good at school and parents who had college or university education, which suggests that many had in their social network people who had both the motivation and the required knowledge to help them. Yet, not everyone was lucky enough to benefit from such support in his or her personal network. For the very few adolescents who were in this situation, when they encountered difficulties, they either turned to weak ties (e.g., teachers, tutors, or classmates), or decided not to solicit the help of anyone and hand in an incomplete homework or not hand it in at all.

3.10.2. Do Late Adolescents Use the Resources Embedded in Their Core Social Network When They Need Them for Their Schoolwork?

Most participants did not hesitate to seek the help of people in their social network when they experienced difficulties doing schoolwork. This means that they were able to recognize they needed help but were motivated to make the necessary efforts to obtain this help. However, it appears that they did not always fully take advantage of the resources embedded in their social network: availability often prevailed on competence as the main criteria for deciding who to approach. To use Shenton and Dixon's way of categorizing people that satisfy the information needs of others, adolescents mostly approached people of convenience (2003). This was often the result of doing homework at the last minute, which left them with little time to find the more competent person in their network to help them and, thus, maximize the chances of the experience being beneficial.

Despite the general positive attitude the participants had towards academic help seeking, there were cases where they reported not having sought the help of anyone although they were facing difficulties they could not overcome by themselves. The analysis revealed that different reasons explained this behavior, including avoiding potential conflicts, lack of motivation, the fear of disturbing others, and the fear of looking unintelligent in the eyes of the helper (more specifically of teachers). There were also few participants who greatly valued their independence, thus having a more negative attitude toward help seeking. Some of these reasons were also identified by other researchers as inhibitors to academic help seeking.

The fear of looking unintelligent is certainly one of the most studied barriers to help seeking in learning situations (Newman & Goldin, 1990; Ryan & Pintrich, 1997). Avoiding conflicts could be associated to the conclusions Ryan and Pintrich (1997) reached: adolescents who perceive themselves as having low social competence were less likely to ask people for help with their schoolwork. Ryan and Pintrich also identified perceived benefits of help seeking and intrinsic motivation as factors affecting help seeking. According to Hill and Tyson (2009), the increased desire to be autonomous that characterizes adolescence could also be a factor.

3.10.3. Who Do Late Adolescents Approach When They Need Help with Their Schoolwork?

The participants in this study relied mainly (but not exclusively) on strong ties and more specifically on their classmates to receive the help and information they needed to do their schoolwork. The ties used to get help were also greatly homophilous: the students that were interviewed mainly sought help from people with whom they shared several characteristics. For instance, they almost exclusively requested the help of friends who were in the same school, in the same grade, preferably in the same group. This behavior was particularly prevalent when participants needed help with schoolwork related to mathematics or other sciences. Relying on someone for whom the material covered in class was still fresh, and who had learned it the exact same way was important. It should also be noted that mathematics and sciences were also the subjects in which parents were often considered as not having the competence to help their children, unless these skills were required for their job. For schoolwork related to languages (and especially for essay papers), seeking the help of parents was more frequent although peers remained the primary source of help. Participants only very rarely actively sought the help of teachers to obtain the support they needed, mostly by fear of disturbing them, of looking dumb, or of being reprimanded for not being attentive enough in class.

All these findings mirror those of previous research. As mentioned earlier, Nelson-Le Gall and Gumerman (1984) observed that adolescents had a clear preference for friends over parents and teachers as sources of help in relation to schoolwork. Hill and Tyson (2009) attribute this partly to the transformations that occur in the parent–adolescent relationships. Researchers also found that parents did not always have the required knowledge to help their children: Balli, Demo, and Wedman (1998), who interviewed parents who had been asked to help their adolescent child with mathematics homework, found that they had some difficulty understanding the subject matter and felt challenged by the fact that their children were taught differently from how they had been taught. This could also explain why studies on parental involvement in middle school revealed that homework assistance by parents was not consistently related to achievement (Hill & Tyson, 2009; Xu & Corno, 2003).

The research on generation Y also demonstrates that today's young adults tend to approach their peers for help and have a distrusting attitude toward their teachers (Gardner & Eng, 2005). The lesser importance of teachers in help seeking has also been attributed by researchers to the fear of embarrassment from looking stupid (Newman, 1990; Newman & Goldin, 1990). However, in his literature review on the role of teachers in the development of adaptive help-seeking skills, Newman (2000) affirms that this fear can be attenuated by the attitude of the teacher:

> Teachers' personal involvement with students can have a powerful, facilitating influence on classroom help seeking. Caring and responsive teachers with democratic interaction styles tend to have students who feel relatively comfortable asking for help. (Newman, 2000, p. 378)

This is in line with what some of the participants in the present study expressed in that they were more comfortable to ask certain teachers than others, mostly because of their personality. It suggests that although teachers are weak ties, they seem to be considered more approachable when they take on some attributes usually associated with strong ties, such as attentiveness and the desire to help. In her research on the role of community health nurses as an information provider for seniors, Pettigrew (1997) arrived at the same conclusion saying that nurses played a unique role in the social networks of seniors, exhibiting qualities of both weak and strong ties. She concluded that nurses with these attributes should be qualified as "strong-weak ties."

The participants' preference for close ties was also observed by other researchers. Drawing on the literature on help seeking, Newman (2000) reviewed the role parents, peers, and teachers play in the development of children' skills. He explained that children are often afraid to seek the help for fear of looking dumb in the eyes of the helper. As a result, they prefer to ask close ties, with whom they feel comfortable disclosing their difficulties and their need for help. Granovetter's Strength of Weak Ties theory (1973, 1983) may also explain this behavior in that the late adolescents in this study were probably aware that these persons would be more motivated to help them. However, the preference for strong ties was more evident when procedural help was sought, perhaps because it usually requires more time and patience. For factual help or for comparing answers, it seemed more acceptable to ask any classmate, especially in SNSs as will be discussed.

3.10.4. How Do Late Adolescents Use and Perceive Online SNSs to Get the Help They Need with Their Schoolwork?

The participants often used the SNS *Facebook* as a medium to approach people for help. As mentioned before, SNSs have made it easier to maintain weak ties, which usually translate in an increased social capital (Ellison et al., 2007). However, although most participants used this media platform to stay in contact with weak ties, they did not fully use the resources to which they had access through their larger social network to get the help they needed for their schoolwork. Indeed, they tended to seek help from people with whom they had frequent contacts (i.e., their classmates) and who were available when the need to seek help arose, even if they believed there were other persons in their network that had an expertise that would have been helpful in that situation.

This study showed that, compared to face-to-face or telephone communication, *Facebook* seemed to lower barriers to interaction, confirming previous research on computer-mediated communication (Tidwell & Walther, 2002). Hence, although participants only occasionally called friends to seek help, many reported feeling confident in contacting any of their classmates who were connected to *Facebook* at a given moment for that purpose. As a result, *Facebook*, especially the Chat feature could be seen as a facilitator in seeking help, which has both benefits and drawbacks. As demonstrated by previous research, help seeking can play an instrumental role in learning and be perceived as a sign that the student is aware that his or her needs for help and that he or she is motivated enough to actively seek help (Nelson-Le Gall, 1981). However, the barriers to interaction in *Facebook* seemed to be so low that several participants reported seeking the help of their peers very frequently and almost immediately after the need was recognized, and often without trying to find a solution themselves.

In certain situations, the services *Facebook* offers were, nevertheless, considered too limited by some participants. They indicated that phone calls or in-person visits remained the most appropriate means to provide and receive help, especially when procedural help was sought, supporting the findings of Luckin et al. (2009). In studying how high school students used Web 2.0 technologies for learning, they concluded that, because of the lack of synchronous communication means, SNSs "may not be ideal arenas through which to conduct collaborative learning" (p. 97).

3.11. Conclusion

This study revealed a wide variety of help-seeking behaviors and motivations in relation to schoolwork among late adolescents. Nevertheless, some common patterns emerged from the analysis. The findings of this study are congruent with those of previous research, which revealed that late adolescents mostly rely on their peers and more specifically on classmates to obtain the help they need with schoolwork. More importantly, the findings of this study illustrate that in many cases, in the last high school years, adolescents can no longer rely on their parents for help, especially in mathematics or sciences. They also find more convenient to ask people who are easily available and who have the same homework to do so that they do not have to provide the instructions. In addition, by examining academic help seeking in the light of SNA, this study revealed that adolescents oftentimes feel more comfortable soliciting "close ties" when seeking procedural help because it requires lengthier explanations, and that by doing so the fear of disturbing others or of looking dumb in the eyes of the helper are removed. Moreover, the findings showed that for adolescents who have a small and dispersed social network (no close ties willing to help), finding help with schoolwork can be challenging.

This study shed new light on late adolescents' academic help seeking by examining the role SNSs play in the process. At first glance, SNSs appear to act as facilitators, allowing adolescents easier access to their classmates while lowering barriers to interaction. However, these tools (e.g.,Facebook) were also found to be inadequate in certain circumstances, especially in providing procedural help. Consequently, SNSs could sometimes encourage non-instrumental help seeking: it is certainly easier when chatting with a classmate to ask for the answer to a problem than to ask how to solve the problem. Although it seems to be acceptable to ask any classmate some help on SNSs, soliciting procedural help or any form of explanation was mostly reserved for "close ties."

By providing a more thorough understanding of the resources available in adolescents' social networks and the process through which they draw on these resources to support their learning, the findings of this study have implications for how educators (teachers) and school libraries could better support high school students with their schoolwork.

Since the help adolescents seek from classmates through SNSs is not always instrumental, and because adolescents with poor social skills could be less likely to find the help they need in their social network, it seems important to offer an alternative form of support that will be instrumental and that will be provided in ways that will meet the needs of adolescents. A service like *Allô prof*, which allows elementary- and high-school students the possibility of receiving distant help from teachers, by phone, chat or forum, should be considered by teachers and be promoted broadly, to both students and their parents. Since availability was the main criteria for selecting the person to approach for help, such services should offer extended hours, especially during the time when students are more likely to be working on their schoolwork to provide help. Additionally, the fact that electronic mediums of communication seem to lower barriers to interaction indicates that providing services by chat or forum is likely to positively affect the chances of students using the service. Considering the limitations of chat in certain situations, adolescents should nevertheless continue to have the possibility of contact tutors by phone. Similarly, results seem to support the idea that school and/or public libraries should also offer chat reference services, which should be available during extended hours, and actively promote these services to high school students and their parents.

3.12. Limitations

This study is based on interviews conducted with a small purposive sample. Dealing with a small sample enables the researcher to obtain rich descriptions from each participant, which is essential to gain a deep understanding of motivations and behaviors. However, it limits the external validity of the results.

The fact that the participants were selected from the same urban area in Quebec, Montreal, and that they were enrolled in the same school, certain behaviors or perceptions late adolescents revealed in this study may be limited to this population of students.

Another limitation resides in use of interviews which tend to provide subjective accounts of experiences and behaviors.

Acknowledgments

The author gratefully acknowledges the contribution of the young adults who participated to this study and the pedagogical consultant who helped with the recruitment process. This research project received financial support from the Fonds Québécois pour la Recherche sur la Société et la Culture.

References

Abbas, J., & Agosto, D. E. (2013). Everyday life information behavior of young people. In J. Beheshti & A. Large (Eds.), *The information behavior of a new generation: Children and teens in the 21st century* (pp. 65–91). Lanham, MD: The Scarecrow Press.

Agosto, D. E., & Hughes-Hassell, S. (2005). People, places, and questions: An investigation of the everyday life information-seeking behaviors of urban young adults. *Library and Information Science Research*, *27*, 141–163.

Agosto, D. E., & Hughes-Hassell, S. (2006). Toward a model of the everyday life information needs of urban teenagers, part 2: Empirical model. *Journal of the American Society for Information Science and Technology*, *57*(11), 1418–1426.

Balli, S. J., Demo, D. H., & Wedman, J. F. (1998). Family involvement with children's homework: An intervention in the middle grades. *Family Relations*, *47*(2), 149–157. doi:10.2307/585619

Bilal, D. (2000). Children's use of the Yahooligans! Web search engine: I. Cognitive, physical, and affective behaviors on fact-based search tasks. *Journal of the American Society for Information Science and Technology*, *51*(7), 646–665. doi:10.1002/(sici)1097-4571(2000)51:7 <646::aid-asi7> 3.0.co;2-a

Bilal, D. (2001). Children's use of the Yahooligans! Web search engine: II. Cognitive and physical behaviors on research tasks. *Journal of the American Society for Information Science and Technology*, *52*(2), 118–136. doi:10.1002/1097-4571(2000)9999:9999 <::aid-asi1038> 3.0.co;2-r

Bilal, D. (2002). Children's use of the Yahooligans! Web search engine. III. Cognitive and physical behaviors on fully self-generated search tasks. *Journal of the American Society for Information Science and Technology*, *53*(13), 1170–1183. doi:10.1002/asi.10145

Bowler, L. (2011). Into the land of adolescent metacognitive knowledge during the information search process: A metacognitive ethnography. In A. Spink & J.

Heinström (Eds.), *New directions in information behaviour* (pp. 93–125). Bingley, UK: Emerald Group Publishing Limited.
Burt, R. S. (2005). *Brokerage and closure: An introduction to social capital.* Oxford, NY: Oxford University Press.
Carrasco, J. A., Hogan, B., Wellman, B., & Miller, E. J. (2008). Collecting social network data to study social activity-travel behavior: An egocentric approach. *Environment and Planning B: Planning and Design, 35*(6), 961–980.
Chung, J. S., & Neuman, D. (2007). High school students' information seeking and use for class projects. *Journal of the American Society for Information Science and Technology, 58*(10), 1503–1517. doi:10.1002/asi.20637
Donath, J., & boyd, D. (2004). Public displays of connection. *BT Technology Journal, 22*(4), 71–82. doi:10.1023/B:BTTJ.0000047585.06264.cc
Ellison, N. B., Steinfield, C., & Lampe, C. (2007). The benefit of Facebook "friends": Social capital and college students' use of online social network sites. *Journal of Computer-Mediated Communication, 12*(4), 1143–1168.
Flanagan, J. C. (1954). The critical incident technique. *Psychological Bulletin, 51*(4), 327–358. doi:10.1037/h0061470
Gardner, S., & Eng, S. (2005). What students want: Generation Y and the changing function of the academic library. *Portal: Libraries and the Academy, 5*(3), 405–420. doi:10.1353/pla.2005.0034
Gibbons, S. (2007). *The academic library and the net gen student making the connections.* Chicago, IL: American Library Association.
Glaser, B. G., & Strauss, A. L. (1967). *The discovery of grounded theory: Strategies for qualitative research.* Chicago, IL: Aldine Publishing Company.
Granovetter, M. (1973). The strength of weak ties. *American Journal of Sociology, 78*(6), 1360.
Granovetter, M. S. (1983). The strength of weak ties: A network theory revisited. *Sociological Theory, 1*, 201–233.
Greenhow, C., & Robelia, B. (2009). Old communication, new literacies: Social network sites as social learning resources. *Journal of Computer-Mediated Communication, 14*(4), 1130–1161. doi:10.1111/j.1083-6101.2009.01484.x
Haythornthwaite, C. (1996). Social network analysis: An approach and technique for the study of information exchange. *Library & Information Science Research, 18*(4), 323–342.
Hill, N. E., & Tyson, D. F. (2009). Parental involvement in middle school: A meta-analytic assessment of the strategies that promote achievement. *Developmental Psychology, 45*(3), 740–763. doi:10.1037/a0015362
Holliday, W., & Li, Q. (2004). Understanding the millennials: Updating our knowledge about students. *Reference Services Review, 32*(4), 356–366. doi:10.1108/00907320410569707
Howe, N., & Strauss, W. (2000). *Millennials rising: The next great generation.* New York, NY: Vintage Books.
Julien, H., & Michels, D. (2000). Source selection among information seekers: Ideals and realities. *Canadian Journal of Information & Library Sciences, 25*(1), 1–18.
Large, A., & Beheshti, J. (2000). The web as a classroom resource: Reactions from the users. *Journal of the American Society for Information Science and*

Technology, *51*(12), 1069–1080. doi:10.1002/1097-4571(2000)9999:9999<::aid-asi1017>3.0.co;2-w

Lenhart, A., Madden, M., Smith, A., Purcell, K., Zickuhr, K., & Rainie, L. (2011). *Teens, kindness and cruelty on social network sites*. Washington, DC: Pew Research Center's Internet & American Life Project.

Lin, N. (2009). *Social capital: A theory of social structure and action*. Cambridge: Cambridge University Press.

Luckin, R., Clark, W., Graber, R., Logan, K., Mee, A., & Oliver, M. (2009). Do Web 2.0 tools really open the door to learning? Practices, perceptions and profiles of 11–16-year-old students. *Learning, Media and Technology*, *34*(2), 87–104.

Manuel, K. (2002). Teaching information literacy to generation Y. *Journal of Library Administration*, *36*(1–2), 195–217. doi:10.1300/J111v36n01_12

Nelson-Le Gall, S. (1981). Help-seeking: An understudied problem-solving skill in children. *Developmental Review*, *1*, 224–246.

Nelson-Le Gall, S. (1985). Help-seeking behavior in learning. *Review of Research in Education*, *12*, 55–90. doi:10.2307/1167146

Nelson-Le Gall, S., & Gumerman, R. (1984). Children's perceptions of helpers and helper motivation. *Journal of Applied Developmental Psychology*, *5*(1), 1–12.

Newman, R. S. (1990). Children's help-seeking in the classroom: The role of motivational factors and attitudes. *Journal of Educational Psychology*, *82*(1), 71–80. doi:10.1037/0022-0663.82.1.71

Newman, R. S. (2000). Social influences on the development of children's adaptive help seeking: The role of parents, teachers, and peers. *Developmental Review*, *20*(3), 350–404.

Newman, R. S., & Goldin, L. (1990). Children's reluctance to seek help with schoolwork. *Journal of Educational Psychology*, *82*(1), 92–100. doi:10.1037/0022-0663.82.1.92

Patton, M. Q. (2002). *Qualitative research and evaluation methods* (3rd ed.). Thousand Oaks, CA: Sage.

Pettigrew, K. E. (1997). *The role of community health nurses in providing information and referral to the elderly: A study based on social network theory*. Unpublished doctoral dissertation, University of Western Ontario, London, ON, Canada.

Prensky, M. (2001). Digital natives, digital immigrants Part 1. *On the Horizon*, *9*(5), 1–6. doi:10.1108/10748120110424816

Ryan, A. M., & Pintrich, P. R. (1997). "Should I ask for help?" The role of motivation and attitudes in adolescents' help seeking in math class. *Journal of Educational Psychology*, *89*, 329–341.

Savolainen, R. (2008). Source preferences in the context of seeking problem-specific information. *Information Processing & Management*, *44*(1), 274–293. doi:10.1016/j.ipm.2007.02.008

Shenton, A. K., & Dixon, P. (2003). Youngsters' use of other people as an information-seeking method. *Journal of Librarianship and Information Science*, *35*(4), 219.

Statistics Canada. *Table 282-0004 — Labour force survey estimates (LFS), by educational attainment, sex and age group, annual (persons unless otherwise noted)*.

Retrieved from CANSIM (database), http://www5.statcan.gc.ca/cansim/a26?lang=eng&id=2820004. Accessed on January 28, 2014.

Tidwell, L. C., & Walther, J. B. (2002). Computer-mediated communication effects on disclosure, impressions, and interpersonal evaluations: Getting to know one another a bit at a time. *Human Communication Research*, *28*(3), 317–348. doi: 10.1111/j.1468-2958.2002.tb00811.x

Wasserman, S., & Faust, K. (1994). *Social network analysis: Methods and applications*. New York, NY: Cambridge University Press.

Wellman, B. (1983). Network analysis: Some basic principles. *Sociological Theory*, *1*, 155–200. doi:10.2307/202050

Wellman, B., Carrington, P. J., & Hall, A. (1997). Networks as personal communities. In B. Wellman & S. D. Berkowitz (Eds.), *Social structures: A network approach* (pp. 130–184). Greenwich, CT: JAI Press.

Xie, I., & Cool, C. (2009). Understanding help seeking within the context of searching digital libraries. *Journal of the American Society for Information Science and Technology*, *60*(3), 477–494. doi:10.1002/asi.20988

Xu, J., & Corno, L. (2003). Family help and homework management reported by middle school students. *The Elementary School Journal*, *103*(5), 503–517. doi:10.2307/1002115

Zipf, G. K. (1949). *Human behavior and the principle of least effort*. Upper Saddle River, NJ: Addison-Wesley.

SECTION II

SPECIAL POPULATION

Chapter 4

Young Girls' Affective Responses to Access and Use of Information and Communication Technology (ICT) in Information-Poor Societies

Dania Bilal and Valerie Jopeck

Abstract

Purpose – To identify research work on Information and Communication Technology (ICT) in the context of young girls' affective responses to access and use of ICT in developing countries.

Methodology/approach – A literature search covering the period from early 1990s to date in fields of information science, human–computer interaction, ICT, and educational technologies was performed using relevant databases and Google Scholar. Related literature in the context of specific theoretical frameworks was retrieved and analyzed.

Findings – Abundant research exists on ICT in developing countries. However, little empirical work was found on young girls' affective responses to access and use of ICT. The gendered digital divide in relation to ICT showed differing perspectives on this issue. Generally, affective information behavior is much less observed in empirical research than the cognitive behavior, regardless of age, gender, or culture.

Practical implications – Young girls' affective responses to access and use of ICT in these countries warrant additional research in this area of study. Findings from research on youth information behavior in Western countries may have little or no bearings on youth in developing countries. The study of young girls' access and use of ICT in

New Directions in Children's and Adolescents' Information Behavior Research
Library and Information Science, Volume 10, 107–133

ISSN: 1876-0562/doi:10.1108/S1876-056220140000010048

developing countries should account for cultural, socioeconomic, and institutional differences among countries and between societies or communities in a given developing country.

Originality/value – Minimal research exists on young girls' affective responses to accessing and using ICT in developing countries. The literature review covered in this chapter is grounded in theoretical frameworks derived from varied disciplines, including the field of library and information science.

Keywords: Young girls; ICT; affective responses; information-poor societies; developing countries; gendered digital divide

4.1. Introduction

Affect is central to learning about the user's experience with technology. Affect, as defined in Merriam-Webster Dictionary, is "the conscious subjective aspect of an emotion considered apart from bodily changes. [It is] a set of observable manifestations of subjectively experienced emotions" (http://www.merriam-webster.com/dictionary/affect). The study of human affect is not a new phenomenon. Nahl (2007) noted that the concept "affective revolution" has been used by researchers in the field of social history and culture in the 19th-century to mark a shift from suppression of feelings imposed by a society's *feelings rules* to expression of feelings (*feelings norms*) that are important for maintaining social systems. Nahl and Bilal's book (2007), *Information and Emotion: The Emergent Affective Paradigm in Information Behavior Research and Theory*, has charted new research territories on the emergent affective paradigm in information sciences and related fields and provided evidence of the role emotions play in users' information behavior and interacting with technologies.

Recently, the study of people's affect has become of importance not only to academic researchers, but also to marketers interested in learning about the emotions people express in watching movies, television shows, and videos (Affectivo, 2014) so that they develop products and services that meet their needs (Picard, 2011). Advances in technology have provided new opportunities for researchers to capture and measure users' emotional states through deployment of software such as Affdex Facial Coding (http://www.affdex.com/technology), Emotient Facial Expression Recognition (http://www.emotient.com), and Emotiv EEG that "uses sensors to tune into electrical signals produced by the brain to detect user thoughts, feelings, and expressions" (http://emotiv.com).

While access to and use of Information and Communication Technology (ICT) is ubiquitous in the United States, such access is considered a privilege in many developing countries, especially in poor communities or societies. Despite numerous studies on ICT in developing countries, little is known about young girls' affective responses to access and use of ICT. The term ICT is defined in the context of this chapter as technologies that provide access to information through the internet, wireless networks, mobile devices such as cellular phones and tablets, and computers.

The purpose of this chapter was to identify the state of published research on young girls' affective information behavior in developing countries, in general, and on young girls' affective responses to access and use of ICT in these countries' information-poor societies, in particular. Findings from this review identified gaps that researchers should consider to fill in order to develop understanding of the issues and challenges surrounding access to and use of ICT by young girls.

The literature covered in this chapter focuses on young girls aged 5–12 because development economics shows that educated girls have a profound impact on a society's economic recovery, and that the poorest girls have the least chance of completing primary school education in information-poor societies (EFA Global Monitoring Report Team, 2014; Psacharopoulos & Patrinos, 2002). In a recent study of 430 children, parents, and teachers in rural southern India about use of computers, Pal (2012) found that most parents interviewed agreed that "becoming computer literate positively affected the girl's choice." A laborer father from Shimoga in Karnataka [spoke on empowering girls by saying]: "A girl who has learnt computers is a more competent and powerful person and she does not have to accept whatever man the family gets for her, including one who want more dowry. She can instead choose to wait till she gets the right man" (http://firstmonday.org/ojs/index.php/fm/article/view/3733/3152). In addition, children, in general, begin schooling at age five in the United States, and between this age and age twelve, they will have developed social, emotional, and physical abilities to successfully engage with technology in a research setting (Bjorklund, 2011; Erikson, 1963; Piaget & Inhelder, 1969; Strommen, Revelle, Medoff, & Razavi, 1996; Vygotsky, 1978). This engagement with technology may hold true for young girls of this age group in information-poor societies (Pal, 2012).

4.2. Research Questions

This chapter addressed the following overarching research question: What is the state of published research on young girls' affective responses to access and use of ICT in information-poor societies?

4.3. Theoretical Frameworks

The significant role of emotions in the process of learning and seeking meaning has been recognized by constructivist theorists in the early 20th century, notably by Dewey's theory of Reflective Thinking (1933) and Kelly's phases of construction (1963), and Bruner's theory of the Interpretive Task (1986). In 1963, Erikson's work, *Youth*: *Change and Challenge*, describes the socio-emotional theory of child development that occurs from infancy to older adulthood. In later years, a number of theorists emphasized the interplay of emotions and thinking, decision-making, and creativity (see, e.g., Bandura, 1989; Simon, 1967). A number of researchers in the field of information sciences have used one or more of these theories to develop models of user information behavior or provide interpretation of certain information phenomenon. For example, Nahl's Affective Coping Skills measure (1996) combines Bandura's self-efficacy theory and optimism (1997) as factors influencing user's success during information seeking. In addition, her Affective Load Theory (Nahl, 2004, 2005) measures users' affective states based on multiple dimensions including satisficing (Simon, 1967) and self-efficacy (Bandura, 1993).

Kuhlthau's Information Search Process (ISP) is another model that is grounded in the constructivist approach to learning (1988, 2004). It consists of six stages users experience during the information seeking process and includes thoughts, feelings, and actions at each stage. The model shows that users experience uncertainty, frustration, apprehension, and other negative emotions in the early stages of the process. These states diminish as users become more confident in their topic pursuit and find relevant information. At the last stage of the process, users may develop a high level of certainty and satisfaction or become disappointed and dissatisfied as the process turns out to be unsuccessful. Kuhlthau's model is rooted in the works of Dewey (1933), Kelly (1963), and Brunner (1986).

The affective paradigm introduced by Nahl and Bilal (2007) is relevant to the study of young girls' affective responses to use of ICT resources in information-poor societies. The book focuses on affective dimensions and affective issues applied in information behavior research and theory in a variety of contexts and populations, including children. In this book, Bilal (2007) reviewed cognitive and affective theories on child development and suggested ways to apply them in examining children's information behavior in using technology. She provided grounds for designing ICT that support children at various stages of cognitive, emotional, and motor skills development. Bilal noted that emotions are integral to human development and are interwoven within each individual regardless of age, context, or culture (Bilal, 2007).

Erikson (1968) posited that meaningful technology should support every child's feeling of competence. It should also allow the child to demonstrate intelligence so that the child does not develop a sense of inferiority. This can be challenging because regardless of how effective technology may be and how well computers and devices are designed, people will always experience frustration (Picard, 1999). To enliven the user experience, researchers in affective computing have developed devices that sense people's emotions and feelings in interacting with computers so that they provide ways to minimize negative affect and design interfaces that support positive human emotional experience.

As to ICT *per se*, Nsibirano (2009) argued that it has created a gendered digital divide in developing countries, including Uganda. Nsibirano posited that this divide is rooted in the "inequitable distribution of benefits that come with the use of ICT" (p. 33). Her explanation of this divide was approached from the Gender Symbolism and Feminist Standpoint Theory, noting that girls and women have far lower levels of ICT access and use than their male counterparts. "This has been in part a result of a long standing male dominated science and technology culture and of biased socialization processes that stereotype female and male potential and capacity for ICT" (p. 34). The "gendered digital divide" in developing countries (EFA Global Monitoring Report Team, 2014; Hafkin, 2002; Nsibirano, 2009) is relevant to exploring young girls' access and use of ICT as marginalized populations in the context of Chatman's information poverty theory (1996). Chatman's concepts of "risk-taking" and "situational relevance" provide explanation for adoption or rejection of technology in these societies. Chatman conceptualized "risk-taking" as "an attribute affecting the acceptance of an innovation based on our perception of whether it is worthwhile or not. It does not seem to merit consideration if, weighted against personal or negative cost, the result would be negative" (p. 196). Thus, technology should have meaning to the individual in order to accept and engage with it.

Viable to the acceptance notion of technology is the Technology Acceptance Model (TAM) introduced by Davis (1989) to investigate factors that influence acceptance of computers by people. TAM is based on two key constructs, *perceived ease of use* and *perceived usefulness*. Park, Roman, Lee, and Chung (2009) explored the influence of affective factors (computer self-efficacy, intrinsic motivation, and computer anxiety) on users' *perceived ease of use* and *perceived usefulness* of technology. They found that these affective factors influenced the users' perceived ease of use and perceived usefulness of technology. In another study, Park, Roman, Lee, and Chung (2009) applied TAM to examine the factors that influence people's adoption and use of a digital library system in developing countries, specifically Africa, Asia, and Central/Latin America. In addition to the two key constructs in TAM, the authors examined experience in computer use, domain knowledge, English literacy, interest in publishing, visibility, accessibility, library assistance, and relevance to use of the digital library. However, they precluded affective factors from their investigation.

In retrospect, situating the published literature in the context of the aforementioned theoretical frameworks provided a focus for examining young girls' affective responses to access and use of ICT in developing countries, and unraveled issues and challenges of access to and use of ICT in developing countries.

4.4. Method

A literature search was performed in varied sources covering the period from early 1990s to date. The search was structured around topics that were combined with specific terms to find relevant literature. These included, but were not limited to, affective information behavior, children affective behavior/reactions/responses/emotions/feelings; ICT, developing countries, information-poor societies, technology infusion/technology adoption/technology implementation; young children, girls/young girls; gender differences/gender parity; digital divide/gendered digital divide; information access/information use/interaction; Internet/web/engines; computer-based resources, digital resources/technology resources, and cross-culture/culture, among others. Based on the findings, the body of literature most relevant to the theoretical frameworks and for the purpose of this chapter was reviewed.

4.5. Literature Review

The literature was reviewed in relation to work published on affective information behavior, young children's affective behavior, children's affective behavior in cross-cultural environments, interface design and children's affective reactions, children's affective responses to ICT in information-poor societies, gender differences and gendered digital divide in use of technology, and cross-cultural studies on use of digital and print resources.

4.5.1. Affective Information Behavior

Information seeking is one component of information behavior. It is rooted in an individual's information need that manifests itself due to a knowledge gap (Belkin, 1980; Belkin, Oddy, & Brooks, 1982). In 1981, Wilson published his first model describing the factors that lead an individual to seek information in a system. Putting the individual's information need at the core of information seeking, he outlines three intertwined dimensions that trigger the need: physiological, cognitive, or affective. Wilson revised his model in 1994 and 1996, and in both revisions he accounted for the interplay of these three dimensions (Case, 2012).

Kuhlthau (1988, 2004) introduced the affective dimension of information seeking in the ISP model. She iterated six steps delineating a progression in affective states the students experienced at each step of the process, from topic formulation to search closure. Kuhlthau's research focuses on imposed assignments or projects a user engages in over a period of time and the progression of feelings, thoughts, and actions experienced throughout the stages of the process. Her model has been validated in numerous studies, contexts, cultures, and users of varied age levels (see, e.g., Heinström, 2002; Kracker, 2002; Kracker & Wang, 2002; Todd, 2006). More recently, Kuhlthau, Heinström, and Todd (2008) examined the usefulness of the ISP model in a technologically-rich school environment with 574 students ages 6–12 who performed inquiry-based tasks requiring knowledge construction. Based on interviews at three stages of the ISP, the authors identified a similar progression of feelings, thoughts, and actions as suggested in the original ISP model. However, the model was not tested with young children in information-poor societies.

Using a different perspective, Nahl (2007) presented a social-biological information technology model of information behavior. She used a unified theoretical framework with three intersecting zones of today's information environment: technology, human biology, and social structures. The intersection zone in human biology described in the model includes activities such as the user's affective, cognitive, and sensorimotor procedures during information seeking and use. She noted that "individuals perform sensorimotor, cognitive, and affective procedures in unique adaptation to information ecology" (p. 3). This adaptation is relevant to young girls' affective responses to access and use of ICT in developing countries.

4.5.2. Young Children's Affective Behavior

Children have personal and emotional responses to their learning activities (Piaget & Inhelder, 1969). This is echoed by Vygotsky (1978), who noted that a child's processing "does not in the least resemble the adult process" (p. 34). In a study that compared the affective behaviors of middle school children to the behaviors of adults (graduate students), Bilal and Kirby (2002) found that adults have greater resiliency than the children to setbacks that occurred during the information seeking process, but children exceeded the adults' capacity in processing disappointment. Abbas (2005) found that children had very different preferences for metadata elements than did adults and preferred using color, genre, age level, or emotional response in selecting books. Druin (2005b) noted that younger children who are in the concrete stage of development and who rely on perceptual cues (visual and auditory) have needs that are different from those of adult users. The study findings by Flatoff (2007) concluded that the subject index terms that children had developed differed from the index that their parents created for the same terms.

Cooper (2002b) recognized that children's affective responses to information resources are stronger in the early elementary grades. A young child may not persevere in an information resource environment if the child is not having a largely positive experience. The range of emotional responses children experience may influence how they may or may not understand an intellectual task, or felt motivated and challenged in using technology. Conducting research that tracks affective responses to the task children undertake is central to the understanding of the affective issue. Large and Beheshti's (2000) study of sixth graders in a well-to-do neighborhood showcased the varying emotions children expressed in searching the Web for schoolwork. Although initially enthusiastic about using computers for assigned information seeking tasks, they experienced frustration and tedium. Many children preferred the organization of printed resources to the disorganized nature of the Web. In this study, Large and Beheshti's work focused more on cognitive and physical interaction behaviors than on children's emotional responses (Julien, McKechnie, & Hart, 2005).

Bilal's study (2000) of middle school children's use of Yahooligans! search engine/directory (now defunct) revealed that while children enjoyed using the Web, found it easier to use than print resources, more convenient, challenging, and motivating; they experienced confusion and frustration. In subsequent studies, Bilal (2001, 2002a) reported that when the children chose their own search tasks, they were not only more successful, but also more positive about their experiences. Children's success was also attributed to learning about the engine and skill gain by the time they performed the fully self-generated task. The engine's inadequate design and content impacted on children's affective reactions. Subsequent work has found that children of various age levels had more positive affective responses to digital information resources than print ones when factors important to them (e.g., topics of interest) and their cognitive abilities are taken into account (see, e.g., Bilal, 2002a; Bilal & Bachir, 2007a, 2007b; Bilal & Wang, 2005; Cooper, 2002a, 2002b; Large & Beheshti, 2000; Massey, Druin, & Weeks, 2007; Reuter & Druin, 2004). Nonetheless, studies showed a dichotomy in children's responses to print and computer-based resources. For example, the studies by Cooper (2002a, 2002b) uncovered that although children preferred locating information in print resources, they found the computer to be more fun to use. In another work, Cooper (2005) noted that children feel more secure during information seeking when significant adult supervision was present, prior instruction on resources took place, and positive results were easy to come by. Other researchers found that children exhibited a mixture of feelings toward using print materials or digital resources like the Web. Large and Beheshti's (2000) study of middle school children's use of search engines revealed similar results. Cooper (2002a) found that seven-year-old children who browsed the library's bookshelves were more successful and more efficient in finding books on topics (e.g., spiders) than searching online. Preference to print over digital was also revealed in studies of adult users. Liu and Huang (2008), for example, uncovered that in selecting books, males and females preferred information received in print over that they read online, while Astleitner and Leutner (2000) demonstrated how the computer, when appropriately used, can reduce negative affective responses. They developed the term *emotionally sound instruction* to encapsulate its implementation and proposed the Fear-Envy-Anger-Sympathy-Pleasure (FEASP) approach for use in emotionally sound instruction. The approach proposed a highly concrete set of emotional strategies to pair with instructional technology features. Underlying this study is the idea that, for young children, the emotions of fear, envy, and anger should be reduced to the extent possible during technology interactions, while sympathy and pleasure should be enhanced. Bilal (2000, 2007) and Cooper (2005) echoed these statements by saying that although children receive some degree of ultimate satisfaction in overcoming setbacks, these experiences should be fewer and less deterrent emotionally.

4.5.3. Children's Affective Behavior in Cross-cultural Environments

Cultural differences can be reflected in system interface design based on meanings, design representations, language, and visual cues. People from different cultures may have different experiences in using digital technology (Bilal & Bachir, 2007a). Massey et al. (2007) examined the affective responses of twelve children from the United States, Honduras, New Zealand, and Germany to reading and reviewing books in the International Children's Digital Library (ICDL). The ICDL is a multilingual and multicultural library for reading books online that is co-designed with children (Druin, Bederson, Rose, & Weeks, 2009). The authors found that children's emotional response to book cover design plays a role in book selection. Children relied on images and colors to understand book stories and to express how it made them feel. The way children interpreted book images influenced their emotional classifications of the books. In an earlier study of the ICDL, Reuter and Druin (2004) investigated the searching and book selection behavior of 96 first- through fifth-grade children in the United States. Children liked the ICDL but younger children experienced more frustration than older children in searching for books. In addition, children's book searching and selection varied by age and gender. Younger children, for example, favored the simple interface, whereas older children preferred the more complex interfaces.

Use of the ICDL by elementary and middle school Arabic-speaking children in Alexandria, Egypt, showed that older children understood the meaning of 80% of its design representations (e.g., icons, buttons), but younger children found these difficult to understand (Bilal & Bachir, 2007a). Children's book searching on four tasks revealed that they were uncertain about their ability to use the ICDL to complete the tasks. Children expressed that the ICDL made them feel happy and enthusiastic, and that they were more confident about their knowledge of how to use it and satisfied with their performance after completing the tasks. In terms of success on the tasks, children were more successful on the fully self-generated task than on the assigned or semi-assigned tasks. Children made suggestions for improving the interface design and content of the ICDL to support their cultural understanding and information needs. Based the findings of these two studies, Bilal and Sarangthem (2009) developed task-based models of the children's information seeking of and interaction with the ICDL that integrate cognitive, affective, and physical behaviors. The model consists of seven modes of behavior that characterized children's interaction: Start, Recognize, Browse, Differentiate, Read, Explore, and Finish. Each mode is associated with moves based on task characteristics and reflects the children's information needs and affective responses that were clouded with uncertainty and anxiety in the beginning of information seeking and transitioned to certainty and satisfaction upon completing the tasks.

More recently, Martens (2013) examined how the ICDL design supports searching for books by seven ten-year-old Danish children and their teacher. The author sought to find whether the ICDL can be a valuable resource for the children in relation to transnational reading. Children were given a booklet of 10 tasks to complete. Findings revealed that children successfully completed the tasks, but needed the assistance of an adult to move beyond the "read books" page. They experienced difficulty browsing the globe (geographical interactive interface), and found the thumbnail pictures of book covers too small for choosing book titles. Since language was a barrier for the children, their reliance on book covers to judge retrieved books is a normal behavior. This study did not report on children's affective reactions to the tasks or use of the ICDL.

4.5.4. Children's Involvement in Interface Design and Affective Responses

In the field of human–computer interaction, Druin (2002) noted that a child's role in the design of technology includes four categories: user, tester, informant, and design partner. She posited that children are able to articulate their emotions and feelings about the design of interfaces, and that their affective responses can be tracked if they are involved as equal stakeholders in the design of new technology (Bilal, 2005; Druin, 2005b). The design of the International Children's Library (ICDL) is based on what Druin et al. (2003) called Cooperative Inquiry method, where children are involved as active and full design partners alongside a team of educators, graphic designers, and computer scientists in the design process. Of importance in the design of the ICDL is a focus on children's affective responses to specific elements of the interface design. In a study of 12 children's responses to books in the ICDL in four countries (Germany, Honduras, New Zealand, and the United States), Massey et al. (2007) found that all children often experienced more than one emotion when reading a book. Children were able to review books and rate them by feelings such as happy, funny, sad, or scary. Learning about children's affective responses provided insights into the interaction between emotions and both book selection and reading. The ICDL has a mobile App that was designed by involving children in the design process (Fails, Druin, Bederson, Weeks, & Rose, 2009).

In the library and information science field, few researchers worked with children to design new technologies. Large, Beheshti, and Rahman (2002a) gathered the reactions of children ages 10–13 to four Web engines. Children expressed their feelings about each engine and provided suggestions for improving its design. Based on these reactions and other findings from the study, Large, Beheshti, Nesset, and Bowler (2007) designed two portals for elementary school students using a new design methodology they called Bonded Design. Working with each other and with adults, children were able to design two low-tech prototypes for portals on Canadian history, one prototype was generated by a team of grade-three elementary students and another by a team of grade-six students. These prototypes were transformed into working web portals by interface designers. Children evaluated the appearance of History Trek and expressed their likes using words such as cool, attractive, and funny. History Trek is operational on the Web (see http://www.historytrek.ca) and provides access to information in both English and French (Large et al., 2007).

Using a participatory design approach, Bilal (2002b, 2003) involved 11 middle school children in the design of a web search engine interface. Using a paper-based, low-cost prototyping, children created drawings of their own engines, personalized them, and provided descriptions of what they wanted the engines to do for them and their friends. Personalization of the engines was a motivating factor in drawing the interfaces. Individual follow-up interviews with the children uncovered likes for the features they included in the interfaces and dislikes for certain features embedded in existing search engines. Fisher, Bishop, Magassa, and Fawcett (2013) provide another perspective on involving youth in the design process using Teen Design Days methodology.

4.5.5. Children's Affective Responses to Access and Use of ICT

A survey of the literature reveals little attention has been given to children's affective experiences in accessing and using ICT in information-poor societies. Prinsloo (2005) observed the conversations of six- and seven-year-old children attending a computer class in Khayelitsha Township in Cape Town, South Africa. He held conversations with the children en route to a class and observed their reactions while a teacher demonstrated for the children how to use a computer. He found that children exhibited excitement, jealousy, frustration, and shame. The negative affective responses to the computers far outweighed the positive. He argued that computers are information resources that have been placed in schools with a hope of reducing the digital divide, but with little actual local or cultural value. Digital literacy requires a higher degree of facility with information resources than print materials (Pigato, 2001; Warschauer, 2002) and is, perhaps, of greater utility in communities where strong general literacy indicators exist. Snyder and Prinsloo's (2007) argued that the development of digital literacy is a necessary precursor to the implementation of computer-based information resources in marginalized communities. Their argument is based on the study they conducted in poor regions (low socioeconomic conditions) of Brazil, Greece, Uganda, and Australia.

Seeking information can be deterring to youth with HIV/AIDS. Mnubi-Mchombu, Mostert, and Ocholla's (2009) study of the information needs and seeking behavior of HIV/AIDS orphans and vulnerable children in Okahandja, Namibia, found that children relied on other children/friends and surviving parents (who they fundamentally trusted), community organizations, and extended family caregivers for information. They also found that children experienced frustration, hopelessness, and indignation in seeking information. Children in this study were accessing print materials, as computer-based resources were not available.

More recently, Pal (2012) reported that children (boys and girls) in rural India attached "significant social capital" to the effective use of computers, similar to success in athletic pursuits, and they tended to over-report success with technology to maintain self-esteem. Although Pal did not utilize specific vocabulary related to affective behaviors, the positive experience children had with computers implicitly suggests positive affective reactions on the part of boys and girls. While this study did not find gender differences in using computers, these differences were prevalent in other studies.

Published literature on children's use of technology, in general, and access and use of ICT in developing countries, showed differing views on gender differences. The next section reports on studies that considered gender as a variable in children's use of technology.

4.5.6. Gender Differences in Information Behavior Research

Studies that examined the differences between female and male students' attitudes toward the Internet revealed that across national borders females report both lower affinity with and less positive attitudes toward computers than males. For example, Li and Kirkup (2007) surveyed 500 British and Chinese students and collected data on their computer experience, attitude to and use of both email and chat rooms and playing computer games. Participants were asked to assess their degree of self-confidence and whether using computers were a gender-related activity or skill. They found that the students in the United Kingdom reported the lowest levels of self-confidence and were least likely to identify computer activity or skill as a female trait.

In examining use of the web by boys and girls in a Canadian elementary school, Large, Beheshti, and Rahman (2002b) found differences between girls' and boys' search formulations, the time it took them to complete search tasks, and number of links they activated. In addition, they reported that girls tended to favor natural language in searching and to use more keywords than did boys. Boys were more frequent "clickers" of hyperlinks than girls and did not spend as much time as girls either reading or processing the content of the web pages. Agosto's study (2004) of male and female youths' behaviors in using computers found that females play less computer games than their male counterparts. Conversely, in the context of public libraries, Dresang, Gross, and Holt (2004) uncovered that girls and boys, ages 9–13, were equally positive about computers and their ability to use them effectively. The authors cautioned about using generic statements regarding gender. They noted that assumptions based on studies in traditional environments may not transfer accurately to the digital environment. While this may be true, the study by Cooper two years later (2006) uncovered differences between the male and female students in using computers. He noted that being aware of one's girl-ness can make a girl less comfortable using computer resources, and that this difference makes it more challenging for girls and women to succeed in an increasingly technologically oriented economy. In a more recent work, Foss et al. (2012) found that affect is one of eight strands impacting the search behaviors among boys and girls ages 7, 9, and 11 in using Google. They reported that while girls and boys have similar responses to search tasks, girls reported higher degrees of boredom than boys. Boys responded to games as "triggers" and refused to search more often. Nonetheless, statistical testing of gender differences found in these studies alongside confounding variables warrants further investigation.

If gender differences were found in most studies on children's information behavior, could be that these differences are more prominent in the literature on ICT in developing countries?

4.5.7. Gender Differences in ICT Research on Developing Countries

In developing countries, information poverty lacks gender parity in educational opportunities (EFA Global Monitoring Report Team, 2014). Morahan-Martin and Schumacher (2001, 2007) found that between 2001 and 2007, a steadily decreasing, though still significant, difference existed between male and female expertise in using computer technology. Gillard, Howcroft, Mitev, and Richardson (2008) echoed these findings by saying that in developing countries there is "continued absence of women in the design and control of ICTs" (p. 275). Later work by Dlodlo (2009) found that in rural South Africa, girls' and women's access to information and ICT resources is culturally different and that "technology is a masculine activity" (p. 172). Taking the issue from the feminist movement perspective, Nsibirano (2009) noted that while "many studies have shown that males and females differ in both access to and use of ICTs ... there has been no satisfactory attempt to explain why the observed differences between female and male students exist" (p. 38). She argued that in order to develop understanding of these differences, one should examine students' perspectives on using computers and the internet based on "meanings" of their situated experiences with ICT. She posited that "attempts to integrate of ICTs in the teaching, learning and research activities of the universities globally and Uganda in particular will be a waste of time and resources" (p. 38) without understanding these "meanings." Conversely, Hilbert (2011) vied the findings in published literature on access to and use of ICT by women in developing countries, noting that "misleading statistics mask the reality about the gender divide" (p. 481). His study of 25 developing countries, 12 Latin American and 13 African countries from 2005 to 2008, representing varied levels of development, geography, culture, and social structure revealed that ICT *per se* does not pose barriers for keeping women and girls from using it. On the contrary, women embrace digital technology more enthusiastically than men. By controlling for variables such as literacy, employment or studying, and income to study the gender divide, he found no difference between men and women in African countries. He explained that "the reason why fewer women access and use ICT is a direct result of their unfavorable conditions with respect to employment, education and income" (p. 479). Thus, one concludes that there are continued differing perspectives on the issue of gendered digital divide when it comes to access to and use of ICT in developing countries.

Regardless of gender, however, there have been major efforts to narrow the digital divide between the "haves" and "have-not" in many developing countries. These are discussed in the next section.

4.5.8. Narrowing the Digital Divide in Access to and Use of ICT

The digital divide goes beyond gender disparity to include access to and use of computers across geographical regions within a country and at the global level. This section describes two key technology programs implemented in the information-poor societies to empower children with technology skills. Programs developed in the United States and Western countries are beyond the scope of this chapter.

In an effort to narrow the digital divide and provide learning opportunities to children, Sugata Mitra developed the *Hole-in-the-Wall* (HiWEL) ICT-based program "to create a new paradigm in the learning process by providing unrestricted computer access to groups of children in an open playground setting" (http://www.hole-in-the-wall.com/new-way-to-learn.html). This program is rooted in the theory of Minimally Invasive Education (Mitra, 2000), meaning that it is integrated with traditional schooling and furnishes educational software, allowing children to access, retrieve, and use information collaboratively and on their own. The program provides computer learning stations in India, Cambodia, Bhutan, and the Republic of Central Africa (HiWEL, 2013). Learning Stations are set up in an outdoor playground and can be accessed anytime, providing better opportunities for girls, "who would generally be sent to close room housing a computer" (http://www.hole-in-the-wall.com/new-way-to-learn.html) to easily access information in an open setting, thus ensuring equality in access between girls and boys. Warschauer (2002) criticized this project for its failure to take into account the real social and learning needs of the children it seeks to impact. However, since that time, the program has changed dramatically as it became integrated with schooling (http://www.hole-in-the-wall.com/new-way-to-learn.html).

Empirical studies published between 2005 and 2011 (http://www.hole-in-the-wall.com/Publications.html) that examined the impact of this ICT-based program (based on data collected over a four-year period, from 2000 to 2004) showed that children were able to understand how computers work, had higher academic achievements, and had positive affect, especially girls who reported high confidence and pride (http://www.hole-in-the-wall.com/Findings.html). In addition, girls often took on the role of "Connector, who initiates younger children and siblings (usually novices with little or no exposure to computers) and connects them to the leaders in the group" (http://www.hole-in-the-wall.com/Findings.html).

While the HiWEL program was initiated by an entrepreneur in India, the *One Laptop per Child* (OLPC) Project was developed in 2005 by Nicholas Negroponte, founder of the Massachusetts's Institute of Technology's Media Lab (U.S.). OLPC provides low-cost, high-durability laptops to school children around the world (Warman, 2009). Negroponte has donated over two million laptops to date in 42 countries (OLPC, 2013). Evaluations of the OLPC in Uruguay, the country which has received the most laptop donations to date, suggest that laptops are given to schools where additional and costly security measures must be implemented, children are not given total possession of the laptops (they remain at the school), and teachers lack adequate training to usefully incorporate the laptops' technology into the curriculum (Johnson, 2008).

Earlier research by Prinsloo (2005) in the Khayelitsha Township in Cape Town, South Africa, revealed similar findings. He found that one computer resource teacher served multiple schools in one area; and when the resource teacher was absent, computer use did not take place because teachers reported feelings of insecurity concerning their own technological skills. In the United States, Warschauer (2007), Mouza (2008), and Grimes and Warschauer (2008) reached similar conclusions about the placement of technology in low-income schools. They argued that without fundamental and ongoing teacher training and a team of technology personnel in a school, laptop programs in the schools are of marginal usefulness. This argument is in line with what Prinsloo (2005) calls *placed resources* in the era of the internet. Using the concept "new literacies," he noted: "despite their global impact, the new literacies are best studied as resources situated in social practices that have local effect ... the new literacies don't have an intrinsic resourcefulness. Whether they offer opportunities for particular users is something that has to be established by situated research, not assumed" (p. 87). Nonetheless, in January 2014, over 2.4 million children and teachers in different parts of the world had XO Tablets through OLPC. The XO Tablet is a learning tool with more than 200 educational applications and 200 books designed for children ages 3–12. The Tablet became available in September 2013. In October of the same year, the

Tablet was chosen as the winner in the Parents' Choice Award by the Parents' Choice Foundation (http://one.laptop.org/summary).

Hourcade, Beitler, Cormenzana, and Flores (2008) examined use of XO laptops by children, teachers, and staff in a small rural town in Uruguay. The laptops were provided through the OLPC program. They found that despite the problems with software, hardware, and technology infrastructure children had a positive experience with computers. Children voiced their opinions about the features they liked and disliked, and were motivated to perform the activities the researchers assigned them. They indicated the need to localize the technology, change the user interface to the file browser, and adopt better touchpads, which were too complex for the children to use. Teachers commented on children's motivation to search online and find information about topics of interest to them rather than rely only on books available in their classroom. Internet connectivity and mobility contributed to students' success in using the XO laptops.

Negroponte's dedication to narrowing the global digital divide is reflected in the announcement that he made on March 17, 2014, to provide free satellite-based internet access to Africa to serve 100 million people including those in low density and rural areas (Wakefield, 2014).

Narrowing the digital divide has also been undertaken by academic libraries, non-profit organizations (NGOs), and aid organizations. In information- and economically poor sub-Saharan Africa, for example, these agencies have provided key print resources through a variety of mobile services (Anunobi & Okoye, 2008; Arunachalam, 2002; Makenzi, 2004; Meyers, 2009). Most recently, in Karnataka, Bangalore, India, mobile libraries have been successful in reaching out to women, housewives, and senior citizens to deliver books in locations where no local libraries are available. These services have been particularly helpful to older people who prefer reading books and perceive that using new technology does not match their requirements (Sharadhaa, 2014), like mobile library services that provide laptops and WiFi internet connection to rural and deprived communities.

ICT as a field of study includes use of not only computers and wireless networks, but also mobile devices to access information. The next section provides an overview about the impact mobile technologies are having on the lives of many societies in developing countries.

4.5.9. Mobile Technologies Use in Developing Countries

The increased penetration of mobile technologies in developing countries has bridged isolation and improved the lives of people in many information- and economically poor communities. A recent report by eMarketer estimated that in 2014, smartphone users alone will total 1.75 billion worldwide (http://www.emarketer.com/Article/Smartphone-Users-Worldwide-Will-Total-175-Billion-014/1010536#TGJhrTFH6O8Rk25r.99). In 2013, mobile phone penetration worldwide was 61.1%. In January 2014, this increased to 63.5% and it is predicted to rise to 69.4% by 2017. New users in developing regions such as Asia-Pacific, Middle East, and Africa are expected to drive further increases in smartphone adoption. Among the top 14 countries in the world with over 100 million mobile subscriptions, China, India, and the United States are on the top list, respectively. Studies of use of mobile technologies begin to offer insights into reshaping the ICT landscape. In Bhor, a remote rural community in India, for example, Potnis (2011) found that girls and women earning less than $2 a day rely on cell phones to meet the information needs of everyday life such as staying in touch with family and friends, for emergency situations and employment purposes, as well as to acquire and/or offer emotional support and ensure safety and security. In Kenya, farmers use social media via cell phones to connect with others in order to boost their crops (Routh, 2011).

Many developing countries are investing in information technology to improve socioeconomic conditions (Donner, 2008). Examples are Mauritius' investment in education to make schools and universities cyber ready and Mongolia's plan to become the IT leader in Asia (Routh, 2011). In India, women are empowering themselves as IT entrepreneurs, and the *Open Mind Programme's Question Box Project* (established in 2007) continues to empower illiterate youth, girls and boys, who live in poor villages in India by connecting them to the Internet.

4.6. What Do We Conclude from the Reviewed Research on Young Girls' Affective Responses to Access and Use of ICT in Information-Poor Societies?

Study findings culled from the reviewed literature show that, while empirical research on children's information behavior and interaction with digital technologies is well established in the United States, minimal empirical work exists in these areas in developing countries. Recognizing that affective information behavior is generally less observed in empirical research than the cognitive behavior, very little attention has been given to young girls' affective responses to access and use of ICT in developing countries, aside from the work by Mitra (2000) and that of few researchers who studied the impact of the HiWEL program (http://www.hole-in-the-wall.com/Publications.html). As to the program, One Computer per Child, the authors found one empirical study. Additional research is needed on the latter program to develop understanding of its effectiveness and influence on children's learning and empowerment, in general, and on young girls, in particular.

The literature also showed differing perspectives on the gendered digital divide in relation to access and use of ICT in developing countries. While most research on this topic provided evidence of this divide, Hilbert (2011) refuted the findings from this research, suggesting that, unless researchers control for variables such as income, education, employment, among others, in examining gender differences, finding that there are inequalities between men and women in the context of access to and use of ICT in developing countries is misleading. Future research should consider the variables suggested by Hilbert, and possibly additional relevant ones, in determining significant differences between males and females in accessing and using ICT.

Unlike the culminating body of literature on youth information behavior, interaction with technology, and participation in system design in the United States, minimal research exists in these areas in developing countries, and research on young girls' affective responses to access and use of ICT is almost nonexistent. This could be due to the fact that information behavior *per se* is an understudied area of research in these countries. It is believed that with the fast penetration of mobile technologies in developing countries brings new opportunities for researchers to study young girls' mobile access to and use of ICT.

In researching the topic of this chapter, the authors did not find literature on ICT in Arabic-speaking countries, women and ICT, or youth and ICT. This is an area of research that warrants future investigation. Research on females, in general, and young girls' affective responses, in particular, is "one that needs a voice within the 'landscape and prospects' of ICTs in developing countries research" (Gillard, Howcroft, Mitev, & Richardson, 2008, p. 276).

Study findings from the United States or other Western countries may have no bearings on youth in developing countries. According to Snyder and Prinsloo (2007), "Western scholarship on children is not applicable to information-poor societies because such communities lack the in- and out-of-school experiences with computers and digital technologies so necessary for appropriate implementation and use." Though written in 2007, the authors' statement is still valid today. Indeed, research on youth in the context of access to and use of ICT should account for variations in social, cultural, and economic infrastructures across the communities or societies being studied in developing countries.

In researching the topic of this chapter, the authors experienced difficulty searching the term "affect" and "affect"-related terms. This is because major LIS databases do not include affect, or any "affect"-based variation, in controlled vocabularies or thesauri. This issue was noted by Julien et al. (2005) who found that access to the literature on affective behavior in the field of information sciences is difficult. One may only access the term by doing a keyword full-text search. The major LIS databases assessed by the authors did not provide this option. A search by the authors of this chapter in 2014 found that, of the major databases in LIS, the Library and Information Science and Technology Abstracts (*LISTA*) and Library and Information Science Abstracts (*LISA*) lack the term affective behavior in their thesauri. Among the education databases, only *ERIC* included affective behavior in its thesaurus. This may be because affective behavior is a topic explored in the field of education (e.g., affective education).

Another issue was finding studies that have focused exclusively on young children's affective behavior, including young girls, in use of technology, in general, is not an easy task. Bilal (2000) posited that it is difficult to ascertain the emotional or affective responses of children because they may lack the ability to adequately express themselves. Another issue in this area of study is noted by Druin (2002) who found that research that captured children's affective responses already had adult-driven factors in play. Adults, as the researchers, determine the set of questions to be asked and the emotions to be reported. Despite these issues, children's affective behavior, especially in the context of young girls' access to and use of ICT in developing countries warrants further investigation. Studies should consider the "distinct" elements that characterize information access to and use of ICT in developing countries. According to Wilson (2004), these include physical access, financial access, cognitive access, design access, content access, production access, and institutional access. Generally, in the study of user information behavior, emphasis is placed more on the cognitive, design, and content access than on the other elements of access. This leads one to question how girls' affective responses to ICT in developing countries are embraced in Wilson's framework? While there is no answer to this question, adding the "affective access" to the framework is a case in point.

References

Abbas, J. (2005). Creating metadata for children's resources: Issues, research, and current developments. *Library Trends*, *54*(2), 303–317.

Affectivo. (2014). *Media measurement*. Retrieved from http://www.affdex.com/solutions/media-measurement

Agosto, D. E. (2004). Gender, technologies, and the school library. *School Libraries Worldwide*, *10*(1–2), 39–51.

Anunobi, C. V., & Okoye, I. B. (2008). The role of academic libraries in universal access to print and electronic resources in the developing countries. *Library Philosophy & Practice*, *10*(2), 1–5.

Arunachalam, S. (2002). The role of leadership and innovative management in building rural knowledge centers to reach the "unreached". *Science & Technology Libraries*, *23*(2–3), 17–24.

Astleitner, H., & Leutner, D. (2000). Designing instructional technology from an emotional perspective. *Journal of Research on Computing in Education*, *32*(4), 497–510.

Bandura, A. (1989). Human agency in social cognitive theory. *American Psychologist*, *44*, 1175–1184.

Bandura, A. (Ed.). (1997). *Self-efficacy: The exercise of control*. New York, NY: W.H. Freeman.

Bandura, A. (1993). Perceived self-efficacy in cognitive development and functioning. *Educational Psychologist*, *28*(2), 117–148.

Belkin, N. (1980). Anomalous states of knowledge as the basis for information retrieval. *Canadian Journal of Information Science*, *5*, 133–143.

Belkin, N. J., Oddy, R. N. & Brooks, H. M. (1982). ASK for information retrieval: Part I. Background and theory. *Journal of Documentation*, *38*(2), 61–71.

Bilal, D. (2000). Children's use of the Yahooligans! Web search engine: I. Cognitive, physical, and affective behaviors on fact-based search tasks. *Journal of the American Society for Information Science*, *51*(7), 646–665.

Bilal, D. (2001). Children's use of the Yahooligans! Web search engine: II. Cognitive and physical behaviors on research tasks. *Journal of the American Society for Information Science and Technology*, *52*(2), 118–136.

Bilal, D. (2002a). Children's use of the Yahooligans! Web search engine. III. Cognitive and physical behaviors on fully self-generated search tasks. *Journal of the American Society for Information Science and Technology*, *53*(13), 1170–1183.

Bilal, D. (2002b, May). Children design their interfaces for Web search engines: A participatory approach. *Proceedings of the 30th annual conference of the Canadian Association for Information Science*, Toronto, Canada (pp. 204–214).

Bilal, D. (2003, October 19–22). Draw and tell: Children as designers of web interfaces. *Proceedings of the 66th ASIST annual meeting*, Long Beach, CA (pp. 135–141).

Bilal, D. (2005). Children's information seeking and the design of digital interfaces in the affective paradigm. *Library Trends*, *54*(2), 197–208.

Bilal, D. (2007). Grounding children's information behavior and system design in child development theories. In D. Nahl & D. Bilal (Eds.), *Information and emotion: The emergent affective paradigm in information behavior research and theory* (pp. 39–50). Medford, NJ: Information Today.

Bilal, D., & Bachir, I. (2007a). Children's interaction with international and multilingual digital libraries. I. Understanding interface system design representations. *Information Processing & Management*, *43*(1), 47–64.

Bilal, D., & Bachir, I. (2007b). Children's interaction with international and multilingual digital libraries. II. Information seeking, success, and affective experience. *Information Processing & Management*, *43*(1), 65–80.

Bilal, D., & Kirby, J. (2002). Differences and similarities in information seeking: Children and adults as web users. *Information Processing & Management*, *38*, 649–670.
Bilal, D., & Sarangthem, S. (2009). Meditating differences in children's interaction with digital libraries through modeling their tasks. *Proceedings of the American Society for Information Science and Technology*, *46*(1), 1–19.
Bilal, D., & Wang, P. (2005). Children's conceptual structures of science categories and the design of web directories. *Journal of the American Society for Information Science and Technology*, *56*(12), 1303–1313.
Bjorklund, D. (2011). *Children's thinking: Cognitive development and individual differences* (5th ed.). Boston, MA: Cengage Learning.
Brunner, J. (1986). *Actual minds: Possible worlds*. Cambridge, MA: Harvard University Press.
Case, D. O. (2012). *Looking for information: A survey of research on information seeking, needs, and behavior* (3rd ed.). Bingley, UK: Emerald Group Publishing Limited.
Chatman, A. E. (1996). The impoverished life-world of outsiders. *Journal of the American Society for Information Science*, *47*(3), 193–206.
Cooper, J. (2006). The digital divide: The special case of gender. *Journal of Computer Assisted Learning*, *22*, 320–334.
Cooper, L. Z. (2002a). A case study of information-seeking behavior in 7-year-old children in a semistructured situation. *Journal of the American Society for Information Science and Technology*, *53*(11), 904–922.
Cooper, L. Z. (2002b). Methodology for a project examining cognitive categories for library information in young children. *Journal of the American Society for Information Science and Technology*, *53*(14), 1223–1231.
Cooper, L. Z. (2005). Developmentally appropriate digital environments for young children. *Library Trends*, *54*(2), 286–302.
Davis, F. (1989). Perceived usefulness, perceived ease of use, and user acceptance of information technology. *MIS Quarterly*, *13*(3), 319–339.
Dewey, J. (1933). *How we think*. Lexington, MA: Heath.
Dlodlo, N. (2009). Access to ICT education for girls and women in rural South Africa: A case study. *Technology in Society*, *31*, 168–175.
Donner, J. (2008). Research approaches to mobile use in the developing world: A review of the literature. *The Information Society*, *24*, 140–159.
Dresang, E., Gross, M., & Holt, L. E. (2004). *The information-seeking behavior of youth in the digital environment*. Retrieved from https://www.ideals.illinois.edu/bitstream/handle/2142/3475/Dresang_InfoSeeking.pdf?sequen
Druin, A. (2002). The role of children in the design of new technology. *Behaviour & Information Technology*, *21*(1), 1–25.
Druin, A., Bederson, B., Weeks, A., Farber, A., Grosjean, J., Guha, M., … Zhang, L. (2003). *The international children's digital library: Descriptions and analysis of first use*. Retrieved from http://firstmonday.org/ojs/index.php/fm/article/view/1050
Druin, A. (2005a). Children's access and use of digital resources. *Library Trends*, *54*(2), 173–177.

Druin, A. (2005b). What children can teach us: Developing digital libraries for children with children. *The Library Quarterly*, *75*(1), 20–41.

Druin, A., Bederson, B., Rose, A., & Weeks, A. (2009). From New Zealand to Mongolia: Co-designing and deploying a digital library for the world's children. *Children, Youth and Environments: Special Issue on Children in Technological Environments*, *19*(1), 34–57.

EFA Global Monitoring Report Team. (2014). *Teaching and learning: Achieving quality for all.* Paris, France: UNESCO. Retrieved from http://unesdoc.unesco.org/images/0022/002256/225660e.pdf

eMarketer. (2014). *Smartphone users worldwide will total 1.75 billion in 2014.* Retrieved from http://www.emarketer.com/Article/Smartphone-Users-Worldwide-Will-Total-175-Billion-014/1010536#TGJhrTFH6O8Rk25r.99

Erikson, E. H. (1963). *Youth: Change and challenge.* New York, NY: Basic Books.

Erikson, E. H. (1968). *Identity: Youth and crisis.* New York, NY: W. W. Norton & Company.

Fails, J., Druin, A., Bederson, B. B., Weeks, A., & Rose, A. (2009). A child's mobile digital library: Collaboration, community and change. In A. Druin (Ed.), *Mobile technology for children: Designing for interaction and learning* (pp. 125–146). Burlington, MA: Morgan Kaufmann Publishers.

Fisher, K. E., Bishop, A., Magassa, L., & Fawcett, P. (2013, December 7–10). InfoMe @ teen design days: A multi-variable, design thinking approach to community development. *ACM ICTD 2013: International conference on Information and Communication Technologies for Development*, Cape Town, South Africa. ACM. Retrieved from http://dx.doi.org/10.1145/2517899.2517914

Flatoff, J. (2007). Do children use indexes differently than adults? Summary of an informal survey of index users. *Key Words*, *15*(1), 19–25, 30.

Foss, E., Druin, A., Brewer, R., Lo, P., Sanchez, L., Golub, E., & Hutchinson, H. (2012). Children's search roles at home: Implications for designers, researchers, educators, and parents. *Journal of the American Society for Information Science and Technology*, *63*(3), 558–573.

Gillard, H., Howcroft, D., Mitev, N., & Richardson, H. (2008). "Missing women": Gender, ICTs, and the shaping of the global economy. *Information Technology for Development*, *14*(4), 262–279.

Grimes, D., & Warschauer, M. (2008). Learning with laptops: A multi-method case study. *Journal for Educational Computing Research*, *38*(3), 305–332.

Hafkin, N. (2002, November 11–14). Gender issues in ICT policy in developing countries: An overview. United Nations Division for the Advancement of Women (DAW), *Expert group meeting on information and communication technologies and their impact on and use as an instrument for the advancement and empowerment of women*, Seoul, Republic of Korea. Retrieved from http://www.un.org/womenwatch/daw/egm/ict2002/reports/Paper-NHafkin.PDF

Heinström, J. (2002). *Fast surfers, broad scanners and deep divers — Personality and information seeking behaviour.* Doctoral dissertation, Åbo Akademi University Press, Åbo (Turku), Finland. Retrieved from http://www.abo.fi/~jheinstr/thesis.htm

Hilbert, M. (2011). Digital gender divide or technologically empowered women in developing countries? A typical case of lies, damned lies, and statistics. *Women's Studies International Forum*, *34*(6), 479–489.

Hole-in-the-Wall Education, Ltd. (HiWEL). (2013). *Solution. Hole-in-the-Wall: Lighting the spark of learning*. Retrieved from http://www.hole-in-the-wall.com/solution.html

Hourcade, J. P., Beitler, D., Cormenzana, F., & Flores, P. (2008). Early OLPC experiences in a rural Uruguayan school. In A. Druin (Ed.), *Mobile technology for children: Designing for interaction and learning* (pp. 225–243). Boston, MA: Morgan Kaufmann Publishers.

Johnson, J. (2008). Can a laptop change how the world teaches? *Knowledge Quest*, *36*(4), 72–73.

Julien, H., McKechnie, L., & Hart, S. (2005). Affective issues in library and information science systems work: A content analysis. *Library & Information Science Research*, *27*, 453–466.

Kelly, G. A. (1963). *A theory of personality: The psychology of personal constructs*. New York, NY: W.W. Norton & Company.

Kracker, J. (2002). Research anxiety and students' perceptions of research: An experiment. Part I. Effect of teaching Kuhlthau's ISP model. *Journal of the American Society for Information Science and Technology*, *53*(4), 282–294.

Kracker, J., & Wang, P. L. (2002). Research anxiety and students' perceptions of research: An experiment. Part II. Content analysis of their writings on two experiences. *Journal of the American Society for Information Science and Technology*, *53*(4), 295–307.

Kuhlthau, C. C. (1988). Developing a model of the library search process: Cognitive and affective aspects. *Reference Quarterly*, *28*(2), 232–242.

Kuhlthau, C. C. (2004). *Seeking meaning* (2nd ed.). Westport, CT: Libraries Unlimited.

Kuhlthau, C. C., Heinström, J., & Todd, R. J. (2008). The information search process revisited: Is the model still useful? *Information Research*, *13*(4) paper no. 355. Retrieved from http://www.informationr.net/ir/13-4/paper355.html

Large, A., & Beheshti, J. (2000). The web as a classroom resource: Reactions from the users. *Journal of the American Society for Information Science*, *51*(12), 1069–1080.

Large, A., Beheshti, J., Nesset, V., & Bowler, L. (2007). Children's web portals: Can an intergenerational design deliver the goods? In M. K. Chelton & C. Cool (Eds.), *Youth information-seeking behavior II: Context, theories, models, and issues* (pp. 279–311). Lanham, MD: Scarecrow Press.

Large, A., Beheshti, J., & Rahman, T. (2002a). Design criteria for children's web portals: The users speak out. *Journal of the American Society for Information Science and Technology*, *53*(2), 79–94.

Large, A., Beheshti, J., & Rahman, T. (2002b). Gender differences in collaborative web searching behavior: An elementary school study. *Information Processing and Management*, *38*, 427–443.

Li, N., & Kirkup, G. (2007). Gender and cultural differences in Internet use: A study of China and the UK. *Computers & Education*, *48*(2), 301–317.

Liu, Z., & Huang, X. (2008). Gender differences in the online reading environment. *Journal of Documentation*, *64*(4), 616–626.
Makenzi, M. (2004). *Reaching out to the less advantaged: Reading tents in Kenya.* Retrieved from http://archive.ifla.org/IV/ifla70/papers/081e-Makenzi.pdf
Martens, M. (2013). Considerations of how children think: Danish responses to the international children's digital library. *New Review of Children's Literature and Librarianship*, *19*, 139–156.
Massey, S. A., Druin, A., & Weeks, A. C. (2007). Emotion, response, and recommendations: The role of affect in children's book review in a digital library. In D. Nahl & D. Bilal (Eds.), *Information and emotion: The emergent affective paradigm in information behavior and theory* (pp. 135–160). Medford, NJ: Information Today.
Meyers, J. K. (2009). The Lubato library project creating excellent and sustainable libraries for vulnerable African children and youth. *Focus on International Library & Information Work*, *40*(1), 4–8.
Mitra, S. (2000). *Children and the Internet: New paradigms for development in the 21st century.* Retrieved from http://www.hole-in-the-wall.com/docs/Paper03.pdf
Mnubi-Mchombu, C., Mostert, J., & Ocholla, D. (2009). Information seeking needs and information-seeking behaviour of orphans and vulnerable children and their caregivers in Okahandja, Namibia. *African Journal of Library, Archives and Information Science*, *19*(1), 39–52.
Morahan-Martin, J., & Schumacher, P. (2001). Gender, Internet and computer attitudes and experiences. *Computers in Human Behavior*, *17*(1), 95–110.
Morahan-Martin, J., & Schumacher, P. (2007). Attitudinal and experiential predictors of technological expertise. *Computers in Human Behavior*, *23*(5), 2230–2239.
Mouza, C. (2008). Learning with laptops: Implementation and outcomes in an urban, under-privileged school. *Journal of Research on Technology in Education*, *40*(4), 447–472.
Nahl, D. (1996). The user-centered revolution: 1970–1995. In *Encyclopedia of microcomputing* (Vol. 19, pp. 143–200). New York, NY: Marcel Dekker.
Nahl, D. (2004, November 12–17). Measuring the affective information environment of Web searchers. *Proceedings of the 67th annual meeting of the American Society for Information Science and Technology*. Providence, RI (pp. 191–197).
Nahl, D. (2005). Affective load theory. In K. E. Fisher, S. Erdelez, & L. E. E. McKechnie (Eds.), *Theories of information behavior* (pp. 39–43). Medford, NJ: Information Today.
Nahl, D. (2007). The centrality of the affective in information behavior. In D. Nahl & D. Bilal (Eds.), *Information and emotion: The emergent affective paradigm in information behavior research and theory* (pp. 3–37). Medford, NJ: Information Today.
Nahl, D., & Bilal, D. (Eds.). (2007). *Information and emotion: The emergent affective paradigm in information behavior research and theory.* Medford, NJ: Information Today.
Nsibirano, R. (2009). Him and Her — Gender differentials in ICT uptake: A critical literature review and research agenda. *International Journal of Education and*

Development Using ICT, *5*(5), 33–42. Retrieved from http://ijedict.dec.uwi.edu/viewarticle.php?id=858

One Laptop per Child (OLPC). (2013). About the project. *Countries*. One Laptop per Child. Retrieved from http://one.laptop.org/about/countries

Pal, J. (2012). The machine to aspire to: The computer in rural South India. *First Monday*, *17*(2), February 6, 2012. Retrieved from http://journals.uic.edu/ojs/index.php/fm/article/view/3733

Park, N., Roman, R., Lee, S., & Chung, J. E. (2009). User acceptance of a digital library system in developing countries: An application of the technology acceptance model. *International Journal of Information Management*, *29*, 196–209.

Piaget, J., & Inhelder, B. (1969). *The psychology of the child*. New York, NY: Basic Books.

Picard, R. W. (1999). *Affective computing for HCI*. Retrieved from http://affect.media.mit.edu/pdfs/99.picard-hci.pdf. Accessed on March 30, 2014.

Picard, R. (2011). *Want marketers to measure your emotions? That technology's coming*. Retrieved from http://venturebeat.com/2011/03/30/mit-researcher-shows-how-to-measure-emotions-with-technology

Pigato, M. A. (2001). *Information and communication technology, poverty, and development in Sub-Saharan Africa and South Asia*. Africa Region Working Paper Series No. 20. World Bank, Washington, DC.

Potnis, D. L. (2011). Cell-phone-enabled empowerment of women earning less than 1$/day. *IEEE Technology and Society Magazine*, Summer, pp. 39–45. Retrieved from http://web.utk.edu/~dpotnis/IEEE

Prinsloo, M. (2005). The new literacies as placed resources. *Perspectives in Education*, *23*(4), 87–98.

Psacharopoulos, G., & Patrinos, H. A. (2002). *Returns to investment in education: A further update*. Policy Research Working Paper No. 2881. World Bank, Washington, DC.

Reuter, K., & Druin, A. (2004, November 13–18). Bringing together children and books: An initial descriptive study of children's book searching and selection behavior in a digital library. *Proceedings of the 67th annual meeting of the American Society for Information Science and Technology (ASIST)*, Providence, RI (pp. 339–348).

Routh, D. (Ed.). (2011). *Southern innovator issue 1: Mobile phones and information technology*. New York, NY: United Nations Development Program. Retrieved from http://www.scribd.com/doc/95410448/Southern-Innovator-Magazine-Issue-1-Mobile-Phones-and-Information-Technology

Sharadhaa, A. (2014). Books on wheels: Mobile library, a hit. *The New Indian Express*, June, 10, 2013. Retrieved from http://www.newindianexpress.com/cities/bangalore/Books-on-wheels-Mobile-library-a-hit/2013/06/10/article1627519.ece

Simon, H. A. (1967). Motivational and emotional controls of cognition. *Psychological Review*, *71*(1), 29–39.

Snyder, I., & Prinsloo, M. (2007). Young people's engagement with digital literacies in marginal contexts in a globalised world. *Language and Education*, *21*(3), 171–179.

Strommen, E. F., Revelle, G. L., Medoff, L. M., & Razavi, S. (1996). Slow and steady wins the race? Three-year-old children and pointing device use. *Behaviour & Information Technology*, *15*(1), 57–64.

Todd, R. (2006). From information to knowledge: Charting and measuring changes in students' knowledge of a curriculum topic. *Information Research*, *11*(4) paper no. 264. Retrieved from http://InformationR.net/ir/11-4/paper264.html

Vygotsky, L. S. (1978). *Mind in society: The development of higher psychological processes*. Cambridge, MA: Harvard University Press.

Wakefield, J. (2014). *Ted 2014: Negroponte on plans to connect last billion*. Retrieved from http://www.bbc.com/news/technology-26357363

Warman, M. (2009). One laptop per child: How technology and the One Laptop per Child (OLPC) movement have become key factors in Rwanda's economic growth. *The Telegraph*, October 1, 2009. Retrieved from http://www.telegraph.co.uk/technology/6247728/One-laptop-per-child.html

Warschauer, M. (2002). Reconceptualizing the digital divide. *First Monday*, *7*(7), July 1, 2002. Retrieved from http://firstmonday.org/ojs/index.php/fm/article/view/967

Warschauer, M. (2007). Information literacy in the laptop classroom. *Teacher College Record*, *109*(11), 2511–2540.

Wilson, E. J. (III). (2004). *The information revolution and developing countries*. Cambridge, MA: MIT Press.

Wilson, T. D. (1981). On user studies and information needs. *Journal of Documentation*, *37*(1), 3–15.

Chapter 5

InfoMe: A Field-Design Methodology for Research on Ethnic Minority Youth as Information Mediaries

Karen E. Fisher, Ann Peterson Bishop, Philip Fawcett and Lassana Magassa

Abstract

Purpose – InfoMe is an innovative research program that explores and facilitates how ethnic minority youth help members of their social networks, especially elders, with everyday life situations through information and technology.

Methodology/approach – The project employs mixed methods, iteratively using Teen Design Days and a stratified random, classroom-based survey ($n = 500$) in six schools, with multiple community partners in King County, WA.

Findings – InfoMe inductively demonstrates how ethnic minority youth help others with situations of daily living through information and technology.

Practical and social implications – The findings are being used to develop InfoMe applications with the youth and InfoMe Train-the-Trainer workshops for professionals who work with youth.

Originality/value – The research is developing a model of how ethnic minority youth engage as information mediaries in different community settings, how individuals and communities benefit; and it is

New Directions in Children's and Adolescents' Information Behavior Research
Library and Information Science, Volume 10, 135–156

ISSN: 1876-0562/doi:10.1108/S1876-056220140000010053

contributing to our general understanding of specific concepts related to the human information experience.

Keywords: Immigrants; refugees; teens; design thinking; mixed methods; information behavior

5.1. Introduction

The InfoMe (Information Mediary) program is designed to understand how ethnic minority teens provide everyday information to members of their social networks (families, friends, neighbors, strangers) and how this propensity can be supported by library services. We have examined how teens surface the information needs of others; and how they seek, share, manage, and re-purpose information about and for others. In this chapter, we describe and discuss InfoMe's methodology: an innovative, mixed-methods, community-based approach for research on teens' information behavior. While the study includes a statistically generalizeable, paper-based survey of youth that is being conducted in school classrooms, we focus here on our innovative Teen Design Day method, which involves ethnic minority teens articulating and reflecting on their roles as information mediaries, with the aim of designing applications and services that support them. Teen Design Days expands on our earlier ALA Jesse Shera award winning research known as Tween Days, which is conducted with a younger population (c.f. Meyers, Fisher, & Marcoux, 2007, 2009).

In the United States, one in nine residents is foreign born. While diversity brings incredible richness, it also carries responsibility for helping immigrants and ethnic minorities participate fully in American life. The need for help, particularly through effective information services, is acute for several reasons. First, today's immigrant population is vastly more culturally and linguistically diverse than in earlier decades. In 1960, 8 of the top 10 source countries were in Western Europe, with only Mexico (#1) and Cuba (#6) from outside; in 2009, the top countries (Mexico, China, Philippines, India, Dominican Republic, Cuba, Vietnam, Colombia, Korea, Haiti) were located across several continents, with none from Western Europe (Migration Policy Institute, 2010). For U.S. public libraries today, 75% have patrons from over 30 countries, some serving up to 200 nationalities (Burke, 2008).

Second, immigrants face ever more complex everyday life issues. As "information poor" (Chatman, 1996; Childers, 1975), immigrants' needs for practical information related to becoming settled in their new communities are pronounced, including: English language instruction, employment and business, schools, adult education and training, health, transportation, social services, housing, civic engagement, protection of civil rights, immigration, and citizenship (Burke, 2008; Caidi, Allard, & Quirke, 2010; City of Seattle, 2007; Srinivasan & Pyati, 2007).

Third, immigrants still face an array of barriers to seeking assistance due to language and cultural differences, finances, transportation, unwelcoming environments, technology access and skills, agency complexity, and knowledge itself of what is available — including libraries and other agencies.

Fourth, immigrants are settling outside of traditional gateway cities where fewer services exist to facilitate integration, including instruction in English and citizenship preparation; these places have "little history or identity with immigration" (Singer, 2009). Given the 9214 public library systems in the United States — in traditional and emerging gateway areas — "there is an even greater role for public libraries in welcoming and educating immigrants" (U.S. Citizenship and Immigration Services and Institute of Museum & Library Services, 2006) and promoting social inclusion.

For decades, libraries have supported immigrant communities through providing multilingual collections, staff, and programming (Borrett & Milam, 2008; Burke, 2008; Courtright, 2005; Koontz, Jue, & American Library Association, 2008; McCook, 2004; Plummer, 1999, 2004). Ashton and Milam's (2008) Urban Libraries Council report identified five strategies employed by libraries for working with immigrant transitions: understanding immigration dynamics, bringing cultural and language sensitivity to service delivery, building English capacity, creating connections to local institutions, and encouraging civic engagement. Fisher, Durrance, and Hinton (2004) showed how the Queens Public Library's New Americans Program found its tremendous success was due to the welcoming and secure nature of the library, which in turn served as building blocks for achieving outcomes pertaining to everyday life skills. The U.S. Citizenship and Immigration Services and IMLS (2006) discussed how libraries serve immigrants through partnerships, collections, information services, programs and events, outreach, and planning. As was recently reported in the *New York Times*, public libraries face increasing service demand by immigrants but lack budgetary support (Gonzalez, 2013).

Despite the outstanding work of library staff, the evolving diversity, settlement patterns, and complex everyday life situations of immigrants present new service and policy challenges that require a community-wide response. Librarians — as information experts — are poised to provide solutions and local leadership that can benefit entire immigrant communities and affect policy making. One part of the solution lies with empowering immigrant youth through information literacy, computer and Internet services, and other design innovations at public libraries, based on findings gleaned through research in which immigrant youth are active partners in the design of improved and new library services. This emphasis on enriching the information experiences of immigrant youth and strengthening their potential to serve as information mediaries assumes broader significance when considered in context of the increasing aging U.S. population and its associated health, human services and other needs. Thus, not only can youth assist themselves and their social networks through serving as information mediaries, but also they are needed to help society at-large.

5.2. Theoretical Understanding Behind InfoMe

5.2.1. The Everyday Information Worlds of Youth

The everyday information worlds of youth in general are little understood, despite the plethora of examinations of their scholastic needs. Meyers et al. (2007, 2009) fieldwork generated the Tween Day Methodology and five library service principles focusing on social, affective, and credibility aspects. Tangential studies include Todd and Edwards' (2004) work on Australian teenage girls' experience with drug information; Hamer's (2003) and Mehra and Braquet's (2007) examinations of the coming-out experiences of queer youth; and Shenton and Dixon's (2003) research on interpersonal information sharing of youth ages 7–17 in a British town. A Kaiser Family Foundation study (Rideout, Foehr, & Roberts, 2010) reported two-thirds of youth ages 8–18 years own a cell phone for conversing, listening to/playing/watching other media, and texting (90 minutes daily for middle and high schoolers).

Regarding ethnic minority youth, Agosto & Hughes-Hassell (2005, 2006) found urban, racial minority teens preferred friends and family as information sources, and cell phones for tool-mediated communication. Fisher, Marcoux, Miller, Sanchez, and Cunningham (2004) studied migrant Hispanic farm workers and their families in Washington state. Elaborating on Bates' berry-picking model (1989), they found immigrants engaged in interpersonal berry-picking, using individuals instead of documents in formal information retrieval systems and often maintaining that relationship over a lifetime instead of relying on single or a short series of interactions with a variety of people. Focusing on the farm workers' children, they echoed Chu's (1999) work on immigrant child mediators, explaining that once immigrant youth become comfortable speaking English, they may become their families' primary information mediary, bilingually carrying out adult or mature responsibilities, often requiring sophisticated vocabulary. Upon immigrating, often, neither parents nor children speak English; due to school, however, the children soon become fairly proficient in

English. Parents then turn increasingly to them for help with cashing checks, getting directions, ordering food, completing applications, and so forth. Yet this child-rendered service can handicap parents as they may never develop independent survival skills. Moreover, the interpretation and, hence, presentation of their information needs to the system, and the information given later to the parents is through the lens of the child and may not reflect the parent's or adult's personal framing of the situation.

The recently completed Youth Community Informatics (YCI) Project (Bruce, Bishop, & Budhathoki, 2014) studied the use of information media by marginalized youth to engage with their local communities and the issues affecting their lives. Of particular relevance here is YCI's community-based methodology, as well as its focus on youth as designers and creators of media to share their perspectives on, and address, critical local information needs. For example, one group of African-American youth created a multimedia digital directory of community assets for teens. Another created a library in the local juvenile detention center. Teen males representing the Haitian Diaspora in Chicago created a video about the use of surveillance cameras in their neighborhood. Ethnic minority high school students created podcasts dealing with health, identity, and other everyday needs.

5.2.2. Information Mediaries

Information mediaries (Abrahamson & Fisher, 2007; Abrahamson, Fisher, Turner, Durrance, & Turner, 2008; Coward & Fisher, 2010) are people who seek information and perform instrumental tasks on behalf of others, without necessarily being asked or engaging in follow-up discussion. Glimpses of information mediary behavior have been observed as gatekeepers (Metoyer-Duran, 1991), proxy searchers (van Doorn, Stappers, & Gielen, 2013), information-acquirers-and-sharers, and encounterers (Erdelez, 1997; Erdelez & Rioux, 2000; Marshall & Bly, 2004). Technology, web 2.0 specifically, has facilitated information mediary behavior exponentially, as well as made it easier to study by, for example, having information exchanges automatically recorded as tweets, texts, and emails.

5.2.3. The U.S. Impact Study: Evidence of Ethnic Minority Youth as Information Mediaries

The information mediary behavioral framework was used in the *U.S. Impact Study* (Becker, Crandall, & Fisher, 2010) to understand how people use public access computing services, specifically terminals, internet access, digital resources, databases, networked and virtual services, training, technical assistance, and other staff support in public libraries. The study, which was supported by the IMLS and the Bill & Melinda Gates Foundation, gathered over 50,000 responses from people ages 14 and older via a household phone survey, an online survey of users of over 400 libraries, and four case studies. It showed that two out of every three people acted as information mediaries within the past 12 months, using public access computers for informational and instrumental purposes on behalf of someone else, including strangers. Moreover, information mediaries tend to be young (ages 14–18 are twice as likely), non-white and non-Asian (from 38% to 75% more likely), and non-native English speakers (30% more likely). In addition, 79% use library computers on a daily or near daily basis, while their level of education is insignificant. These findings are highly significant for immigrant communities. They suggest that youth may be key pathways for understanding the information needs of their respective populations, passing on needed information to otherwise hidden users (especially non-English speakers and those who do not use libraries), and identifying the greater range of how libraries help overall.

The information mediary behavior findings in the *U.S. Impact Study* informed the structure of the InfoMe instruments and are guiding analysis. They reveal that instead of the traditional equating of one person per public computer workstation (or usage), each user actually represents multiple users and hence, beneficiaries. Understanding how, why and to what effect people use library computers on behalf of others is a fundamental path to obtaining a complete view of the library's public value. By establishing such parameters in questioning with both users and service providers (including library staff), the framework enabled a deeper dissection of the information needs and instrumental purposes which library computers play in people's everyday lives. By integrating the information mediary framework with computer use, a substantially greater, more holistic view was gained of the reach of computers through familial and community networks. In addition, at the variable level, information mediary behavior enabled comparison across demographics and situations to aid understanding of the types of people who are more likely to assist others in information seeking and problem solving.

5.3. InfoMe Methodology

5.3.1. Overview

InfoMe is guided by the following primary research question:

How do ethnic minority youth serve as information mediaries?

More specific questions include:

- On whose behalf do ethnic minority youth find information/carry out instrumental tasks?
- How do they identify those who need help?
- How frequently do they help others?
- Is their information mediary relationship with others dependent on topic?
- How do ethnic minority youth surface/determine information needs?
- Why do they engage in information mediary behavior and relationships?
- How do ethnic minority youth identify, assess, and use particular sources to meet the needs of others?
- How do ethnic minority youth create, share, remix, and give information?
- How do ethnic minority youth manage and curate information about those they help and the information/help they provide?
- What are the patterns in information mediary behavior among different immigrant groups?
- How are ethnic minority families and others affected by youth serving as information mediaries?
- How are schools and communities affected by youth information mediaries?
- How can library-generated and youth-generated resources be shared and integrated?

We are investigating these questions using a mixed-method design (Creswell & Plano Clark, 2007; Fidel, 2008), which offers the advantage of offsetting methodological weaknesses and stimulating policy insight by identifying convergences, that is, the extent to which qualitative themes support quantitative results from survey data. This approach offers an iterative process and provides contextual information to help understand areas of convergence or divergence between disparate data collection activities.

5.3.2. Participants' Recruitment

All youth participants are being drawn from the Seattle/King County area in Washington State, which includes a multitude of immigrant communities in King County. African immigrants are found to be the highest percentage (52.4%) of library computer users (Burke, 2008). This offers a useful comparison group when examining InfoMe behaviors and need for and receptivity to information literacy training. The Seattle area is an ideal environment to conduct this study: the percentage of foreign-born residents has increased from 11% in 1980 to 20% in 2010; people come from more than 70 countries, speaking more than 90 languages (City of Seattle, 2007). Seattle Public Library and King County Library System have needed to respond to this increasing influx and diversity of people.

5.3.3. Partners

Our primary project partners include:

- *Seattle Public Library* (SPL) and *King County Library System* (KCLS): SPL serves a population of 600,000 people, 20% of whom are foreign born. KCLS serves a population of 1.2 million. Administrators, teen librarians, and diversity staff are providing project guidance, assisting with recruiting youth, participating in interviews about their ethnic minority patrons and hosting InfoMe Teen Design Days and community organization workshops.
- *Northwest Communities of Burma* and *Horn of Africa Services*: The Northwest Communities of Burma is a nonprofit organization that builds community among refugees and immigrants from Burma by providing opportunities to come together, enjoy friendly activities, and become more familiar with those who come from different ethnicities, faiths, and backgrounds. Horn of Africa Services is a multilingual, multicultural nonprofit organization offering individual and family counseling and referral services for communities from Djibouti, Eritrea, Ethiopia, Somalia, Sudan, and neighboring countries. The staff at both organizations have helped recruit immigrant youth, host Teen Design Days, participate in interviews, and provide feedback on outreach strategies, program design, and other activities.

5.3.4. Data Collection and Training

InfoMe has two primary data collection components:

(1) Teen Design Days (groups of 15–20) based on youth developmental needs where information worlds and InfoMe behavior are being discovered and design ideas for new information services generated and developed. Teens are provided food and receive monetary and other incentives.
(2) A survey with 500 King County youth. To obtain generalizable data about the extent to which all youth engage in InfoMe behavior, a 30-minute, paper-based survey is being administered with youth ages 14–19 in six Seattle and Tukwila schools. The schools were selected

> via stratified random sampling of low, medium, and high density ethnic minority populations. Though the survey results will be generalizable to the entire youth population in the area, the survey specifically targets ethnic minorities by asking questions about whether the youth or his/her parent(s) were born outside the United States, or if a language other than English is spoken in his/her home. In addition to questions about the youths' demographics, social networks, and computing background, the survey will comprise both closed- and open-ended questions about their InfoMe experiences. These questions are based around activities of daily living that we modified for immigrant situations, such as needs for help with social norms, legal situations, shopping, healthcare, housing, education, child-rearing, managing finances, and so on, set against different information activities (seeking, sharing, managing, giving, using, etc.). In lieu of individual compensation for survey participation, classroom cash gifts are being given.

InfoMe also has a training component that includes Train-the-Trainer Workshops with public library and community organization staff on how to use the Teen Design Day method themselves, and how to design services for ethnic minority youth.

5.3.5. Institutional Review Board

We have worked extensively with the Institutional Review Board at the University of Washington in developing both the teen workshops and survey. With such vulnerable populations, great care must be taken to protect the rights of youth participants. The Institutional Review Board has helped in creating consent and assent forms that clearly describe InfoMe workshop activities to youth and guardians, and encompass the survey, student access methods, and data protection measures.

5.3.6. InfoMe Status

Thus far, we have completed two multi-day Teen Design Day workshops (Fisher, Bishop, Magassa, & Fawcett, 2014). The InfoMe survey has been approved by the Institutional Review Board and will be conducted through the public school system in fall 2014, with data analysis to occur over winter 2015. Our Train-the-Trainer Workshops with InfoMe partners — library and community organization staff — intended to help them implement Teen Design Day and survey findings are scheduled to begin in fall 2014. We anticipate creating an Online Toolkit to complement the Train-the-Trainer Workshop Series as we continue hosting Teen Design Days with further youth populations and conduct refined versions of the survey to further generalize its results.

We have also conducted several preliminary sessions with library and community organization staff. These include an in-depth discussion with staff and administrators of King County libraries, whose purpose was to learn about current library understanding of, services for, and institutional needs regarding immigrant youth. We also conducted several Train-the-Trainer workshops, one in the United States at the MacArthur Digital Media and Learning (DML) Conference (Fisher, Dresang, et al., 2013) and one internationally at the European Council on Information Literacy (Fisher, Bishop, Magassa, & Fawcett, 2013), in order to help others learn how to conduct their own Teen Design Days. We learned more about the InfoMe teen design methodology through these workshops, because they generate feedback from a wide range of professionals about how Teen Design Days could be appropriated for different settings, as well as about anticipated barriers to implementing the methodology across a variety of venues, each with their own set of institutional goals and constraints.

In the remainder of this chapter, we focus on the Teen Design Days component of InfoMe; our program's survey is discussed in forthcoming reports.

5.3.7. Teen Design Days

InfoMe employs a *design thinking* framework to gain a deeper understanding of how ethnic minority youth serve as information, technology, language, and cultural mediaries within their social networks and larger communities. The concept of design thinking originated from the design discipline and the term was coined by Dave Kelly and Tim Brown of IDEO in 2001. It was popularized in a *Harvard Business Review* article written by Brown (2008) when IDEO was called to solve a variety of problems outside the traditional realm of most design firms. Since then, design thinking has been used to solve problems in business, address social issues (e.g., equitable public housing), and support international development (e.g., sanitary water to rural villages in India), as well as in product design spaces. Design thinking involves three major steps: inspiration, ideation, and implementation. Our use of design thinking with teens also draws on the rich research of Allison Druin and colleagues around involving children in the design process (e.g., Druin, 1999, 2002, 2005, 2009; Guha, Druin, & Fails, 2013; Hourcase, 2008; Large, Nesset, Beheshti, & Bowler, 2006;

Van Doorn et al., 2013). Bilal (2003) provides another example of involving children in the design of information systems.

More broadly, Teen Design Days (TDD) draw from a range of research methods: participatory design (Schuler & Nakimoka, 1993; Simonsen & Robertson, 2013), community-based action research (Hacker, 2013; Ledwith & Springett, 2010), social networking analysis (Haythornthwaite, 1996), and rapid prototyping. Our approach integrates these perspectives and methods into a multi-day workshop format developed specifically for youth. TDD workshops are designed to gain an understanding of how and why immigrant and refugee youth act as InfoMes to members of their social networks, especially their ethnic communities (and elders), and how they can be supported through technology and information services.

TDDs involve capturing in-depth data about ethnic minority youth's information mediary behavior, including surfacing information needs; information encountering; information creating and remixing; information management; curating; and information sharing and giving. In the TDDs, youth represent and discuss their InfoMe experiences using a variety of techniques and participate in low-tech prototyping of potential InfoMe services and applications. Like the survey data described above, these data are being analyzed quantitatively and qualitatively — as appropriate — using social network analysis and according to theories of information behavior.

As noted above, the TDDs are being held at libraries and community centers in the Seattle area. Such locations are gathering places or "information grounds" (Fisher, Landry, & Naumer, 2007) for many immigrant communities across the United States. At the TDDs, participants reflect on their InfoMe behavior using social network mapping tools and cultural probes (Gaver, Dunne, & Pacenti, 1999; Graham, Rouncefield, Gibbs, Vetere, & Cheverst, 2007), which involve storytelling, images, and dramatic play, as well as design, prototyping, and programming principles. Smartphones, laptops, Kinect controllers, Microsoft Surface, and other devices are also being used and technology experts from the University of Washington and Microsoft Research are being invited to devise ways of facilitating teens' current and future InfoMe behaviors.

At each of the TDDs, project staff and community members assist in meeting the teens' developmental needs (Davidson & Koppenhaver, 1992) for physical activity, competence and achievement, self-definition, creative expression, positive social interaction, and structure and clear limits. Three types of research notes are kept: field notes (our contextual observations while interacting with teens), method notes (reflections on techniques for collecting data), and theory notes (documentation of ideas and connections with the study's theoretical frameworks and other phenomena) (Chatman, 1992).

5.4. Implementation of Teen Design Days

5.4.1. Teen Design Days I

Our first TDD workshop took place over the course of two days. It was hosted by the Horn of Africa Services and included 12 teenagers, ages 14–18, from East African families. We planned activities that we hoped would be fun and engaging for the youth. The workshop was videotaped, from which we produced a short film. Our primary goals were to test techniques of gathering data about InfoMe behavior and to gain a better understanding of how young people think about their information behaviors. After an initial icebreaker game and participative policy setting for the workshop, we began by asking youth how they defined key terms, including *information*, *technology*, *social network*, and *design*. Next we initiated a discussion about the different kinds of people the youth knew and communicated with. This was followed by a more specific exercise in which the youth combined the "inspiration" stage of design thinking with telling a story about a specific incident involving InfoMe behavior (with and without digital technology). Here, youth were invited to use any method that felt comfortable to them, such as drawing a picture, sketching a diagram, or creating a skit. Their results were presented within the group and discussed. At the end of the first day, youth were given a task to complete for the next day: to create either a diagram or a story about their social network and how information was exchanged within it.

Those teens who chose stories to illustrate their InfoMe behavior narrated incidents involving: helping a young cousin who just arrived from Africa get oriented to U.S. schools; teaching a new student how to play basketball; showing an aunt how to use the internet to look for a job (and then accompanying her to a job interview); and helping a friend learn how to use the latest social media, such as Facebook and Twitter.

The sketches produced by the young people combined social network diagrams with flowchart processes and written annotations. One diagram described helping a mother with understanding medical information. Another mapped out Facebook relationships and communication purposes. Another depicted helping a mother communicate with a cashier at the store. Another placed the teen in the center and showed the large network of people with whom information of various types was shared.

The second day of the workshop included a debriefing session in which youth shared the diagrams and stories they created, as well as an in-depth session on design thinking. For the latter, the youth first learned the process of design thinking in a hands-on fashion in which they worked in groups to create a better paper clip. They then applied design thinking to their InfoMe experiences by brainstorming a few improvements in technology and libraries that would support their work in finding and sharing information with their family, peers, and others in their local community.

As noted above, the TDDs include attention to the developmental needs of youth. To meet participants' need for physical activity, for example, we included games that had them on their feet and moving around. In the obstacle course game, one youth was blindfolded. The others each chose an object from the room and placed it in the way of the person who couldn't see. Then, everyone had to work together to give the blindfolded youth instructions to navigate safely from one side of the room to the other. Our TDD also used some fairly traditional short written questionnaires. One collected demographic data and included a few basic items on technology use and information behavior. Another was used to evaluate the TDD itself.

5.4.2. Teen Design Days II

The second TDD was expanded to three days (Fisher, Bishop, Fawcett, & Magassa, 2013). Youth were recruited from the public high school in Tukwila, WA. We recruited youth ages 15–18 at a school job fair, and held the TDD in the Foster Public Library located next door. Participating youth (14 girls, 9 boys) came from families that were originally from East Africa and Nepal. All youth completed all three Teen Design Days and each received a $150 cash stipend. The TTD II was video and audio recorded, yielding three terabytes of data to accompany researchers' field notes and youth artifacts and evaluations.

The expanded TDD agenda included pre-testing our forthcoming school survey on InfoMe behavior, more in-depth design sessions on creating "the perfect cell phone" and "any tool or resource that would help you as an InfoMe," and an introduction to the TouchDevelop programming language, which allows you to create apps for computers and mobile devices by tapping on your screen. The new design and programming sessions were facilitated by volunteer industry experts. We also expanded the reflection period of the "light and lively" games to include discussion of information behavior in the games. For example, in the brief reflection period after the obstacle course game, youth noted such things as "you have to trust the person giving you information."

Youth presented InfoMe stories and skits based on their own experiences. These included explaining a telephone bill to a parent, searching the internet to find medical information when a snowstorm prevented the family from going to the doctor's, sharing religious and cultural information, giving tips to peers about sports and how to avoid fights, helping relatives find their way around town, assisting tourists with local information, and helping friends with their homework. Translating for parents, other relatives, and friends was a regular occurrence.

InfoMe tool prototypes designed by the youth with craft supplies included a wristwatch cell phone, a multimedia information kiosk at bus stops, and a free van for the elderly equipped with "comfy seats" and information monitors that would take the seniors to/from their homes and various information and educational hubs (including museums and classes). These ideas reinforced those from the pilot work with Somali youth about creating and posting YouTube videos about cooking, travel and music for their mothers and others illiterate in both English and native languages.

5.5. What Have We Learned about the TDD Methodology?

In addition to the preliminary findings on the nature of the information mediary behavior of ethnic minority youth, we have also been noting lessons related to the TDD methodology itself:

- Youth are largely unaware of their InfoMe behavior but are able to articulate it easily in multiple ways once it "clicks."
- By and large, all of the TDD youth participated actively in the sessions, though there was a range of levels of engagement, which seemed related to both shyness and/or lack of interest.
- Youth were able to describe their InfoMe behavior with diagrams, role-playing skits, and brief written narratives. Role-playing appeared to be the most enjoyable; in one skit, youth re-enacted a scene from riding a public bus in which an old lady asked her young seat-mate for help finding her desired location and communicating with the bus driver.
- Because participants were minors, signed assent forms from the youth were required as well as signed consent forms from their guardians; this created a little mayhem at the outset of the TDD as not all youth had been sent the appropriate forms ahead of time.
- We need greater cultural sensitivity in planning the TDD schedule: while we built prayer time into the daily schedule, and planned Halal food to meet the religious needs of specific participants, more time should have been added and thought given to how cultural norms might affect group dynamics.
- Information concepts and vocabulary seemed foreign to most youth. The use of the term "social networks" was particularly problematic as the young people immediately fixed certain digital applications in their brains (e.g., Facebook), making it difficult to think more broadly about the entire spectrum of their social relationships and the means they used

for communicating with different people they encountered in daily life. At TDD II we described the same idea as a "social circle" and were able to avoid that pitfall.

- TDDs provide a viable way to study and collaborate with youth, but we need to do more to put together outcomes related to InfoMe behavior and youth-designed prototypes in usable formats; and
- To be successful, all of the TDD elements are important, including: building group coherence and youths' comfort with voicing their views by, for example, having youth themselves create the rules for behavior during the TDDs; providing youth with good local food; building in physical exercise; promoting creativity and self-expression; and pushing for ongoing reflection to generate and make sense of research connections.

The majority of youth in both TDDs said they wanted to participate in further InfoMe activities. They also noted how TTDs enhanced their individual well-being and development.

We were somewhat surprised to learn all of the benefits of videotaping the TDD workshop and have decided to continue recording video of future workshops. As a methodology, it provides another data source from which we can learn. The youth were clearly comfortable with it and appreciated getting still shots they could use for various purposes. We have also found that the film we created from the video footage is an effective dissemination tool for communicating with sponsors, parents, partners, and other interested researchers.

5.6. Summary

InfoMe provides a deeper understanding of how ethnic minority youth serve as information, technology, language, and cultural mediaries within their social networks and larger communities. Our multidisciplinary, experiential approach integrates perspectives from computer science, information science, design, and information behavior. It engages immigrant and refugee youth in the Seattle area and focuses on public library and community agency innovation.

Summarizing what we have learned about the Teen Design Day methodology, we can say at this point that we believe TDDs are highly helpful in understanding the social and information worlds of ethnic minority youth. In addition, they proved useful for testing concepts, vocabulary, and instruments for later project activities. TDDs appear to be scalable by number of participants and length of time (having mapped out a six-day workshop, we condensed it to two days, and then expanded again to three). We found the methodology useful for developing relationships and ongoing partnerships with youth and community groups. For example, three youth participated in the Train-the-Trainer workshop about the TDD method at the MacArthur Digital Media and Learning Conference in Chicago. In addition to serving as table facilitators, they gave brief presentations on their TDD participation and reflected on what they had learned.

5.7. Implications for Information Services

InfoMe aims to further understanding of the relationships among information, technology, design, and empowerment in immigrant and refugee youth populations, and to assist those who act as information and technology mediaries for others in their social circles. It is poised to make future contributions to the fields of information science, computer science, human–computer interaction, design, education, family studies, the health sciences, and other cognate fields.

We found, first and foremost, that youth are both active information mediaries (even though they often do not realize it) and that they are competent design partners. Youth serve as info mediaries on behalf of different types of people, including relatives, friends, other known adults, and complete strangers, and they do so across contexts.

InfoMe includes developing and leading workshops for supporting InfoMes with Seattle Public Libraries, the King County Library System, and other community agencies. We anticipate the workshops will help us integrate InfoMe's findings with seminal work from the LIS literature, in order to better inform our understanding of the nature of information mediary behavior and how it can be used to design library services and applications. Three such ripe areas for support are information needs, personal information management, and information sharing/giving — none of which are adequately supported from an InfoMe perspective. Taylor's (1968) work on the development of users' information needs could be substantially revisited from an information mediary perspective and integrated into today's library services (Naumer & Fisher, 2009). Such an expansion of the concept of information needs would explore social contexts, specifically the roles of other people in the emergence, iterative development, communication, and maturation of information needs.

InfoMe can make a meaningful difference to people — locally and globally — by increasing our understanding of the information worlds of today's immigrants, particularly regarding service and policy implications. The findings can help in elaborating the model of how and why people engage in InfoMe behavior and its inherent micro-behaviors. InfoMe helps modify the Tween Day methodology for teens, with their distinctive socio-demographic characteristics. Additionally, it provides a mechanism for developing specifications for tools that library and community organization staff can use in support of immigrants and other patrons.

Similarly, software applications could be developed employing principles of personal information management (Jones, 2007; Naumer & Fisher, 2007) to inform how information mediaries organize and keep track of the needs of people they are helping, and all the information they seek and share. Fisher/Pettigrew's (2000) work on information giving can further inform InfoMe services' functionality.

Supporting InfoMes suggest an expanded role for traditional information literacy. Indeed, information literacy as an essential ability was echoed throughout President Obama's (2009) National Information Literacy Awareness Month Proclamation: "rather than merely possessing data, we must also learn the skills necessary to acquire, collate, and evaluate information for any situation." Despite observations on the growing importance of context (corporeal and social sources) in understanding and promoting information literacy, the prevailing paradigm focuses on individual users engaged in learning about tools and problem-solving processes on their own behalf, sometimes for life-long learning.

Regarding public libraries, Lloyd and Williamson (2008, p. 7) concluded, "information literacy research is still in its infancy, with very little research pertaining to community perspectives of information literacy being reported … there is a major gap in the community sector, exacerbated by the wide range of societal groups and organizations" adding, "in community and cross-cultural settings, [information literacy] may also take on a different shape that cannot be accommodated by library-driven frameworks and standards" (p. 8).

Building on the library field's substantial record in information literacy, a key contribution of InfoMe is that we will be articulating information literacy to reflect people's information seeking on behalf of the needs of other people. Its core elements of being able "to identify, locate, evaluate, and effectively use information" (National Forum on Information Literacy, 2010), might include how individuals are attuned to the information situations of others, have the skills to surface people's information needs, know how to optimally provide information (i.e., the right information, in the best format, in the right way at the right time). Broadened in this way, information literacy training can reflect people's natural range of everyday information experience.

Acknowledgments

We wish to thank the following agencies for financially supporting our research: the U.S. Institute of Museum and Library Services, Microsoft

Global Community Affairs, Microsoft Research, and the University of Washington.

References

Abrahamson, J., & Fisher, K. E. (2007). "What's past is prologue": Towards a general model of lay information mediary behaviour. *Information Research, 12*(4). Retrieved from http://informationr.net/ir/12-4/colis/colis15.html

Abrahamson, J. A., Fisher, K. E., Turner, A. G., Durrance, J. C., & Turner, T. C. (2008). Lay information mediary behaviour uncovered: Exploring how non-professionals seek health information for themselves and others online. *Journal of the Medical Library Association, 96*(4), 310–323.

Agosto, D. E., & Hughes-Hassell, S. (2005). People, places, and questions: An investigation of the everyday life information seeking behaviors of urban young adults. *Library & Information Science Research, 27*(2), 141–163.

Agosto, D. E., & Hughes-Hassell, S. (2006). Toward a model of the everyday life information needs of urban teenagers, part 2: Empirical model. *Journal of the American Society for Information Science and Technology, 57*(11), 1418–1426.

Ashton, R. J., & Milam, D. P. (2008). *Welcome, stranger: Public libraries build the global village*. Chicago, IL: Urban Libraries Council. Retrieved from http://urbanlibraries.org/associations/9851/files/ULC_WS.pdf

Bates, M. J. (1989). The design of browsing and berrypicking techniques for the online search interface. *Online Review, 13*(5), 407–424.

Becker, S., Crandall, M. D., & Fisher, K. E. (2010). The users and uses of public access computing in public libraries. *Report one from the U.S. IMPACT studies: A research initiative examining the impact of free access to computers and the Internet in public libraries*. Seattle, WA: University of Washington Information School.

Bilal, D. (2003, October 18–22). Draw and tell: Children as designers of Web interfaces. *Proceedings of the 66th annual meeting of the American Society for Information Science and Technology*, Long Beach, CA (pp. 135–141).

Borrett, R. M., & Milam, D. P. (2008). *Welcome, stranger: Public libraries build the global village toolkit*. Chicago, IL: Urban Libraries Council. Retrieved from http://urbanlibraries.org/associations/9851/files/ws_toolkit.pdf

Brown, T. (2008). Design thinking. *Harvard Business Review, 86*(6), 8–92.

Bruce, B. C., Bishop, A. P., & Budhathoki, N. R. (2014). *Youth community inquiry: New media for community and personal growth*. New York, NY: Peter Lang.

Burke, S. K. (2008). Public library resources used by immigrant households. *Public Libraries, 47*(4), 32–41.

Caidi, N., Allard, D., & Quirke, L. (2010). Information practices of immigrants. *Annual Review of Information Science & Technology, 44*, 493–531.

Chatman, E. A. (1992). *The information world of retired women*. New York, NY: Greenwood Press.

Chatman, E. A. (1996). The impoverished life-world of outsiders. *Journal of the American Society for Information Science, 47*(3), 193–206.

Childers, T. (1975). *The information-poor in America*. Metuchen, NJ: Scarecrow Press.

Chu, C. M. (1999, August 20–28). Immigrant children mediators (ICM): Bridging the literacy gap in immigrant communities. Paper presented at the 65th IFLA Council and General Conference, Bangkok.

City of Seattle. (2007). *Immigrant & refugee (I/R) report and action plan 2007–2009*. Seattle, WA. Retrieved from http://www.seattle.gov/neighborhoods/immigrants/docs/I&R_Report.pdf

Courtright, C. (2005). Health information-seeking among Latino newcomers: An exploratory study. *Information Research, 10*(2). Retrieved from http://informationr.net/ir/10-2/paper224.html

Coward, C. T., & Fisher, K. E. (2010, August 10–15). *Measuring indirect access: Indicators of the impacts of lay information mediary behavior*. Gothenburg, Sweden: 2010 IFLA World Library and Information Congress. Retrieved from http://www.ifla.org/files/hq/papers/ifla76/72-coward-en.pdf.

Creswell, J. W., & Plano Clark, V. L. (2007). *Designing and conducting mixed methods research*. Thousand Oaks, CA: Sage.

Davidson, J., & Koppenhaver, D. (1992). *Adolescent literacy: What works and why* (2nd ed.). New York, NY: Garland.

Druin, A. (1999). Cooperative inquiry: Developing new technologies for children with children. In *CHI '99: Proceedings of the SIGCHI Conference on Human Factors in Computing Systems* (pp. 592–599). New York, NY: ACM Press.

Druin, A. (2002). The role of children in the design of new technology. *Behavior and Information Technology*, *21*(1), 1–25.

Druin, A. (2005). What children can teach us: Developing digital libraries for children with children. *Library Quarterly*, *75*(1), 20–41.

Druin, A. (Ed.). (2009). *Mobile technology for children: Designing for interaction and learning*. Amsterdam: Elsevier.

Erdelez, S. (1997). Information encountering: A conceptual framework for accidental information discovery. In P. Vakkari, R. Savolainen, & B. Dervin (Eds.), *Information seeking in context: Proceedings of an international conference on research in information needs, seeking and use in different contexts* (pp. 412–421). London: Taylor-Graham.

Erdelez, S., & Rioux, K. S. (2000). Sharing information encountered for others on the web. *New Review of Information Behaviour Research, 1*, 219–233.

Fidel, R. (2008). Are we there yet?: Mixed methods research in library and information science. *Library & Information Science Research*, *30*(4), 265–272.

Fisher, K. E., Bishop, A., Fawcett, P., & Magassa, L. (2013, October 22–25). Teen design days: Engaging youth in information literacy through design thinking. *European Council on Information Literacy*, Istanbul, Turkey. All-day workshop. Retrieved from http://www.ecil2013.org/

Fisher, K. E., Bishop, A., Magassa, L., & Fawcett, P. (2013). InfoMe @ Teen design days: A multi-variable, design thinking approach to community development. *ACM ICTD 2013: International conference on information and communication technologies for development*, Cape Town, South Africa. ACM. Retrieved from http://dx.doi.org/10.1145/2517899.2517914. Accessed on December 7–10, 2013.

Fisher, K. E., Bishop, A., Magassa, L., & Fawcett, P. (2014). Action! Co-designing interactive technology with immigrant teens. In *CHI interaction design and children*. Denmark: Aarhus/Billund. Retrieved from http://idc2014.org/. Accessed on June 17–20, 2014.

Fisher, K. E., Dresang, E., Davis, K., Fawcett, P., Bishop, A., & Magassa, L. (2013). Teen design days: Promoting youth civic engagement through design thinking. *MacArthur Digital Media & Learning Conference*, Chicago, IL. Retrieved from http://dml2013.dmlhub.net/. Accessed on March 14–16, 2013.

Fisher, K. E., Durrance, J. C., & Hinton, M. B. (2004). Information grounds and the use of need-based services by immigrants in queens, New York: A context-based, outcome evaluation approach. *Journal of the American Society for Information Science and Technology*, *55*(8), 754–766.

Fisher, K. E., Landry, C. F., & Naumer, C. M. (2007). Social spaces, casual interactions, meaningful exchanges: An information ground typology based on the college student experience. *Information Research*, *12*(2). Retrieved from http://informationr.net/ir/12-2/paper291.html

Fisher, K. E., Marcoux, E., Miller, L. S., Sanchez, A., & Cunningham, E. R. (2004). Information behavior of migrant Hispanic farm workers and their families in the Pacific Northwest. *Information Research*, *10*(1). Retrieved from http://informationr.net/ir/10-1/paper199.html

Fisher, K. E., Naumer, C., Durrance, J., Stromski, L., & Christiansen, T. (2005). Something old, something new: Preliminary findings from an exploratory study about people's information habits and information grounds. *Information Research*, *10*(2). paper 223. Retrieved from http://InformationR.net/ir/10-2/paper223.html

Gaver, B., Dunne, T., & Pacenti, E. (1999). Design: Cultural probes. *Interactions*, *6*(1), 21–29. doi:10.1145/291224.291235

Gonzalez, D. (2013, October 27). Budgets challenge libraries, a "point of integration" for libraries. *New York Times*. Retrieved from http://nyti.ms/17rl33o

Graham, C., Rouncefield, M., Gibbs, M., Vetere, F., & Cheverst, K. (2007). How probes work. In *Proceedings of the 2007 conference of the computer-human interaction special interest group (CHISIG) of Australia on Computer-human interaction: Design: Activities, artifacts and environments*, ACM, Adelaide, Australia (pp. 29–37).

Guha, M. L., Druin, A., & Fails, J. A. (2013). Cooperative inquiry revisited: Reflections of the past and guidelines for the future of intergenerational co-design. *International Journal of Child-Computer Interaction*, *1*(1), 14–23.

Hacker, K. (2013). *Community-based participatory research*. Thousand Oaks, CA: Sage.

Hamer, J. S. (2003). Coming-out: Gay males' information seeking. *School Libraries Worldwide*, *9*(2), 73–89.

Haythornthwaite, C. (1996). Social network analysis: An approach and technique for the study of information exchange. *Library & Information Science Research*, *18*, 323–342.

Hourcase, J. P. (2008). Interactive design and children. *Foundations and Trends in Human-Computer Interaction*, *1*(4), 277–392.

Jones, W. (2007). *Keeping found things found: The study and practice of personal information management*. San Francisco, CA: Morgan Kaufmann Publishers.

Koontz, C. M., Jue, D. K., & American Library Association. (2008). *Serving non-English speakers in U.S. public libraries: 2007 analysis of library demographics, services and programs: A report*. Chicago, IL: American Library Association.

Large, A., Nesset, V. Beheshti, J., & Bowler, L. (2006). "Bonded design": A novel approach to intergenerational information technology design. *Library & Information Science Research*, *28*, 64–82.

Ledwith, M., & Springett, J. (2010). *Participatory practice: Community-based action for transformative change*. Portland, OR: Policy Press.

Lloyd, A., & Williamson, K. (2008). Towards an understanding of information literacy in context: *Implications for research. Journal of Librarianship and Information Science*, *40*(1), 3–12.

Marshall, C. C., & Bly, S. (2004). Sharing encountered information: digital libraries get a social life. *Proceedings of the 4th ACM/IEEE-CS joint conference on digital libraries* (pp. 218–227).

McCook, K. d. l. P. (2004). *Introduction to public librarianship*. New York, NY: Neal-Schuman.

Mehra, B., & Braquet, D. (2007). Process of information seeking during "queer" youth coming-out experiences. In M. K. Chelton & C. Cool (Eds.), *Youth information-seeking behaviors: Theories, models and issues* (pp. 93–131). Lanham, MD: The Scarecrow Press.

Metoyer-Duran, C. (1991). Information-seeking behaviour of gatekeepers in ethnolinguistic communities: Overview of a taxonomy. *Library & Information Science Research*, *13*, 319–346.

Meyers, E. M., Fisher, K. E., & Marcoux, E. (2007). Studying the everyday information behavior of tweens: Notes from the field. *Library & Information Science Research*, *29*(3), 310–331.

Meyers, E. M., Fisher, K. E., & Marcoux, E. (2009). Making sense of an information world: The everyday life information behavior of preteens. *The Library Quarterly*, *79*(3), 301–341.

Migration Policy Institute. (2010). *Ten source countries with the largest populations in the United States as percentages of the total foreign-born population: 2008. MPI data hub: Migration facts, stats, and maps*. Washington, DC: Migration Policy Institute. Retrieved from http://www.migrationinformation.org/DataHub/charts/10.2008.shtml

National Forum on Information Literacy. (2010). *What is information literacy?* Retrieved from http://www.infolit.org/index.html

Naumer, C. M., & Fisher, K. E. (2007). Field methods for investigating personal information management. In W. Jones & J. Teevan (Eds.), *Personal information management* (pp. 76–88). Seattle, WA: University of Washington.

Naumer, C. M., & Fisher, K. E. (2009). Information needs: Conceptual and empirical developments. In M. Bates & M. N. Maack (Eds.), *Encyclopedia of library and information science*. London: Taylor & Francis.

Obama, B. (2009). *Presidential proclamation: National information literacy awareness month, 2009*. Washington, DC: U.S. Government Printing Office. Retrieved from http://www.whitehouse.gov/assets/documents/2009literacy_prc_rel.pdf

Pettigrew, K. E. (2000). Lay information provision in community settings: How community health nurses disseminate human services information to the elderly. *Library Quarterly*, *70*(1), 47–85.

Plummer, A. J. Jr. (1999). *Libraries, immigrants, and the American experience*. Westport, CT: Greenwood Press.

Plummer, A. J. Jr. (2004). *Still struggling for equality: American public library services with minorities*. Westport, CT: Libraries Unlimited.

Rideout, V., Foehr, U., & Roberts, D. (2010 January). *Generation M2: Media in the lives of 8- to 18-year-olds. A Kaiser family foundation study*. Menlo Park, CA: Henry J. Kaiser Family Foundation. Retrieved from http://www.kff.org/entmedia/upload/8010.pdf

Schuler, D., & Nakimoka, A. (Eds.). (1993). *Participatory design: Principles and practices*. Hillsdale, NJ: Lawrence Erlbaum.

Shenton, A. K., & Dixon, P. (2003). "Youngsters" use of other people as an information-seeking method. *Journal of Librarianship and Information Science*, *35*(4), 219–233.

Simonsen, J. & Robertson, T. (Eds.). (2013). *Routledge handbook of participatory design*. New York, NY: Routledge.

Singer, A. (2009). *New geography of United States immigration* (Vol. 9). Brookings Immigration Series. Washington, DC: Brookings Institute. Retrieved from http://www.brookings.edu/~/media/Files/rc/papers/2009/07_immigration_geography_singer/07_immigration_geography_singer.pdf

Srinivasan, R., & Pyati, A. (2007). Diasporic information environments: Reframing immigrant-focused information. *Journal of the American Society for Information Science and Technology*, *58*(12), 1734–1744.

Taylor, R. (1968). Question negotiation and information seeking in libraries. *College and Research Libraries*, *29*, 178–194.

Todd, R. J., & Edwards, S. (2004). Adolescents' information seeking and utilization in relation to drugs. In M. K. Chelton & C. Cool (Eds.), *Youth information-seeking behaviors: Theories, models and issues* (pp. 353–386). Lanham, MD: Scarecrow Press.

U.S. Citizenship and Immigration Services, and Institute of Museum & Library Services. (2006). *Library services for immigrants: A report on current practices*. Retrieved from http://www.uscis.gov/files/nativedocuments/G-1112.pdf

van Doorn, F., Stappers, P. J., & Gielen, M. (2013). Design research by proxy: Using children as researchers to gain contextual knowledge about user experience. *CHI'13*, Paris, France (pp. 2883–2891).

Chapter 6

Perspectives of Rural Librarians about the Information Behaviors of Children with Special Needs in the Southern and Central Appalachian Region: An Exploratory Study to Develop User-Centered Services

Bharat Mehra

Abstract

Purpose – This chapter explores the perspectives of rural librarians about the information behaviors of children with special needs (CSN) and services available for the disenfranchised population in the Southern and Central Appalachian (SCA) region.

Methodology/approach – Qualitative feedback is collected from 31 SCA rural librarians via phone interviews and a web-based survey about: (1) The most important information needs/wants of the CSN in the SCA rural libraries; (2) The most important information resources and services that the CSN seek/use in the SCA rural libraries; (3) Extent of perceived need for effective library services for the CSN in rural areas; (4) Ways that the SCA rural libraries can improve to better serve the CSN in their local communities.

Findings – Content analysis of the data generated quantitative representation of response counts for specific themes that resulted in practical user-centered suggestions for positive change in delivering effective library services for the CSN in the SCA region.

New Directions in Children's and Adolescents' Information Behavior Research
Library and Information Science, Volume 10, 157–189

ISSN: 1876-0562/doi:10.1108/S1876-056220140000010054

Originality/value – Research significance lies in its first-time effort to understand the information needs and information uses of the CSN in the SCA rural library environments from the perspective of a rural librarian immersed in an American society that perceives a parochial regional work setting. This research presents data that challenges notions stereotyping and marginalizing of the "South" in its documentation of positive and meaningful efforts that rural librarians suggest should be made to improve the conditions experienced by the CSN in this region.

Keywords: Rural librarians; Southern and Central Appalachian region; children with special needs; user-centered services

6.1. Introduction

This chapter explores the perspectives of rural librarians about the information needs and information uses of children with special needs (CSN) (that are implicitly and/or explicitly expressed in their information behaviors) in the Southern and Central Appalachian (SCA) region and discusses the implications of the findings for developing effective user-centered services for this underserved population. CSN is an umbrella term that includes a wide range of definitions and diagnoses addressing a myriad array of medical, behavioral, physical, emotional, developmental, learning, and/or mental health-related issues (Gargiulo & Kilgo, 2010; Greenspan, Wieder, & Simons, 1998). The Center for Children with Special Needs in Glastonbury, Connecticut (http://www.autismct.com/), recognizes the complex and intertwining nature of these concerns and focuses on individuals with (1) Autism, Asperger Syndrome, and related Pervasive Developmental Disorders; (2) Pediatric Chronic Illness (including Spina Bifida, Prader Willi Syndrome, Cerebral Palsy, Muscle Disease, Diabetes); (3) Developmental Disabilities and severe behavioral difficulties including aggression and self-injury. This research acknowledges these varied differences in CSN and includes how one or more of these factors impact the ability of the person to communicate, socialize, and interact with others, posing challenges in the person's information seeking processes and barriers to becoming independent, self-reliant, and self-motivated individuals (National Center for Health Statistics, 2009; Zambone & Jones, 2010).

The U.S. Bureau of the Census defines "rural" as areas with fewer than 2500 people and open territory (Economic Research Service, 2007). *The Encyclopedia of Rural America* defines the related concept of "nonmetropolitan" counties to describe the spread of housing developments outside the boundaries of metro areas that have no cities with as many as 50,000 residents (Rathge, 1997, p. 627), in addition to being non-urbanized (Office of Management and Budget, 1998). The word "rural" in this chapter is used with regard to both meanings. The Appalachian Regional Commission (ARC) (1974), created as a Unites States federal-state partnership, identifies *Central Appalachia* to include: West Virginia's nine southernmost counties, eastern Kentucky, Virginia's southwestern tip, and the northwestern portion of Tennessee's Appalachian area (Bush, 2003), while *Southern Appalachia* includes most of Appalachian Virginia and Tennessee as well as the western Carolinas and the northern parts of Georgia, Alabama, and Mississippi.

6.2. Problem Statement and Research Significance

The SCA belt has traditionally faced excruciating economic, social, and cultural conditions that have adversely affected library services and the population living in these areas (Eller, 2008; Scruggs, 2010). Extreme information poverty and unemployment, low levels of information literacy and educational attainment (Spatig et al., 2009), a lack of access and use of information technology (Mehra, Singh, & Parris, 2010), and other unique environmental circumstances (Bardwell et al., 2009; Black, Mather, & Sanders, 2007; Herzenberg, Price, & Wial, 2005; Kusmin, 2008; Lichter & Campbell, 2005; Schwartz, 2004) have resulted in the region's rural librarians experiencing critical information needs and concerns (Mehra, Black, & Lee, 2010) that have been inadequately represented in the library and information science professions (Mellon & Kester, 2004). For example, findings of a recent qualitative study of rural librarians' perspectives in Tennessee about efforts to improve their library services in the 21st century included a need for greater user-centered community analysis, information technology competencies, training in managerial//public administration, public services, and technical services (Mehra, Black, Singh, & Nolt, 2011a). Fifty-two counties in Tennessee are within the SCA region (ARC, 2008), of which 16 are economically distressed, 16 are economically at-risk, and another 16 contain distressed areas (ARC, 2013). These improvements, however, are needed across the entire SCA belt and other major challenges experienced by rural libraries in the region include limited money; lack of diverse library services to meet varied information needs, wants, and expectations; few qualified staff; and poor collections and equipment (American Library Association, 2004; National Center for Education Statistics, 2006). If the SCA rural libraries can develop assets to extend themselves in these domains (ARC, 2004) they can play a significant leadership role in the planning and implementation efforts to achieve the goals and objectives identified in the Appalachian Regional Commission's Strategic Plan 2011–2016 (2010) to foster the development, access, and effective use of innovative information services and telecommunications technologies toward community building, community development, economic revitalization, and enhancing workforce skills through training and education. Some steps for rural librarians to overcome their experienced challenges include (American Library Association Office for Literacy and Outreach Services, 2011): developing familiarity with their user and community base, nurturing leadership skills and influencing decision-makers, using all available media outlets in its diverse forms to tell their stories effectively, applying information technology for advocacy to meet underserved needs, and building powerful collaborations and partnerships in resource sharing efforts.

Research in contextualizing and understanding how the SCA rural libraries differ from libraries elsewhere in the United States calls for regional library professionals to expand their current practice and service design to represent a diversity of needs and expectations, integrate information-related management skills, and develop information technology-related competencies in their work environments (Oden, Strover, Inagaki, & Lucas, 2004). The Institute of Museum and Library Services' (IMLS) new research brief, *Service Trends in U.S. Public Libraries, 1997–2007* (Publication No. IMLS-2010-RB-01), examined key service differences in urban and rural communities and benchmarked for more place-based analysis and detailed studies of rural library trends to provide greater evidence for planning library services to meet local needs (Henderson, 2009).

Further, the CSN in the SCA region experience harsh conditions since their numbers are large and the health information resources available to them are few (Heflinger & Christens, 2006). A recent study found that the SCA region averaged much higher with 15.6% of the children and youth in the general population with special health care needs, as compared to the national average of 13.9% (U.S. Department of Health and Human Services, Health Resources and Services Administration, Maternal and Child Health Bureau, 2008). Also, the CSN in the SCA rural libraries tend to be underserved and their information and special needs are often unmet (Allen & Hughes-Hassell, 2010; Brind'Amour, 2010) due to the unique debilitating social and cultural circumstances, geographic and psychological isolation, low literacy and educational levels, information poverty, and lack of public awareness or adequate social support (Kotch, 2005; Skinner & Slifkin, 2007).

The State of America's Children 2011 published by the Children's Defense Fund (2011) provides a "comprehensive compilation and analysis of the most recent and reliable national and state-by-state data" on children's health topics that include uninsured children, children's access to health care, children's dental health and access to dental health, overweight and obesity, immunization, children's mortality rates, amongst others, though a discussion of children's special needs is conspicuous by its absence. Similarly, data and research concerning published library standards for services to CSN patrons are limited and few. The *Standards for the 21st Century Learner* published by the American Association of School Librarians (AASL) (2007) provides a broad understanding of a homogenous group of learners in its reference to "All children deserve equitable access … in an environment that is safe and conducive to learning" ("Common Beliefs") without any acknowledgement or guidance to address differences and diversity of children and their special needs and learning styles. Similarly, the AASL's (2008) *Learning4Life: A National Plan for Implementation for the 21st Century Learner and Empowering Learners: Guidelines for School Library Programs* identifies one of its guiding principle in terms of "One size does not fit all" though its reference is toward how "implementation efforts must be able to adapt to state and local conditions" and consideration of "diversity and multicultural makeup of the various communities we seek to serve" ("Guiding Principles & Position Statement") without any further description or discussion about the learner or her/his diverse needs, expectations, values, practices, or special needs behavior. Hill (2012) identified select strengths and opportunities for school librarians serving students with special needs in Central New York State, finding that the analysis of the feedback collected from the 43 respondents via an electronic survey revealed that they showed some strength in specific areas such as their knowledge levels, use of resources, instructional accommodations, and collaboration with special educators. The *Competencies for Librarians Serving Children in Public Libraries* published by the Association for Library Service to Children (2009), a division of the American Library Association, identifies "patrons with special needs as a basis for designing and implementing services following the Americans with Disabilities Act (ADA) and state and local regulations where appropriate" as one important skill related to the "Knowledge of the Client Group" that library staff should gain through specialized coursework in undergraduate and graduate study, on-the-job training, and/or continuing education opportunities, without specifying the "hows" of such a skill as it may be implemented in practice or associated details.

In the face of the marginalizing conditions faced by the CSN in the SCA environment and rural libraries, and limited research on applicable standards of practice, details, or operationalization information available for library service design, how do rural SCA libraries experience (and respond to) children with special information needs, information uses, and information seeking behaviors? What efforts can they make to more effectively meet the expectations of this disenfranchised group in their rural library environments? This chapter shares qualitative data collected from 31 SCA rural librarians via phone interviews and a web-based survey about: (1) The most important information needs/wants of the CSN in the SCA rural libraries; (2) The most important information resources and services that the CSN seek/use in the SCA rural libraries; (3) Extent of perceived need for effective library services for the CSN in rural areas; (4) Ways that the SCA rural libraries can improve to better serve the CSN in their local communities.

The significance of the research reported in this chapter lies in its first-time effort to understand the information needs and information uses of the CSN in the SCA rural library environments from the perspective of a rural librarian immersed in an American society that perceives a parochial work setting in the region (Cash, 1991; Cobb, 2007; Wyatt-Brown, 2008) with its limited availability of resources and technology applications (Fritsch & Gallimore, 2007; Mehra et al., 2012a, 2012b) in a religiously and politically conservative climate with its often hostile cultural conditions toward anyone who is different (Fisher & Smith, 2012; Ludke & Obermiller, 2012). Moreover, the stereotyping and marginalizing of the "South" and of the SCA region has been long documented (Cooper & Terrill, 2009; Escott, Goldfield, McMillen, & Turner, 1999) and this research presents data that challenges such notions in its documentation of positive and meaningful efforts that rural librarians suggest should be made to improve the conditions experienced by the CSN in this region.

6.3. Research Questions

This study addressed the following questions:

1) What are the most important information needs/wants of the CSN in the SCA rural libraries?
2) What are the most important information resources and services that the CSN seek/use in the SCA rural libraries?
3) What is the extent of perceived need for effective services to meet the needs of the CSN in the SCA rural libraries?
4) What are the ways that the SCA rural libraries can improve to better serve the CSN in rural communities?

6.4. Theoretical Framework

Several aspects are worthy of attention when placing this research on the perspectives of rural librarians about the information needs and information uses of the CSN in the context of a framework or theories of information behavior.

First, the research explores connections between information behavior theory, library practice, and library service design, an approach that has been limited in past work that has compartmentalized these areas as separate and unrelated domains of knowledge (Crowley, 2004; Winston, 2002). It draws implications from an analysis of select information behavior constructs and explores its application on the conceptualization and construction of service design, and in the process, helps bridge connections between the two (Case, 2012; Savolainen, 2008). For example, Glanz, Rimer, and Viswanath (2008) explored the impact of health behavior theories in areas as diverse as health communication, e-health, health promotion and social marketing, health service evaluation and assessment, and health practices in culturally diverse communities, on the design and development of health service education curricula and practice at individual, interpersonal, and community and group levels.

From the earliest time of "use studies" (Davis & Bailey, 1964) information behavior and information seeking research has recognized information needs and information uses as important components (Menzel, 1966) of "people's interaction with information" (i.e., information behavior) (Bates, 2010, p. 2387) since often in direct and/or indirect response to their information *needs* people *behave/seek/search* for information in a particular manner to effectively *use* it for various purposes (Bates, 1989; Belkin, Oddy, & Brooks, 1982; Kuhlthau, 1991; Wilson, 1981). Dervin (1992) has clearly articulated these connections in her triangulated "situation/gap/use" framework (Mehra, Bishop, & Bazzell, 2000): this research applies that understanding in a new direction in its exploration of the existing information needs and uses of the CSN (i.e., the select information behavior constructs representing the associated characteristics shaping the situation experienced by members in the group) to propose suggestions for the design and development of effective library services. The goal is to eventually address the gaps that have emerged in not meeting the situational information needs of the CSN user community, and thereby, improve the existing conditions of their limited use of the available library and information services in the rural settings.

Second, the research extends the approach of "linking theories to action" (Wilson, 2005, p. 35) by documenting an analysis of select information behavior of a particular marginalized group in order to identify user-centered strategies and suggestions (the proposed action component) that can improve library services for the CSN population in the SCA rural areas. It furthers an understanding of *user-centered design* as an example of metatheory and its "does it work?" engineering question goes beyond that described by Bates (2005) in terms of "Does it work so well that people can concentrate on what they are doing rather than on operating the system or device?" (p. 14); this research presents user-centered design in its broader focus on not just technological systems and applications, but, to identify improvements in the entirety of library services and experiences (including technology-related) based on an analysis of select information behavior of a population that has traditionally been overlooked in past design processes (Deisinger, Burkhardt, & Wahlberg, 2012; Khare & Fletcher, 2010). The focus on user-centered improvements and changes to existing rural library services based on the select information behavior analysis for an under-served group in this research represents another example of a metatheory (as identified by Bates, 2005), namely, a *critical theory* approach founded upon critique "to liberate human beings from the circumstances that enslave them" (Horkheimer, 1982, p. 244) that is "adequate only if it meets three criteria: it must be explanatory, practical, and normative, all at the same time. That is, it must explain what is wrong with current social reality, identify the actors to change it, and provide both clear norms for criticism and achievable practical goals for social transformation" (Bohman, 2012, para. 3). Further, this research is informed by critical theory as it (Leckie, Given, & Buschman, 2010; Mehra, 2007; Mehra & Bishop, 2007): (1) involves a reflective process to question, scrutinize, and propose changes to traditional understandings and existing values, practices, ideological frameworks, and processes (Geuss, 1981; Habermas, 1993; McCarthy & Hoy, 1994); (2) recognizes the perspectives of the under-represented in order to "do justice to a diversity of socially defined perspectives while providing a grounding for the evaluation of controversial problems" (Endres, 1996, p. 24). Representing the voices of disenfranchised CSN users in this research becomes "the fact of pluralism" and an effort, limited and scaled as it is, to identify an important stakeholder point of view in the diversity of experiences in a modern society that is directly relevant to the political order because its conditions "profoundly affect the requirements of a workable conception of justice" (Rawls, 1999, p. 424). This research provides evidence-based analysis (Rycroft-Malone & Bucknall, 2010) of select information behavior patterns and experiences observed of a group of users "left out" in past design efforts (Mehra, Merkel, & Bishop, 2004; Smith, 2008) in order to develop and implement library services and information practices that can become more conducive of use (Johnston & Carrico, 1988) for the children in this area who are currently getting overlooked in having their information needs met in an adequate manner (Druin, 2005; Johnson, 2007; Schenk, 2005).

Third, both the qualitative and quantitative datasets and resulting analysis about the CSN patrons collected in this research and its impact on the design of rural library services presents the library institution and its services as a "socio-technical system" that connects "networks of technology, information, documents, people, and practices" and finds "multidisciplinary ways of talking about heterogeneity: of talking, at the same time, of social and technical relations even-handedly without putting one or the other in a black box whose contents we agree not to explore" (Van House, Bishop, & Buttenfield, 2003, p. 1). This includes the "socio" or human component (e.g., the CSN, parents/teachers of the CSN, library staff), the newer, emerging technologies and their electronic library applications, the traditional print-based services, the rural library programming and policies, as well as the resulting human–computer–service interactions beyond those seen in past LIS research (Ackerman, 2000; Bates, 2002; Carroll, 2002; Marchionini, 2005; Rogers, 2004).

Lastly, this research focuses on the perspectives of rural library practitioners and not on direct feedback gathered from the CSN. The role of mediators (i.e., parents, teachers, therapists, and family volunteers), who are seen as "information seeking proxies" and valid and reliable information sources about the CSN and their information landscape, is only recently been recognized (Bilal, 2010, p. 42). This research adds to the list of mediators to include feedback about the CSN from library professionals embedded in rural work environments. The psychological, social, and environmental difficulties experienced by the CSN that create challenges in their communication and interactions with others necessitates the intervention and information gathering from mediators (library professionals) about their behaviors (Reiff & Tippins, 2004; Yau, 2012). The concept of information mediaries defined as a lay-person who seeks information in a non-professional (i.e., informal capacity) or professional setting (i.e., a formal association) "on behalf (or because) of others without necessarily being asked to do so, or engaging in follow-up" (Fisher & Abrahamson, 2007, Background Literature section, para. 1) includes the rural librarians experiencing a range of work-related behaviors and expected roles that directly/indirectly involve seeking information on behalf of the CSN and/or their mediators (Wathen, Wyatt, & Harris, 2008). The role of the librarian as an information intermediary has been acknowledged in past research (White, 1992) though gathering feedback from this group of information professionals in the SCA work context of the rural library environment becomes all the more relevant in today's marginalizing conditions experienced in the region (Mehra, Black, Singh, & Nolt, 2011b) while also highlighting their role as a "connecting link between information seekers and the resources that provide answers to their questions" (Katz, 1992, p. 5).

Moreover, this focus on the perspectives of rural library practitioners embedded in the everyday workplace practices experienced in rural library settings follows Davenport and Cronin's (1998) call for library and information science workplace studies to examine "the world of work *per se,* not […] 'information seeking,' 'information needs,' information uses,' and 'information use environments'" (p. 266); in this research the latter are explored not for their own sake but in the context of integrating information behavior analysis to improve service design in the rural library work settings. Additionally, the rationale for the methodology of gathering data about the needs and uses of the CSN from the librarians who serve them is based on the fact that the librarians have the closest interactions with the information services designed for these patrons and any suggestions for service improvements should include this group of professionals and some level of analysis of their feedback. It may identify and conceptualize an extended role of the rural librarian as a facilitator (Chang & Wu, 2012; Currie, 2000; Eldredge, 2004) on behalf of the CSN easing the process of meeting their information needs via effectively interpreting and analyzing their information seeking behaviors and information use.

6.5. Research Methods

This study employed a mixed method of quantitative and qualitative research design using interviews (qualitative) and survey questionnaire (quantitative). Initially, semi-structured phone interviews lasting 45–60 minutes with five staff members working in Tennessee's rural libraries provided feedback from a narrow and focused sample. Participants were elicited via the author's personal social networks and provided basic information about the CSN in their library/community, their awareness of how CSN seek/use information in their libraries, and what programs/services they provided to meet the expectations/wants of this traditionally underserved population. Based on the interview feedback, a self-administered web-based survey consisting of 11 open-ended questions (similar to those used during the phone interviews) was developed (see Appendix 6.A).

Use of phone interviews and web-based survey helped generate complementary datasets that were both qualitative in nature. The former provided an initial glimpse into the complexity of experienced realities via a detailed discussion of issues and the latter identified themes that became instrumental in understanding exploratory patterns and trends. Using similar questions during both data collection methods allowed for gathering valid datasets that provided for appropriate comparisons and juxtaposition. Specific examples and narrative voices presented in the form of quotations in this chapter were selected from the transcriptions of the phone interviews and the open-ended feedback collected from the survey.

6.5.1. Population and Sample

The population size consisted of the total number of members of select electronic mailing lists of the five SCA state library networks and library associations in Georgia, North Carolina, South Carolina, Tennessee, and Virginia. There are no exact numbers of this total membership though they account for more than 300 SCA rural librarians of which 31 participated in the study. Those who agreed to participate were contacted via email and individual telephone interviews were scheduled. Five librarians participated in the interviews. The answers to the questions posed during the interviews (nearly the same as those included in the survey) were captured by using written notes.

Twenty-six rural librarians agreed to participate in the study. They were directed to the link of the web-based survey hosted on a secure password-protected server at the author's institution.

6.5.2. Instrument

The survey instrument (Appendix 6.A) included 11 questions. It focused on gathering data about the following: the type of library (of the participant) and its geographical location; most important information needs/wants of the CSN in the participant's library/community; critical challenges facing the CSN in the library/community; common types of information (resources and services) that the CSN seek/use in the library; effectiveness of the participants' library in meeting the needs and/or wants of the CSN; and ways that their library can improve to better serve the CSN in the SCA rural libraries.

The questionnaire was tested with five participants and the average time for completing it was 30 minutes. The testing of the questionnaire allowed for refining the questions. The final version of the questionnaire was used to collect data using a web-based survey.

This study followed appropriate ethical procedures and protocols for research involving human subjects that were approved by the institutional review board at the author's place of work. Both the participants in the phone interview and respondents to the web-based survey completed an informed consent form prior to data collection — the interview participants received and completed the form via email while the survey respondents read the informed consent message at the beginning of the survey, prior to the presentation of its content, and granted permission to participate. Research involvement was voluntary, and both participants and respondents were free to drop out of the study anytime without any penalty. No personally identifiable information was requested in the web-based survey and even though the researcher knew the identity of the interview participants they all were insured confidentiality regarding what they individually shared during the research. No compensation was offered for involvement in the study that was expected to pose minimal risks to the human subjects.

Even though this chapter is not based on a methods-focused study, it is important to note that it applies a data collection method of a web-based survey that has traditionally been used to collect quantitative datasets (Barrios, 2011; Cook, Heath, & Thompson, 2000) to gather qualitative feedback. Mixed method strategies were also applied in the use of both phone interviews, a qualitative method of data collection (Berg, 2008; Sturges & Hanrahan, 2004), with a web-based survey. Use of mixed methods or a combination of the two methods in the same research (Creswell, 2009) provided a holistic understanding of the context of study by generating complementary datasets that compensated for the weaknesses of each method when used independently (Creswell & Clark, 2007; Tashakkori & Teddlie, 2003).

6.6. Data Analysis

Data analysis of the feedback collected via the web-based survey involved applying a "mixed methods" approach in using content analysis that has traditionally been employed in qualitative research (Glaser, 1965; Holsti, 1969; Neuendorf, 2002) to generate quantitative representation of response counts for the themes identified for each question (listed above). This helped to generate findings that can be appreciated for both their quantitative and qualitative attributes (Mertens, 2010).

The patterns and trends in respondents' responses to the web-based survey were documented as themes that were recorded quantitatively as response counts to the four research questions addressed in this study. Several respondents provided more than one response to the various questions that were listed in the survey. Response counts were generated based on content analysis of open-ended feedback for emerging themes that resulted in practical user-centered suggestions for positive change in delivering effective library services for the CSN in the SCA region.

6.7. Findings

Table 6.1 identifies the geographical state of rural libraries where all participants worked. These included those who were interviewed by phone and those who responded to the web-based survey. Some of the libraries (e.g., in Knoxville) were located in semi-urban settings or on the outskirts of the city boundaries, yet they provided some focused services that were especially for rural clients and/or had a majority of patrons who resided in rural areas. For the purpose of distinguishing, the term "participant(s)" is used while referring to those individuals who were interviewed during this

Table 6.1: The geographical state of the SCA rural libraries where the research subjects worked.

Geographical state	No. of subjects (*n*) and percentage
Tennessee	13 (41.94%)
Virginia	6 (19.36%)
Georgia	4 (12.90%)
North Carolina	4 (12.90%)
South Carolina	4 (12.90%)
TOTAL	31 (100%)

research and the word "respondent(s)" is utilized to identify those who shared their responses via the web-based survey.

In terms of the types of rural libraries where subjects worked, there were 18 librarians working in public libraries, 10 librarians in school libraries, and three librarians in academic libraries. Of these, two participants each in public libraries and school libraries were interviewed, while one participant working in an academic library was interviewed. All five participants interviewed were working on their master's degree in library and information science while out of the 21 survey respondents' who identified their educational and professional qualifications, seven had their master's degree in library and information science with an additional two who were working on their master's degree at the time of data collection, six had a master's degree in other disciplines (four in education and one each in business administration and history), three had only a bachelor's degree, and three did not have an undergraduate degree. All the five interview participants had worked more than three years in a rural library and their current job titles included branch manager, circulation clerk, library director, reference librarian, and technology coordinator. Twenty out of the 26 survey respondents identified their length of work and current job titles in rural libraries. Of these, four respondents had worked in a rural library for more than ten years, eight had worked in a rural library for 5–10 years, five had worked in a rural library for at least two years and less than five years, and three respondents had worked in a rural library for less than two years. Their job titles included assistant directors (2), branch managers (2), community librarians (2), genealogist (1), information services supervisor (1), librarians (4), library clerks (4), library directors (2), medical and health librarian (1), and reference librarian (1).

Survey respondents provided a range of responses in various formats while responding to the question of how many and how often the CSN used their library. Table 6.2 summarizes the respondents' feedback collected

Table 6.2: Respondent feedback collected from the web-based survey about how many and how often the CSN used the SCA rural libraries.

Categories	Respondent responses	No. of respondents (n) and percentage
Based on daily encounters	None per day	1 (3.85%)
	25–50 per day	3 (11.54%)
	50–75 per day	4 (15.38%)
Based on weekly encounters	15–20 per week	2 (7.69%)
	20–25 per week	6 (23.07%)
	25–50 per week	4 (15.38%)
	>200 per week	2 (7.69%)
Based on monthly encounters	1–5 per month	2 (7.69%)
Based on yearly encounters	75–100 sporadically per year	2 (7.69%)
	TOTAL	26 (100%)

Note: The above percentages were rounded up for the individual categories, hence do not add to 100.

from the web-based survey about how many CSN used the SCA rural libraries in terms of categories of daily, weekly, monthly, and yearly encounters. A majority of respondents of the web-based survey ($n = 14$, 53.85%) reported on weekly encounters with the CSN in their rural libraries.

Tables 6.2–6.4 report on the results from the 26 survey respondents.

Both the interview participants and the respondents to the web-based survey identified measurement problems related to the kind and form of special needs of the children and youth patrons that they experienced in their rural libraries. Two interview participants mentioned how some special needs (e.g., mild cerebral palsy, autism) are not readily visible. Interview participants discussed how it was difficult to identify their patrons in the CSN category since the CSN were not necessarily identified as "special needs" to the librarians. One interview participant did not know how many CSN used her library. As the following interview participant stated:

> Our library does not keep any statistics concerning special needs youth information behavior, so any information I have is based on assumptions that the child may have special needs, except for a few isolated instances where a parent or caretaker has specially identified the child as special needs and asked for help on the child's behalf.

Another interview participant excellently summarized:

> I work in an elementary school and there are approximately 520 students in my school from grades K-5. I do not know the percentage of those considered with special needs. But we have special "levels" for lack of a better description. There are probably 20 students who are considered learning disabled in one way or several who spend the majority of the school day in an extended resources classroom. There are probably up to 70 other students with lesser disabilities that are served in resource class for part of the day.

Responses to qualitative data collected from survey respondents are reported in the context of the research questions posed.

RQ1: *What are the most important information needs of the CSN in the SCA rural libraries?*

Based on content analysis of the open-ended feedback respondents shared via the web-based survey, 56 different response counts were recorded for this question. Three themes emerged from the application of the content analysis process and data coding. First, the CSN have very specific information needs (as expressed in their behaviors) that have to be acknowledged in the SCA rural libraries. This theme received the highest response count of 22 (39.29%) based on the feedback provided by the respondents. Specific information behaviors of the CSN they noted included: inability of the CSN to handle structure, easily distracted by library displays, less ability to find and understand information materials, difficulty to communicate needs to staff, inability to read or reading levels below peer levels, inability to write, short attention spans, limited motivation to "look" for answers, disinterested in topics assigned for school homework, tending to get "stuck" on one particular topic while looking for items, unwilling to accept alternative options, keeping materials checked for extended periods, unable to use OPACs, often served indirectly by intermediaries (e.g., teachers, parents), and poor traditional information skills (e.g., analysis of their own information needs, information seeking, information searching, critical reflection).

Second, the SCA rural libraries have to provide special services for meeting the majority of information needs of the CSN that are unmet in their local and regional communities. This was identified as the second most important theme with a response count of 20 (35.71%) based on the feedback provided by the research respondents. Special services noted by the respondents included: more audio books/adaptive technology, computer programming to read to the CSN, appropriate entertainment materials (e.g., DVDs, fun resources), basic skill materials for the CSN, special programming with direct interactions, more hi/lo books that are not babyish yet straight to the point, books that have been made into play-a-ways and with interesting images, as well as available books on different reading levels. This theme also included greater special physical space requirements that are needed in the SCA rural libraries; it received a response count of two (3.57%). Specific examples of special physical space requirements for the CSN mentioned doors and obstacles that needed to be manipulated to accommodate the CSN and several of the CSN did not physically know how to operate the computer. The issue about the limited physical space requirements at the library was also discussed by the five interviewees.

Third, the SCA rural librarians themselves have to individually develop special attention in meeting the majority of the information needs of the CSN that are currently being unmet in the local and regional communities. This theme had the response count of 14 (25%) based on the respondents' feedback. The focus of aspects suggested by respondents in this category required the SCA rural librarians pay attention individually to their own behavior (as compared to what strategies and services their institutions could develop as identified in the above theme). Such behavioral modifications required of the SCA rural librarians at an individual level included the following:

- Extra care needed to work with the CSN;
- Need to hand the CSN materials such as movies and books instead of directing them to find the materials on their own;
- Instructions need to be simple and short since the CSN require more attention in locating resources and finding websites;
- Better communication efforts are required to interact with the CSN;
- Extra strategies are required to keep the attention of the CSN;
- More patience and identification of shortcuts needed;
- Need for giving quick answers, where to find "easy" books, and efforts to better understand what the CSN are saying.

The information needs of the CSN in the SCA rural library and community and the challenges the respondents reported are shown in Table 6.3. Based on content analysis, 79 different response counts were recorded for challenges experienced by the CSN in the rural communities. These included: a lack of appropriate information support services to meet the needs of the CSN in the SCA rural libraries, of which, a majority and particular forms are not getting met; inadequate use of communication channels and the development of time-activity services; limited personal and social support; few trained professional staff and mentors; moderate to high community tolerance; economic shortcomings and budget restraints; application of

Table 6.3: Respondents' feedback collected from the web-based survey about the challenges the CSN faced in the SCA rural library and community.

Challenge	**Response count/ percentage**	**Examples**
Lack of appropriate information, support, resources, and accessible materials	19 (24.05%)	Few hi/lo non-babyish books that cover relevant content; few adaptive technology (touch screen, listening station); lack of friendly programming; few alternative media (audio books).
Particular forms of special needs not being met and traits unacknowledged	15 (18.99%)	No skills to identify ADHD, Autism, Asperger Syndrome, patron with disabilities, etc.; low reading ability and comprehension (e.g., inability to garnish information from reading).
Lack of appropriate communication channels, time, and activities	9 (11.39%)	Productive activities for all ages missing; CSN inability to communicate with others and use tech to communicate; too much unoccupied, unstructured time (especially during summer) leads to loss of skills acquired during school year; limited time for accessing library resources (due to over-scheduled core class time).
Personal and social support lacking	8 (10.12%)	Parent involvement missing; lack of transportation; organized support to assist CSN to fully integrate into society missing; parents reluctant to bring CSN to public places; socially, families in crises and CSN living with grandparents, non-parents; parents on drugs or in jail; few materials to meet needs of parents.

Table 6.3: (*Continued*)

Challenge	**Response count/ percentage**	**Examples**
Limited professional staff and mentors	7 (8.86%)	Limited staff awareness about the needs of CSN.
Community intolerance	6 (7.6%)	Lack of positive adult attitudes, acceptance, and community understanding; prejudice against kids looking and behaving different.
Economic limitations and budget restraints	6 (7.6%)	No financial support of CSN families; not enough money in library to buy play-a-things etc. for CSN.
Universal spatial design standards missing	5 (6.33%)	Need wider spaces in shelving to accommodate wheelchairs.
Lack of tailored specialized support services	4 (5.06%)	Not enough service providers to help parents identify issues and solve problems; lack of housing and employment opportunities for CSN.
TOTAL	79 (100%)	

universal spatial design standards missing; and, lack of uniquely tailored and specialized information support services.

RQ2: *What are the most important information resources and services that the CSN seek/use in the SCA rural libraries?*

Fifty-three different response counts were recorded in response to this question. The respondents ranked the physical materials and collections as the most important resources and services that the CSN sought and used in the SCA rural libraries with 31 response counts (58.49%). These included materials specifically created and developed for the CSN based on particular characteristics associated with: traits/genre/type (e.g., current and new, dictionaries and encyclopedias, easy to read/listen/find materials, fun resources, and interactive novelty and non-fiction resources); topic-based (e.g., animals, basic skills, specific topics of interest such as dragons and pirates); and format (e.g., books, companion audio books, DVDs and videos of films, magazines, and story-telling resources). Additionally, catalogs and programs for the CSN, television presentation areas, and development of a Parent Resource Center were also identified as important resources and services needed in the physical library. Online and electronic resources (technology-based) were identified as the next most important resources and services that the CSN sought and used in the SCA rural libraries with 11 response counts (20.76%). These included computers with adaptive technology, appropriate computer games, easy to use websites, game cheats, homework help for the CSN, and culturally relevant Internet services and online library catalogs for the CSN. Lastly, though not least, specific information resources for the population were identified as the next most important resources and services that the CSN sought and used in the SCA rural libraries with nine response counts (16.98%). Such resources and services were categorized based on: audience (CSN, parents), functional domains (entertainment, socializing), purposes of use (recreational reading, school report-writing), topics (animals, disabilities, sports, transportation), and type (local, non-local).

RQ3: *What is the extent of perceived need for effective services to meet the needs of the CSN in the SCA rural libraries?*

Table 6.4 summarizes the extent of perceived need for effective services to meet the needs of the CSN in the SCA rural libraries based on feedback provided by the survey respondents.

Based on the five-point scale (very effective, effective, neutral, ineffective, very ineffective) used, 12 (46.16%) believed that their libraries were effective in meeting the needs of the CSN in the SCA region. None of the respondents selected "very effective" or "very ineffective." This finding was

Table 6.4: Extent of perceived need for effective rural library services for the CSN in the SCA region.

How effective is your library?	No. of respondents (*n*) and percentage
Effective	12 (46.16%)
Neutral	8 (30.77%)
Ineffective	5 (23.08%)
TOTAL	26 (100%)

Note: One respondent did not provide feedback to this question.

somewhat puzzling when viewed along with the lengthy descriptions and detailed feedback the respondents described regarding gaps and challenges experienced by the CSN in their rural libraries and communities, and given the improvements they suggested to make their rural libraries more responsive to the CSN and their needs and expectations.

The complexity and difficulties in providing appropriate resources and services for the CSN in the SCA region was aptly described by one interview participant: "This library meets ADA requirements for physical access. Challenges come in understanding what the child might be saying, or in interpretation of the child's needs … served indirectly as their teachers, librarians, and parents use the collection and the web page more … we have targeted this group for improvement in developing their information skills as well as providing more accessible materials … we could do more to reach out to the autistic community. They would come if they knew staff were accommodating and informed about their needs."

RQ4: *What are the ways that the SCA rural libraries can improve to better serve the CSN in their communities?*

Fifty-seven different response counts were documented for ways that the respondents' libraries could improve to better serve the CSN in the SCA region. This feedback, in conjunction with the responses to the other questions, helped draw implications of relevance from the research findings for the SCA rural libraries to deliver more effective services for the CSN in their regions. It helped identify practical user-centered suggestions for positive change that are discussed in the next section. The call for adopting user-centered services requires greater involvement and participation of the CSN and their representatives (e.g., parents, teachers) in the planning, design, delivery, implementation, and operationalization of services to make them more effective in meeting the needs/wants of the CSN in the SCA rural communities.

6.8. Discussion

Based on the findings of this study, the key areas in developing and implementing practical user-centered improvements for effective rural library services for the CSN in the SCA region include:

- Staff development and training;
- Collections and services;
- Programming and events planning;
- Physical resources and appropriate policies and implementation;
- Partnerships and community involvement;
- Alternative and creative revenue streams.

Staff development and training was identified as most important component in user-centered services for the CSN in the SCA rural libraries with the highest response count of 19 (33.33%) based on feedback provided by the research respondents. Specific strategies suggested by respondents include:

- Develop training and education of professionals to become aware of the particular forms of special needs and associated characteristics;
- Show the CSN patrons extra and personal attention and care;
- Learn to serve the CSN patrons and communicate with them and help parents;
- Patience, awareness, and understanding of their needs is required;
- Treat every person with respect and courtesy;
- Hire a special education teacher/librarian and hire welcoming and supportive staff.

The respondents recognized both collections and services, on the one hand, and programming and events for the CSN, on the other, as important user-centered components for the CSN in the SCA rural libraries with a respective response count each of 10 (17.54%). These included the need for:

- Developing culturally appropriate and accessible print and electronic materials based on feedback from parents and providers and by understanding of their information needs/wants, barriers and challenges, and information behaviors/seeking/uses;
- Providing alternate media options;
- Identifying resources for parents' audio needs and hi/lo materials for their CSN;
- Listening to the children's requests for proposing special book clubs for the CSN.

Suggestions for programming and events for the CSN included: Inviting them to many events; advertising and attracting the CSN via innovative publicity efforts; supporting the development of a welcoming environment; making inclusion a key strategy in all activities; and, making it easy to use the library at no cost.

Physical resources, appropriate policies, and their implementation were the next important user-centered efforts that were needed for the CSN identified by the respondents with eight response counts (14.04%). This involved flexibility in policies formulation and operationalization and included: applying universal spatial design standards by observing and understanding the behaviors of the population; making the facility fully accessible; replacing unusable furniture; and, making the environment physically comfortable (e.g., lighting, colors, sound).

Partnerships, collaborations, and community involvement were also considered important with seven response counts (12.28%). Efforts identified by the respondents included: encouraging parents to get involved; building stronger ties with K-12 schools; promoting adult usage of library to get the CSN involved; communicating with parents; encouraging class visits; and, identifying other organizations to partner with.

Pursuing alternate and creative revenue streams were the last component identified by research participants with three response counts (5.26%). This included: increasing budgets for the CSN services; looking for grants for needed materials; and, using book fair and parent-teacher organization funds to sponsor reading contests, buying medals, prizes, and books, etc.

6.9. Conclusion

Exploratory evidence collected from the participants/respondents suggests that there are a significant number of the CSN with different kinds and levels of "special needs" who are using the SCA rural library services, though no systematic documentation had been made of their information behaviors, or of the effectiveness of library services they used to meet their needs. Future research should address this gap and respond to the urgent need to develop systematic data collection efforts about the CSN in the SCA rural libraries. This should include triangulation efforts to collect data from rural librarians alongside data from mediators (e.g., parents or caregivers of the CSNs, classroom teachers, special education teachers, and the CSNs themselves).

Much education and training is needed amongst library professionals and the lay community to address ignorance and dispel stereotypes in order to develop a better understanding of the CSN in the SCA region (Allen, 2008). Physical resources and print collections for the CSN are still the focus of the limited efforts and few resources available in the SCA region and there is also a need to develop the yet untapped availability and use of online and other digital tools and resources. Additionally, it is important to create culturally appropriate resources and services for intermediaries (e.g., parents) since they play a major role in mediating the everyday lives of the CSN in the SCA rural libraries. As one research respondent stated: "We have had parents also ask for required reading list books on audio for the middle or high school students who are dyslexic or have other reading disabilities, but, again, our interaction is with the adult instead of the child."

The findings of this study served as a basis for identifying some practical improvements to library service design based on the rural librarians' viewpoints about the information needs of the CSN in rural settings. Future research should extend these findings to include other geographical settings and library environments to enrich our understanding of the effective services provided for the CSN in different regions. In addition, future research should consider exploration of the CSN information needs through their own lenses, and explore their information seeking behaviors in using varied digital tools.

References

Ackerman, M. S. (2000). The intellectual challenge of CSCW: The gap between social requirements and technical feasibility. *Human-Computer Interaction*, *15*(2–3), 179–203.

Allen, K. L. (2008). *The school library media program and special education programs*. Unpublished master's thesis, University of North Carolina, Chapel Hill. Retrieved from http://dc.lib.unc.edu/cdm/singleitem/collection/s_papers/id/1117. Accessed on July 28, 2012.

Allen, K. L., & Hughes-Hassell, S. (2010). Meeting the needs of students with disabilities. *School Library Monthly*, *27*(1), 52−54.

American Association of School Librarians. (2007). *Standards for the 21st century learner*. Chicago, IL: American Association of School Librarians. Retrieved from http://www.ala.org/aasl/sites/ala.org.aasl/files/content/guidelinesandstandards/learningstandards/AASL_LearningStandards.pdf. Accessed on October 20, 2013.

American Association of School Librarians. (2008). *Learning4Life: A national plan for implementation for the 21st century learner and empowering learners: Guidelines for school library programs*. Chicago, IL: American Association of School Librarians. Retrieved from http://www.ala.org/aasl/sites/ala.org.aasl/files/content/guidelinesandstandards/learning4life/document/l4lplan.pdf. Accessed on October 20, 2013.

American Library Association. (2004). *The American Library Association Task Force on Rural School, Tribal and Public Libraries: Final report to the Council of the American Library Association*. Chicago, IL: American Library Association. Retrieved from http://www.ala.org/ala/aboutala/offices/olos/outreachresource/docs/rural tf_finalrpt.pdf. Accessed on March 10, 2010.

American Library Association Office for Literacy and Outreach Services. (2011). *The small but powerful guide to winning big support for your rural library*. Chicago, IL: American Library Association. Retrieved from http://www.ala.org/offices/sites/ala.org.offices/files/content/olos/toolkits/rural/2011RuralWeb_FINAL.pdf. Accessed on March 10, 2012.

Appalachian Regional Commission. (1974). The new Appalachian subregions and their development strategies. *Appalachia, a Journal of the Appalachian Regional Commission*, *8*, 11–27.

Appalachian Regional Commission. (2004). *Appalachia: Turning assets into opportunities*. Washington, DC: Appalachian Regional Commission. Retrieved from http://www.arc.gov/images/newsroom/publications/assets/assets.pdf. Accessed on March 10, 2010.

Appalachian Regional Commission. (2008). *Counties in Appalachia*. Washington, DC: Appalachian Regional Commission. Retrieved from http://www.arc.gov/counties. Accessed on March 10, 2010.

Appalachian Regional Commission. (2010). *Moving Appalachia forward: Appalachian Regional Commission strategic plan 2011–2016*. Washington, DC: Appalachian Regional Commission. Retrieved from http://www.arc.gov/images/newsroom/publications/sp/ARCStrategicPlan2011-2016.pdf. Accessed on March 10, 2011.

Appalachian Regional Commission. (2013). *County economic status and number of distressed areas in Appalachian Tennessee, Fiscal Year 2014*. Retrieved from http://www.arc.gov/images/appregion/economic_statusFY2014/County EconomicStatusandDistressAreasFY2014Tennessee.pdf. Accessed on October 20, 2013.

Association for Library Service to Children. (2009). *Competencies for librarians serving children in public libraries*. Chicago, IL: American Library Association. Retrieved from http://www.ala.org/alsc/edcareeers/alsccorecomps. Accessed on October 10, 2013.

Bardwell, G., Morton, C., Chester, A., Pancoska, P., Buch, S., Cecchetti, A., … Branch, R. A. (2009). Feasibility of adolescents to conduct community-based participatory research on obesity and diabetes in rural Appalachia. *Clinical and Translational Science*, *2*(5), 340–349.

Barrios, M. (2011). Response rates and data quality in web and mail surveys administered to PhD holders. *Social Science Computer Review*, *29*, 208–220.

Bates, M. J. (1989). The design of browsing and berrypicking techniques for the online search interface. *Online Review*, *13*, 407–424.

Bates, M. J. (2002). The cascade of interactions in the digital library interface. *Information Processing and Management*, *38*, 381–400.

Bates, M. J. (2005). An introduction to metatheories, theories, and models. In K. E. Fisher, S. Erdelez, & L. McKechnie (Eds.), *Theories of information behavior* (pp. 1–24). Medford, NJ: Information Today.

Bates, M. J. (2010). Information behavior. In M. J. Bates & M. N. Maack (Eds.), *Encyclopedia of library and information sciences* (3rd ed., Vol. 3, pp. 2381–2391). New York, NY: CRC Press.

Belkin, N. J., Oddy, R. N., & Brooks, H. M. (1982). ASK for information retrieval: Part I. Background and theory. *Journal of Documentation*, *38*(2), 61–71.

Berg, B. L. (2008). *Qualitative research methods for the social sciences* (7th ed.). Boston, MA: Allyn & Bacon.

Bilal, D. (2010, July 19–23). The mediated information needs of children on the Autism Spectrum Disorder (ASD). *Proceedings of the 31st ACM SIGIR workshop on Accessible Search Systems*, Geneva, Switzerland (pp. 42–49). Retrieved from http://personal.cis.strath.ac.uk/~ir/accessiblesearch/final_proceedings.pdf#page=46. Accessed on January 11, 2013.

Black, D. A., Mather, M., & Sanders, S. G. (2007). *Standards of living in Appalachia, 1960 to 2000*. Washington, DC: Appalachian Regional Commission. Retrieved from http://www.arc.gov/images/reports/2007/standardsliving/Standards_Living_Appalachia.pdf. Accessed on November 8, 2008.

Bohman, J. (2012). Critical theory. In E. N. Zalta (Ed.), *The Stanford encyclopedia of philosophy* (Spring 2012 ed.). Stanford, CA: Metaphysics Research Lab, Stanford University. Retrieved from http://plato.stanford.edu/archives/spr2012/entries/critical-theory/. Accessed on January 12, 2013.

Brind'Amour, C. (2010). Special education students and the school media center. *Current Studies in Librarianship*, *30*(1–2), 49–67.

Bush, W. S. (2003). *Bridging the gap between culture and mathematics: The Appalachian perspective*. Athens, GA: Appalachian Collaborative Center for Learning, Assessment, and Instruction in Mathematics, Ohio State University.

Carroll, J. M. (2002). *Human-computer interaction in the new millennium*. New York, NY: ACM Press.

Case, D. O. (2012). *Looking for information: A survey of research on information seeking, needs, and behavior* (3rd ed.). Library and Information Science. Bingley, UK: Emerald Group Publishing Limited.

Cash, W. J. (1991). *The mind of the South*. New York, NY: Vintage Books.

Chang, C. L., & Wu, M. M. (2012). Integrating service learning into teaching information literacy: The librarian as designer and facilitator for information literacy instruction. In R. Gwyer, R. Stubbings, & G. Walton (Eds.), *The road to information literacy: Librarians as facilitators of learning* (pp. 33–48). Berlin, Germany: Walter de Gruyter.

Children's Defense Fund. (2011). *The state of America's children 2011*. Washington, DC: Children's Defense Fund. Retrieved from http://www.childrensdefense.org/child-research-data-publications/data/state-of-americas-children-2011-report.html. Accessed on October 20, 2013.

Cobb, J. C. (2007). *Away down south: A history of Southern identity*. Oxford, UK: Oxford University Press.

Cook, C., Heath, F., & Thompson, R. L. (2000). A meta-analysis of response rates in web or Internet-based surveys. *Educational Psychological Measurement*, *60*(6), 821–836.

Cooper, W. J. Jr., & Terrill, T. E. (2009). *The American South: A history* (4th ed., Vol. 2). Lanham, MD: Rowman & Littlefield Publishers.

Creswell, J. W. (2009). *Research design: Qualitative, quantitative, and mixed methods approaches*. Thousand Oaks, CA: Sage.

Creswell, J. W., & Clark, V. L. P. (2007). *Designing and conducting mixed methods research*. Thousand Oaks, CA: Sage.

Crowley, B. (2004). *Spanning the theory-practice divide in library and information science*. Summit, PA: Scarecrow Press.

Currie, C. L. (2000). Facilitating adult learning: The role of the academic librarian. *The Reference*, *33*(69–70), 219–231.

Davenport, E. & Cronin, B. (1998). Some thoughts on just for you service in the context of domain expertise. *Journal of Education for Library and Information Science*, *39*(4), 264–274.

Davis, R. A., & Bailey, C. A. (1964). *Bibliography of use studies* (Issue 18). Drexel Library School Series. Washington, DC: National Science Foundation, Office of Science Information Service.

Deisinger, A., Burkhardt, S., & Wahlberg, T. J. (2012). *Autism spectrum disorders: Inclusive community for the twenty-first century*. Charlotte, NC: Information Age Publishing.

Dervin, B. (1992). From the mind's eye of the user: The sense-making qualitative-quantitative methodology. In J. D. Glazier & R. R. Powell (Eds.), *Qualitative research in information management* (pp. 61–84). Englewood, CO: Libraries Unlimited.

Druin, A. (2005). What children can teach us: Developing digital libraries for children. *Library Quarterly*, *75*(1), 20–41.

Economic Research Service. (2007). *Measuring rurality: What is rural?* Washington, DC: Economic Research Service, The Economics of Food, Farming, Natural Resources, and Rural America, U.S. Department of Agriculture. Retrieved from http://www.ers.usda.gov/Briefing/Rurality/WhatIsRural/. Accessed on January 23, 2011.

Eldredge, J. D. (2004). The librarian as tutor/facilitator in a problem-based learning (PBL) curriculum. *Reference Services Review*, *32*(1), 54–59.

Eller, R. D. (2008). *Uneven ground: Appalachia since 1945*. Lexington, KY: The University Press of Kentucky.

Endres, B. (1996). Habermas and critical thinking. *Philosophy of Education*. Retrieved from http://ojs.ed.uiuc.edu/index.php/pes/article/view/2259/954. Accessed on June 30, 2014.

Escott, P. D., Goldfield, D. R., McMillen, S. G., & Turner, E. H. (1999). *Major problems in the history of the American South: Documents and essays, Volume II: The New South* (2nd ed.). Boston, MA: Houghton Mifflin Harcourt.

Fisher, K. E., & Abrahamson, J. A. (2007). What past is prologue: Towards a general model of lay information mediary behaviour. *Information Research*, *12*(4). Retrieved from http://informationr.net/ir/12-4/colis/colis15.html. Accessed on January 12, 2012.

Fisher, S. L. & Smith, B. E. (Eds.). (2012). *Transforming places: Lessons from Appalachia* (1st ed.). Champaign, IL: University of Illinois Press.

Fritsch, A., & Gallimore, P. (2007). *Healing Appalachia: Sustainable living through appropriate technology*. Lexington, KY: The University Press of Kentucky.

Gargiulo, R., & Kilgo, J. L. (2010). *An introduction to young children with special needs: Birth through age eight* (3rd ed.). Belmont, CA: Wadsworth Publishing.

Geuss, R. (1981). *The idea of a critical theory*. Cambridge: Cambridge University Press.

Glanz, K., Rimer, B. K., & Viswanath, K. (Eds.). (2008). *Health behavior and health education: Theory, research, and practice* (4th ed.). Indianapolis, IN: Jossey-Bass.

Glaser, B. G. (1965). The constant comparative method of qualitative analysis. *Social Problems*, *12*(4), 436–445.

Greenspan, S. I., Wieder, S., & Simons, R. (1998). *The child with special needs: Encouraging intellectual and emotional growth*. Reading, MA: Addison-Wesley/ Addison Wesley Longman.

Habermas, J. (1993). *Justification and application: Remarks on discourse ethics* (C. Cronin, Trans). Cambridge, MA: The MIT Press.

Heflinger, C. A., & Christens, B. (2006). Rural behavioral health services for children and adolescents: An ecological and community psychology analysis. *Journal of Community Psychology*, *34*(4), 379–400.

Henderson, E. (2009). *Service trends in U.S. public libraries, 1997–2007*. Research Brief No. 1. Washington, DC: Institute of Museum and Library Services. Retrieved from http://www.imls.gov/pdf/ Brief2010_01.pdf

Herzenberg, S., Price, M., & Wial, H. (2005). *Displacement in Appalachia and the non-Appalachian United States, 1993–2003: Findings based on five displaced workers surveys*. Washington, DC: Appalachian Regional Commission. Retrieved from http://www.arc.gov/images/reports/2006/displacement/pdf/displacement_arc.pdf. Accessed on November 2, 2008.

Hill, R. F. (2012). Strengths and opportunities: School librarians serving students with special needs in Central New York. *School Library Research: Research Journal of the American Association of School Librarians*, *15*, 1–14.

Holsti, O. R. (1969). *Content analysis for the social sciences and humanities*. Reading, MA: Addison-Wesley.

Horkheimer, M. (1982). *Critical theory*. New York, NY: Seabury Press.

Johnson, M. A. (2007). The social ecology of acculturation: Implications for child welfare services to children of immigrants. *Children and Youth Services Review*, *29*(11), 1426–1438.

Johnston, H. R., & Carrico, S. R. (1988). Developing capabilities to use information strategically. *MIS Quarterly*, *12*(1), 37–48.

Katz, L. S. (1992). *The reference librarian and implications of mediation*. Reference Librarian Series. Florence, KY: Routledge.

Khare, R., & Fletcher, V. (2010). *Designing inclusive educational spaces for Autism*. Boston, MA: Institute for Human Centered Design.

Kotch, J. B. (2005). *Maternal and child health: Programs, problems, and policy in public health*. Sudbury, MA: Jones and Bartlett Publishers.

Kuhlthau, C. C. (1991). Inside the search process: Information seeking from the user's perspective. *Journal of the American Society for Information Science*, *42*(5), 361–371.

Kusmin, L. (2008). Rural America at a glance 2008 Edition. *Economic Information Bulletin*, *40*(6). Retrieved from http://www.ers.usda.gov/Publications/EIB40/. Accessed on November 2, 2008.

Leckie, G. J., Given, L. M., & Buschman, J. E. (2010). *Critical theory for library and information science: Exploring the social from across the disciplines*. Library and Information Science Text. Englewood, CO: Libraries Unlimited.

Lichter, D. T., & Campbell, L. A. (2005). *Changing patterns of poverty and spatial inequality in Appalachia*. Washington, DC: Appalachian Regional Commission. Retrieved from http://www.arc.gov/index.do?nodeID=2914. Accessed on November 2, 2008.

Ludke, R. L., & Obermiller, P. J. (Eds.). (2012). *Appalachian health and well-being* (1st ed.), Lexington, KY: The University Press of Kentucky.

Marchionini, G. (2005, July 28–29). Leveraging context for adaptive multimedia retrieval: A matter of control. In M. Detyniecki, J. M. Jose, A. Nürnberger, & C. J. van Rijsbergen (Eds.), *Third international workshop on* adaptive multimedia retrieval: User, context, and feedback (pp. 35–43). Revised Selected Papers. Glasgow, UK: Springer 2006 Lecture Notes in Computer Science.

McCarthy, T., & Hoy, D. (1994). *Critical theory*. London: Basil Blackwell.

Mehra, B. (2007). Affective factors in information seeking during cross-cultural learning of international doctoral students in library and information science education. In D. Nahl & D. Bilal (Eds.), *Information and emotion: The emergent affective paradigm in information behavior research and theory* (pp. 279–301). ASIST Monograph Series. Medford, NJ: Information Today.

Mehra, B., & Bishop, A. P. (2007). Cross-cultural perspectives of international doctoral students: Two-way learning in library and information science education. *International Journal of Progressive Education*, *3*(1), 44–64. Retrieved from http://inased.org/v3n1/mehrabishop.htm. Accessed on February 1, 2011.

Mehra, B., Bishop, A. P., & Bazzell, I. (2000). The role of use scenarios in developing a community health information system. *Bulletin of the American Society for Information Science*, *26*(4). Retrieved from http://www.asis.org/Bulletin/May-00/mehra_et_al.html. Accessed on January 11, 2012.

Mehra, B., Black, K., & Lee, S. (2010). Perspectives of East Tennessee's rural public librarians about the need for professional library education: An exploratory study. *Journal of Education for Library and Information Science*, *51*(3), 142–157.

Mehra, B., Black, K., Singh, V., & Nolt, J. (2011a). What is the value of LIS education? A qualitative analysis of the perspectives of rural librarians in Southern and Central Appalachia. *Journal of Education for Library and Information Science*, *52*(4), 265–278.

Mehra, B., Black, K., Singh, V., & Nolt, J. (2011b). Collaboration between LIS education and rural libraries in the Southern and Central Appalachia: Improving librarian technology literacy and management training [Brief communications and research in progress]. *Journal of Education for Library and Information Science*, *52*(3), 238–247.

Mehra, B., Black, K., Singh, V., Nolt, J., Williams, K. C., Simmons, S., & Renfro, N. (2012a, May 22–25). The social justice framework in the Information Technology Rural Librarian Master's Scholarship Program: Bridging the rural digital divides. *Proceedings of the Qualitative and Quantitative Methods in Libraries International Conference (QQML 2012)* [Abstract], Limerick, Ireland.

Mehra, B., Black, K., Singh, V., Nolt, J., Williams, K. C., Simmons, S., & Renfro, N. (2012b, February 23–25). Computer-enabled innovations in the Information Technology Rural Librarian Master's Scholarship Program: Bridging rural digital divides in the Southern and Central Appalachia. *Proceedings of the 57th Indian Library Association Annual Conference*, Mangalore, Karnataka, India.

Mehra, B., Merkel, C., & Bishop, A. P. (2004). Internet for empowerment of minority and marginalized communities. *New Media & Society*, *6*(5), 781–802.

Mehra, B., Singh, V., & Parris, H. (2010). Open source software collaborations in Tennessee's regional library system: An exploratory study. *Library Review*, *59*(9), 690–701.

Mellon, C. A., & Kester, D. D. (2004). Online library education programs: Implications for rural students. *Journal of Education for Library and Information Science*, *45*(3), 210–220.

Menzel, H. (1966). Information needs and uses in science and technology. *Annual Review of Information Science and Technology*, *1*, 41–69.

Mertens, D. M. (2010). *Research and evaluation in education and psychology: Integrating diversity with quantitative, qualitative, and mixed methods*. Thousand Oaks, CA: Sage.

National Center for Education Statistics. (2006). *Public libraries in the United States fiscal year 2004*. Washington, DC: National Center for Education Statistics, Institute of Education Sciences, U.S. Department of Education. Retrieved from http://www.nces.ed.gov/pubs2006/2006349.pdf. Accessed on March 10, 2010.

National Center for Health Statistics. (2009). *Design and operation of the national survey of children with special health care needs 2005–2006*. Washington, DC: Department of Health and Human Services.

Neuendorf, K. A. (2002). *The content analysis guidebook*. Thousand Oaks, CA: Sage.

Oden, M., Strover, S., Inagaki, N., & Lucas, C. (2004). *2004 update of links to the future: The role of information and telecommunications technology in Appalachian economic development*. Washington, DC: Appalachian Regional Commission. Retrieved from http://www.arc.gov/images/reports/telecomupdate/links.pdf. Accessed on March 10, 2010.

Office of Management and Budget. (1998, December 21). Part III alternative approaches to defining metropolitan and nonmetropolitan areas. *Federal Register*. 63 (6370526-70561). Retrieved from http://www.whitehouse.gov/omb/inforeg/msa.pdf. Accessed on January 12, 2013.

Paisley, W. J. (1968). Information needs and uses. *Annual Review of Information Science and Technology*, *3*, 1–30.

Rathge, R. W. (1997). Rural demography. In *Encyclopedia of rural America: The land and the people* (pp. 626–629). Santa Barbara, CA: ABCCLIO.

Rawls, J. (1999). The idea of an overlapping consensus. In *Collected papers* (pp. 421–448). Cambridge, MA: Harvard University Press.

Reiff, M. I., & Tippins, S. (Eds.). (2004). *ADHD: A complete and authoritative guide*. Washington, DC: American Academy of Pediatrics.

Rogers, Y. (2004). New theoretical approaches for human-computer interaction. *Annual Review of Information Science and Technology*, *38*, 87–143.

Rycroft-Malone, J., & Bucknall, T. (2010). *Models and frameworks for implementing evidence-based practice: Linking evidence to action*. The Evidence Based Nursing Series. Hoboken, NJ: Wiley-Blackwell.

Savolainen, R. (2008). *Everyday information practices: A social phenomenological perspective*. Summit, PA: The Scarecrow Press.

Schenk, K. (2005). *Ethical approaches to gathering information from children and adolescents in international settings: Guidelines and resources*. Durham, NC: Family Health International.

Schwartz, J. H. (2004). *Development and progress of Appalachian higher education network*. Washington, DC: Appalachian Regional Commission. Retrieved from http://www.arc.gov/images/newsandevents/publications/ahen/AHENetwork.pdf. Accessed on November 2, 2008.

Scruggs, C. E. (2010). *The view from Brindley Mountain: A memoir of the rural south*. North Charleston, SC: BookSurge Publishing.

Skinner, A. C., & Slifkin, R. T. (2007). Rural/urban differences in barriers to and burdens of care for children with special health care needs. *Journal of Rural Health*, *23*, 150–157.

Smith, L. J. (2008). How ethical is ethical research? Recruiting marginalized, vulnerable groups into health services research. *Journal of Advanced Nursing*, *62*(2), 248–257.

Spatig, L., Gaines, S., MacDowell, R., Sias, B., Olson, L., & Adkins, C. (2009). Like a mountain: Performing collaborative research with youth in rural Appalachia. *Collaborative Anthropologies*, *2*, 177–212.

Sturges, J. E., & Hanrahan, K. J. (2004). Comparing telephone and face-to-face qualitative interviewing: A research note. *Qualitative Research*, *4*(1), 107–118.

Tashakkori, A., & Teddlie, C. (2003). *Handbook of mixed methods in social and behavioral research*. Thousand Oaks, CA: Sage.

U.S. Department of Health and Human Services, Health Resources and Services Administration, Maternal and Child Health Bureau. (2008). *The national survey of children with special health care needs chartbook 2005–2006*. Rockville, MD: U.S. Department of Health and Human Services. Retrieved from http://mchb.hrsa.gov/cshcn05/. Accessed on May 20, 2010.

Van House, N., Bishop, A. P., & Buttenfield, B. (2003). Introduction: Digital libraries as sociotechnical systems. In A. P. Bishop, N. Van House, & B. Buttenfield (Eds.), *Digital library use: Social practice in design and evaluation* (pp. 1–24). Cambridge, MA: MIT Press.

Wathen, N., Wyatt, S., & Harris, R. (2008). *Mediating health information: The go-betweens in a changing socio-technical landscape* (1st ed.). Health, Technology and Society. New York, NY: Palgrave Macmillan.

White, H. S. (1992). The reference librarian as information intermediary: The correct approach is the one that today's client needs today. *The Reference Librarian*, *17*(37), 23–35.

Wilson, T. D. (1981). On user studies and information needs. *Journal of Documentation*, *37*(1), 3–15.

Wilson, T. D. (2005). Evolution in information behaviour modeling: Wilson's model. In K. E. Fisher, S. Erdelez, & L. McKechnie (Eds.), *Theories of information behavior* (pp. 31–39). Medford, NJ: Information Today.

Winston, M. (2002). *Leadership in the library and information science professions: Theory and practice*. Florence, KY: Routledge.

Wyatt-Brown, B. (2008). *Southern honor: Ethics and behavior in the Old South*. History E-Book Project Reprint Series. New York, NY: ACLS Humanities E-Book.

Yau, A. (2012). *Autism: A practical guide for parents*. Los Angeles, CA: CreateSpace Independent Publishing Platform.

Zambone, A. M., & Jones, J. L. (2010). Special Ed 101 for school librarians. *School Library Monthly*, *26*(6), 19–22.

APPENDIX 6.A: SURVEY INSTRUMENT

1. Circle the type of library you work in (academic, public, school, other) and identify its geographical location (i.e., city, state) ____________
2. How long have you worked in a rural library and what is your current job title? __________
3. What are your educational and professional qualifications? ____________
4. How many children with special needs use your library and how often do they use your library? ___________________
   Provide any additional comments: ___________________
5. What are the three most important information needs of children with special needs in your library?
   Most important information need: ___________________
   Most important information need: ___________________
   Most important information need: ___________________
   Provide any additional comments: ___________________
6. What are the three most critical challenges that children with special needs face in their everyday life in your community?
   Most critical challenge: ___________________
   Most critical challenge: ___________________
   Most critical challenge: ___________________
   Provide any additional comments: ___________________
7. What are the three most critical challenges that children with special needs face in their everyday life in your library?
   Most critical challenge: ___________________
   Most critical challenge: ___________________
   Most critical challenge: ___________________
   Provide any additional comments: ___________________
8. What are the three most common information resources and services that children with special needs seek/use in your library?
   Most common information resource and service: _______________
   Most common information resource and service: _______________
   Most common information resource and service: _______________
   Provide any additional comments: ___________________

9. How effective is your library in meeting the needs of children with special needs? (check the category that applies)
   ___ Very Effective ___ Effective ___ Neutral ___ Ineffective
   ___ Very Ineffective
   Provide any additional comments: ____________________
10. What are the three most important ways that your library can improve to better serve children with special needs?
    Most important way that the library can improve: _______________
    Most important way that the library can improve: _______________
    Most important way that the library can improve: _______________
    Provide any additional comments: __________________
11. Provide any other comments you wish to share: ___________________

Thank you for your participation and feedback!

Chapter 7

The Social Information Grounds of Māori Secondary School Students

Spencer C. Lilley

Abstract

Purpose – This chapter presents results of a study that investigated the social information grounds of 45 Māori students ages 16–18 when they are at school.

Methodology – A mixed research method was used. The quantitative approach was based on a survey questionnaire that was distributed to the students to gather data about their social information behaviour in four schools. The qualitative approach used six focus groups of students to discuss the behaviour.

Findings – Māori students exchange, share and seek information within their social networks in six different places in their schools. These places are best described as social information grounds, as defined by Fisher, Naumer, Durrance, Stromski, and Christiansen (2005).

Social implications – The research identifies the importance that Māori students place on information obtained through interpersonal transactions particularly within their social networks. These social networks play an integral role in assisting Māori students to understand the social and educational environment of which they are part.

Originality/value – This chapter focuses on information grounds and indigenous teenage youth, an understudied area of research. It uses

New Directions in Children's and Adolescents' Information Behavior Research
Library and Information Science, Volume 10, 191–213

ISSN: 1876-0562/doi:10.1108/S1876-056220140000010055

the information grounds theory to explore the social networks of Māori secondary school students in New Zealand.

Keywords: Māori information behaviour; indigenous peoples; information grounds; New Zealand; social networks; youth

7.1. Introduction

New Zealand's population statistics (Statistics NZ, 2012) identify that the Māori population is youthful in comparison to other ethnic groups in New Zealand, with 37% of its population being under twenty years of age, as opposed to 27% of New Zealand's total population. The statistics also demonstrate that New Zealand has a rapidly ageing population and in the future the social and economic well-being of the nation will be increasingly dependent on the current youthful generation to support them. It is, therefore, imperative that Māori youth be given every opportunity to be successful academically so that they can make a strong contribution to New Zealand's future prosperity.

Although extensive research has taken place on various aspects of Māori society and culture, very few studies have focused on Māori information behaviour, particularly relating to how youths engage with information. In addition, there has been an extensive body of research published on the academic under achievement of Māori students, particularly at the secondary school level where approximately 47% of Māori students leave school without achieving a qualification that would enable them entry into university level study. This is in stark contrast to their non-Māori peers where the failure rate is 23% (Ministry of Education, 2013). The difference in achievement rates is further exacerbated by higher levels of Māori students leaving school without attempting to achieve these qualifications. Critical to achieving higher levels of qualifications is the need for the retention of Māori students in the compulsory schooling sector. There are many reasons for leaving school at an earlier stage than other students, including failure to make sufficient academic progress, expulsion and a perception that school is uninspiring and irrelevant due to a lack of emphasis on tikanga Māori (Māori culture). The study presented in this chapter is framed around the question, what role does information play in lifting the level of Māori students' achievement? However, before answering this question, it is important to firstly focus more widely on the value that Māori youth place on information by looking at how they seek, share and exchange information in a social context. Findings from this study should contribute to our understanding of the social information behaviour of this group of users.

7.2. Research Questions

This study addressed one overarching research question:

What sources do Māori students use when seeking information in a social context?

a. Where at school do the students meet to share, exchange and seek information?
b. What type of information do they share, exchange and seek?

7.3. Related Literature

Very few studies exist on the information seeking behaviour of Māori. Tamaira's study (2007) investigated the information seeking needs of *whakapapa* researchers. She found that like other genealogists, they are high users of public libraries and the resources available there. Her research revealed that the most popular information sources were other people encountered at the library, and most notably librarians, volunteers from genealogy societies, and other *whakapapa* and genealogy researchers. Lilley (2008) examined the information behaviour of Māori secondary school students with a focus on information barriers, the cultural values that influence their information seeking (2012) and the information resources they used for seeking career-related information (2013). These three studies also demonstrated a significant emphasis on interpersonal information seeking within the context of Māori cultural values.

Studies by Savolainen (1995) and Chatman (1999) (Fisher, Naumer, Durrance, Stromski, & Christiansen, 2005), although they do not relate to indigenous groups, provide frameworks for considering how cultural differences in information seeking and sharing environments can be taken into account. Chatman's 'life in the round study' (1999) and 'information poverty' (1996); and the study of Hispanic immigrant farmers (Fisher, Marcoux, Miller, Sanchez, & Cunningham, 2004) involved minority and at-risk populations. Chatman's (1990, 1991) studies of janitors, prisoners and retired women (1992) focused on how culture, social norms and the role played by key individuals resulted in the development of information environments firmly entrenched in the worldview shared by those in these circumstances. Chatman's description of these as a 'small world' indicated a high degree of dependence between these group members for information flow and interaction.

Fisher's theory of information grounds is based on research conducted in foot clinics (Pettigrew, 1999, 2000). It involves situations and places where people may gather for one purpose, and end up sharing and exchanging information while they are there. This has been applied to immigrants in New York (Fisher, Durrance, & Hinton, 2004) and the Pacific Northwest (Fisher, Marcoux, et al., 2004), as well as to other social groups and situations (Fisher et al., 2005) that include public facilities such as hair salons, airports, sports fields, classrooms and churches.

Fisher's information grounds theory is heavily influenced by social networking theory, particularly the writings of Granovetter (1973, 1982) on the strength of weak ties. Granovetter was deeply influenced by the work of Rapoport (1954) and Rapoport and Horvath (1961). Rapoport (1954, p. 75) commented on the 'well known fact that the likely contacts of two individuals who are closely acquainted tend to be more overlapping than those of two arbitrarily selected individuals'. Rapoport and Horvath's (1961, p. 290) hypothesis was based on the expectation that 'the friendship relations and, therefore the overlap basis of the acquaintance circles tend to become less tight with increasing numerical rank-order (i.e., best friend, second-best, third-best, etc.)'. Granovetter's studies concluded that individuals and social groups received information from both strong ties (individuals that are well known to them) and weak ties (individuals that are not well known). However, the information received from weak ties is of a richer vein as it is sourced from outside the social network's normal information sources.

Johnson's (2004) study of the social networks of urban residents in Mongolia found that, when it came to choosing from organisations, friends, acquaintances or media sources for their information, they tended to deliberately choose individuals who were not well known to them and whom they considered to have better access to information resources. Johnson's study reinforced the weak ties theory promulgated by Granovetter (1973, 1982).

Like Chatman's theories, Fisher's information grounds theory takes into account the social and cultural status of the individuals gathered, thus normalising the information behavioural practices. Those who are gathered set the tone for the interactions that take place at the information ground, with Fisher's theory effectively establishing that these can occur at any time or place. Information grounds theory includes indigenous places and peoples, as the present study demonstrates through its explorations of the information grounds that Māori students participate in at school, as well as the studies of information grounds in marae and social settings (Lilley, 2008, 2010, 2012, 2013).

Chatman's and Fisher's studies and theories are viewed by Savolainen (2009) as being based in the context of everyday life information seeking. Savolainen (1995, pp. 266–267) describes his Everyday Life Information Seeking (ELIS) model as the 'acquisition of various informational (cognitive and expressive) elements which people employ to orient themselves in daily life or to solve problems not directly associated with the performance of occupational tasks'. Daily life in this context can cover everything from domestic and household issues, financial problems and questions, and personal health information seeking. Although occupational information needs are not normally included, Savolainen does concede that it is not normally possible to easily separate work from everyday life.

The ELIS model has been utilised by a number of information seeking researchers in a variety of contexts, demonstrating its adaptability. Studies have been undertaken involving a range of different ethnic and social groups including young adults (Agosto & Hughes-Hassell, 2006a, 2006b), African-American households (Spink & Cole, 2001) and Korean graduate students (Jeong, 2004). However, like the other major models created by Wilson (1981, 1999a, 1999b), Krikelas (1983), Dervin (1992), Ellis (1989) and Kuhlthau (1991), ELIS has not been applied to indigenous populations.

Savolainen (2009), in reviewing the role of social factors in Fisher's and Chatman's studies, concludes that these factors are normative constraints in Chatman's concept of the small world, as the presence of people outside the normal group is viewed with suspicion by the social network. However, unknown individuals are at times absolutely necessary to the success of information grounds, as the co-presence of other individuals is essential to the seeking and sharing of information, regardless of whether these opportunities are planned or serendipitous.

In summary, very little research has examined the information grounds and social networks of Māori students in school settings. In addition, existing models in the context of everyday life information seeking have not been tested with indigenous people including Māori population. This study is an attempt to fill this literature gap.

7.4. Method

7.4.1. Description of the Method

This study employed both quantitative and qualitative research methods. The quantitative approach allowed for gathering data through a questionnaire instrument. The qualitative approach generated data through use of focus groups.

7.4.2. Participants

The study was conducted over an eighteen month period and involved participation by Māori students aged 16–18. These students were drawn from four different state funded secondary schools. These schools were selected on the basis of their student profiles, with all four having substantial numbers of Māori students. Two of these schools were single sex (one for males and the other for females) and pre-dominantly Māori focused (more than 95% of the students identified as Māori), and two were co-educational schools where 30% of the student population were Māori. The two Māori focused schools were located in rural settings, as was one of the co-educational schools. The other school is situated in an urban centre.

Potential participants were identified by the schools using their student management systems, which allowed for finding all students who were ethnically identified as Māori and were sixteen years of age and over. In total, there were 190 eligible participants across the four schools. Of these, 139 agreed to participate in this study and completed the questionnaire. This instrument was distributed at hui (meetings) to those who were identified as eligible. It should be noted that not all 190 potential participants were present at the hui, due to absence from school or because of other engagements at the times these meetings took place. In addition to the questionnaire, each student at the hui was provided with an invitation form to participate in a focus group discussion.

7.4.3. Data Gathering

With the assistance of each school, eligible students were invited to complete a questionnaire. The purpose of this questionnaire was to obtain some 'big picture' data about what information sources Māori students use when seeking information and how useful these are. All students that participated in the questionnaire phase of the research were also invited to participate in a focus groups discussion.

7.4.4. Focus Groups

There were 61 expressions of interest to take part in the focus groups, but only 45 participants actually took part across the four schools. Non-participation by the 16 students was due to absence from school or other reasons such as detention, sports practice and attending an assessment. Three of the students had left school in the time between the distribution of the questionnaire and the focus groups meeting. In total, six focus group sessions were held, with a varied number of participants in each group (Table 7.1). The focus groups were facilitated by the author and were audio-recorded. Also present was a research assistant who took notes, particularly when the facilitator used the whiteboard to record answers.

Table 7.1: Focus group participants.

Focus group	No. of participants	School type
1	6	Girls' school
2	6	Girls' school
3	5	Urban co-educational school
4	11	Boys' school
5	9 (5 boys, 4 girls)	Rural co-educational school
6	8 (3 boys, 5 girls)	Rural co-educational school

7.4.5. Setting

This study was conducted in four secondary schools. Each school provided a room where the focus groups were held. At two schools (the co-educational schools) this was a classroom and at the other two (single sex schools) the school library was used as the venue. The focus groups sessions involved a series of prepared questions that addressed what information sources the participants found valuable, and where and how they accessed each of them. It also provided the researcher with an opportunity to investigate themes that were identified from analysis of the data generated from the completed questionnaires.

7.5. Analysis

The 139 completed questionnaires were coded and entered into SPSS for analysis. The focus group transcripts were entered into HyperResearch and links between the themes were identified. The data and themes from both the quantitative and qualitative phases were then compared for synergies between two sets of data

7.6. Results

7.6.1. What Information Sources Are Used?

Like many other studies involving youth (Julien, 1999; Julien & Michels, 2000; Agosto & Hughes-Hassell, 2005, 2006a, 2006b); Shenton, 2004; Shenton & Dixon, 2003), this study found that the main source of information for most participants was interpersonal interactions. This information was mostly obtained from friends, parents, siblings, teachers and members of the whānau (extended family).

When exploring their information behaviour at school, it was revealed that the participants' interpersonal interactions varied depending on the environment in which they found themselves. Within the school, these environments were identified as formal learning places, boarding (two schools had hostels attached to them), and social and recreational places. The participants indicated that they had most control over the social and recreational places, whereas other environments were determined and, in some cases, imposed on them by others (school leadership team, teachers and hostel staff members).

7.6.2. Where at School Do Students Meet to Share, Exchange, or Seek Information?

The participants were asked in an open-ended question to indicate their preference for interpersonal interactions. Students in the focus groups were not directly asked where these places were, as the initial aim was to get them to identify what they did at break times (before and after school, intervals and lunchtimes) and where these activities took place. Once they identified these locations and activities, they were probed further to uncover what they discussed while they were in these places.

Based on these discussions, six main places were identified as gathering points. These are: the school grounds, outside the school shop,[1] restrooms, gymnasium, sports practice and the smokers' hangout. It should be noted that all of these places are within the schools precincts and, therefore, the students' activities and behaviours are expected to be within the boundaries of the school rules. These social information grounds are characterised by the fact that, in these places, students are not engaged in any formal educational practices. In most cases, although there is an element of pre-determination, students' presence in these areas is largely voluntary.

7.6.3. School Grounds

Although the amount of space varies from school to school, all secondary schools in New Zealand are fortunate enough to have substantial areas within their precincts for students to use before and after school, and during common break times. Although these grounds must be shared with

1. In New Zealand schools, the school shop is commonly referred to as a tuck shop, where food and minor stationery items can normally be purchased.

other pupils at the school, they become highly valuable venues in themselves for information sharing and exchange. Due to the extent of space, it is not unusual to expect that several information grounds are in operation at any one time, as participants prefer to mix with their own social group.

Focus group participants indicated that, on the whole, they were 'creatures of habit', in that they tended to mix with the same people each day and normally met up at the same spot. If for some reason they were unable to meet there (such as rain), they would switch to somewhere appropriate. However, it was stated by one participant that this latter situation normally resulted in a tendency to be less inclined to have a full and frank exchange because there was no guarantee of privacy. The other aspect of the school grounds is that, at the time that the students were there sharing information, they were also normally undertaking a variety of activities.

7.6.4. What Information Is Shared, Exchanged or Sought?

Some students indicated that they used these breaks in different ways, with the morning break only being a chance to have a quick catch up with each other, talk about what had been going on in different classrooms and catch up on anything that happened the previous day (especially if they had not all been in the same class in the first couple of hours of the school day).

During the lunchtime break, discussions were more likely to be far wider and the activities being undertaken more varied, ranging from reasonably passive discussions while sitting to being physically active by way of a sport or a game (see Table 7.2).

Students participating in activities that can be described as less active indicated that this was normally out of choice. Four students in one focus group said that if at all possible they would work on their homework and '*help each other finish what we can*'. This was often achieved through '*us doing something* [homework activity] *each and then swapping the answers*'.

Table 7.2: School grounds by information type and percentage of participants.

Information type	Group 1	Group 2	Group 3	Group 4	Group 5	Group 6
Schoolwork	50%	50%	40%	27%	44%	50%
Sport	33%	50%	60%	54%	33%	38%
Gossip	100%	17%	40%	18%	33%	50%
Media (TV, Net)	50%	66%	80%	45%	222%	38%
Fashion	66%	50%	60%	0%	22%	38%

A student in another focus group said that her group did not play sport '*but just like to talk about different things*'. When asked what these 'things' might be, she admitted that it largely depended who was there but '*it is mainly based around gossip, TV shows, music and clothes*'.

The focus groups also had individuals that liked to play sports at lunchtimes and sometimes this meant they did not have time to talk. However, at other times they talked about '*who we are playing this weekend and whether they're any good*'. Sometimes the discussions revolved around '*who has been picked for the team and who hasn't and why*'. Occasionally information was passed on from one of the group about how to perform or improve different skills, with them taking on a role more like a 'coach' or a 'tuakana' (mentor). Situations like these depended on who was present as '*not everyone in the group stops and listens*'.

7.6.5. The Gymnasium

Although higher year levels in secondary schools are not normally timetabled for physical education, students did find themselves at the gymnasium at odd times (before and after school and the occasional lunchtime break). These occasions normally related to when they were undertaking some physical activity, or an exercise programme with weights or other fitness equipment. When probed for information about how often they used the gymnasium in their breaks, the answered varied from once or twice a week to everyday. Depending on what activity they were undertaking and the degree of concentration required, there was always scope for chatter and the exchange of information with the others gathered there. Two students in the same focus group agreed that, although it was possible to arrange to meet people at the gym, you could not always control who was there, and you could end up sharing the facilities with other year groups and the occasional teacher. This was particularly true if students were there before or after the school day.

One advantage of the gymnasium was that individuals were normally there for similar purposes. Depending on what these individuals were doing, their presence at the gym could be regular or irregular. If regular, it was more likely that the activities were organised and, therefore, it was probable that those they were interacting with were either members of the same team or participating in the same sport (in another team).

Those who used the gymnasium in a less structured manner (i.e. less frequently or just as frequently but at irregular intervals) added an element of unpredictability to the information exchanges.

The types of information shared in the gymnasium were centred on three different themes: to physical activity, schoolwork and social chatter.

Information relating to physical activity depended on the type of exercise the students were involved in. For instance, if they were in the weights room, their information exchanges quite often involved techniques for using weights. Another example was the student who stated that they often discussed the 'different gyms around town and what they have there'. If the students were engaged in playing a game in the gymnasium, such as basketball or indoor soccer, the nature of the exchange could be tactical in nature, pointing out the weaknesses in the play of their opponents, and there was a level of banter that was less serious in nature.

Like other places in the school where students congregated, the discussion around schoolwork related to talking about homework activities or the results of assessments that students had received back from their teachers, as well as what was going to be in the (forthcoming) test for an academic subject. Those with older siblings who had already done these subjects were able to share what they knew from the experience of their brothers or sisters.

Social chatter was also prevalent, including gossip about others in the school and talking about films, television, music and computer games. The boys in one of the focus groups at the rural based co-educational schools said that they often engaged in a fair amount of teasing of each other with some of the information being shared about each other was made up (see Table 7.3).

Although information could be exchanged in the process of practicing sports, some of the richest exchanges came when different groups of users came together in the same space. One area where this occurred was in the weights room where users of the equipment could come together, with teams present at the same time as other users. More users in the room could quite often mean that information was exchanged while waiting to use the next piece of equipment. A similar situation occurred in the changing areas, where gymnasium users were changing before or after the particular activity they participated in or were waiting to use the showering facilities. It seems that, even though people find waiting in queues frustrating, they were a natural location for an information grounds to occur as people were likely to strike up a conversation with those standing next to them.

Table 7.3: Gymnasium by information type and percentage of participants.

Information type	Group 1	Group 2	Group 3	Group 4	Group 5	Group 6
Schoolwork	33%	50%	40%	18%	33%	50%
Physical activity	66%	33%	40%	45%	44%	38%
Social chatter	100%	50%	60%	36%	44%	38%

7.6.6. Restrooms

Every person at school at some time during the day needs to use the restroom, and arranging to all meet in the same restroom is hard to organise unless it is pre-arranged for one of the common breaks. Although it is possible to leave class to go to the restroom it is normally at the discretion of the classroom teacher, and this is not always forthcoming. Milling around in restrooms is not encouraged at most schools as it can cause congestion, can be deemed to be unhygienic and unhealthy and restrooms are not really deemed to be an appropriate place to congregate (especially if someone is eating). However, in every focus group restrooms were identified as being a place where information is shared and exchanged.

The types of information exchanged and shared was again mainly around the topics of idle gossip about others at school and people they knew from outside school, schoolwork (especially if someone was having trouble understanding or getting something right in an academic subject) and what they had seen on television or had been listening to (musically).

It was noted that in the restrooms for females there were never enough cubicles to meet the demand, particularly at morning tea time, and this led to queuing for the cubicles and the wash basins. While in the act of queuing conversations were held and, although at times these were only between individuals who were friends, occasionally they were between people who were not members of the same group of friends or social network.

Male students at the co-educational schools noted that they were less likely to have to queue unless there was a demand for cubicles. If they were there to simply to use the urinals, the amount of time they spent in the restrooms was relatively brief and, although some information was exchanged, it was normally quite light and casual rather than 'deep and meaningful'. However, it was indicated by several of the male participants the focus groups that these conversations could sometimes continue outside the restrooms (see Table 7.4). This was dependent on the topic of the conversation, the participants involved and how much time was available before they had to be somewhere else (such as the next class).

Table 7.4: Restrooms by information type and percentage of participants.

Information type	Group 1	Group 2	Group 3	Group 4	Group 5	Group 6
Schoolwork	66%	50%	40%	36%	44%	38%
Gossip	100%	50%	40%	27%	44%	50%
Media (TV, Net)	33%	50%	40%	27%	33%	38%

A cluster of six students in one of a focus group at the single sex girls' school noted that the restrooms were '*safe from teachers*',[2] and that they could carry out conversations there about teachers and '*things we wouldn't want them* [teachers] *to know about*'.

7.6.7. Outside the School Shop

Most secondary schools in New Zealand have a school shop and these are colloquially known as the 'tuck shop'. This shop normally sells food, beverages and minor stationery items to the staff and students of the school. As such, the tuck shop is a space where individual students are likely to congregate and queue to buy their morning tea or lunch.

Students at only one of the schools mentioned that outside the school tuck shop was a good place for them to share and exchange information (note that two schools did not have school shops). For the students who mentioned it, it was a natural gathering space for them. This was because there was a specific need that was being fulfilled (food purchase and consumption), and students not only had time for sharing information but also had a natural inclination to share resources, pool money and buy items that they could consume together.

As a gathering and selling point, the area around the tuck shop is busy and the queues to purchase items quite long. In one focus group, the participants indicated that they would share responsibility for standing in line to purchase items while the other members of the group protected their 'space'. As a result, participants in any one social interaction and information exchange could vary from day to day depending on whose turn it was to be in the queue and who was looking after the space. This could affect the quality of the information being exchanged, as the most valuable participant could be the one standing in the queue rather than with the group. However, it was also recognised that some members of their social group were much better than others in eliciting information from others while they were standing in the queue, so the information they picked up while fulfilling this task could be useful when they returned to their social group.

There was a strong tendency for conversations around the tuck shop to focus on food, including its cost, best value for money and tastes. The other focus of conversation was gossip about others or what had happened in their classes or assembly that morning, particularly if someone had been asked to see one of the senior staff (see Table 7.5).

---

2. Normally because at most schools the teachers had their own restrooms.

Table 7.5: School shop by information type and percentage of participants.

Information type	Group 1	Group 2	Group 3	Group 4	Group 5	Group 6
Food	0%	0%	0%	0%	33%	0%
Gossip	0%	0%	0%	0%	55%	0%

Someone else's trouble was often a strong source of gossip and information exchange throughout the whole school as '*we want to know what they have done wrong and what's going to happen to them*'. If the person in question or one of their friends was there '*we will try and find out from someone that knows them*'. This may lead to some form of reciprocal information exchange between two individuals or groups, or an expectation that the favour will be returned at a later date.

Information was also often exchanged with other students who had either already purchased their food or were in line, about whether anything special was available or whether things had run out. This was particularly useful as '*if we don't have enough money we will either have to buy something else or try and borrow some off someone else*' [like another friend].

7.6.8. The Smokers' Hangout

Although smoking is not an approved activity at schools and being caught will result in punishment, it does occur. At most schools there are places where those wishing to smoke will congregate with a view to not being detected by teachers. This results in clandestine gatherings of students of all year levels at various points during the day (before and after school, lunchtime and during other breaks).

As a gathering point, the 'smokers' hangout' not only serves as a venue for flouting the school rules but also serves a number of other purposes. As the students who gather there become well known to each other, they become part of a social network that would in all likelihood not exist if it was not for the common activity they are partaking in. Although those they gather with might not be part of their normal network of contacts in the school, their mere presence places another layer of communication into the pre-existing networks within the school.

Although some of the discussion at the 'hangout' mirrors other information exchange activities in the school, it is one of the few places that pupils of different ages congregate. As the participants are from different year levels, the 'hangout' is a place where several information channels come together and information is exchanged while smoking occurs.

Table 7.6: Smokers' hangout by information type and percentage of participants.

Information type	Group 1	Group 2	Group 3	Group 4	Group 5	Group 6
School activities	13%	25%	20%	18%	22%	33%
People (personalities)	25%	25%	20%	18%	33%	25%
Gossip (general)	25%	25%	40%	18%	22%	33%

Like many other 'information grounds' within the school precinct, the information exchanged revolved around school activities, personalities and gossip. The content of these exchanges always had the potential to be more rewarding than others within the school, as those present from the different year groups would be able to make contributions from their respective groups. This information otherwise would not always be available to them all and provided a rich vein of information that they could disseminate to other social groups of which they were part (see Table 7.6).

Other information shared in the hangout was related to the act of smoking and included '*shops where under-age smokers can safely buy cigarettes from*', '*what happens if you're caught smoking*' and practical tips such as '*how to stop smelling like an ashtray*'.

7.6.9. Sports Practice

Every New Zealand secondary school fields teams across a range of sporting codes. The more popular sports include basketball, cricket, football (soccer), field hockey, netball and rugby. Entry into the elite teams fielded by schools is highly competitive and places in these teams are normally held by the senior students. However, selection into these teams is based on merit and it is possible for some students from the earlier year groups to be included. Schools also typically field teams in lower and social grade competitions. Every team fielded by a school has a practice at some stage during the week, with some of the elite teams sometimes having multiple practices. These practices are typically held after the school day has ended, but some teams also fit in practice during the lunch break. In truly exceptional circumstances the school will allow a team to practice during the school day (but this is highly irregular). Every focus group at every school identified sports practice as a place where they exchanged information with their teammates, friends and peers.

Sports practice is a regular activity and will be normally held at the same time and place every time it is scheduled. With this regular time slot established, students will typically know who will be present, resulting in a pattern.

The most opportune time for this information exchange to take place was before and after the sports practice. This was due to the fact that some coaches of the sports teams did not condone any frivolous discussion during the practice sessions. However, it was noted that students in some lower teams did not have an actual coach, and the training and practice sessions were not always as focused as they could be. This could lead to quite robust discussions being held by those present at times. For the more serious teams, it was noted by students in four different focus groups that they needed to wait for the time after the practice when the players were getting changed or preparing to go home.

Like most other 'information grounds' around the school, the types of information being exchanged was about individuals, social lives and schoolwork. However, of particular value was the performance of other teams, and the strengths and weaknesses of the team being played next. The latter information was normally sought from people in other teams who had already played them, or were in representative trials or in teams with them (see Table 7.7).

Timing of discussions was sometimes delayed on purpose to ensure that not too much information was spilled in front of the coach, particularly if they did not want their coach/teacher to know what they were up to (especially when discussing their social lives). One student stated that if they waited until after practice to talk to the friends in their network, they quite often had more to discuss as they were in different teams and sometimes '*we will pick up some gossip from our team mates and we can pass that on*'.

Self-coached teams (some only had a manager) would use practice as a means of ensuring that the team had a full contingent of players and to make sure everybody knew where the weekend's game was to be played. There was also a learning element to some of these team practices, whereby focus group members stated that they would '*pass on new moves to the other players*'.

Table 7.7: Sports practice by information type and percentage of participants.

Information type	**Group 1**	**Group 2**	**Group 3**	**Group 4**	**Group 5**	**Group 6**
Schoolwork	38%	50%	40%	22%	33%	25%
Skills	25%	25%	60%	33%	22%	38%
Social lives	50%	38%	40%	22%	44%	38%
Gossip	50%	50%	60%	33%	33%	25%

7.7. Discussion

Fisher's (2005) definition of information grounds states that they are temporary in nature, can occur anywhere and normally occur where people have come together for one purpose and serendipitously share information. For many of the social information grounds identified in the school environment, there may be less serendipity in the students coming together. However, the nature of the information they share, exchange or gather is dependent on who is present, where they have been, and who they have been associating with in class and other places in or out of school. Those with broader connections beyond their social networks at school will be able to make contributions mined from these other social acquaintances, which will enrich the information being shared and exchanged within their school group. These broader social networks go beyond the 'small world' concept as defined by Chatman (1990, 1991, 1992). Although the serendipity in bringing them together in one place may be missing, it is undoubtedly present in the content of the information available at these information grounds. Recent studies on teenage information seeking activities have been more highly focused on how these are closely aligned with the everyday life information seeking practices as defined by Savolainen (1995). Studies by researchers including Julien (2004), Agosto and Hughes-Hassell (2005), Shenton and Dixon (2003) and Meyers, Fisher, and Marcoux (2007) demonstrate that information seeking and exchange behaviour is very heavily weighted towards the use of interpersonal interaction as the preferred form of information behaviour. The different information grounds at school provide a rich vein of information. The information shared is sourced and shared, not only in these places, but also across other activities inside and outside of school. As classes for the individuals change from one school period to the next, information is gained and exchanged in these places and is then able to be shared at a social information ground during the next break. Participants in the focus groups mentioned that they often hear the same information in the social information grounds as they have in other places, but sometimes in more detail and from a number of perspectives. The overlap is probably best attributed to a snowballing effect, where information is developed and added to over the course of a day (or sometimes longer) and its exchange in these social information grounds is part of this process.

Currently, little is known about the information seeking behaviour of non-Māori students in New Zealand. Due to the fact that most New Zealand secondary schools have similar structures and schedules to the four schools used in this study, it would be surprising if there were any distinct differences in the way information is shared or exchanged.

The transmission of information across the social information grounds within the school precincts is assisted largely by the role played by what I call 'information carriers'. Agada (1999), Metoyer-Duran (1993) and Shoemaker (1991) refer to these carriers as 'gatekeepers'. As carriers, they assume responsibility for taking information from one information ground to another; as gatekeepers they can decide what information is worthy of sharing or of likely interest to those whom they choose to share it with. Depending on the number of information grounds they are involved with, it might be that carriers choose to vary the information they share with the different groups of which they are part. Their motivation for acting in this manner is also likely to vary. Reasons for this behaviour include not betraying the confidence of close friends, maintaining reciprocal obligations with other participants, keeping control over the dissemination of information and, in some groups, behaving more as a passive participant by receiving information than spreading it.

Across the six focus groups there were participants who the characteristics of an information carrier. These individuals made significant contributions to the exchanges within each focus group, with a tendency to lead or dominate the direction of the discussions taking place during the sessions and often being the first to offer their views on the question that had been posed. This was notable during the discussions held around the smokers' hangout and the restrooms. Although many of the other participants were not 'shrinking violets' when it came to the discussions, it was clear that those individuals identified as carriers had an extra dimension to them, best described as charisma. While others may have had equally important views, they appeared to defer to these 'characters' before offering their own views. Each focus group included individuals with these features, however at the co-educational schools' focus groups it was the males that were most notable, with the female members of the groups being more reserved. The non-verbal language in these situations was interesting to observe, with there being distinct use of 'eye rolling' and frowning amongst the females (and some other male students) as the very vocal students were speaking.

The range of information shared across the different information grounds is relatively limited in that it focuses heavily on personal information, and gossip about other members of the school community, particularly teachers, and their own families. Gossip within this context is highly valued. Other gossip is centred on well-known individuals in the wider community, such as television personalities and celebrities. Although some people do not approve of gossip, to teenagers and others who engage with it, it fulfils a basic human need of knowing what is going on in the lives of other people, whether or not they are personally known to those discussing and exchanging the information.

Although celebrity gossip is most likely to be sourced from magazines, newspapers or television, its value lies in its ability to 'normalise' the lives of the rich and famous. Information obtained about celebrities gains in value when individual participants are able to provide information that they have observed first hand. However, gossip is not the only information that teenagers choose to share. More serious topics are exchanged, but these discussions are dependent on the right individuals being present at the right location at the right time. This is illustrated where privacy is identified as being crucial to exchanging information with a close friend. This is particularly important when the person sharing the information does not want others to eavesdrop or overhear personal information about them, family or friends. In cases such as this, it is more about exclusion rather than inclusion of others.

Exclusion also emerged as a theme in other aspects of the focus group discussions and is primarily focused on the composition of social networks. At school, social networks evolve over time as the students become more familiar with each other and friendships develop. Some of the networks could have developed over a longer period, particularly if a group had been at other schools together. At secondary school level, a hierarchy of social networks is quite normal. These hierarchies vary, but some common elements that appeared across the four schools studied were year group and age. It was noted by the focus group participants that information was not normally shared outside year groups, particularly senior students who did not wish to share information with younger students. However, being the same age and in the same year group did not always result in the formation of a social network of all students in that category. Further demarcations within age and year group levels were likely to be based on the sharing of similar interests or backgrounds. An example is where a social network at one school consisted of girls that were highly active and interested in sport, whereas another group consisted of girls that were more academically focused. Members of these two networks were frequently in the same classes together but chose to move in different social groups outside class. While in class, depending on the type of information in question, members of the different networks may or may not discuss and exchange information with each other. If this occurred then it was normally ripe for repeating in one of the information grounds that they belong to. This type of behaviour is essentially representative of human nature and includes an element of reciprocity, in that the information and discussions in one environment can then be shared in other networks.

7.8. Conclusion

This study found that Māori teenagers focus heavily on the use of interpersonal information exchange as their preferred form of information sharing, exchanging and seeking in a social context within a school setting. These activities occur in regular places and most often with the same participants. These teenagers prefer to be part of a social network that includes friends and teammates (in the case of sporting activities). These findings are congruent with previous research that uncovered the social information behaviour of teenagers (e.g. Agosto & Hughes-Hassell, 2005). The fact that there was no focus on Māori cultural activities indicates that aspect of their lives may not be important in this particular context. Researchers interested in similar studies should consider probing teenagers about cultural activities to determine their relevance to them both inside and outside of school settings.

Various locations were identified in the schools where information was shared, exchanged or sought. Particular areas for these activities were in the school grounds, gymnasiums, restrooms, at sports practice, outside the school shop and in the smokers' hangout. The types of information centred largely on social chatter, including gossip about people in the school, celebrities and family, and discussions about film, television programs, and music and schoolwork. This information is an integral component of the social networks that Māori students belong to at school. These networks play an instrumental role in the exchange of information. Although each of the schools had their own unique features, the types of information grounds found across the four schools were very similar. Future research should examine the types of social information grounds of teenagers inside and outside of the school setting to obtain better understanding of the differences and similarities between the two settings.

The distinct notion of inclusion and exclusion in information exchange behaviour, whereby members of social groups ensured that the information they shared stayed within their circle of influence deserves further investigation. In addition, the notion of information 'carriers' that was found to be analogous to information 'gatekeepers' should be examined in more depth in future studies in the context of social information behaviour.

References

Agada, J. (1999). Inner-city gatekeepers: An exploratory survey of their information use environment. *Journal of the American Society for Information Science*, *50*(1), 74–85.

Agosto, D. E., & Hughes-Hassell, S. (2005). People, places, and questions: An investigation of the everyday life information-seeking behaviors of urban young adults. *Library & Information Science Research*, *27*(2), 141–163.

Agosto, D. E., & Hughes-Hassell, S. (2006a). Toward a model of the everyday life information needs of urban teenagers, part 1: Theoretical model. *Journal of the American Society for Information Science and Technology*, *57*(10), 1394–1403.

Agosto, D. E., & Hughes-Hassell, S. (2006b). Toward a model of the everyday life information needs of urban teenagers, part 2: Empirical model. *Journal of the American Society for Information Science and Technology*, *57*(11), 1418–1426.

Chatman, E. A. (1990). Alienation theory — Application of a conceptual framework to a study of information among janitors. *Reference Quarterly*, *29*(3), 355–368.

Chatman, E. A. (1991). Life in a small world: Applicability of gratification theory to information-seeking behavior. *Journal of the American Society for Information Science*, *42*(6), 438–449.

Chatman, E. A. (1992). *The information world of retired women*. Westport, CT: Greenwood Press.

Chatman, E. A. (1996). The impoverished life-world of outsiders. *Journal of the American Society for Information Science*, *47*(3), 193–206.

Chatman, E. A. (1999). A theory of life in the round. *Journal of the American Society for Information Science*, *50*(3), 207–217.

Dervin, B. (1992). From the mind's eye of the user: The sense-making qualitative-quantitative methodology. In J. Glazier & R. Powell (Eds.), *Qualitative research in information management* (pp. 61–84). Englewood, CO: Libraries Unlimited.

Ellis, D. (1989). A behaviourial approach to information retrieval design. *Journal of Documentation*, *45*, 171–212.

Fisher, K. E. (2005). Information grounds. In K. E. Fisher, S. Erdelez, & L. McKechnie (Eds.), *Theories of information behaviour* (pp. 185–190). Medford, NJ: Information Today (Published for the American Society for Information Science and Technology).

Fisher, K. E., Durrance, J. C., & Hinton, M. B. (2004). Information grounds and the use of need-based services by immigrants in Queens, New York: A context-based, outcome evaluation approach. *Journal of the American Society for Information Science and Technology*, *55*(8), 754–766.

Fisher, K. E., Marcoux, E., Miller, L. S., Sanchez, A., & Cunningham, E. R. (2004). Information behaviour of migrant Hispanic farm workers and their families in the pacific Northwest. *Information Research*, *10*(1). paper 199. Retrieved from http://InformationR.net/ir/10-1/paper199.html

Fisher, K., Naumer, C., Durrance, J., Stromski, L., & Christiansen, T. (2005). Something old, something new: Preliminary findings from an exploratory study about people's information habits and information grounds. *Information Research*, *10*(2). paper 223. Retrieved from http://InformationR.net/ir/10-2/paper223.html

Granovetter, M. (1973). Strength of weak ties. *American Journal of Sociology*, *78*(6), 1360–1380.

Granovetter, M. (1982). The strength of weak ties: A network theory revisited. In P. Marsden & N. Lin (Eds.), *Social structure and network analysis* (pp. 105–130). Beverly Hills, CA: Sage.

Jeong, W. (2004). Unbreakable ethnic bonds: Information-seeking behaviour of Korean graduate students in the United States. *Library & Information Science Research*, *26*, 384–400.

Johnson, C. (2004). Choosing people: The role of social capital in information seeking behaviour. *Information Research*, *10*(1). Retrieved from http://informationR.net/ir/10-1/paper201.htm

Julien, H. (2004). Adolescent decision-making for careers: An exploration of information behavior. In M. K. Chelton & C. Cool (Eds.), *Youth information-seeking behavior: Theories, models, and issues* (pp. 321–352). Lanham, MD: Scarecrow Press.

Julien, H. E. (1999). Barriers to adolescent information seeking for career decision making. *Journal of the American Society for Information Science*, *50*(1), 38–48.

Julien, H., & Michels, D. (2000). Source selection among information seekers: Ideals and realities. *Canadian Journal of Information and Library Science*, *25*(1), 1–18.

Krikelas, J. (1983). Information seeking behavior: Patterns and concepts. *Drexel Library Quarterly*, *19*, 5–20.

Kuhlthau, C. C. (1991). Inside the search process — Information seeking from the users perspective. *Journal of the American Society for Information Science*, *42*(5), 361–371.

Lilley, S. C. (2008). Information barriers and Maori secondary school students. *Information Research — An International Electronic Journal*, *13*(4). paper 373. Retrieved from http://InformationR.net/ir/13-4/paper373.html

Lilley, S. C. (2010). *The information seeking behaviours of Māori secondary school students.* A thesis presented in partial fulfilment of the requirements for the degree of Doctor of Philosophy at Massey University, Manawatu Campus, New Zealand.

Lilley, S. C. (2012). The impact of cultural values on Maori information behaviour. *LIBRI*, *62*(4), 377–388.

Lilley, S. C. (2013). Māori career information seeking. *MAI Journal*, *2*(1), 32–45.

Metoyer- Duran, C. (1993). Information gatekeepers. *Annual Review of Information Science and Technology*, *28*, 111–150.

Meyers, E., Fisher, K., & Marcoux, E. (2007). Studying the everyday information behavior of tweens: Notes from the field. *Library & Information Science Research*, *29*(3), 310–331.

Ministry of Education. (2013). *Progress against Māori education plan targets: Ka Hikitia — Managing for success.* Retrieved from http://www.educationcounts.govt.nz/statistics/maori_education/36805

Pettigrew, K. E. (1999). Waiting for chiropody: Contextual results from an ethnographic study of the information behaviour among attendees at community clinics. *Information Processing & Management*, *35*(6), 801–817.

Pettigrew, K. E. (2000). Lay information provision in community settings: How community health nurses disseminate human services information to the elderly. *Library Quarterly*, *70*(1), 47–85.

Rapoport, A. (1954). Spread of information through a population with sociostructural bias III. suggested experimental procedures. *Bulletin of Mathematical Biophysics*, *16*, 75–81.

Rapoport, A., & Horvath, W. J. (1961). A study of a large sociogram. *Behavioral Science*, *6*(4), 279–291.

Savolainen, R. (1995). Everyday life information-seeking: Approaching information seeking in the context of way of life. *Library & Information Science Research*, *17*(3), 259–294.

Savolainen, R. (2009). Small world and information grounds as contexts of information seeking and sharing. *Library & Information Science Research*, *31*(1), 38–45.

Shenton, A. K. (2004). Research into young people's information-seeking: Perspectives and methods. *Aslib Proceedings*, *56*(4), 243–254.

Shenton, A. K., & Dixon, P. (2003). Youngsters' use of other people as an information-seeking method. *Journal of Librarianship and Information Science*, *35*(4), 219–233.

Shoemaker, P. J. (1991). *Gatekeeping*. Newbury Park, CA: Sage.

Spink, A., & Cole, C. (2001). Information and poverty: Information-seeking channels used by African American low-income households. *Library & Information Science Research*, *23*(1), 45–65.

Statistics NZ. (2012). *National population estimates: March 2012 quarter*. Retrieved from http://www.stats.govt.nz/

Tamaira, M. (2007). *Searching for tupuna*. MLIS research project, Victoria University of Wellington School of Information Management. Retrieved from http://searching4tupuna.blogspot.com

Wilson, T. D. (1981). On user studies and information needs. *Journal of Documentation*, *37*(1), 3–15.

Wilson, T. D. (1999a). Exploring models of information behaviour: The 'uncertainty' project. *Information Processing & Management*, *35*(6), 839–849.

Wilson, T. D. (1999b). Models in information behaviour research. *Journal of Documentation*, *55*(3), 249–270.

SECTION III

DESIGNING SYSTEMS

Chapter 8

A Failure to Connect: The Elusive Relationship between Broadband Access and Children's Information Seeking in American Academic Research

Laura I. Spears and Marcia A. Mardis

Abstract

Purpose – The purpose of this study was to determine the extent to which academic researchers consider the relationship between broadband access and children's information seeking in the United States. Because broadband has been cited as an essential element of contemporary learning, this study sought to identify gaps in the attention given to the role of broadband in the information seeking environment of youth.

Approach – The researchers conducted a mixed method synthesis of academic research published in peer-reviewed journals between 1991 and 2011 that reported the information seeking of children aged 5–18 years. Quantitative and qualitative data were gathered from leading databases, analyzed separately, and conclusions drawn from integrated results.

Results – The results of this study indicated that broadband is rarely considered in the design of children's information seeking published in peer-reviewed research journals. Only 15 studies showed any presence of broadband in study design or conclusions. Due to the small number of qualifying studies, the researchers could not conduct the

New Directions in Children's and Adolescents' Information Behavior Research
Library and Information Science, Volume 10, 217–263

ISSN: 1876-0562/doi:10.1108/S1876-056220140000010056

synthesis; instead, the researchers conducted a quantitative relationship analysis and qualitative content analysis.

Practical implications – Given the focus of policymaking and public discussion on broadband, its absence as a study consideration suggests a crucial gap for scholarly researchers to address.

Research limitations – The data set included only studies of children in the United States, therefore, findings may not be universally applicable.

Originality/value – Despite national imperatives for ubiquitous broadband and a tradition of information seeking research in library and information science (LIS) and other disciplines, a lack of academic research about how broadband affects children's information seeking persists.

Keywords: Children; youth; broadband; imposed query; information seeking; homework

8.1. Introduction

Benchmarked as one of the worst rates of broadband access and home connectivity among industrialized countries (Organisation for Economic Co-operation and Development [OECD], 2012; Windhausen, 2008), Americans are now at a disadvantage to compete educationally and commercially in a global information economy. Perhaps the most profound illustration of this policy paucity is the persistent 30% of households in the United States that lack high-speed broadband connectivity (Horrigan, 2012; National Telecommunications & Information Administration [NTIA], 2012; OECD, 2012) and reports that informal and formal learning online is drastically hampered by inadequate bandwidth (Ezell, Atkinson, Castro, & Ou, 2009; Windhausen, 2008).

Although the use of digital technology expands through the growth of mobile and handheld devices, The Pew Internet and American Life Project reported that 26% of teens 12–17 years of age did not access the Internet using mobile technology (Madden, Lenhart, Duggan, Cortesi, & Gasser, 2013). While this recent Internet study described increasing use of mobile technology for teens, penetration of use was distinguished by economic and ethnic boundaries. Significantly fewer black teens than white teens owned a desktop or laptop computer (Madden et al., 2013) and mobile technologies do not enable the complex information manipulation allowed by a broadband-enabled computer.

Although broadband has been cited as an essential element of contemporary learning (Gartner Consulting, 2003; Windhausen, 2008) and federal investments in upgrading and expanding availability exist, Internet access in public libraries, homes, and schools has remained relatively flat. Lacking this key affordance, many U.S. citizens are prevented from engaging in activities that promote engagement, citizenship, and lifelong learning. Many of these effects are manifested in "information seeking," the currently preferred term used to describe the many ways in which human beings interact with information, in particular, the ways in which people seek and use information (Bates, 2010).

The larger currents affecting the spread of broadband connectivity have especially disadvantaged schools. Currently, national initiatives that promote the development of 21st century learning focus strongly on children's abilities to find, use, evaluate, analyze, communicate, and create information in activities that require immersive, simultaneous Internet use (LEAD Commission, 2012; U.S. Department of Education, 2013). Although the effect of poor connectivity on children's information seeking may seem obvious or insignificant, to date, the extent to which broadband as either an element of study design or as an expressed study finding has not been specifically examined in American academic research. Cursory review of the mounting broadband literature suggested that very little focus had been given to the impact that access to and adoption of broadband had on information seeking of children. Given this apparent dearth of scholarly work, the present study sought to determine whether and how broadband was considered in research design or reported in research findings. Results gained from this study have implications for the role of broadband access in the information seeking of children aged 5−18 years engaged in schoolwork, in either a self-directed or an imposed query mode (Gross, 2006).

8.1.1. Research Questions

Because anecdotal and fragmented reports have suggested that broadband access is a key determinant of information seeking, this study proceeds from an overarching question: What is the nature of academic research concerning broadband and children's information seeking in the United States?

This overarching question was examined through four specific research questions:

RQ1. To what extent has broadband emerged as a factor in the design and results of studies of children's information seeking?

RQ2. Which information seeking emerged in studies that did consider broadband?

RQ3. Which sites, locales, participant socioeconomic status (SES), and participant genders have researchers considered?

RQ4. How has the role of broadband changed over time in studies of children's information seeking?

8.2. Literature Review

Broadband has been described as the "great infrastructure challenge of the early 21st century" (Federal Communications Commission [FCC], 2010b, p. 3), on par with prior challenges such as a transcontinental railway, an interstate highway system, and the provision of electricity to all communities in America (FCC, 2010a). Unlike these previous occurrences, however, broadband is more than an infrastructure creation problem; the nation's broadband infrastructure is a patchwork of delivery technologies and service providers and requires management and enhancement to ensure that the connectivity is available, stable, and robust. However, "broadband speed has emerged as the single most commonly cited metric for characterizing the quality of broadband offerings" (Bauer, Clark, & Lehr, 2010, p. 5). In the context of this study, broadband is defined as "high-speed Internet access that is always on and faster than the traditional dial-up access" (FCC, n.d.).

In this section, we provide an overview of U.S. broadband policy, of home and school access, and of children's use that considers speed but also includes additional factors that affect access and use.

8.2.1. Broadband in the United States

As early as 1987, the United States was on the forefront of high-speed networked telecommunications with the National Science Foundation's NSFNET project. This decade long initiative not only linked education and research institutions via a robust national data network, NSFNET also changed the work of educators and researchers so profoundly that demand quickly grew for connectivity in schools, libraries, government organizations, and homes. In response, the federal government forwarded a number of initiatives designed to make Internet connectivity more accessible and affordable. Once technology had advanced sufficiently to allow citizens to envision uses of broadband in every aspect of their lives, the demand for high-speed, continuously available, high-capacity connectivity grew (Frazer, 1996).

8.2.1.1. Universal Service Fund The Universal Service Fund (USF) was created by the Federal Communications Commission (FCC) in 1997 to meet the universal service goals mandated by Congress in the 1996 Telecommunications Act. The 1996 Act states that all providers of telecommunications services should contribute to federal universal service in some equitable and nondiscriminatory manner; there should be specific, predictable, and sufficient federal and state mechanisms to preserve and advance universal service; all schools, classrooms, health care providers, and libraries should have access to advanced telecommunications services; and finally, that the Federal-State Joint Board and the FCC should determine those other principles that, consistent with the 1996 Act, are necessary to protect the public interest.

Although the USF has been credited with infusing $20 billion into schools and libraries, demand for funding has remained strong despite controversial elements of the policy. Early detections of fraud and abuse resulted in increased accountability and auditing layers and revealed that often, some funding was wasted through poorly executed good intentions and occasional malfeasance. In 2011, the FCC approved a six-year transfer process that would transition money from the USF to a new $4.5 billion a year Connect America Fund for broadband Internet expansion, effectively putting an end to the USF by 2018.

8.2.1.2. National Broadband Plan In 2009, Congress directed the FCC to provide the critical infrastructure needed to deliver broadband Internet connectivity to every citizen in the United States. This National Broadband Plan (NBP) lays out short- and long-term goals to ensure that "every American has access to broadband capability" (FCC, 2010b). The NBP aims to improve competition among broadband service providers with innovative policies designed to ensure efficient development of infrastructure; to address income inequities preventing adoption through streamlined universal service assistance; and, to reform laws and standards as well as provide incentives for all stakeholders under governmental influence including educators, health care providers and insurers, and, government service agencies (FCC, 2010b). The NBP also includes a strong emphasis on raising awareness about broadband's benefits, especially for citizens who may be slow to adopt it for reasons other than cost and access. To wit, in an attempt to appeal to many communities experiencing the stagnant economic performance, the FCC touted broadband's potential to yield economic benefit in the NBP's initial paragraph.

8.2.1.3. National Education Technology Plan Soon after the release of the NBP, in 2010, the U.S. Department of Education released *Transforming American Education: Learning Powered by Technology*, also known as The National Education Technology Plan (NETP), which set a national agenda for digital learning. Digital learning is defined as educational programs and technology that "enable engaging individual learners' personal interests by connecting web learning resources to learning standards, providing options for adjusting the challenge level of learning tasks to avoid boredom or frustration, and bridging informal and formal learning in and outside of school" (U.S. Department of Education, 2010, p. 17). The NETP presents five goals with recommendations for states, districts, the federal government, and other stakeholders. The goals pertain to learning, assessment, teaching, infrastructure, and productivity.

The infrastructure goal reflects the U.S. Department of Education's vision for an education system enabled by the same kind of "cyberinfrastructure" that the (National Science Foundation [NSF], 2007) has promoted to undergird scientific research. The NETP's digital learning vision also mimics the rhetoric surrounding NSFNET's catalyzing of Internet use in non-research contexts nearly 25 years earlier. Indeed, the Department of Education's conception of digital learning parallels the FCC's definition of broadband, that is "a crucial element of … an infrastructure for learning is always on and makes learning opportunities available to learners, educators, and administrators regardless of their location, the time of day, or the type of access devices" (U.S. Department of Education, 2010, p. 52). The NETP concludes that research and development on technology and learning is essential for scaling of effective practices and reducing education costs.

8.2.2. Broadband Deployment in the United States

Thirty years of U.S. broadband policy initiatives have resulted in an environment that can be assessed from many angles including availability, access, adoption, and infrastructure. For the purposes of this review, the focus in this chapter is on youth access to broadband at home and school, but it begins with a general look at the evolution of the state of broadband adoption in the United States

8.2.2.1. Home broadband In its *Eighth Broadband Progress Report*, the FCC (2012) reported that broadband availability has significantly increased but that one in six Americans still lacked home access to broadband at the FCC's acceptable speed threshold. This means that almost 19 million Americans, in over 7 million households, did not access broadband at home (FCC, 2012). Still, over the last decade, home broadband adoption has risen steeply from slightly less than 4% to almost 64% of homes having high-speed connections. Broadband adoption has risen to 5.6 million homes despite variations in income, race and ethnicity, gender, employment status, and location (NTIA, 2012). While these reports reflect adults in the home who access broadband, since many of these adults are parents and because parents are financial gatekeepers, understanding home broadband adoption is key to exploring the nature of children's use of technology for schoolwork and at home (Livingstone, 2003; Livingstone & Helsper, 2007).

Availability does not result in adoption. At the time of the crafting of the NBP, 100 million Americans did not have household broadband; 14 million did not even have broadband infrastructure access; and up to 10 million school age children did not have home access (FCC, 2010b). This slow adoption has been attributed to a lack of federal effort to streamline policy and incentivize industry to make broadband available and affordable. The impact of nonresponsive, complicated national policy initiatives is stagnant home broadband adoption. While many citizens may be eager to bring broadband into their homes, it seems that a sector of the public does not recognize the potential of broadband to add value to their lives.

In 2010, researchers at Connected Nation, a broadband consulting company, compared early adopters to new adopters in a 2010 representative nationwide survey (Joshi, Lane, McGovern, Noriega, & Walker, 2011). The researchers reported new adopters tended to be female; live in a rural area; have a low annual income; and be Hispanic or African-American. In contrast, late adopters used fewer applications and were online less frequently unless enrolled in online education. As the authors observed, some users required a significant amount of time to recognize the value of household broadband, especially in delivering high-quality digital content for educational purposes. Household broadband adoption enhances users' Internet skills, even if home Internet is used for entertainment rather than practical endeavors (Hsieh, Rai, & Keil, 2008; Van der Heijden, 2004; Venkatesh & Brown, 2001).

A host of causes could account for the apparent plateau of the dissemination of expensive broadband service too hard to reach communities: a much larger expanse of expensive, physical infrastructure has yet to be installed and home broadband installation requires additional technologies and skill. For these reasons and likely many others, a lack of coherent national broadband policy has very real consequences for home adoption.

No study conclusively points to effective adoption promotion strategies or to the value of broadband either as a policy directive or a personal choice. However, with the migration of institutional education to digital platforms, including virtual classrooms, online and distance learning, and digital textbooks in K-20 classrooms, the barriers to household adoption loom as significant concerns to educators and parents.

Children's Internet use at home. According to the 2010 Current Population Survey (CPS), about one quarter of households with children had Internet access (NTIA, 2012). Mardis (2013) conducted an integrated secondary analysis of Census and NCES data and found that the presence of home broadband had compelling relationships with student achievement, even when a major predictor of student achievement, SES, was considered. These findings were affirmed by Selwyn, Potter, and Cranmer (2010), and Livingstone and Helsper (2007), whose research had similar results:

> In other words, children from lower SES homes who have home internet access use it just as much as those from higher SES homes: it seems that providing home internet access in low SES households helps to close the gap in use, potentially reducing disadvantage .... SES differences in amount of use disappear if just those with home access are compared .... We conclude that providing home access can alleviate but not overcome the relative disadvantage of coming from a low SES household in terms of the breadth of internet use, this warranting continued attention to socioeconomic disadvantage in relation to internet use. (pp. 7,12,13).

These findings were not surprising in light of other research that refutes contemporary perceptions that children use the Internet at home purely for leisure purposes (Tripp, 2011) and youth self-reports of engaging in risky online seeking (Livingstone & Helsper, 2007). Many researchers have found that the top three reasons children use their home Internet connections are completing schoolwork, gathering information about hobbies, and communicating with peers (Livingstone & Helsper, 2007; O'Keeffe, Clarke-Pearson, & Council on Communications Media, 2011) and that each of these applications offers powerful potential to redress technology and information skills not gained in school (Livingstone & Helsper, 2010). When parents understood the impact broadband could have on student learning and how students with broadband at home were at an educational advantage, they were more willing to invest in it, even if they had concerns about online safety (Cranmer, 2006).

Results of other research conducted with youth (Selwyn, 2006) yielded surprising results: although students recognized that their home technology environments and their school technology environments were often in stark contrast, for the most part, students accepted their schools as technology-limited environments. They expressed resignation and few expectations that schools could or should be places where technology is integrated widely and deeply. Selwyn's (2006, 2011) research suggested that students who were "net-savvy" also grew to be "school-savvy"; students saw their schools as places where technology was only as good as its educational applications required. This pragmatism was balanced by children's interest in using technology at home and a lack of home technology was seen as a far worse condition than poor school technology (Lewin, Mavers, & Somekh, 2003; Livingstone, 2003). Lacking opportunities at school, in some instances, children did not develop the capacity to envision how the Internet would help them find information, communicate with others, or entertain themselves (Holmes, 2011; Livingstone & Helsper, 2007; Project Tomorrow, 2012).

A synthesis of prior research suggested that regardless of time or context, home broadband has clear advantages for student learning but adoption was hindered by parents' lack of perceived value (Livingstone & Bober, 2006). An absence of home broadband access also affected children's desire to use the Internet at school because they had not experienced online activities enough to understand how the Internet might be helpful and did not possess enough skills to confidently accomplish desired tasks. Studies of how well Internet use at school related to Internet use at home found that when students performed sophisticated activities on the Internet at school, they were able to further the case for broadband's value at home. These studies pointed to the need for curriculum, not connectivity, to be the constant linking home and school experience for maximum student benefit (Lewin et al., 2003).

8.2.2.2. School broadband Many calls have been made to fundamentally redefine the meaning of schooling and re-envision the infrastructure of education to include immersive experiences; informal opportunities; and greater continuity between home, school, and workforce, all of which are enhanced by ubiquitous, reliable high-speed networks (NSF, 2007). However, when schools are connection rich but equipment and management poor, children's experiences with technology at school are negatively impacted (Kozma, 2011).

In many schools, bandwidth capacity dictates the extent to which teachers are able to foster high-level information, communications, and technology "21st century" skills among their students. While 99% of public schools in the United States reported having Internet access, less than one-third of schools reported top tier broadband speeds (Brenchley, 2011); rural and high poverty schools reported 88–96% Internet penetration (U.S. Department of Education, 2010). Classroom connections were less frequent in all schools (National Center for Education Statistics, 2011) and even when classroom access was available, many building-level bandwidth capacity management policies impede the integration of the Internet into teaching and learning. In 2010, the FCC reported that many (over 80%) school connections were not meeting school officials' needs because the connections were overloaded and poorly managed, leading to slow performance or restricted use (FCC, 2010c). For example, in a study done in Michigan, education officials reported having to develop and enforce bandwidth use policies that limited video streaming and other high-capacity uses; the Michigan finding was confirmed by the overwhelming majority of respondents to a nationwide survey of school officials who reported that their networks were too slow to support video streaming (FCC, 2010c). Broadband capacity influenced teachers' use of the Internet in their classrooms as much as their skills with technology integration (Mardis, 2009).

Many school administrators reported that they would like to scale up the use of digital learning objects, handheld devices, and information resources, but lacked the funds to do so (FCC, 2010c; Project Tomorrow, 2013). Reflecting the rapidly increasing adoption of multimedia digital resources within the classroom, 71% of district technology leaders in a nationally representative sample said they could not ensure that their future needs for classroom connectivity can be met. Eleven percent said that their current connectivity did not even address current district needs; in 2010, only 10% of these leaders identified that same issue as critical (Project Tomorrow, 2013). School officials understood the potential benefits of increased Internet connectivity. If students and teachers had the bandwidth that they needed, school administrators reported they would be able to better utilize online curriculum, offer online learning opportunities for student and teachers, and strengthen school-home linkages, in addition to supporting usage of multimedia in the classroom (Project Tomorrow, 2013).

As technology and Internet have gained presence in classrooms, instructional materials and activities have become digitally rich and the use of digital textbooks is rapidly gaining ground in education at all levels. A lack of adequate broadband access is complicated by information needs that occur beyond the school day or in the case of schooling that occurs in a virtual format (Moyle, 2010). The number of districts enrolling students in distance or online education classes has grown from 36% to 55% in 2010 (U.S. Department of Education, 2010); several million K-12 students (over 5%) participated in different types of digital learning programs (Watson, Murin, Vashaw, Gemin, & Rapp, 2012). In 2012, many states enacted legislation that ranged from planning some form of online education initiative in an unstated time frame to immediately implementing a comprehensive digital learning mandate. Eight states (Alabama, Arkansas, Florida, Maine, Michigan, New Hampshire, North Carolina, Virginia) currently have statewide implementation plans and/or established virtual schooling (Watson et al., 2012) and the move toward digital textbooks is a juggernaut (Fletcher, Schaffhauser, & Levin, 2012).

But even the FCC states that it lacks "comprehensive data regarding the actual or desired level of broadband service our nation's elementary and secondary schools" (FCC, 2012, p. 59) need. Therefore, to date, little data have been gathered on the extent to which delivery of learning and subsequent knowledge creation has been constrained (Somekh, 2007). Less clear from current research are what the Internet connection to the actual end user in school is like and what type of instruction and learning it has the capacity to support. However, researchers and policymakers must acknowledge the pivotal role of broadband in contemporary elementary and secondary education in order to prepare students for work and life in the 21st century (Fox, Waters, Fletcher, & Levin, 2012).

8.2.3. The Information Search Process: A Framework for Digital Information Seeking

Adequate, reliable broadband is a key affordance of a digital learning environment and the activities it enables within this environment deserve exploration. Whether at home or at school, teacher-directed activities function as a learning bridge that connects home and school Internet activity (Peters, 2008). Investigations into children's Internet information seeking have a long history and can be roughly grouped into what Kuhlthau (2004) called stages of the Information Search Process (ISP). In order, the stages are: Initiation; Selection; Exploration; Formulation; Collection; and Closure.

8.2.3.1. Stage 1: Initiation During the first stage, initiation, the information seeker recognizes the need for new information to complete an assignment (Kuhlthau, 2004). Previous research has shown that children mainly use the Internet for schoolwork (Project Tomorrow, 2012). This task functions as a *de facto* "imposed query," that is, an information task generated by someone other than the information seeker (Gross, 1996, 2006). For children, these imposed queries take the form of homework assignments, research paper topics, and other teacher-driven information explorations. While self-generated questions may emerge from within the confines of an assignment, the nature of the assignment still drives students' information investigations (Gross, 1999; Project Tomorrow, 2012).

8.2.3.2. Stage 2: Selection In the second stage, selection, the individual begins to decide what topic will be investigated and how to proceed (Kuhlthau, 2004). Some information retrieval may occur at this point. Because children are predominantly seeking information in an imposed query environment, the selection phase is particularly meaningful in situations where students have the option of selecting a topic within the bounds of the assignment. Mardis (2008) found that children often sought help from librarians in selecting a topic for their assignments, particularly in the instance of science projects assigned in middle school. Gross (2006) explained that the successful completion of this phase is essential for all subsequent information seeking activities. Topic selection is often a reflection of children's confidence in the subject domain (Hirsh, 2004). In this phase, children often begin a recursive process of Internet use in which they gauge the viability of potential topics by initial keyword searches of databases and the Web (Bilal, 2004; Shenton, 2007).

8.2.3.3. Stage 3: Exploration In the third stage, exploration, information on the topic is gathered and a new personal knowledge is created (Desjarlais, Willoughby, & Wood, 2008). Students endeavor to locate new information and situate it within their previous understanding of the topic (Kuhlthau, 2004). Early studies of children's information seeking in electronic environments focused mainly on their abilities to navigate conceptually organized browsing interfaces and drew conclusions about children's seeking based on their topic selections (Cool, 2004). As the Internet became more commonly used in information seeking, and the sophistication of information presentation developed accordingly, research turned to children's abilities to form search queries that reflected their questions. These early studies suggested that children tended to excel in information environments created for and by them and that when they were faced with less intuitive interfaces, tended to construct short searches that often lacked the flexibility and sophistication experienced searchers used to get results (Bilal, 2002, 2005; Nahl & Harada, 2004). Prior research has also suggested that successful completion of this phase depends on the extent to which children encounter problems they cannot resolve throughout their searches. That is, when children make the effort to master the search strategies they are taught and unexpected technical problems hinder search problems, children can become discouraged and either abandon the investigation or engage in satisficing seeking based on weak and incomplete search results (Selwyn, 2011; Shenton, 2007; Watson, 2004).

8.2.3.4. Stage 4: Formulation and Stage 5: Collection During the formulation stage, the information seeker starts to evaluate the information that has been gathered. Formulation is considered to be the most important stage of the process because it is in this stage that the information seeker formulates a personalized construction of the topic from the general information gathered in the exploration phase (Kuhlthau, 2004). During the fifth stage, collection, the information seeker has a focused topic and can proceed with a greater sense of ownership over the information seeking process and a clearer sense of desired outcome (Kuhlthau, 2004).

The main instantiation of these phases is the ability to identify relevant search results. Shenton (2007) traced the change in published literature of relevance assessment discussed as a generic skill, to one situated in the child's prior knowledge of the topic, confidence in the information seeking process, trust of the information source, and other personally constructed ideas toward the information seeking process. Underlying this change, Shenton contended, was researchers' growing familiarity with the complexity of children's processes and willingness to propose more sophisticated conceptions of children's information seeking. In short, he posited that researchers tended to report results in the areas they were examining and did not often note results that did not fit within the frames of their studies, especially when those results took the shape of search failures. While Shenton noted that search failure has been documented by a handful of researchers (e.g., Cool, 2004 and, more recently, Bilal & Sarangthem, 2009) but that exploring the causes of those failures had not been a focus of research.

8.2.3.5. Stage 6: Closure In the sixth and final stage, search closure, the individual has completed the information search. Now the information seeker will summarize and report on the information that was found through the process. The information seeker will experience a sense of relief and, depending on the fruits of their search, either satisfaction or disappointment (Kuhlthau, 2004). This phase is one in which the most current research relating to children's learning in an online environment is important. While not necessarily always considered part of information seeking, children's use of social media as a means by which to communicate what he/she has learned as a result of schoolwork functions as an expression of closure. In 2012, Project Tomorrow reported results of its nationwide survey of school-aged children. Among their findings was a strong preference for using Internet-mediated tools for schoolwork, but especially for communication and assessment of learning:

- 1 in 10 students in grades 6–12 have sent out a Tweet about an academic topic that interests them;
- 15 percent have informally tutored other students online or found an expert to help them with their own questions;
- 18 percent have taken an online assessment to evaluate their own self-knowledge;
- One-fifth have used a mobile app to organize their schoolwork;
- 1 in 4 have used a video that they found online to help with homework;
- 30 percent of middle school students and 46 percent of high school students have used Facebook as an impromptu collaboration tool for classroom projects; and
- Almost half of the high school students have sought out information online to help them better understand a topic that is being studied in class (p. 4).

Robust connectivity allows children to personalize their approaches to learning (Nesbit & Winne, 2008); and the potential to blur the distinction between home and school learning (Project Tomorrow, 2012). Inadequate or unreliable access can distract from the ISP and contribute to frustration and a lack of persistence that may be credited to poor task definition, weak search strategy, or any number of other failures that describe the downside of children's information experiences. Positive Internet experiences, on the other hand, lead children to a sense of success and accomplishment that results in a willingness to be self-directed, independent learners (Selwyn, 2011; Warschauer & Matuchniak, 2010) who understand the relationship between schooling and the rest of their life experiences (Somekh, 2007).

8.3. Methods

In this section, the systematic approach used to select the literature for the synthesis and to analyze the results is described. The researchers chose to focus on peer-reviewed articles available through leading periodical databases to mimic a primary information gathering strategy used commonly by academic researchers (Ge, 2010; Head, 2008; Niu et al., 2010).

8.3.1. Data Collection

To collect data, the researchers first defined the target sample, developed a search strategy, and gathered the initial sample.

8.3.1.1. Definition of the target sample The first step of collecting the data was to clearly define the criteria for inclusion in the study.

Publication date. The first criterion of selecting the study sample was publication date. This criterion was framed by dates that frame the growth of the Internet. As Crandall and Jackson (2001) pointed out, "The obvious candidate for the sudden acceleration in economic growth after 1994 is the Internet" (p. 8). One indication of the phenomenal impact of network connectivity was in 1990, the first World Wide Web server was deployed in Geneva, Switzerland (Berners-Lee, 1996). In 1989, 12 years after Apple introduced the first personal computer in 1977, only 12% of American households possessed any type of home computer (Crandall & Jackson, 2001); by 1994, this figure quickly jumped to over 40% three years after the Internet began connecting users.

Inclusion characteristics. After determining the sampling frame using the databases as boundaries, criteria for study inclusion in a systematic review required that the study participants be located in the United States, and be comprised of participants between the ages of 5–18 years. No restriction was placed on methods used or any other aspect of the study participants. As a truly exploratory search, and in order to fully expose the hypothesis to scrutiny, the sample selection process was broadly derived. Clear inclusion criteria were established at the outset in order to demonstrate reliability and avoid the bias that can occur with selectively sampled studies (Littell, Corcoran, & Pillai, 2008).

8.3.1.2. Search strategy With the sample criteria clearly defined, the next step was to define the search strategy. Definition of the search strategy was a two-step process: (1) identify the relevant databases that index research literature; and, (2) identify relevant articles.

Target databases. Based on this background, we devised the sites for the literature search. Eleven databases that contained full-text, peer-reviewed research articles published between the years 1991 through 2011 were considered, based upon the Joint Information Systems Committee's (JISC) Academic Database Assessment Tool (ADAT). ADAT was used to determine suitability based on the journals included, extent of full-text peer-reviewed journal content, and availability through the Florida State University (FSU) Library system. FSU academic librarians were also consulted on database choice to ensure the widest possible coverage of the subject. The 11 database names and their publishers are listed in Table 8.1.

Table 8.1: Target database names and publishers used in this study.

Database name	Publisher
ACM Digital Library	Association for Computing Machinery
EBSCOHost	EBSCO
Emerald Library E-journals	MCB Publications
Gale Databases	Gale Cengage
Google Scholar	Google
IngentaConnect	PublishingTechnology
OmniFile Full Text Mega Edition	Wilson
ProQuest	ProQuest
SAGE Journals	SAGE Publications
ScienceDirect	Elsevier
Web of Knowledge	Thomson Reuters

Query formation. We purposefully chose very broad search terms to enable the database search to gather a rich selection of articles about children's information seeking in the United States. The terms were broadened to include youth and teens in order to collect studies that may not specifically refer to ages in the metadata.

The query used in each database, "child* OR youth OR teen*" AND "seek* W1 information" retrieved far more results than were relevant. Reasons for this include lack of effective search engine interfaces to adequately and consistently refine and filter the results; lack of comprehensive metadata, particularly with older or foreign articles, that did not adequately identify basic elements of the journal's study sample; and, library collection discontinuities that indicated possession of the full text of the article when the article was not actually available. Two databases were eliminated from the preliminary list: Google Scholar and Emerald were removed because they each yielded an extremely large number of results without providing effective features to filter results to meet the inclusion criteria.

8.3.1.3. Sample collection Given the wide range of terms used to refer to the key concepts of broadband, youth, and information seeking, the researchers intentionally kept the search terms very broad and manually reviewed the search results to determine which studies included broadband in their designs and/or results. Each researcher independently reviewed the results.

Using the FSU databases, the researchers' query yielded a combined total of 3290 articles from nine databases. This group of articles was refined to a final sample of 15 articles using the process illustrated in Figure 8.1. The list of articles included in the final sample is shown in Appendix 8.A.

As Figure 8.1 illustrates, in the systematic review process, the researchers narrowed the total number of search results ($n = 3290$) by discarding obviously irrelevant articles ($n = 3054$). Articles were deemed irrelevant if they did not pertain to any aspect of information seeking; if they did not include any aspect of youth; and if they focused on a site outside of the United States. The researchers then examined the titles and abstracts from the resulting group of articles ($n = 236$) and identified more articles to exclude, leaving 199 full-text, peer-reviewed articles that were available at FSU. Of this group, 46 articles included the use of computer mediation in the study of children, youth, or teens seeking information.

This group was then reviewed to determine whether broadband was considered in the study design or the study results. Broadband was considered broadly, taking into account mentions of high Internet connection speed, "ubiquity," "connectivity," or other expressions of high speed or capacity. Once the researchers excluded articles that did not consider broadband in any way, the sample size was reduced to 15 articles. The Appendix lists the

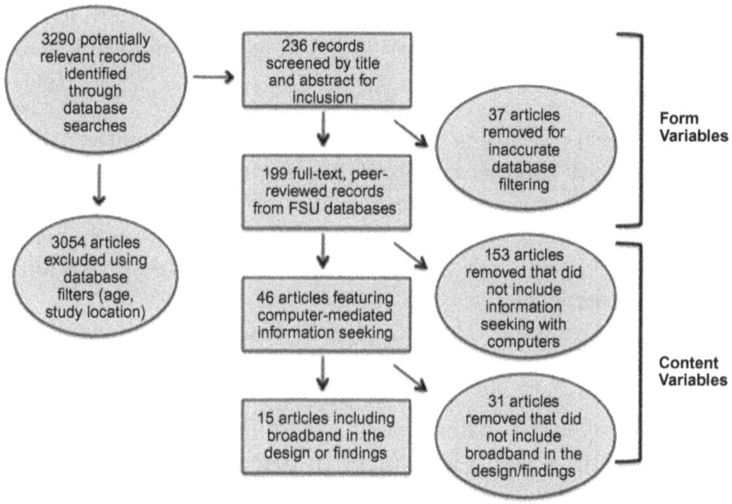

Figure 8.1: Systematic review steps using integrative content analysis. *Form variables*: Design attributes including study location, age of sample, full-text availability, and peer-reviewed articles. *Content variables*: Computer-mediated information seeking: presence of broadband. *Source*: Adapted from Shoemaker and Reese (1996).

full citations and assigned article numbers (A1–A15) for the 15 articles eligible for further analysis.

8.3.2. Data Analysis

The researchers conducted content analysis on the 15 articles that included children's computer-related information seeking to determine the presence and to determine the change of this presence over time.

8.3.2.1. Content analysis Content analysis is "the systematic, objective, quantitative analysis of message characteristics" (Neuendorf, 2002, p. 1). The purpose of content analysis was to determine the nature of broadband's consideration in the study, the type of information seeking activity being described by the study, and the difference between study settings and participants. The unit of analysis was a single, peer-reviewed, full-text article.

Broadband in design and/or use. The researchers were interested in studies in that reflected broadband as an explicit element of study design and/or broadband as an explicitly stated element of a finding or conclusion. Broadband may have been discussed in the design or findings on a study in the following ways:

- Quality of access resulting from descriptions of ubiquitous, effective, fast, slow, speedy Internet connectivity associated with computer use by children/youth/teens seeking information;
- Quantity of features that work singularly effectively with high-speed Internet connectivity such as multimedia, interactive applications, and presences of a network.
- Type of access resulting from description of technology including bandwidth, latency, and fiber optic networks.

Importance of broadband. After the researchers determined how broadband was included in the study, they sought to determine how important of a consideration broadband was to the study. Importance was classified into three levels and defined as Table 8.2 describes.

Research method. The researchers also noted the research methods used in each study. The method names were taken from study authors' descriptions of the research methods employed in the study.

Classification into Kuhlthau's ISP stages. Once researchers identified reports that included broadband in design or findings, the reports were classified into one of Kuhlthau's ISP stages: Initiation; Selection; Exploration; Formulation; Collection; and Closure. These six stages are described in detail in Section 8.2. The ISP is a useful framework for

Table 8.2: Broadband levels and definitions used in data analysis.

Level	Design	Findings
Low	Broadband was mentioned as a data point to be collected	Broadband is mentioned in passing in results report
Medium	Broadband was mentioned as a data point with explanation as to why it was important to the study	Broadband is discussed as a result but did not have a significant bearing on results interpretation
High	Broadband was mentioned as a data point and with substantial explanation about its importance to the study	Broadband is discussed as a result and had a significant bearing on results interpretation

designing, framing, and analyzing the investigation of information seeking behavior in complex tasks and has been validated in a number of contexts in the last 20 years (Kuhlthau, Heinström, & Todd, 2008).

Description of sites, locales, number of participants, participant gender, and participant SES. The content analysis concluded with an examination of the study settings. That is, researchers noted: study site (e.g., elementary school, middle school, high school, public library, home); locale (urban, suburban, rural); SES (high poverty, low poverty, both); and gender (male, female).

8.3.2.2. Frequency analysis The publication dates of research reports used in the content analysis were frequency analyzed to determine change over time. Then, journal titles were visually inspected for frequency of publication years as well as the names of authors.

8.4. Results

This section presents the results of the content analysis and frequency analysis procedures.

8.4.1. Content Analysis Phase 1

All subsequent analyses were performed on the final group of 15 articles. The first phase of content analysis, summarized in Table 8.3, captured the role of broadband in study design or study findings as well as the data collection methods, query types, and ISP stages.

8.4.1.1. Broadband in study design and results The researchers analyzed the content each of the 15 eligible studies to determine whether broadband was included in the study design or the study results or findings. Table 8.3 illustrates the number of studies that included broadband in study design, in study results, or in both study design and results. As the table demonstrates, the majority of the eligible studies ($n = 9$ or 60%) included broadband in both the study design and the study findings. Only one study included broadband in design but did not also report it in findings. The remaining five studies reported broadband as part of a study finding.

Importance of broadband. Once the researchers established broadband's role in each of the content analyzed methods, the researchers sought to

Table 8.3: Broadband articles by study method, broadband inclusion type, broadband importance, query type, and ISP stage.

Article number	Design	Finding	Importance	Method(s)	Query type	ISP stage
A1	Yes	Yes	High	Survey Interview	Unimposed	1–5
A2	Yes	Yes	High	Systematic review	N/A	N/A
A3	Yes	Yes	High	Systematic review	N/A	N/A
A4	Yes	No	Low	Interview	Imposed/ Unimposed	2,4,5
A5	Yes	Yes	Medium	Survey	Unimposed	5,6
A6	Yes	Yes	High	Observation	N/A	N/A
A7	No	Yes	High	Observation Interview	Imposed	3–5
A8	Yes	Yes	Low	Observation Interview	Unimposed	1,4,6
A9	No	Yes	High	Survey Content analysis	Unimposed	2–5
A10	Yes	Yes	High	Interview	Unimposed	6
A11	No	Yes	Medium	Observation Interview Content analysis	Unimposed	1–5
A12	No	Yes	Medium	Survey Interview	Unimposed	6
A13	Yes	Yes	High	Survey	Imposed/ Unimposed	4,5
A14	No	Yes	Low	Observation Interview	Imposed/ Unimposed	4,5
A15	Yes	Yes	High	Survey	Unimposed	4,6

determine the extent to which broadband played a role. As described in Table 8.3, the presence of broadband was classified into three levels: low, medium, and high. For the nine articles that included broadband in both study findings and study results, seven had a high presence of broadband, one had a medium presence of broadband, and one had a low presence of broadband. The one article in which broadband was included in study design but not in study results reflected a low presence of broadband. The remaining five articles included broadband only in the results reporting and of those articles, two had a high presence of broadband, two had a medium presence of broadband, and one had a low presence of broadband.

To further illustrate how the researchers discerned broadband presence, Table 8.4 includes example quotes from the eligible articles that reflect each level. Each quote is appended with the article number and article page number.

8.4.1.2. Study method Next, the researchers examined each of the studies to determine the methods used in data collection. As Table 8.3 indicates, the majority ($n=9$) of the eligible studies used two or more data collection methods. Study A13 used three data collection methods. The remaining six studies employed a single data collection method.

The most common data methods were interview ($n=7$), survey ($n=6$), and observation ($n=5$). For both data collection and data analysis methods, published research was the basis for systematic review ($n=2$) and participant-provided artifacts informed content analyses ($n=2$).

8.4.1.3. Query type The researchers also reviewed the content of the eligible articles to determine the types of queries that guided the tasks under study. The majority ($n=8$) of the eligible studies were based on activities in which children were defining their own search tasks in unimposed queries while only two studies looked at children working on an imposed query. Three of the studies described situations in which children were using the Internet in tasks driven by both imposed and unimposed queries. The remaining two studies (A2 and A3), both systematic reviews, were not focused on a particular type of query. While each systematic review synthesized prior research that reflected both kinds of queries, the researchers determined that a secondary assignment of query was not meaningful for this study.

8.4.1.4. ISP stage The final task the researchers conducted during the content analysis phase of the data analysis was to note the stages of the ISP (Kuhlthau, 2004) were reflected by the activities reported in the eligible articles. These stages are Stage 1: Initiation; Stage 2: Selection; Stage 3: Exploration; Stage 4: Formulation; Stage 5: Collection; and Stage 6: Closure. Each stage is detailed in Section 8.2 of this research report.

Stage 4: Formulation ($n=9$) and Stage 5: Collection ($n=8$) were most often included in the eligible studies. Stage 6: Closure was reflected in five of the studies. Stage 2: Selection and Stage 3: Exploration were reflected in four studies while Stage 1: Initiation was included in three studies: A1, A6, and A13.

Table 8.4: Example quotes of levels indicating broadband inclusion in design or results.

Level	Design	Results
Low	*The group discussion guide was broad, including the following sections ... Self-reported challenges encountered when using the Internet.* (A10, p. 243, e3)	*A lack of Internet experience, however, often led to quick abandonment of the Internet as an information source.* (A15, p. 415)
Medium	*In addition, participants were asked (1) the speed of their Internet connection, (2) if the line they use to connect to the Internet is ever needed for phone use, and (3) the extent to which parental rules restricted their weekday leisure time allocation* (A4, p. 637)	*For example, if the average participant reported spending 46 min online, she or he might spend 36 of those minutes IMing, 30 min downloading music from a favorite website, and, during this activity, visit a chat room for 5 min (all the while ostensibly conducting research for her social studies homework).* (A4, p. 641)
High	*Respondents were asked to complete a pencil-and-paper survey to describe their access, frequency of use and comfort levels regarding general Internet use.* (A1, p. 54)	*Although T-1 lines connected the school's computers, sometimes the system was overloaded; graphics frequently took a long time to load. Slow connect times quickly tried students' patience, especially when they had only 45 minutes to use the school's library during their regularly scheduled library visits; waiting for the computer to load limited the amount of research students could accomplish. In some cases, slow connections caused students to abort their search or to shy away from Internet sites that could have contained useful information because they did not want to wait for them to load.* (A11, pp. 1270–1271)

8.4.1.5. Study participants In the second phase of the content analysis, the researchers examined each of the eligible studies to characterize their participants. Table 8.5 summarizes the study locales and sites as well as the participants' numbers and characteristics. Studies A2 and A3 are systematic reviews and this did not have participants, locations, or sites to record.

Number of participants. As Table 8.5 shows, the eligible studies included a wide range of participants, from 4 to 2416 children. Studies A2 and A3 are systematic reviews and this did not have participants. Study A5 was a case study that described the activities of children within an educational program at a homeless shelter and did not provide the number of participants.

Locale. The majority of the studies took place in suburban settings ($n=5$), and as many took place in urban locales ($n=5$). Only one study was conducted in a rural location. Three studies did not report a location.

Site. Public schools ($n=5$) were popular study sites as were health centers and agencies ($n=3$). Home was the site on two studies while a homeless shelter and a public library provided the sites of the two remaining studies.

Age. With the exception of study A15 that reported an age group as "Under 13," all studies that reported age ($n=11$) included specific ages. The lowest age specifically reported was nine years old and five studies included eighteen-year-old participants. The majority of the studies included participants between 13 and 17 years old.

Gender. All of the studies that reported participant gender ($n=11$) included both male and female participants. Two studies did not report gender.

SES. Seven studies specifically reported SES and five of those studies mentioned including both high and low SES participants. Two studies' participants were described as having high SES.

8.4.2. Relationship Analysis Results

The researchers visually inspected the publication dates and journal titles for frequency. Table 8.6 depicts the results by article number for frequencies of authors, publications years (Year), and journal title.

Table 8.5: Eligible studies' number of participants (*N*), locale, site, age, gender, and SES.

Article number	Study *N*	Study locale	Study site	Participant age	Participant gender	Participant SES
A1	319	Urban	Health center	13–18	Male Female	High Low
A2	N/A	N/A	N/A	N/A	N/A	N/A
A3	N/A	N/A	N/A	N/A	N/A	N/A
A4	157	Suburban	Public school	11–18	Male Female	High Low
A5	261	Suburban	Public school	12–13	Male Female	High
A6	Not reported	Urban	Homeless shelter	13–18	Male Female	Not reported
A7	10	Suburban	Public school	10–12	Male Female	Not reported
A8	7	Not reported	Home	15–17	Male Female	Not reported
A9	255	Suburban	Home	13–15	Not reported	High
A10	4	Not reported	Health agency	14–16	Male Female	Not reported
A11	16	Suburban	Public school	14–18	Not reported	High Low
A12	2416	Urban	Public school	9–12	Male Female	High Low
A13	405	Rural	Health agency	13–18	Male Female	Not reported
A14	11	Urban	Public library	Under 13 13–17	Male Female	Not reported
A15	1501	Not reported	Home	10–17	Male Female	High Low

Table 8.6: Broadband articles by author, publication year, and journal title.

Article	Author(s) (Year)	Journal title
A1	Borzekowski and Rickert (2001)	*Journal of Applied Developmental Psychology*
A2	Chan, Hue, Chou, and Tzeng (2001)	*Computers & Education*
A3	Dresang (2005)	*Library Trends*
A4	Gray, Klein, Noyce, Sesselberg, and Cantrill (2005)	*Journal of Adolescent Health*
A5	Gross (2004)	*Journal of Applied Developmental Psychology*
A6	Hendry et al. (2011)	*Children and Youth Services Review*
A7	Hirsh (1999)	*Journal of the American Society for Information Science*
A8	Jacobs (2006)	*Journal of Literacy Research*
A9	Marshall and Reday (2007)	*Young Consumers*
A10	O'Conner-Von (2009)	*Journal of Pediatric Oncology Nursing*
A11	Pickard (2008)	*Popular Narrative Media*
A12	Radford (2006)	*Library Trends*
A13	Rushing and Stephens (2011)	*The Journal of Primary Prevention*
A14	Slone (2003)	*Library & Information Science Research*
A15	Ybarra, Alexander, and Mitchell (2005)	*Journal of Adolescent Health*

As Table 8.6 shows, no author contributed to more than one of the publications in the analysis.

The publication dates reflected 2005 ($n = 3$) most frequently, followed 2006, 2001 ($n = 2$), and 2011 with two years. Finally 1991, 2003, and 2004 each had one publication per year.

The *Journal of Applied Developmental Psychology* and the *Journal of Adolescent Health* each published two of the publications in the analysis while *Computers & Education*; *Children and Youth Services Review*; *Journal of the American Society for Information Science*; *Journal of Literacy Research*; *Journal of Pediatric Oncology Nursing*; *Library & Information Science Research*; *Library Trends*; *Popular Narrative Media*; and *Young Consumers* represented only one publication per journal title.

8.5. Discussion

In this section, the results of the analyses in the context of each of the research questions are examined. The section concludes with some possible limitations and cautions to results interpretation.

RQ1. To what extent broadband emerged as a factor in the design and results of studies of children's information seeking?

Broadband is increasingly considered a cornerstone affordance of contemporary life and learning. Based on the number of studies first retrieved, the number of studies that had to be examined, and the subsequent analyses of method, no evidence suggests that academic researchers consistently consider broadband in study design or results. While there is a growing body of work that provide reasons for adoption and the new seeking that individuals adopt (Bennett, Stewart, & Atkinson, 2013), the ways in which broadband impacts imposed information seeking upon children in K-20 environments is not widely considered in scholarly studies.

As indicated in the literature, the lag between broadband availability and broadband adoption appears to parallel the study of broadband in research of children's information seeking. The results of this study showed that researchers considered broadband in only 15 studies over 20 years and that only four of those years had more than one broadband-inclusive study. Equally remarkable is that despite the fact that broadband began spreading into homes in 1991, no study considered broadband's role in children's information seeking until 1999. Only three journals produced any more than one study and no journal produced more than two broadband reflective research reports in 20 years. Health-related journals produced six studies, information studies journals provided five, and the remaining studies were published in communication- or education-related publications. Non-imposed information seeking comprised at least 11 of the studies. Queries were imposed in 5 of the 15 studies and three of these included mixed queries.

In spite of Internet availability mandate of national and state policy plans (FCC, 2010a) and the specific technology-enhanced educational mission, as outlined by NETP, the number of studies in which researchers examined broadband in any aspect of children's information seeking is minimal. With such scant research, it is simply not possible to determine the extent to which broadband's "always on" nature or the sluggishness of an insufficient connection affects children's decisions to remain engaged in an information seeking task or undertake any online information-related activities. While the U.S. Department of Education (2010) stressed that broadband connectivity was a crucial aspect of anytime, anywhere learning, only 60% of the focused on computer-mediated information seeking by children examined this element. The fact that four of the five research reports examined in this study studies reported a broadband-related finding of high and two of medium importance suggests that broadband may emerge as an important element, even if not intentionally studied. These findings can be seen to mirror the FCC (2012) report's conclusion that broadband speed measurement is confusing and often misrepresented and may not always be considered or understood by consumers, researchers, and policymakers. Perhaps this "measurement confusion" (Carmichael, McClure, Mandel, & Mardis, 2012) is why so few authors of the research reports targeted for this study considered broadband as a factor in study design or findings.

Broadband policy clearly favors increasing adoption and nascent research has demonstrated that broadband has strong potential to enrich household activities and children's learning (Joshi et al., 2011). However, as more states increase the number and size of their digital learning initiatives, the inconclusive nature of this research does not support that communities, schools, and homes are prepared to offer the ubiquitous access necessary to use broadband to its potential. Equally unclear is whether researchers study the effects of the absence or presence of broadband factor with the intensity or frequency it deserves.

RQ2. Which information seeking emerged in studies that considered broadband?

In this study, we used the search "information seeking" as a proxy in order to capture activity that is distinguished from a broad span of information behavior for its often intentional and high stakes nature (Case, 2012). In spite of Peters' (2008) assertion that teacher-directed activities connect home and school Internet use, 12 of the 15 studies were driven by unimposed queries derived from activities based on the ISP Stage 1 of Initiation. Study A1 described the use of the Internet for personal health care information. Study A8 explored adolescents' use of digital text messaging to focus the initiation process while Study A11 described this type of iterative query construction as a disruptive, stating that teachers felt that sharing query ideas encouraged "'messing about' and 'getting no work done'" (p. 59) and wasting bandwidth on frivolous pursuits. Natural curiosity and personally developed search seeking will likely become more prominent as statewide digital learning initiatives increase students' need to seek information for a larger number of learning tasks. Project Tomorrow has indicated that teachers will face technical challenges but this seeking will likely pose some as well.

The ISP Stage 2 process of Selection was explored in four articles (A1, A4, A9, and A11). In spite of the Mardis (2008) finding that children often sought help from librarians for help with assignments, Study A11's findings indicated that students preferred to use social "trial and error" methods of search refinement instead of asking for help. Because teachers and librarians found this type of collaboration to be inefficient use of time and bandwidth, teachers and librarians advocated limiting student Internet access to curtail this information seeking. However, studies A1, A4, and A9 all indicated that when children had positive experiences while information seeking for health information, they became confident information seekers and were elevated to the position of family technology decision-maker due to their familiarity with Internet use. These findings extended the Rompaey, Roe, and Struys (2002) and Tripp (2011) studies of children's influence on home technology adoption, demonstrating uses beyond schoolwork completion to practical, everyday decision-making support. Home broadband offers the entire family greater opportunity to increase Internet use (Hsieh et al., 2008; Van der Heijden, 2004; Venkatesh & Brown, 2001).

ISP Stage 3, Exploration was characterized in studies A1, A7, A9, and A11. While previous research indicated that children may abandon searches if their search strategies are not successful or they encounter technical difficulties (Selwyn, 2011; Shenton, 2007; Watson, 2004), Pickard (2008) found that peer interaction was beneficial to students in overcoming this challenge (A11); A1's study of adolescents seeking health information found that users referred back to family, peers, and health care professionals when faced with questionable information (A1). However, Study A8 reinforced the need for increased media literacy skills in a digital environment that could deliver information in a quantity commensurate with broadband capacity, as youths of all ages struggled to accurately assess the authority of this information (A7). Risky online seeking and online safety concerns (Cranmer, 2006; Livingstone & Helsper, 2007) were mitigated by an increase in digital literacy skills and Study A8's findings extended this concern to the use of the Internet for schoolwork as well. In each of these studies, broadband access was a backdrop for skills and abilities for digital learning.

ISP Stages 4 and 5 were strongly captured in the many studies in which ubiquitous connectivity enabled, and in some instances, seemed almost to require personalization. Overwhelmingly, the ability to independently seek information in preferred modes appeared in several of the studies, especially those focused on seeking health-related information (A1, A2, A10, A13). Personalized health-related information seeking allowed youth to take advantage of interactive features that filtered out irrelevant information for them (A1, A13). Personalization demonstrates the user's query formulation in response to information problems, adopting findings into a personally curated collection of perceived, credible resources. A13's focus on Native American teens provided a rich discussion of possible avenues for further research that begin to address Shenton's (2007) concerns that search failures are underreported, thus neglected in future studies (2007).

The ability to seek information independently and confidently, a foundation of digital literacy, was heavily impacted by youth and teen preference for interactive, bandwidth-intensive web resources and applications. For youth, "Internet sites must include and merge attention keeping qualities" (A1, p. 57). In fact, Study A15 reported that in comparison to other age groups, children 13 and under preferred websites that were light on text and had few graphics to download so that they could quickly decide whether to stay on the web page or view another site. A15 clearly showed how the act of information seeking is very much intertwined with the connectivity along which the query is transmitted and search resulted returned.

The research reports examined in the study also expanded the idea ISP Stages 4's Formulation and Stage 5's Collection. For example, A8's case study of instant messaging for homework suggested the constant background tasking functioned as a basic literacy skill. The need for simultaneous simulation and online social interaction was also reflected in a study of homeless youth (A6). The collaborative, social use of digital content and applications in information seeking, enabled by broadband, can be viewed as seeking enhanced by digital environments and offering stronger formulation and collection processes in achieving the user's desired outcomes, as described by Kuhlthau (2004).

The ISP Stage 6 Closure process also focuses on communication. Research reports examined in this study described the use of email and chat to obtain information from peers and friends as a form of search closure (A4, A5, A15). A finding of A3 noted that, contrary to current concern that youth may be isolating themselves with intensive Internet use, youth find greater connectivity in a social, online environment. The creative nature of networked learning also contributed to increased involvement in designing materials, and especially in a collaborative process (A2, A6, A11). In A10, study participants used online forums to communicate advice for cancer patients and families and this contributed to the work of the pediatric oncology nurse workforce (A10). These studies provided a rich complement to the findings Project Tomorrow's (2012) national survey of school-aged children in which the researchers reported that youth value the Internet as a means to enhance knowledge and skills beyond what was needed to complete homework (Livingstone & Helsper, 2010).

Jacobs' case study exemplifies the need to understand new seeking, especially youths as "text producers, distributors and consumers," so that they can be used and taught in the classroom. She also suggests that understanding how these activities are culturally meaningful may help avoid the barriers posed for students with limited or no access (A8). Hendry et al.'s study of a computer drop-in center for homeless youth reinforces the need for engaging, stimulating settings that include interactive, visually appealing web resources; and that in learning how to use information technology and digital media provides a means to learn relationship skills and possibly helps to create a path out of homelessness (A6).

While they may be verifying information accuracy with other sources, there remains a concern about inaccurate information in this area (A10, A13). Gross's study of Internet use by depressive youths found that often, vulnerable youth would exhibit seeking activity called "solitary pretending" (A5). Other problematic behaviors include information overload (A11), and increased meetings with strangers (A15). But youths who seek health-related information like the private nature of Internet searches. Lacking the ability to use the Internet at home would likely deny most youths the opportunity to conduct this search, further diminishing youth perception of Internet value (Holmes, 2011; Livingstone & Helsper, 2007; Project Tomorrow, 2012).

RQ3. Which sites, locales, participant socioeconomic status (SES), and participant genders have researchers considered?

Availability of household broadband is a necessary, but not sufficient, condition for household broadband adoption. As many studies have indicated, broadband adoption, both in the United States and globally, is drawn largely on socioeconomic lines, primarily income (Connected Nation, 2011; OECD, 2013). Further, both the NETP (U.S. Department of Education, 2010) and Project Tomorrow's (2012) and (2013) reports, all broadband focused position papers and reports, reinforced the potential broadband had to improve the educational prospects for all students. In light of these contentions, few studies in the small sample fully described their participants or documented the role demographic differences may have played in study results. Seven of the 15 studies indicated a distinction between SES factors; of these seven, five study samples indicated a combination of SES factors. Study A1 presented two distinct SES groups of high school students, one group from an elite population for which the annual school tuition cost was nearly $21,000 and, another group of high school students who used public computers in a health center while they waited for free medical care (A1). The authors reported that most of the significant differences in Internet use between the two groups were drawn along "income lines" (A1, p. 56) and that ethnic and racial differences were not significant factors in Internet use. In A1, the researchers suggested that the low SES group experienced a "digital divide" (A1, p. 56) but did not elaborate further on how increased or improved access might diminish this separation. On the other hand, in A4, researchers found that adolescents who sought information about health and medicine did not exhibit differences along SES lines — A4 participants' experience were focused on participation in a "common online experience" (A4 p. 1474) in which their differences were not apparent.

Five of the studies did not distinguish locale (i.e., urban, suburban, or rural). Two studies noted the inclusion of all locales but did not report results based on locale. Locale was noted in A1 as an element for further study, particularly between groups located in urban, suburban, and rural settings (A1). A15 reported demographic characteristics but the primary intent of the study was to examine relationships between health symptoms and use of the Internet, thus the technology was not the focal point and no relationship was reported, a practice repeated by several of the studies (A5, A9, A11).

Public schools and libraries were the sites for 6 of the 15 broadband studies, while health agencies hosted three studies. For the students described by A11, the study design was purposely heterogeneous by site type as well as locale. The A11 researchers reported SES indicators as well, in an attempt to gather information on "unique cases that could provide valuable insight into specific instances" (A11, p. 53). However, these demographic characteristics were not commented on in the findings. A11's researchers described the study site choice in great detail and indicated that the students used the location at times when supervision would be least present and this absent supervision seemed to break down barriers to learning in an online environment (A11). Building on A11's reports of personal, unaudited approaches to information seeking, A9's researchers drew strong correlations between home use of the Internet and youth competence in information seeking, just as Project Tomorrow (2013) reported.

A5, along with A15 and A9, presented studies in which gender and age appeared as strong factors the intensity of and the type of activity in Internet use (A1, A5, A9, A15). A9's researchers purposefully sought out male youths as participants but acknowledged this selection as a limitation due to upon prevailing data indicating stronger computer skills among young males (A9). In A15, the study sample was mostly male, but this study was focused on the relationship of all characteristics to symptoms of depression, but participant gender was not considered in relation to Internet use. Study A5 reported participant gender and age, and ethnicity. A5's researcher reported by gender and age, how youth spent their time on the Internet, distinguishing similar trends of use: boys played more games; girls used more social media and communication tools; and, activities trended similarly along different age groups. Interestingly, the A5 study examined the use of an online avatar to transcend identity and assume different personae (A5). In A5, the researcher attempted to extend the challenge issued by Livingstone (2003) and further the research on details of Internet use by youths in order to "illuminate critical, subjective aspects of adolescent Internet use (e.g., motives) that may be difficult to capture" (A5, p. 646).

Overall, gender and age are most highly reported characteristics in this sample but relationships are often drawn to variables other than use of broadband technology. However, the studies that do focus on computer intensive information seeking make connections that support the NCES data linking the effects of home Internet use with student abilities in manipulating the digital environment (A5, A7, A9, and A15).

RQ4. How has the role of broadband changed over time in studies of children's information seeking?

Based on the results, there was not enough evidence to answer this question. Based on the evidence presented, in five of the studies, when children's learning seeking was the focus of a study, broadband deployment emerged as a facilitating condition, that is, as a high-level of Internet connection, even when broadband was not included in the study design. Based on the 15 research reports examined in this study, broadband's occurrence in study design or finding began in 1998 and did not increase over time, and no relationship can be discerned using the study's publication year.

8.6. Limitations

A few external factors influenced the data collection for this study. The researchers excluded research published in monographs, dissertations, and open access publications because we decided such a wide-ranging search would not represent an information gathering strategy common to academic researchers (Ge, 2010; Head, 2008; Niu et al., 2010). Because data were drawn from 11 different databases, searches had to be adjusted to suit the various search algorithms and indexing practices employed by different database publishers. Similarly, the researchers had no way of knowing if all possible articles in the database that met the search criteria were retrieved due to possible human or machine generated metadata generation inconsistencies. It should also be noted that periodical databases are dynamic and while data were collected from each database individually in separate single retrieval sessions, subsequent efforts to replicate the article counts described in Figure 8.1 may not be possible. Despite these cautions, a number of measures were taken to ensure that the data collection and analysis adhered to high standards, was valid, and could be considered reliable.

8.6.1. Validity

The intent of this study was to identify the research contained in the scholarly journal databases available at a prominent academic institution's library. While abundant data about the deployment of broadband are being published through a variety of outlets, our aim was to describe the possible gap in the literature for research that reflected the impact of broadband on children's information seeking. To accommodate term variants common in developing research areas, the retrieved studies were coded using an open and axial method. The study team created a preliminary codebook and then revised it as the articles were analyzed. Further, inter-rater reliability was addressed and minimized by the researchers conducting searches using the agreed upon search string to compare use of the database search interface. By taking these steps, researchers minimized bias and agreed upon the descriptive presentation of results. While descriptive statistics were generated about the study designs, the only conclusions drawn are that the studies are inconsistent in implementation of characteristics that are known to be important to the study of children's use of technology and information seeking in general. Factors like SES, gender, and detailed variable measurements of the technology observed were not always included in the study design or in the findings, thus it is important not to overstate the results based on the number of studies included in the review but to gather characteristics that are emerging in scholarly research.

8.6.2. Reliability

Reliability of this study is based upon setting clear inclusion criteria and insuring that results can be discerned upon replication. The researchers simultaneously conducted searches to ensure consistent use of the different search interfaces of each database. Further, with a relatively unstudied topic like the influence of broadband on children's information seeking, the likelihood that the results of searches conducted today would yield greater numbers in the future cannot be predicted. Agreement rate with systematic reviews is the clearest technique to assure reliability and the authors worked together, reviewing all the included articles to minimize inconsistencies. In gathering data from each study, a table of terms was compiled to view the language being used to indicate the presence of broadband in the study; these terms were discussed several times by the authors to reduce discrepancies.

8.7. Conclusion: A Failure to Connect?

The intent of this study was to examine the corpus of 20 years of academic research conducted about children's information seeking in relation to the role of broadband in schoolwork. In light of the recognition that the Internet is an essential affordance of modern society and instrumental for learning, the United States has undertaken an array of initiatives to encourage organizational leaders and citizens of the importance of adopting and making meaningful use of broadband Internet that is "always on." Quite simply, broadband is an unquestionable high-level national imperative that requires swift and decisive action to ensure that citizens in the United States can compete and are educated to thrive in a global society infused with robust connectivity that enables commerce, scientific pursuit, lifelong learning, civic engagement, and social exchange.

Policy initiatives have established the basis for high-speed connectivity to homes and schools that is present, but not always adequate. Continued adoption and demand for connection improvement and stability are frustrated by a layer of community members, many of whom are parents, who do not believe that broadband is a valuable home utility for their families. In the last two decades, schools have progressed to nearly complete adoption of broadband, thus allowing children primary and complementary sites for access, but school connections are often inadequate in bandwidth and quantity for the kind of multimedia-rich learning that fuels virtual coursework, digital textbooks, distributed collaborations, and other activities of 21st century learners. Without adequate broadband, children are unable to truly integrate the available technology in their lives (Kozma, 2011).

However, in the same way that the current national infrastructure for broadband tends to be sparse, so too is the research literature about the relationship between broadband and children's efforts to use computers ($n = 46$), especially broadband Internet ($n = 15$), to gather information. In the few occurrences of published research, broadband appeared to have at least a minimal role in children's use of the Internet to seek information for school, especially in the question formation and refinement stages of the Kuhlthau's (2004) Information Search Process.

8.7.1. Implications for Research

At this point in the research report, the reader may be confused or perhaps feel a bit betrayed by the less than overwhelming findings and concise discussion presented here. However, rather than abandon the study as a failure to connect broadband to children's information seeking, the researchers carefully considered every aspect of the results and subsequent discussion and found them revealing of the immanent need to consider broadband in the research designs and in the analyses of research results. They came to this conclusion after reflecting on their own research process to ensure that it was appropriately motivated and properly conducted and, therefore, solid enough to issue meaningful implications for research and policy. This reflection yielded the following implications for further research:

8.7.1.1. "Failed" studies yield important results A "failed" study is one in which the conclusions are not clear or the study did not go as planned, that is, "pear-shaped" (Cameron, 2007). Encountering failed studies in scholarly publications is rare. All too often, as Boman and Jevne (2000) noted:

> [B]y the time the research is presented or written-up, all the perils and pitfalls of the research experience have been omitted or smoothed out in a tidy report outlining what went right rather than what went wrong in the research endeavor. (p. 547)

Certainly the small number of studies eligible for our systematic review gave the researchers pause. The researchers are aware that "personal investment in research might blinker researchers from issues in study design" (Cameron, 2007, p. 74) and they carefully reviewed the procedures and motives. Ultimately, they chose to present this research in line with the sentiments of experienced education researchers Shenton (2004) and Lee, Croninger, and Smith (1997) who stated:

> [I]t is unusual to discuss misgivings about data and findings in a journal venue, which is typically the place where authors make arguments that engender confidence in their study's results and in the appropriateness of the data used to generate their findings. We suggest, however, that being candid about difficulties during the conduct of a study, and about … misgivings about the data, may be useful to other researchers. (p. 113)

With this conviction, we further investigated the supporting and explanatory literature for the method and found that the term "empty review" has been used to describe a meta-analytic study in which there are few or no eligible results (Cooper, 1984; Lang, Edwards, & Fleiszer, 2007; Schlosser & Sigafoos, 2009; Yaffee, Montgomery, Hopewell, & Shepard, 2012). Cooper (2010) suggested that, while systematic review may be premature with a body of literature that is young or undeveloped, for a more established body of literature, a systematic review may provide appraisal of the literature and tripe directions for research questions. Even when few or no conclusions may be drawn from the review results, a dearth of results may indicate unrealized research potential or need. Especially in the instance of a disruptive, dynamic technology like broadband, empty systematic reviews may allow researchers to identify gaps in the knowledge related to the effects of a new technology on a particular user group. Certainly in the case of this study, one conclusion is that despite its identification as a key affordance, the role of broadband in children's information seeking is the subject of little research.

Empty systematic reviews may also help researchers to see creative methodological applications or important unstudied variables. In addition to connection speed, details such as device type, broadband technology in use, applications used, hardware employed, and state of the data network providing connectivity all affect ubiquity and user experience in information seeking. Even when broadband was discussed in the small number of results in this study, those discussions were not in depth enough to plumb these additional factors. Therefore, another conclusion that can be drawn from this study is that the absence of research concerning invisible or less obvious structural influences on children's information seeking in digital environments is a warrant for further study.

8.7.1.2. Broadband research is imperative and challenging The importance of broadband to American life, established by numerous policy directives, two decades of reports, federal and nongovernmental agency missions, and a mounting body of scholarly research, is hardly up for debate. Likewise undeniable is the need to prepare children to function in an information rich, hyper-connected world in which children in many peer nations have access to broadband for learning and communication and gain a level of digital literacy that surpasses that of children in the United States. While the need for more research may be self-evident, conducting more research on the impact of broadband in children's learning and getting a clearer idea of the interplay between technology, connectivity, and educational attainment is far from simple.

Just as the research about information seeking would benefit from a specific consideration of broadband in study design and results analysis, so too would research benefit from considering the nature of children's access, not just what happens with the access they have. As the NTIA (2012) pointed out in a recent report:

> Until recently, research on broadband availability has typically taken a binary approach, i.e., whether it is or is not available … [C]onsumers, businesses, and institutional users have a variety of broadband requirements, and faster speeds are among the most important … others require significantly higher speeds to access a more advanced set of applications,

> including real-time video streaming and video conferencing, distance learning, and telemedicine. This variation in user needs underscores the importance of evaluating broadband availability across multiple speed tiers, not just the baseline speed level. (p. 16)

Castells (2000) exhorts in his acclaimed treatise on networked society that technology, especially for younger generations, is an "augmentation of the body and mind." However, to date, published research in peer-reviewed journals has not extensively explored the role of broadband as a key facilitator. This paucity of research may indicate that researchers are disconnected from fundamental questions that will allow a greater understanding of information seeking. Broadband's role is a subtly complex one that goes beyond a simple conception of a have/have not digital *divide*; rather, a more accurate descriptive term is *disconnect*, because there are multiple points at which an individual must disconnect from obstacles to promised benefits (Warschauer, 2003). This study not only issues a call for more research, but also for more kinds of research that take into account a greater number of factors that affect the role of broadband in learning.

Slone (2003) pointed out, "[P]eople who do not understand the Internet often cannot truly access it" (p. 415). If researchers fail to connect broadband to children's information needs, then policymakers will fail to connect the economic impact of depriving the United States' children access to the information access they require.

Acknowledgments

This research was supported, in part, by NSF Grant #1044315 and IMLS Grant RE-04-09-0055-09.

References

References marked with an asterisk indicate studies included in the research synthesis.

Bates, M. J. (2010). Information. In M. J. Bates & M. N. Maack (Eds.), *Encyclopedia of library and information sciences* (pp. 2381–2391). New York, NY: CRC Press.

Bennett, R., Stewart, L. A., & Atkinson, R. D. (2013, February). *The whole picture: Where America's broadband networks really stand.* Retrieved from http://www2.itif.org/2013-whole-picture-america-broadband-networks.pdf. Accessed on June 30, 2014.

Berners-Lee, T. (1996). WWW: Past, present, and future. *IEEE Computer Magazine*, *29*(10), 69–77.
Bilal, D. (2002). Children's use of the Yahooligans! Web search engine. III. Cognitive and physical behaviors on fully-self generated search tasks. *Journal of the American Society for Information Science and Technology*, *53*(13), 1170–1183.
Bilal, D. (2004). Research on children's information seeking on the web. In C. Cool & M. K. Chelton (Eds.), *Youth information-seeking behavior: Theories, models, and issues* (pp. 271–292). Lanham, MD: Scarecrow Press.
Bilal, D. (2005). Children's information seeking and the design of digital interfaces in the affective paradigm. *Library Trends*, *54*(2), 197–208.
Bilal, D., & Sarangthem, S. (2009). Meditating differences in children's interaction with digital libraries through modeling their tasks. *Proceedings of the American Society for Information Science and Technology*, *46*(1), 1–19. doi:10.1002/meet.2009.1450460394
Boman, J., & Jevne, R. (2000). Ethical evaluation in qualitative research. *Qualitative Health Research*, *10*(4), 547–554. doi:10.1177/104973200129118633
*Borzekowski, D. L. G., & Rickert, V. I. (2001). Adolescents, the Internet, and health: Issues of access and content. *Journal of Applied Developmental Psychology*, *22*(1), 49–59. doi:10.1016/S0193-3973(00)00065-4
Brenchley, C. (2011, March 23). Broadband availability to U.S. schools and colleges. *Homeroom* [Weblog]. Retrieved from http://www.ed.gov/blog/2011/03/broadband-availability-to-u-s-schools-and-colleges/
Cameron, M. (2007). When research goes pear-shaped: Report and reflections on a failed study of exercise and manual therapies for rheumatoid arthritis. *Complementary Practice Review*, *12*(63), 63–77. doi:10.1177/1533210107302439
Carmichael, L. R., McClure, C. R., Mandel, L. H., & Mardis, M. (2012). Practical approaches and proposed strategies for measuring selected aspects of community-based broadband deployment and use. *International Journal of Communication*, *6*, 2445–2466.
Case, D. O. (2012). *Looking for information: A survey of research on information seeking, needs, and behavior* (3rd ed.). Bingley, UK: Emerald Group Publishing Limited.
Castells, M. (2000). *The rise of the network society* (2nd ed.). Oxford, UK: Blackwell.
*Chan, T.-W., Hue, C.-W., Chou, C.-Y., & Tzeng, O. J. L. (2001). Four spaces of network learning models. *Computers & Education*, *37*(2), 141–161. doi:10.1016/S0360-1315(01)00044-6
Connected Nation (CN). (2011). *Broadband readiness index*. Retrieved from http://www.connectednation.org/sites/default/files/broadband_readiness_index.pdf
Cool, C. (2004). Information-seeking behaviors of children using electronic information services during the early years: 1980–1990. In C. Cool & M. K. Chelton (Eds.), *Youth information-seeking behavior: Theories, models, and issues* (pp. 1–36). Lanham, MD: Scarecrow Press.
Cooper, H. M. (1984). *The integrative research review* (Vol. 2). Beverly Hills, CA: Sage.
Cooper, H. M. (2010). *Research synthesis and meta-analysis* (Vol. 2). Thousand Oaks, CA: Sage.

Crandall, R., & Jackson, C. (2001). *The $500 billion opportunity: The potential economic benefit of widespread diffusion of broadband Internet access.* Washington, DC: Criterion Economics.

Cranmer, S. (2006). Children and young people's uses of the internet for homework. *Learning, Media & Technology*, *31*(3), 301–315. doi:10.1080/17439880600893358

Desjarlais, M., Willoughby, T., & Wood, E. (2008). Domain knowledge and learning from the internet. In T. Willoughby & E. Wood (Eds.), *Children's learning in a digital world.* Malden, MA: Blackwell.

*Dresang, E. (2005). The information-seeking behavior of youth in the digital environment. *Library Trends*, *54*(2), 178–196.

Ezell, S., Atkinson, R., Castro, D., & Ou, G. (2009). *The need for speed: The importance of next-generation broadband networks.* The Information Technology & Innovation Foundation. Retrieved from http://www.itif.org/files/2009-needfor-speed.pdf

Federal Communications Commission. (n.d.). *About broadband: What is broadband?* Retrieved from http://www.broadband.gov/about_broadband.html

Federal Communications Commission. (2010a). *Broadband availability gap.* Washington, DC: Author. Retrieved from http://www.broadband.gov/plan/broadband-working-reports-technical-papers.html

Federal Communications Commission. (2010b). *Connecting America: The national broadband plan.* Washington, DC: Author. Retrieved from http://download.broadband.gov/plan/national-broadband-plan.pdf

Federal Communications Commission. (2010c). *E-rate program and broadband usage survey: Report.* Washington, DC: Author. Retrieved from http://transition.fcc.gov/010511_Eratereport.pdf

Federal Communications Commission. (2012). *Eighth broadband progress report.* Washington, DC: Author.

Fletcher, G., Schaffhauser, D., & Levin, D. (2012). *Out of print: Reimagining the K-12 textbook in a digital age.* Washington, DC: State Educational Technology Directors Association (SETDA).

Fox, C., Waters, J., Fletcher, G., & Levin, D. (2012). *The broadband imperative: Recommendations to address K-12 education/infrastructure needs.* Washington, DC: State Educational Technology Directors Association (SETDA).

Frazer, K. D. (1996). NSFNET: A partnership for high-speed networking: Final report, 1987–1995. Ann Arbor, MI: Merit Network.

Gartner Consulting. (2003). *One gigabit or bust initiative: A broadband vision for California.* Retrieved from http://www.cenic.org/publications/archives/glossies/Gartner_Full.pdf

Ge, X. (2010). Information-seeking behavior in the digital age: A multidisciplinary study of academic researchers. *College & Research Libraries*, *71*(5), 435–455.

*Gray, N. J., Klein, J. D., Noyce, P. R., Sesselberg, T. S., & Cantrill, J. A. (2005). The Internet: A window on adolescent health literacy. *Journal of Adolescent Health*, *37*(3), 243. e241–243, e247. doi:10.1016/j.jadohealth.2004.08.023

*Gross, E. F. (2004). Adolescent Internet use: What we expect, what teens report. *Journal of Applied Developmental Psychology*, *25*(6), 633–649. doi:10.1016/j.appdev.2004.09.005

Gross, M. (1996). The imposed query. *RQ*, *35*(2), 236–243.
Gross, M. (1999). Imposed versus self-generated questions: Implications for reference practice. *Reference and User Services Quarterly*, *39*, 53–61.
Gross, M. (2006). *Studying children's questions: Imposed and self-generated information.* Lanham, MD: Rowman & Littlefield Publishers.
Head, A. J. (2008). Information literacy from the trenches: How do humanities and social science majors conduct academic research? *College & Research Libraries*, *69*(5), 427–446.
*Hendry, D. G., Woelfer, J. P., Harper, R., Bauer, T., Fitzer, B., & Champagne, M. (2011). How to integrate digital media into a drop-in for homeless young people for deepening relationships between youth and adults. *Children and Youth Services Review*, *33*(5), 774–782. doi:10.1016/j.childyouth.2010.11.024
*Hirsh, S. G. (1999). Children's relevance criteria and information seeking on electronic resources. *Journal of the American Society for Information Science*, *50*(14), 1265–1283. doi:10.1002/(sici)1097-4571(1999)50:14 < 1265::aid-asi2 > 3.3.co;2-5
Hirsh, S. G. (2004). Domain knowledge and children's search behavior. In C. Cool & M. K. Chelton (Eds.), *Youth information-seeking behavior: Theories, models, and issues* (pp. 241–270). Lanham, MD: Scarecrow Press.
Holmes, J. (2011). Cyberkids or divided generations? Characterising young people's internet use in the UK with generic, continuum or typological models. *New Media & Society*, *13*(7), 1104–1122. doi:10.1177/1461444813310397649
Horrigan, J. B. (2012). *Recent tech adoption trends and implications for the digital divide.* Retrieved from http://papers.ssrn.com/sol3/Delivery.cfm/SSRN_ID2130157_code1499111.pdf?abstractid=2031755&mirid=1. doi:10.2139/ssrn.2031755
Hsieh, J. J., Rai, A., & Keil, M. (2008). Understanding digital inequality: Comparing continued use behavioral models of the socio-economically advantaged and disadvantaged. *MIS Quarterly*, *32*(1), 97–126.
*Jacobs, G. E. (2006). Fast times and digital literacy: Participation roles and portfolio construction within instant messaging. *Journal of Literacy Research*, *38*(2), 171–196. doi:10.1207/s15548430jlr3802_3
Joshi, D., Lane, T., McGovern, C., Noriega, R., & Walker, J. (2011). *Late to the party: How new broadband subscribers compare to early adopters.* Retrieved from http://papers.ssrn.com/sol3/Delivery.cfm/SSRN_ID1995130_code1743069.pdf?abstractid=1995130&mirid=1
Kozma, R. B. (2011). ICT, education transformation, and economic development: An analysis of the U.S. national educational technology plan. *E-Learning and Digital Media*, *8*(2), 106–120. doi:10.2304/elea.2011.8.2.106
Kuhlthau, C. C. (2004). *Seeking meaning: A process approach to library and information services.* Westport, CT: Libraries Unlimited.
Kuhlthau, C. C., Heinström, J., & Todd, R. J. (2008). The "information search process" revisited: Is the model still useful? *Information Research*, *13*(4). Retrieved from http://informationr.net/ir/13-4/paper355.html
Lang, A., Edwards, N., & Fleiszer, A. (2007). Empty systematic reviews: Hidden perils and lessons learned. *Journal of Clinical Epidemiology*, *60*, 595–597. doi:10.1016/j.jelinepi.2007.01.005

LEAD Commission. (2012, September). *Paving a path forward for digital learning in the United States*. Retrieved from http://www.leadcommission.org

Lee, V., Croninger, R. G., & Smith, J. B. (1997). Course-taking, equity, and mathematics learning: Testing the constrained curriculum hypothesis in U.S. secondary schools. *Educational Evaluation and Policy Analysis*, *19*(2), 99–121. doi:10.3102/01623737019002099

Lewin, C., Mavers, D., & Somekh, B. (2003). Broadening access to the curriculum using technology to link home and school: A critical analysis of reforms intended to improve students' educational attainment. *The Curriculum Journal*, *14*(1), 23–53. doi:10.1080/0958517032000055974

Littell, J. H., Corcoran, J., & Pillai, V. (2008). *Systematic reviews and meta-analysis*. New York, NY: Oxford University Press.

Livingstone, S. (2003). Children's use of the internet: Reflections on the emerging research agenda. *New Media & Society*, *5*(2), 147–166. doi:10.1177/14614448030 05002001

Livingstone, S., & Bober, M. (2006). Regulating the internet at home: Contrasting the perspectives of children and parents. In D. Buckingham & R. Willett (Eds.), *Digital generations: Children, young people, and new media* (pp. 93–113). Mahwah, NJ: Lawrence Erlbaum Associates.

Livingstone, S., & Helsper, E. (2007). Gradations in digital inclusion: Children, young people, and the digital divide. *New Media & Society*, *9*, 671–696. doi:10.1177/1461444807080335

Livingstone, S., & Helsper, E. (2010). Balancing opportunities and risks in teenagers' use of the internet: The role of online skills and internet self-efficacy. *New Media & Society*, *12*, 309–329. doi:10.1177/1461444809342697

Madden, A., Lenhart, A., Duggan, M., Cortesi, S., & Gasser, U. (2013, March 13). *Teens and technology 2013*. Retrieved from http://www.pewinternet.org/~/media//Files/Reports/2013/PIP_TeensandTechnology2013.pdf

Mardis, M. A. (2008, October 24–29). Children's questions about science: Preliminary results of an analysis of digital library reference questions. Paper presented at the people transforming information — Information transforming people. *Proceedings of the annual meeting of American Society for Information Science and Technology (ASIST)*, Columbus, OH.

Mardis, M. A. (2009). Viewing Michigan's digital future: Results of a survey of educators' use of digital video in the United States. *Learning, Media & Technology*, *34*(3), 243–257. doi:10.1080/17439880903141539

Mardis, M. A. (2013). What it has or what it does not have? Signposts from U.S. data for rural children's digital access to informal learning. *Learning, Media & Technology*, *38*(2), 1–20. doi:10.1080/17439884.2013.783595

*Marshall, R., & Reday, A. P. (2007). Internet-enabled youth and power in family decisions. *Young Consumers: Insight and Ideas for Responsible Marketers*, *8*(3), 177–183. doi:10.1108/17473610710780927

Moyle, K. (2010). *Building innovation: Learning with technologies* (AER 56). Retrieved from http://research.acer.edu.au/cgi/viewcontent.cgi?article=1009&context=aer.

Nahl, D., & Harada, V. H. (2004). Taxonomy of common Boolean, semantic, syntactic and lexical search errors. In M. K. Chelton & C. Cool (Eds.), *Youth information seeking behavior: Theories, models, and issues* (pp. 119–144). Lanham, MD: Scarecrow Press.

National Center for Education Statistics. (2011). *Digest of education statistics 2010*. Washington, DC: United States Department of Education.

National Science Foundation. (2007). *Cyberinfrastructure vision for 21st century discovery*. Arlington, VA: National Science Foundation.

National Telecommunications & Information Administration. (2012). *Current population survey (CPS) Internet use 2010*. Retrieved from http://www.ntia.doc.gov/files/ntia/data/CPS2010Tables/t11_7.txt

Nesbit, J. C., & Winne, P. H. (2008). Tools for learning in an information society. In T. Willoughby & E. Wood (Eds.), *Children's learning in a digital world* (pp. 173–195). Oxford, UK: Blackwell.

Neuendorf, K. A. (2002). *The content analysis guidebook*. Thousand Oaks, CA: Sage.

Niu, X., Hemminger, B. M., Lown, C., Adams, S., Brown, C., Level, C., & Cataldo, T. (2010). National study of information seeking behavior of academic researchers in the United States. Journal of the Association for Information Science and Technology *(JASIST)*, *61*(5), 869–890. doi:10.1002/asi.21307

*O'Conner-Von, S. (2009). Coping with cancer: A web-based educational program for early and middle adolescents. *Journal of Pediatric Oncology Nursing*, *26*(4), 230–241. doi:10.1177/1043454209334417

OECD. (2013). *OECD communications outlook 2013*. doi:10.1787/comms_outlook-2013-en

O'Keeffe, G. S., Clarke-Pearson, K., & Council on Communications Media. (2011). The impact of social media on children, adolescents, and families. *Pediatrics*, *127*(4), 800–804. doi:10.1542/peds.2011-0054

Organisation for Economic Co-operation and Development (OECD). (2012, July). *OECD broadband portal*. The Organisation for Economic Co-operation and Development. Retrieved from http://www.oecd.org/internet/broadbandandtelecom/oecdbroadbandportal.htm

Peters, L. (2008). Meeting the needs of the learner: The role of the teacher in bridging the gap between informal and formal learning using digital technologies. In T. Willoughby & E. Wood (Eds.), *Children's learning in a digital world* (pp. 104–127). Cambridge, UK: Blackwell.

*Pickard, A. J. (2008). Rich pictures: Researching the role of peer interaction for pupils using the internet. *Popular Narrative Media*, *1*, 169–181.

Project Tomorrow. (2012, May). *Personalizing the classroom experience — Teachers, librarians and administrators connect the dots with digital learning*. Retrieved from http://www.tomorrow.org/speakup/SU11_PersonalizedClassroom_EducatorsReport.html

Project Tomorrow. (2013, April). From chalkboards to tablets: The digital conversion of the K-12 classroom. *Speak up 2012 national findings K-12 educators and parents*. Retrieved from http://www.tomorrow.org/speakup/pdfs/SU12EducatorsandParents.pdf

*Radford, M. L. (2006). The critical incident technique and the qualitative evaluation of the connecting libraries and schools project. *Library Trends*, *55*(1), 46–64. doi:10.1353/lib.2006.0051

Rompaey, V. V., Roe, K., & Struys, K. (2002). Children's influence on Internet access at home: Adoption and use in the family context. *Information, Communication & Society*, *5*(2), 189–206. doi:10.1080/13691180210130770

*Rushing, S., & Stephens, D. (2011). Use of media technologies by Native American teens and young adults in the Pacific Northwest: Exploring their utility for designing culturally appropriate technology-based health interventions. *The Journal of Primary Prevention*, *32*(3–4), 135–145. doi:10.1007/s10935-011-0242-z

Schlosser, R. W., & Sigafoos, J. (2009). "Empty" reviews and evidence-based practice. *Evidence-Based Communication Assessment and Intervention*, *3*(1), 1–3. doi:80/17489530902801067

Selwyn, N. (2006). Exploring the "digital disconnect" between net-savvy students and their schools. *Learning & Media and Technology*, *31*(1), 5–17. doi:10.1080/17439880500515416

Selwyn, N. (2011). *Education and technology: Key issues and debates*. London: Continuum Publishing Group.

Selwyn, N., Potter, J., & Cranmer, S. (2010). *Primary schools and ICT: Learning from pupil perspectives*. London: Continuum Publishing Group.

Shenton, A. K. (2004). Strategies for ensuring trustworthiness in qualitative research projects. *Education for Information*, *22*(2), 63–75.

Shenton, A. K. (2007). Causes of information seeking failure: Some insights from an English research project. In M. K. Chelton & C. Cool (Eds.), *Youth information-seeking behavior II* (pp. 313–364). Lanham, MD: Scarecrow Press.

Shoemaker, P. J. & Reese, S. D. (1996). *Mediating the message: Theories of influences on mass media content* (2nd ed.). White Plains, NY: Longman.

*Slone, D. J. (2003). Internet search approaches: The influence of age, search goals, and experience. *Library & Information Science Research*, *25*, 403–418. doi:10.1016/S0740-8188(03)00051-3

Somekh, B. (2007). *Pedagogy and learning with ICT*. London: Routledge.

S. 652 (104th): Telecommunications Act of 1996. (1996). Retrieved from http://www.govtrack.us/congress/bills/104/s652

Tripp, L. M. (2011). "The computer is not for you to be looking around, it is for schoolwork": Challenges for digital inclusion as Latino immigrant families negotiate children's access to the internet. *New Media & Society*, *13*(4), 552–567. doi:10.1177/1461444810375293

U.S. Department of Education. (2010). Transforming American education: Learning powered by technology. *The National Education Technology Plan*. Retrieved from http://www2.ed.gov/about/offices/list/os/technology/netp.pdf

U.S. Department of Education. (2013). Support rolls in for ConnectEd. *Homeroom* [Weblog]. Retrieved from http://www.ed.gov/blog/2013/07/support-rolls-in-for-connected/

Van der Heijden, H. (2004). User acceptance of hedonic information systems. *MIS Quarterly*, *28*(4), 695–704.

Venkatesh, V., & Brown, S. A. (2001). A longitudinal investigation of personal computers in homes: Adoption determinants and emerging challenges. *MIS Quarterly*, *25*(1), 71–102.

Warschauer, M. (2003). *Technology and social inclusion*. Boston, MA: MIT Press.

Warschauer, M., & Matuchniak, T. (2010). New technology and digital worlds: Analyzing evidence of equity in access, use, and outcomes. *Review of Educational Research, 34*, 179–225. doi:10.3102/0091732X09349791

Watson, J. S. (2004). "If you don't have it, you can't find it": A close look at students' perceptions of using technology. In C. Cool & M. K. Chelton (Eds.), *Youth information-seeking behavior: Theories, models, and issues* (pp. 145–180). Lanham, MD: Scarecrow Press.

Watson, J., Murin, A., Vashaw, L., Gemin, B., & Rapp, C. (2012). *Keeping pace with K-12 online & blended learning: An annual review of policy and practice.* Retrieved from http://kpk12.com/cms/wp-content/uploads/KeepingPace2012.pdf

Windhausen, J. Jr. (2008). *A blueprint for big broadband.* An EDUCAUSE White Paper. Washington, DC: EDUCAUSE. Retrieved from http://net.educause.edu/ir/library/pdf/epo0801.pdf

Yaffee, J., Montgomery, P., Hopewell, S., & Shepard, L. D. (2012). Empty reviews: A description and consideration of Cochrane systematic reviews with no included studies. *PLoS One*, *7*(5), 1–7. doi:10.1371/journal.pone.0036626

*Ybarra, M. L., Alexander, C., & Mitchell, K. J. (2005). Depressive symptomatology, youth Internet use, and online interactions: A national survey. *Journal of Adolescent Health*, *36*(1), 9–18. doi:10.1016/j.jadohealth.2003.10.012

APPENDIX 8.A: Eligible Articles by Article Number, APA Reference, and Database Source

Article number	APA reference	Database
A1	Borzekowski, D. L. G., & Rickert, V. I. (2001). Adolescents, the Internet, and health: Issues of access and content. *Journal of Applied Developmental Psychology*, *22*(1), 49–59. doi:10.1016/S0193-3973(00)00065-4	ScienceDirect
A2	Chan, T.-W., Hue, C.-W., Chou, C.-Y., & Tzeng, O. J. L. (2001). Four spaces of network learning models. *Computers & Education*, *37*(2), 141–161. doi:10.1016/S0360-1315(01)00044-6	ScienceDirect
A3	Dresang, E. (2005). The information-seeking behavior of youth in the digital environment. *Library Trends*, *54*(2), 178–196.	Web of Knowledge
A4	Gray, N. J., Klein, J. D., Noyce, P. R., Sesselberg, T. S., & Cantrill, J. A. (2005). The Internet: A window on adolescent health literacy. *Journal of Adolescent Health*, *37*(3), 243. e241–243, e247. doi:10.1016/j.jadohealth.2004.08.023	ScienceDirect
A5	Gross, E. F. (2004). Adolescent Internet use: What we expect, what teens report. *Journal of Applied Developmental Psychology*, *25*(6), 633–649. doi:10.1016/j.appdev.2004.09.005	ScienceDirect
A6	Hendry, D. G., Woelfer, J. P., Harper, R., Bauer, T., Fitzer, B., & Champagne, M. (2011). How to integrate digital media into a drop-in for homeless young people for deepening relationships between youth and adults. *Children and Youth Services Review*, *33*(5), 774–782. doi:10.1016/j.childyouth.2010.11.024	ScienceDirect
A7	Hirsh, S. G. (1999). Children's relevance criteria and information seeking on electronic resources. *Journal of the American Society for Information Science*, *50*(14), 1265–1283. doi:10.1002/(sici)1097-4571(1999)50:14 < 1265::aid-asi2 > 3.3.co;2-5	Web of Knowledge

Appendix 8.A: (*Continued*)

Article number	APA reference	Database
A8	Jacobs, G. E. (2006). Fast times and digital literacy: Participation roles and portfolio construction within instant messaging. *Journal of Literacy Research*, *38*(2), 171–196. doi:10.1207/s15548430jlr3802_3	SageJournals
A9	Marshall, R., & Reday, A. P. (2007). Internet-enabled youth and power in family decisions. *Young Consumers: Insight and Ideas for Responsible Marketers*, *8*(3), 177–183. doi:10.1108/17473610710780927	IngentaConnect
A10	O'Conner-Von, S. (2009). Coping with cancer: A web-based educational program for early and middle adolescents. *Journal of Pediatric Oncology Nursing*, *26*(4), 230–241. doi:10.1177/1043454209334417	SageJournals
A11	Pickard, A. J. (2008). Rich pictures: Researching the role of peer interaction for pupils using the internet. *Popular Narrative Media*, *1*, 169–181.	Gale
A12	Radford, M. L. (2006). The critical incident technique and the qualitative evaluation of the connecting libraries and schools project. *Library Trends*, *55*(1), 46–64. doi:10.1353/lib.2006.0051	Web of Knowledge
A13	Rushing, S., & Stephens, D. (2011). Use of media technologies by Native American teens and young adults in the Pacific Northwest: Exploring their utility for designing culturally appropriate technology-based health interventions. *The Journal of Primary Prevention*, *32*(3–4), 135–145. doi:10.1007/s10935-011-0242-z	IngentaConnect
A14	Slone, D. J. (2003). Internet search approaches: The influence of age, search goals, and experience. *Library & Information Science Research*, *25*, 403–418. doi:10.1016/S0740-8188(03)00051-3	ScienceDirect

Appendix 8.A: (*Continued*)

Article number	APA reference	Database
A15	Ybarra, M. L., Alexander, C., & Mitchell, K. J. (2005). Depressive symptomatology, youth Internet use, and online interactions: A national survey. *Journal of Adolescent Health*, *36*(1), 9–18. doi:10.1016/j.jadohealth.2003.10.012	ScienceDirect

Chapter 9

Interface Design: The Impact of Images and Catalog Organization on the Information Retrieval of Children Ages Five to Eight While Subject Browsing

Stacy Creel

Abstract

Purpose – This study investigated the design of three online public library catalogs in light of the cognitive ability and success of children ages five to eight.

Methodology/approach – A quasi-experimental approach was employed to examine the influence of system design on children's searching strategies and search success. Interviews were used to explore children's rationale for using icons and taxonomies in the catalogs. Fifty one children from one public library participated in this study. Inferential statistics were utilized to whether significant differences existed between use of the catalogs and the children's success in finding information.

Results – Use of images and text were helpful in searching the catalogs. Results of the ANOVA test indicated no significant difference among children's searching success rates and the three catalogs. Additionally, the participants misidentified representations used in icons in all three catalogs and created valid search paths that did not produce results. There was a disconnect between the children's cognitive abilities and the design representations of the three catalogs.

New Directions in Children's and Adolescents' Information Behavior Research
Library and Information Science, Volume 10, 265–293

ISSN: 1876-0562/doi:10.1108/S1876-056220140000010057

Limitations – The study took place in one location, thus one should not overgeneralize the findings. Use of assigned tasks may have affected children's success rates. Children's searching using printed cards of display screens from the three catalogs instead of real-time interaction with them is also a limitation.

Practical implications – Because of the children's reliance on images, the choice of visual representations is crucial to successful searching. Interface designers should involve young users in the design of today's online catalogs. They should also consider new forms of representations such as auditory icons, verbal mouse overs, and zooms.

Originality/value – In addition to addressing the need for research on young children's information seeking and use of online catalogs in public libraries, this research focuses on the need for an additional layer of visual representation and highlights flaws in currently used catalog designs.

Keywords: Children; cognitive information behavior; catalog interface design; design representations; visual interface design; online catalogs

9.1. Introduction

Over 60% of children — 3–17 years — living in the United States had access to the Internet in 2011 (File, 2013). Children have particular information needs and information seeking behaviors. Some of the problems that children face when searching online catalogs and the Internet are due to cognitive abilities, domain knowledge, and motor skills (Bilal, 2000; Cooper, 2002; Hirsh, 1996; Large, 2005; Rowlands et al., 2008; Solomon, 1991). Information seeking technology specifically designed for children, like children's library catalogs, should be appropriate for "these users' information needs, information seeking behavior, cognitive processes, knowledge structures, and expectations" (Bilal & Wang, 2005, p. 1303). Since the late 1980s, reports have indicated that children struggle when searching online library catalogs (Edmonds, Moore, & Balcom, 1990; Hirsh, 2004; Hooten, 1989; Moore & St. George, 1991; Solomon, 1993).

Researchers have typically focused on children's information seeking using school or subject specific catalogs, like the Science Library Catalog (SLC) or their information seeking on the internet. Literature on very young children and their use of the internet and online catalogs in public library settings is scarce (Large, 2005). This study investigated the design of the three catalogs used in public libraries and involved fifty one children ages 5–8. In order to address issues identified by previous research when searching online, the study used paper versions of the catalogs. Exploring the design issues of the catalogs should contribute to filling this literature gap. In addition, the findings from this study will address the need for an additional layer of visual representation in the existing model proposed by Cooper and O'Connor and modified by Abbas (2002).

9.2. Research Questions

The goal of this study was to investigate the design of the three catalogs in light of children's cognitive ability in the 5–8 age range while removing known issues like spelling, keyboarding, and mouse capabilities. Do current children's online catalog designs function in a manner that is compatible with their information seeking behavior? In order to assess the effectiveness of catalog design, two research questions were addressed:

1. To what extent do the online catalogs and labels of links/features used by selected public libraries assist children ages 5–8 in achieving tasks?
2. To what extent do the subject categories and labels of links/features used in the online catalogs cognitively match the level of development of children ages 5–8?

9.3. Relevant Literature

The reviewed literature cover research work related to children's cognitive development, categorization, interface design representations, and searching different systems.

9.3.1. Children's Cognitive and Developmental Stages

Although cognitive development is sequential, research indicates the traditional view of cognitive development as strictly linear is not entirely correct (Shaffer & Kipp, 2010). More recent research suggests children go through a series of overlapping changes with little consistency within the domains (Shaffer & Kipp, 2010). These changes are influenced by their interaction with external environmental factors and internal factors, and their problem solving abilities are varied and adaptive (Cooper, 2005; Gross, 2006; Shaffer & Kipp, 2010). Children's abilities to recognize, recall, understand, and communicate are dependent on intellect and emotional aptitude (Garbarino, Stott, & Faculty of the Erikson Institute, 1992). Walter,

Borgman, and Hirsh (1996) attribute some of the difficulty experienced in searching by children to their lack of vocabulary and knowledge base, which are dependent on their still-evolving memory functions and are caused by lack of experience (Garbarino et al., 1992). As children grow and encounter different experiences, their knowledge base grows along with their ability to "learn and remember" (Shaffer & Kipp, 2010, p. 327). Even though children gain vocabulary progressively through the school curriculum, this vocabulary does not necessarily match the controlled vocabulary of the online catalog's subject headings (Everhart & Hatcher, 2005).

Young children can be at a disadvantage in that as non-readers or beginning readers, young children under age eight or 3rd grade gain information largely from visual or auditory sources (Cooper, 2002). "Therefore, having tools that ignore children's unique user requirements can severely limit not only children's ability to find what they are looking for but also their possibilities for future cognitive and social development" (Druin, 2005, p. 24).

Categorization is a primary method used by children to make sense of the world around them and it serves as "a means of simplifying the environment, of reducing the load on memory, and of helping us to store and retrieve information efficiently" (Markman, 1989, p. 11). Concepts are organized into categories, which are then further installed into taxonomies. Taxonomies are used by information retrieval (IR) systems to assist in searching and to organize information. It involves the practice of matching groups of items with previously defined labels but can also include the creation and arrangement of the items (Drake, 2003). As stated by Waxman and Hatch (1992), "a fundamental feature of human conceptual and semantic organization is the ability to locate an individual object (e.g. a dog) in multiple taxonomic classes at various hierarchical levels (e.g. collie, dog, animal)" (p. 153). Taxonomic systems are readily found in online environments like the Internet and library catalogs. "Use of icons in conjunction with or instead of alphabetic symbols support children who cannot read or read well, have trouble scanning text on a computer screen, or have trouble with the concept that an alphabetic citation stands for a book that they want" (Cooper, 2005, p. 292).

It is a misconception that young children have inability to categorize and inflexibility in labeling categories; they generally accept the base-level label for objects (e.g., dog) while rejecting non-basic-level labels. Waxman and Hatch's (1992) study of three and four year olds found that 75% of the three year olds and 92% of the four year olds were able to produce more than one label at least half of the time. Their findings support research that revealed children, including young ones, are able to construct conceptual and semantic hierarchical systems of organization (Bilal & Wang, 2005; Bjorklund, 2011; Byrnes & Bernacki, 2013; Garbarino et al., 1992).

People utilize cognitive ability to reflect on experiences and make sense of their environment (Marchionini, 1995). Children's cognitive abilities are developed in stages but are certainly fluid and based on many factors (Broch, 2000; Cooper, 2005; Garbarino et al., 1992; Gross, 2006; Hourcade, 2008).Children must have the ability to understand the taxonomy inherent in the online catalog and must grasp the symbolic representation intended by the designers of the system to use the catalog successfully.

9.3.2. Symbols and Icons

A "symbol is something that someone intends to stand for or represent something other than itself" (DeLoache, 2002, p. 207). Children must be able to understand the intended abstract meaning and know the concrete object, which is called dual representation. Their success with understanding and using symbolic representations is dependent on representational insight or "the recognition of the existence of a symbol-referent relation" (DeLoache, 2002, p. 219). DeLoache (2004) contends that intention is a necessary component of symbolization that "Nothing is inherently a symbol; only as a result of someone using it with the goal of denoting or referring does it take on a symbolic role" (p. 67). In addition to intent, symbols may have iconicity or be impressionistic. In iconicity, the symbol has a close resemblance to the referent, like a picture of a Collie to represent a dog versus impressionistic resemblances that have no real resemblance to the referent, like a picture of a woman to represent poetry. Symbols can be further complicated by the mapping between the symbol and referent, which can be one-to-one, one-to-many, or one-to-none, where a symbol is used to stand for something that is not real or has not existed (DeLoache, 1995).

"*How* the object is represented depends on the *semantics* (intended meaning of the sign), which address the direct relationship between the representation and the sign of the object" (Goonetilleke, Martins Shih, Kai On, & Fritsch, 2001, p. 744). Representation can include the following:

- representation icons express real images of the object;
- abstract icons reflect an idea or concept close to the actual image;
- arbitrary icons that do not have an apparent link to the meaning they are supposed to be representing; and
- text (Goonetilleke et al., 2001).

Research has indicated that text and graphics used together may be more effective (Goonetilleke et al., 2001). The linguistic or text message can be used to stress a specific meaning of the image; the literal message is the actual image and the symbolic message is based on "individual or cultural experience and knowledge" (Ornager, 1997, p. 204). The catalog user must bring their knowledge, experience, and culture to what representations the system is using and its organization of those representations (Kuiper, Volman, & Terwel, 2005; Marchionini, 1995). "Growing up in a specific place and time, socioeconomic status, gender, cultural and religious background, access to health care, education, and support for family life within the larger society all affect the nature of childhood" (Gross, 2006, p. 2).

9.3.3. Children and Searching

Online catalogs for children are designed using the following three methods: subject hierarchy, keyword, or a combination of subject and keyword. Early research on OPAC use from the 1980s reported that over 50% of searches were subject searches. Based on these first reports of a preference for searching by browsing, second-generation OPACs added subject browsing by controlled vocabulary and then moved to include graphic interfaces (Marchionini, 1995).

For children seeking materials in the print form, online catalogs are the "primary access tool" (Everhart & Hatcher, 2005, p. 37). Research studies have reported that success in searching online catalogs varies "from 10% on a touch screen online catalog (Edmonds et al., 1990) to 66% on a standard online catalog (Solomon, 1993) to 80% in some of the SLC experiments (Borgman, Hirsh, Walter, & Gallagher, 1995)" (Hirsh, 1997, p. 725). Children's success rates are affected by the types of search strategies, search tasks, subject being searched, and domain knowledge of the children (Hirsh, 1997) in addition to reading skills (Bilal, 2000). Even though many children are more technologically savvy than those of previous generations, the current research literature does not support that their searching skills or evaluating results skills have dramatically increased (Rowlands et al., 2008).

"Age should not be a barrier to the ability to access, receive, and utilize information" (Hooten, 1989, p. 268). Subject browsing catalogs attempt to incorporate children's cognitive abilities, like lack of recall knowledge, by providing images and text to prompt memory (Busey & Doerr, 1993). Children often use browsing strategies no matter what the information task (Borgman et al., 1995; Schacter, Chung, & Dorr, 1998). Browsing uses a smaller "cognitive load than analytical search strategies do. Browsing is highly dependent on human perceptual abilities to recognize relevant information" (Marchionini, 1995, p. 103). Research indicates that browsing interfaces assist children in searching (Borgman et al., 1995) and recovering from setbacks experienced as a result of keyword searching (Bilal, 2000).

In a study of SearchKids (http://www.searchkids.com), children tried to get the answer in the least number of clicks. They were "strikingly adept" at their ability to construct searches in contrast to previous literature (Revelle et al., 2002). The success of these 2nd and 3rd graders could be the result of several techniques employed by the designers such as scaffolding, the display of "in-progress" search results, and the organization of the information (Revelle et al., 2002). SearchKids also makes use of redundancy by providing multiple pathways to information (Druin et al., 2001).

The SLC was designed to minimize some of the mechanical difficulties children face like spelling, vocabulary knowledge, and typing skills (Borgman, Gallagher, Krieger, & Bower, 1990; Borgman, Gallagher, Walter, & Rosenberg, 1991; Walter & Borgman, 1991). It was also designed to build on children's natural tendencies to explore as well as to increase their existing skills and abilities (Borgman et al., 1995; Hirsh, 1997). The subject browsing design limits the need for specific recall and requires no typing and spelling skills. Children are required to understand categorization of the subject headings and to move from broad to specific subject headings (Borgman et al., 1990; Borgman et al., 1991; Hirsh, 1997; Walter & Borgman, 1991). The studies of the SLC indicated that children used "picture browsing (various icons) almost as much as they did analytical search strategies and that they were highly satisfied with the interface and their results" (Marchionini, 1995, p. 123). Hirsh's (1997) analysis showed that success rates varied by browsing task complexity, but that children with high domain knowledge were more successful searchers whether searching for complex or simple tasks. Additionally, higher domain knowledge was reported as an influence on the children's ability to search using a variety of search techniques instead of using one dominate (and maybe unsuccessful) style (Byrnes & Bernacki, 2013; Hirsh, 2004).

The design of the Kid's Catalog was based on research on children's information seeking and focus group input that indicated computers "needed to be more child-oriented, since children often used online public access catalogs (OPACs) without adult assistance" (Busey & Doerr, 1993, pp. 77–78). "The Kid's Catalog is a graphical user interface that solves many of the problems children encounter when using traditional public access catalogs" (Busey & Doerr, 1993, p. 77). It used a "visual hierarchy" to motivate children through attractive icons and provided autonomy in addition to keyword searching capabilities (Busey & Doerr, 1993).

Beheshti, Large, and Tam (2010) analyzed the transaction logs of History Trek, a Web portal designed for elementary students. Their analysis of over 800,000 transactions indicated that the subject taxonomy was the most frequently used at 42%. While transaction log analysis is limited, it does provide insight into user choice "and willingness to explore," including how deep into the taxonomy users search (p. 398). The authors conclude that like earlier studies, their findings support that youth prefer subject browsing, perhaps because it is "less demanding cognitively" (p. 400).

The International Children's Digital Library (ICDL) was created with children's preference for browsing in mind. The current iteration has a flat interface and allows for building Boolean searches using the icons (Hutchinson, Bederson, & Druin, 2006). In a study of children 6–10 years of age by Bilal and Bachir (2007), one of the research questions addressed the extent in which Arabic-speaking children understood the meaning of the design representations (i.e., icons, buttons) in the ICDL. The study found that younger children ages 6–7 were unable to recognize the representations used in the library and that designers should take younger children's information seeking and understanding into consideration when designing interfaces. In a recent study of the ICDL, Danish children found the book cover thumbnails to be too small to be usable (Martens, 2013). Issues of representation are confounded by the fact that children searching catalogs come from different political, social, and cultural backgrounds (Hutchinson, Rose, Bederson, Weeks, & Druin, 2004).

Historically research has supported the idea that children are more successful with browse searching. It uses a lighter cognitive load and relies on recognition versus recall. In 2010, Jochmann-Mannak, Huibers, Lentze, and Sanders studied five Internet interfaces. The study included a metaphorical navigation interface designed to promote browsing. It proved problematic in several areas. First, children did not get the metaphor of exploring islands via a boat. Second, the site used abstract labels, and third, the site used mouse overs instead of text descriptions (Jochmann-Mannak, Huibers, Lentz, & Sanders, 2010). The authors also proposed that perhaps earlier findings might be different now since children are more familiar with keyword searching in Google. Selwyn (2009) cautions, however, that there is lack of large-scale research on what children are using technology for and their success in using it. The impact of geography, socioeconomic status, gender, environment, and age play a role in the technology use and success due to "social, cultural, and cognitive backgrounds" (Selwyn, 2009, p. 372). Some children may not be the digital natives reported in research, while others might legitimately be.

9.4. Theory

There are many theories and models that may be used to address children's information seeking (Dresang, 2005; Eisenberg & Berkowitz, 1990; Gross, 1995). For the purpose of this chapter, the theories have been limited to those most prevalent in the results in the present study, along with a single model.

In Ingwersen's (1996) exploration of the elements of cognitive IR theory, he explains that polyrepresentation seeks to include the user's information need and knowledge states — recall knowledge and recognition knowledge. These knowledge states and cognitive/emotional structures are "determined by the experiences gained through time in a social and historical context" (Ingwersen, 1996, p. 6). These experiences must be taken into consideration when pictorial representations are being chosen for IR systems for children. The use of redundancy is also a chief concern (Ingwersen, 1996). As applied to children, the task should be logically linked in a variety of paths. As Bilal and Wang (2005) address, "Ingwersen (1992) argues that situational classifications provide contexts, whereas categorical classifications often have the form of abstract relations. He also notes that an IR system designer who has some knowledge of the user population should tailor the classification of topics and concepts accordingly" (p. 1311). The emphasis of the cognitive IR theory is on information retrieval being "a continuous process of *interpretation* and *cognition* in context by all participating" searchers or system users and the system (Ingwersen & Jarvelin, 2005, p. 29).

In Hjorland's socio-cognitive theory of users, children first develop a structure of signs and symbols externally in a culture. "When children learn language and symbols the cognitive processes are increasingly mediated by signs, meaning, and symbols, which are internalized in the individual and then reprogram the way cognitive processes work" (Hjorland, 2005, p. 339). Though it originally develops externally, the structure of signs and symbols is internalized influencing the information seeking process. "It emphasizes the internalization of culturally produced signs and symbols and the way cognitive processes are mediated by culturally, historically, and socially constructed meanings. Less priority is given to hardware whether in brains or computers" (Hjorland, 2004, p. 18). The emphasis on domains and domain analysis "might contribute to making IT and information systems better adapted to different user groups and interests" (Hjorland, 2004, p. 21).

The Cooper and O'Connor model focuses on the various cognitive variables and representation from the aspect of the system and the user in searching (Abbas, 2002). The model "further emphasizes the inherent problem of representation, that of information loss when a document's essence or subject is distilled down into two to three subject terms that is often the practice today" (Abbas, 2002, p. 51). Abbas has further adapted this model to show an emphasis on the following: "the user's developmental and cognitive state, domain and system knowledge, and indexer's knowledge of the user's intended purpose(s) for the objects, or the idea of functional representation, can affect representation and retrieval" (p. 51). There is additional significance placed on the indexer's knowledge of user's cognitive

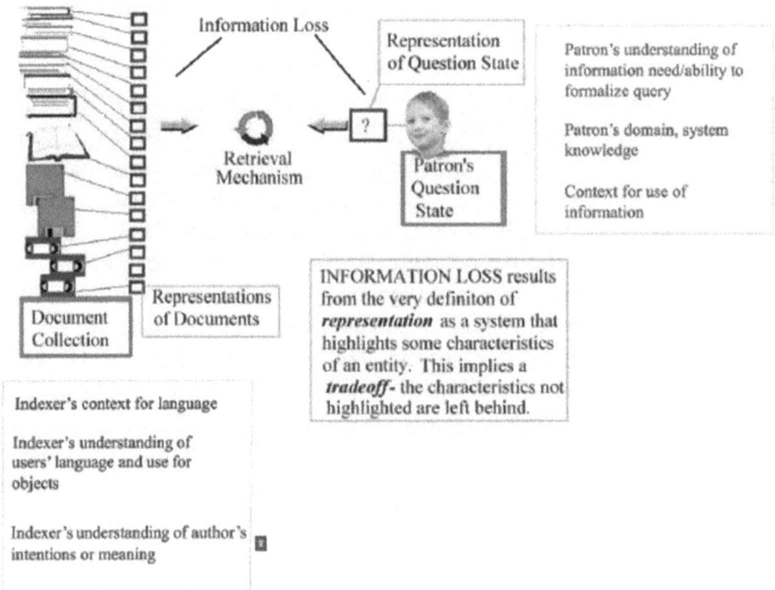

Figure 9.1: Abbas' (2002) modification of the Cooper and O'Connor model.

ability. Her modification of the Cooper and O'Connor model can be seen in Figure 9.1.

9.5. Method

A quasi-experimental approach was employed in this study to examine the influence of the design of three online catalogs on children's searching and their search success rates. Interviews were also used to explore the children's likes and dislikes about finding information in the catalogs.

9.5.1. Participants and Setting

The participants in this study were derived from public library customers outside of Houston, Texas. The study took place in a quiet office in the library during June and July of 2006. Participants were recruited via flyers and from an oral explanation when signing up for the summer reading program. An informal assessment based solely on the parents' responses to being asked if their child(ren) had begun reading and had basic skills took place before interested children and parents were given consent packets. The participants included 30 Caucasians, 11 African Americans, 6 Asian Americans, 2 Hispanic Americans, and 2 other. The participants were ages 5–8 years old (Table 9.1).

Twenty-three of the participants were male and 28 were female. No one was excluded based on race or gender. Children without the minimal required reading skills or not in the age category were excluded.

9.5.2. Public Access Catalogs

Three catalogs were selected because they offered a subject hierarchy with graphical user interfaces and were in use in public libraries. At the time of the study, the three distinct catalogs were supported by two vendors — Innovative Interfaces® and SirsiDynix®. Currently, SirsiDynix still supports the original Dynix and the original Sirsi interfaces for children's subject browsing catalogs. Innovative Interfaces has a new iteration of its subject browsing catalog for children.

9.5.3. Tasks

Each child was given three search tasks to complete. For each correct task, the child was given a score of one. The historically held view is that the majority of children using the public library are there for school assignments. This view is supported by research performed on traditional reference services in the public library. An imposed query "is a question that is developed by one person and then given to someone else who will receive, hold, and transact the query for that person (i.e., the imposer)" (Gross & Saxton, 2001, pp. 170–171). The type of task, well-defined or ill-defined, also has a significant effect on children's search process and success

Table 9.1: Participants by age.

Age	No. of participants	Percent	No. of males	Percent of total participants	No. of females	Percent of total participants
5	9	18	3	0.6	6	12
6	15	29	6	12	9	18
7	12	24	7	14	5	10
8	15	29	7	14	8	16
Total	51	100	23		28	

(Bilal, 2002). "A simple task, also known as fact-based or closed task, has a target answer that the information seeker should find" (Bilal, 2002, p. 110). Children 5–8 years old are in school and may have already experienced imposed queries. In this study, children were tested on fully-assigned closed tasks for evaluation by set criteria such as accuracy of answer and speed (David, Song, Hayes, & Fredin, 2007). However, they were given all the time they needed to complete each tasks. In Cooper's (2004) study, animals were frequently mentioned by Kindergarten through 4th grade students but were especially popular in Kindergarten and 1st grade.

In order to combat low motivation and low domain knowledge, a year's worth of reference statistics in the library where the study took place were analyzed based on which the three most frequent topics: dinosaurs, sharks, and Texas were used as the subject of the tasks. It is important to note that the study of Texas is an annual assignment in all grade levels.

9.5.4. Procedures

Previous studies by Bilal (2000, 2001, 2002), Chen (2003), Hirsh (1997), Kuhlthau (1991), Revelle et al. (2002), and Walter et al. (1996) identified the following issues in an electronic environment as barriers to successful searching: typing/keyboarding, spelling, adequate vocabulary, and wait time. Although these issues were not specific to searching online catalogs, there was the potential for them to exist in this study. This study was conducted using a paper version of the online catalogs to investigate the additional issues affecting success. Every screen was captured and printed on card stock. In order to account for research that shows young children do not scroll down below the top level of results or fold of the display screen, interface choices that went below the fold were shown as one "screen" (Bilal, 2000; Holmes, Robins, Zhang, Salaba, & Byerly, 2006). Since much of the prior research work has indicated that children browse more than they search by keyword, browse using icons and other representations (e.g., buttons) (Bilal & Bachir, 2007) focused only on the browsing interface of the selected online catalogs — not the keyword feature (Borgman et al., 1995; Marchionini, 1995; Schacter et al., 1998).

The researcher randomly assigned the participants a catalog to view. In order to meet children's need to have concrete retrieval cues, they were first shown an example of finding information on the cards to ensure they understood the process. To make certain that the participants had significant knowledge of the search topic, they were shown a card with each search task represented by a collage of images and a text label. The participants were asked to identify the search topic subject to measure for the appropriate knowledge level of the subjects. In all cases, participants were able to identify the search topic. In fact, 24% of the participants also provided additional background information (i.e., identifying types of dinosaurs, sharks, and state images — bluebonnets and Alamo).

From the home screen shot of the assigned browsing catalog, the participants picked the picture that they believed would lead them to information on that task. The selection from the main card led to another set of pictures from which they selected. They continued to select pictures until they felt they had found the one that most represented the topic or requested to stop or go to the next task. They were interviewed during the process and were asked: Which picture do you want to pick? What is it a picture of? Why did you pick it? After completing the task or stopping, they were asked the following questions: What did you like about the pictures used? What didn't you like about the pictures? Did the pictures help you? Did the words help you?

9.6. Results

The results of this study are reported in relation to the two research questions posed.

In order to answer the research questions, the Ordered Probit model was used to predict the effects of categories and labels of links/features in the three catalogs on children's searching success. To gauge the magnitude of the effect on searching success, the coefficients produced by the Ordered Probit are translated into probabilities. These predicted probabilities were calculated using, CLARIFY: Software for Interpreting and Presenting Statistical Results version: 2.1.

The probability of participants reporting that they used both images and text and that these were helpful is 0.80 ($n=41$). Eight participants reported using only the text when searching, and two said they only used the images. The results of ANOVA indicated that no significant difference among the searching success rates and the three catalogs on all three tasks. The between groups variance results in an F of 0.555 (df=2) is statistically insignificant ($p=0.5813$). When holding constant variables such as gender, age, and minority status, the predicted probability that a participant will complete none of the tasks is 0.12, one task is 0.49, two tasks is 0.31, and all three tasks is 0.07 (Table 9.2).

Overall, the participants' success in finding information on the three tasks was very low. Despite this fact, there is a high probability (0.80) that the participants used the images and text when searching. The participants misidentified different representations used in icons in all three catalogs, indicating a disconnect between their cognitive abilities and the interface design of the three catalogs. Table 9.3 summarizes the misidentified icons by catalog.

Table 9.2: Overall probability of task completion.

Number of tasks to complete	Predicted probability	Percent	Absolute number
0	0.12	14	7
1	0.49	31	16
2	0.31	31	16
3	0.07	24	12

Table 9.3: Number of misidentified icons by catalog.

Catalog	Number	Percent
A	5	22
B	7	30
C	11	48
Total	23	100

9.6.1. Catalog A

Participants misidentified five icons. There is a 0.26 probability that the icon for *Animals*, a picture of the Koala bear, will not be successfully identified. The participants were either unfamiliar with what a Koala bear is or based on the image were unable to tell that it was a bear. Sea Animals represented by an *Eel*, a necessary selection for finding information on sharks, was misidentified 3 out of 10 of the time it was viewed by the children.

9.6.2. Catalog B

In this catalog, participants misidentified seven icons. There is a 0.52 probability of misidentification for the icon for the United States (Mount *Rushmore*). However, they did identify it by concepts that were related to the icon — George Washington and the presidents. They knew the people pictured but not the monument. In the same catalog, 15 of the 20 participants looked in Science for answers. The icon for *Science*, a solar eclipse, has 0.40 probability of being misidentified. When looking for *Dinosaurs* in Catalog B, 8 of the 15 participants were unsuccessful at finding dinosaurs under Animals or Fossils. There is a 0.66 probability that the icon for *Reptiles* will be misidentified although the misidentification was related to the actual animal depicted.

9.6.3. Catalog C

The participants misidentified 11 icons. The icon for *Extinct Animals*, a picture of the Dodo bird, was not identified when it was visited and selected. The participants knew what extinct animals were and that dinosaurs are extinct, but did not know or recognize the meaning of this icon.

9.7. Discussion

There are several possible reasons for the misidentification of icons. First is the relationship between the interpretant and their interpretation, which is based on their cultural experience or background. "*Interpretation* also called expression (R-I relationship) is the process of understanding the meaning of a sign" (Goonetilleke et al., 2001, p. 742). The icon is viewed in the context or culture of the viewer to determine the meaning. This is a possible reason for the different (a.k.a. misinterpreted or mislabeled) interpretations of the icons (Goonetilleke et al., 2001). It is possible that the symbol used did not help children infer the correct information about what was being represented (Hourcade, 2008). "The function of *representation* involves emphasizing the relationship between the representation and the object that is represented (O-R relationship). In this relationship, the effectiveness of the representation depends on what is represented and how it is represented" (Goonetilleke et al., 2001, p. 742). "From object to illustration, a viewer of images will search for the features of that object or objects that illustrate its meaning to the viewer in relation to the needs of the situation" (Greisdorf & O'Connor, 2002, p. 10).

For example when looking for sharks, one participant saw the picture of a child sitting in a chair on the beach representing Fun Stuff from Catalog B. The participant had been to the beach with family and was told that sharks come up in the waves at the beach. This was the context or experience for sharks for that participant. Also participants selected A to Z and then went to "S" Words looking for sharks. When they were unable to locate sharks in "S" words, they then looked to the image representing Summer and the image of someone doing laps representing Swimming and in the context of knowing that sharks live in water selected one of those as their choice. This finding confirms the results of a study by Bilal and Wang (2005) who found that middle school children, in some instances, drew maps of concepts and their hierarchical structures based their life experiences. Using Piaget theory of cognitive development (1969), the authors interpreted these structures as based on the children's "experiential" knowledge or learning rather than on the domain or discipline with which the concepts are associated.

Another reason for misidentification is designers may have used the same or similar representations in different contexts. Traditionally, icons have been used as a graphical symbol to symbolize things in a computer or objects, although in recent years actions have been included (Goonetilleke et al., 2001). The icons are designed to convey significant, substantial information in the most basic way so that the icon's image has "perceptual immediacy" (Goonetilleke et al., 2001, p. 743). If icons do not convey the perceptual immediacy, users are unsure what is being represented. "Thus, icons are meant to correspond with real objects with which users are familiar. Limitations may arise due to a lack of a direct mapping between real objects and the system objects. An even greater problem arises if designers use the same or similar metaphor in different contexts thereby causing confusions for the users" (Goonetilleke et al., 2001, p. 743). This use of the same or similar representations in different contexts leads to ambiguity or varied meanings.

An example of this ambiguity and use of the same icon to represent different (and in this case related) concepts includes:

- Fossils and Dinosaurs in Catalog B were both represented by the image of fossil embedded in stone;
- Sharks and Dangerous Fish in Catalog C were both represented by the image of a shark;
- United States Territories and Possessions in Catalog C were both represented by the image of the U.S. flag; and
- Fossils and Dinosaurs in Catalog A were both represented by the image of the skeleton of a dinosaur.

When searching for information on Texas in Catalog C, the icon of the flag for the United States has two distinct separate paths and outcomes. From the main page, selecting United States leads to seven other choices, one of which is "States," which then leads the user to the individual states. Selecting countries from the main page leads to Americas to North America to the United States, which then ends in books about the country as a whole but not to the individual states. When depicting dinosaurs and fossils, Catalog C appropriately uses two separate and meaningful images — a dinosaur eating a plant for dinosaurs, a fossil of a fish for fossils, and a Dodo bird for extinct animals. Unfortunately, the participants were not successful in finding dinosaurs in the catalog, because of the icon representing *Extinct Animals.* Only two participants made their way to dinosaurs in catalog C and only after trying several other avenues under Animals.

While there are many guidelines that should be employed in the creation of icons, the following from Shneiderman and Plaisant (2004) would be especially helpful: "Represent the object or action in a familiar and recognizable manner; make each icon distinctive from every other icon" (p. 237). "To be effective a number of interdependent factors need to be considered, such as level of experience with the graphical representation, the knowledge domain and the type of task" (Scaife & Rogers, 1996, p. 186).

In addition to question complexity; user behavior, possible answers, design and representation further increase the complications. Abbas' (2002) further adaptation of the Cooper and O'Connor model showed an emphasis on the following: "the user's developmental and cognitive state, domain and system knowledge, and indexer's knowledge of the user's intended purpose(s) for the objects, or the idea of functional representation, can affect representation and retrieval" (p. 51). System knowledge and understanding can hinder searching. In this study, a participant selects the icon for Animals (a koala) for dinosaurs but is unsuccessful because the system classifies them as part of Nature (a butterfly) instead of animals. When using words to represent documents or objects in a catalog, there is the ability to generalize or to be more specific — to use antonyms or synonyms, and to define or to describe. There are built in mechanisms to make communication connections based on native elements, but this is not the case with pictures (B. O'Connor, personal communication, June 6, 2007; Wyatt & O'Connor, 2004). "Pictures are not words and words are not native elements of photographs" (Wyatt & O'Connor, 2004, p. 107). When a text document is described, it is done through an "extraction process," and when a picture is described, there are generally no words to extract (Wyatt & O'Connor, 2004).

Linguistics and images are two fundamentally different ways of communicating. Users of a system do not know how the decision was made by the designers to have (blank) represent (blank). Another unknown is whether designers have taken the users' interpretation of the images into account in using them for representation and the accompanying text descriptors of the icons (B. O'Connor, personal communication, June 6, 2007). The complexity of using images in representation is that there "is no general rule for translation of an entire picture or any of its parts into words" (Wyatt & O'Connor, 2004, p. 113). Wyatt and O'Connor (2004) use the example of the following words and pictures: sheep, elephant, and horse. These three words can easily be generalized into the superordinate taxonomic class of mammals or animals. However as images, even if parts are selected or a collage of the sheep, elephant, and horse is constructed, the user must take big cognitive leap to animals since the representation is still of a sheep, an elephant, and a horse (Wyatt & O'Connor, 2004). Icons are not part of the documents or materials being represented. Text representation is a direct path; icon representation is not a direct path.

Culture also plays a role in determining the meaning of an icon (Goonetilleke et al., 2001). In general, a sign should be readily recognized by the recipient no matter what the context or cultural background. This is especially important when children are the users since they may not yet have the cultural or social background necessary to interpret the sign. In contrast to denotation, commonsense, or literal meaning signs, connotation signs likely have multiple meanings and are based on the sociocultural and individuality of the recipient. Signs are interpreted within a code or framework used to make sense of the signs. Thus, "The effectiveness of the representation depends on what is represented and how it is represented" (Goonetilleke et al., 2001, p. 742), and for whom it is represented (Bilal & Bachir, 2007).

In the case of the catalog designs, participants did not always exhibit using the same code as the designers. For the purposes of this study, the Cooper and O'Connor model can be even further modified to include an emphasis on the selection of icons and their text descriptors and subjects selected by the designer as in Figure 9.2.

The information loss is resulting on multiple levels: loss in text descriptors, loss by icon choice, and loss through cognitive mismatch between the user and the system. However, participants in the study took reasonable

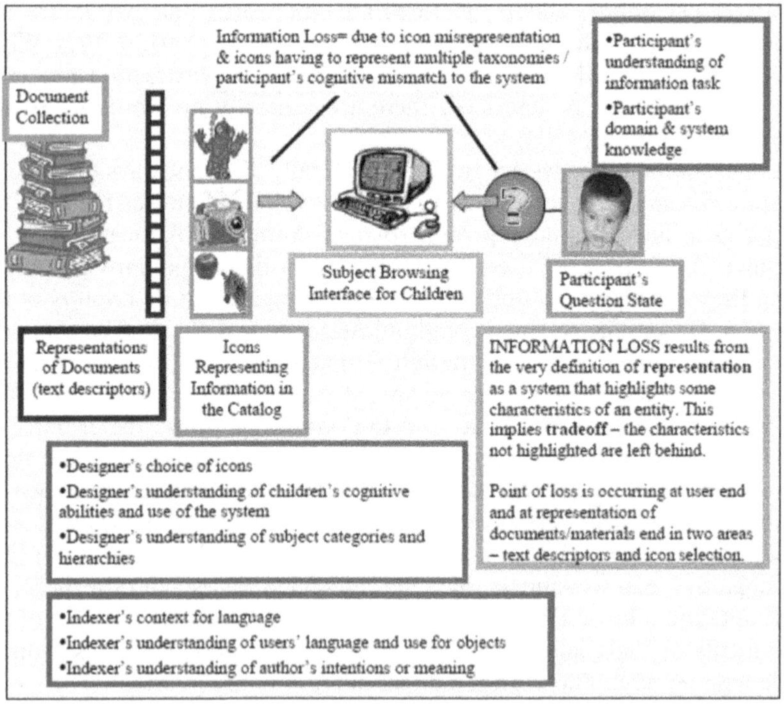

Figure 9.2: Further modification of the Cooper and O'Connor model.

steps to find the tasks but were unsuccessful in part because of this loss of information.

In addition to the loss of information by icon choice and cognitive mismatch, there are definite system design flaws. According to Ingwersen's cognitive IR theory, users' experiences must be taken into consideration when pictorial representations are being chosen for IR systems and redundancy should be used (Ingwersen, 1996). As applied to children, the task should be logically linked in a variety of paths. The taxonomies created, identification of icons, and the catalogs' flawed use of redundancy (not enough redundancy used and identical images/icons not leading to identical results) are examples of some of the problems identified in the study.

Taxonomies are used by IR systems to assist in searching and to organize information (Drake, 2003). An object is placed in a category based on appropriate properties, appearance, role, or behavior. "In either case, to decide whether an object is a member of a given category, it suffices to consider its relevant properties, appearance, function, or behavior. However, many external relations between objects are not captured by this internal analysis of an object's properties" (Markman, 1989, p. 21). Examples of external relations are causal relations, spatial relations, and event relations. "These various types of external relations between objects are referred to as *thematic* relations, to reflect the idea that the objects participate together in a theme or event" (Markman, 1989, p. 21). For children younger than 6 or 7 years of age, categorization is based on some other basis, like life experiences, instead of discipline or domain or shared characteristics (Bilal & Wang, 2005). "These thematic relations emphasize events rather than taxonomic similarity" (Markman, 1989, p. 23). The presentation of the hierarchy or thematic relationship can also impact search success (Beheshti, Large, Julien, & Tam, 2010; Hutchinson et al., 2006) and finding appropriate categories based on children's information needs (Bilal & Wang, 2005).

In this study, 33% of the participants were successful with inclusion understanding that dinosaurs are a subclass of reptiles, under the superordinate class of animals. Almost 51% of participants demonstrated success with inclusion by understanding that sharks are a subclass of fish under the superordinate class of animals. Nearly 72% of the participants were successful with inclusion, understanding that Texas is a subclass of the United States under the superordinate class of North America. Additionally, on task one, almost 22% of the participants were able to correctly identify the correct taxonomic path to dinosaurs on the first try. On task two, 29% of participants correctly went straight to sharks; and on task three, nearly 57% of them followed the correct taxonomic path to Texas.

The participants' creation of thematic relationships based on events and experiences were not accounted for within the catalogs. Examples include sharks being related to swimming, beaches, and scary things, or dinosaurs being related to scary things and places where they are found. In all three catalogs, there is evidence of participants using logic based on experience and knowledge, which while not perfect, certainly held some aspect of truth. Repeatedly, participants looked for dinosaurs under science knowing scientists study dinosaurs. In fact, dinosaurs are found in the broad category of science in Dewey — more specifically 567s Paleontology — so this makes sense. In Catalog B and Catalog C, Science leads to fossils. However, the information found through the Science to Fossils path does not result in the same information discovered through the Animals to the Dinosaurs path, or the Animals to Extinct Animals to the Dinosaurs path. Additionally in Catalog A, Science does not lead to Dinosaurs at all. Users must go through another science category — Nature to Fossils to Dinosaurs. Participants repeatedly looked to Animals and then to Reptiles to locate Dinosaurs. In Catalog A, there is no path to dinosaurs via the Animals taxonomy. In Catalogs B and C, for participants to be successful instead of choosing reptiles they must recognize the meaning of the images in order to find Dinosaurs through the Animals taxonomy.

The participants' cognitive thinking about the taxonomies and their logic for choosing them are illustrated in the following examples taxonomies they created. The taxonomies are pictured along with the participants' logical reasoning. In each of the taxonomies, the participants' reasoning shows that they are relying on their knowledge of the subject matter and on their own personal experiences.

In Figure 9.3, dinosaurs were by fact prehistoric animals that were reptiles (logic a and b). Dinosaurs lived in the past during the Mesozoic era that began about 248 million years ago and ended about 65 million years ago (logic c). Dinosaurs are studied by scientists and found in science studies

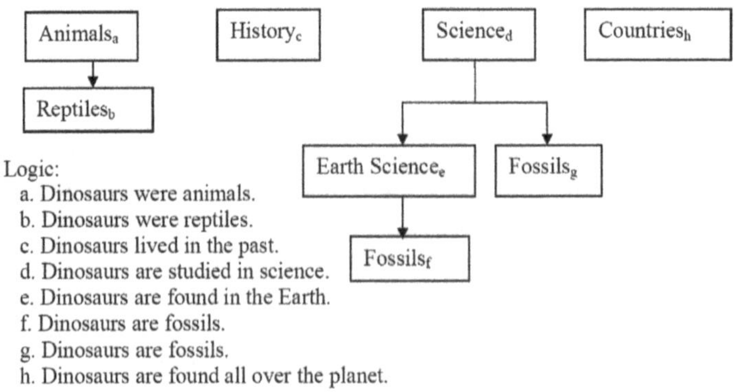

Figure 9.3: Dinosaur taxonomy from Catalog C.

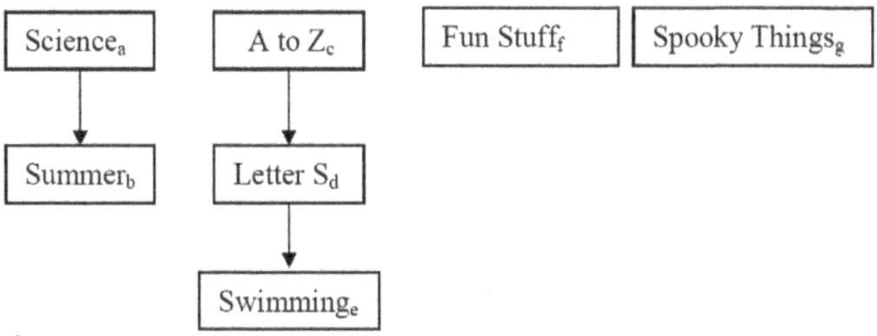

Logic:
a. Sharks are studied in science.
b. It's a picture of the beach where you swim and sometimes see sharks.
c. A to Z means has everything.
d. Sharks starts "s."
e. It's a picture of a shark's fin and sharks swim. (Icon = person swimming laps)
f. It's a picture of a beach and sharks live in salt water and come up in the waves; sharks live near beaches.
g. Sharks are scary.

Figure 9.4: Shark taxonomy from Catalog B.

Logic:
a. Texas is in a country.
b. Texas is on the world. (Icon = a globe)
c. Texas is in North America.
d. Texas is in the United States.

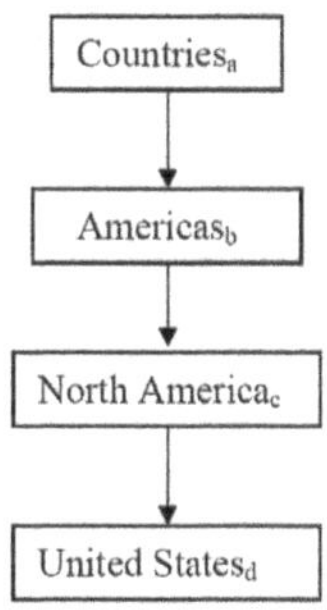

Figure 9.5: Texas taxonomy from Catalog C.

(logic d). Dinosaur fossils were first discovered in the early 1800s in the Earth and have been found in many countries (logic e through h) (Dinosaur, 2007).

In Figure 9.4, sharks are studied in science (logic a). Sharks certainly live in the ocean/salt water and can be seen there (logic b and f) (Shark, 2007). Additionally in Texas, sharks are active during summer months and frequently feed in the shallow waters of the Gulf of Mexico (KGBT 4, 2004). During the summer in Texas, the incidents of shark attacks and warnings are seen on the news.

The A–Z list implies that it has everything; the word shark does start with the letter "s" so the selection of "s" words is sound (logic c and d). If you were unfamiliar with a pool set up for swimming laps, it certainly can be mistaken for something else (logic e). It is water and sharks do swim (logic e). Sharks are dangerous and can be scary (logic g) (Shark, 2007).

In the taxonomy listed in Figure 9.5 (below), there is no doubt that the participants' logic is sound. Texas is in a country in the world on the continent of North America in the United States (logic a–d) (Texas, 2007). The results of this study confirms the findings of the work by Bilal and Wang (2005) about how middle school children built taxonomies for Science categories that were not in line with the structure of the same categories employed by search directories or engines.

9.8. Limitations

This study involved fifty one children ages five to eight in location. Thus, the results, although they confirm in many instances, the findings of previous research, should not be generalized to the whole population of children of that age range in using online catalogs. Extraneous or uncontrolled variables may affect the internal validity of the study (Singleton, Straits, & Straits, 1993). For example, a trip to the pool promised after the library visit could have caused the participants to rush through completing the assigned tasks. Lack of real-time interaction with the catalogs to find information on the three tasks may have influenced children's success rates and information seeking behavior.

9.9. Conclusion

Although research presents conflicting views about the success of children searching online and their preference for browsing interfaces (Cunningham, 2011; Jochmann-Mannak et al., 2010), in this study the results indicated that there is no significant difference among the searching success, or lack of success, and children's use of the three online catalogs. Despite this lack of success in finding information for all three tasks, there is a high probability that the participants use both the catalogs' images and the text, and that these will help them when searching. Because of this degree or predicted reliance on images, symbol choice is crucial to the participants' successful searching. Although these results cannot be generalized, this study indicates that there was a disconnect between the participants' cognitive abilities and the design representations embedded in the three online catalogs used. This disconnect is further exhibited by the taxonomies created and logic behind them. The participants misidentified representations used in icons in all three catalogs search the catalogs using taxonomies based on their experiences.

With icon selection, there is no established mechanism of extraction; children must figure out the representations used in the icons selected to represent materials and items. In these catalogs, the information loss resulted on multiple levels: loss in text descriptors, loss by icon choice, and loss through cognitive mismatch between the participants and the design of the catalogs. The latter is an additional layer that poses cognitive challenges for young participants such as the children who were involved in this study. Therefore, designers of these catalogs should incorporate the tools and innovations of commercial vendors and search engines (Julien, Guastavino, & Bouthillier, 2012). For example, investigations into using auditory icons to test if they reinforce "the visual metaphors in a graphical user interface" need to be explored (Shneiderman & Plaisant, 2004, p. 383). Additionally, the testing and implementation of other auditory-interface tools like verbal mouse overs that display subject categories should be considered by the designers (Hourcade, 2008). Other tools like zooms and 3-D environments to allow users to move and see different levels of representation should be further investigated (Beheshti et al., 2010; Julien et al., 2012; Marchionini, 1995). Although speech recognition was originally created for adults, there are certainly implications for use with children. Bruckman and Bandlow (2002) reported on a study by Nix, Fairweather and Adams which showed that adult software could be modified for use with children ages 5–7 with a success rate of 95% by including common mispronunciations and children's predilection for using multiple words instead of one-word responses. Online catalogs for children that use keyword searching should include spelling correction and question refinement, and subject browsing catalogs should use "real-world categories" that children can understand (Gossen & Nurnberger, 2013, p. 743). Additionally, children as design partners in the creation of future online catalogs (Bilal, 2003; Druin, 2005; Hourcade, 2008; Large, 2005; Large, Beheshti, & Rahman, 2002) and in the design of subject categories or taxonomies (Bilal & Wang, 2005) warrant further investigation. Future studies should consider children's real-time interaction with and information seeking behavior in online library catalogs instead of using printed layouts of these catalogs. In addition, the examination of the children's affective experiences with these catalogs alongside the cognitive information behavior (Absar, 2012; Bilal, 2005, 2007), and allowing children to select their own tasks (Bilal, 2002) deserve future investigation.

While "a child may be exposed to digital technology even before he or she is exposed to books" (Cooper, 2005, p. 286), catalog systems that are appropriate for even the youngest beginning readers need to be designed based on these users' experiences and information behavior. A catalog that provides adequate help, feedback and support scaffolding is necessary.

This scaffolding may end up coming in many different forms, including but not limited to, verbal mouse over and auditory clues.

References

Abbas, J. (2002). *Smoothing the information seeking path: Removing representational obstacles in the middle school digital library environment*. Published dissertation, University of North Texas, Denton, TX.

Absar, R. (2012). *Enhancing navigation using auditory feedback: A case study of a hierarchical information visualization system*. Ph.D. dissertation, McGill University.

Beheshti, J., Large, A., Julien, C. A., & Tam, M. (2010). A comparison of a conventional taxonomy with a 3D visualization for use by children. *Proceedings of the American Society for Information Science and Technology*, *47*(1), 1–9.

Beheshti, J., Large, A., & Tam, M. (2010). Transaction logs and search patterns on a children's portal. *The Canadian Journal of Information and Library Science*, *34*(4), 391–402.

Bilal, D. (2000). Children's use of the Yahooligans! Web search engine: I. Cognitive, physical, and affective behaviors on fact-based search tasks. *Journal of the American Society for Information Science*, *51*(7), 646–665.

Bilal, D. (2001). Children's use of the Yahooligans! Web search engine: II. Cognitive and physical behaviors on research tasks. *Journal of the American Society for Information Science and Technology*, *52*(2), 118–136.

Bilal, D. (2002). Children's use of the Yahooligans! Web search engine: III. Cognitive and physical behaviors on fully self-generated search tasks. *Journal of the American Society for Information Science and Technology*, *53*(13), 1170–1183.

Bilal, D. (2003, October 19–22). Draw and tell: Children as designers of Web interfaces. *Proceedings of the 66th ASIST annual meeting*, Long Beach, CA (pp. 135–141).

Bilal, D. (2005). Children's information seeking and the design of digital interfaces in the affective paradigm. *Library Trends*, *54*(2), 197–208.

Bilal, D. (2007). Grounding children's information behavior and system design in child development theories. In D. Nahl & D. Bilal (Eds.), *Information and emotion: The emergent affective paradigm in information behavior research and theory* (pp. 39–50). Medford, NJ: Information Today.

Bilal, D., & Bachir, I. (2007). Children's interaction with cross-cultural and multilingual digital libraries: I. Understanding interface design representations. *Information Processing and Management*, *43*, 47–64.

Bilal, D., & Wang, P. (2005). Children's conceptual structures of science categories and the design of Web directories. *Journal of the American Society for Information Science and Technology*, *56*(12), 1303–1313.

Bjorklund, D. (2011). *Children's thinking: Cognitive development and individual differences*. Belmont, CA: Wadsworth Publishers.

Borgman, C., Gallagher, A., Krieger, D., & Bower, J. (1990). Children's use of an interactive catalog of science materials. In D. Henderson (Ed.), *Proceedings of the 53rd Annual Meeting of the American Society for Information Science* (pp. 55–68). Medford, NJ: Learned Information.

Borgman, C., Gallagher, A., Walter, V., & Rosenberg, J. (1991, October 27–31). The Science Library Catalog project: Comparison of children's searching behavior in a direct manipulation and a keyword search system. *Proceedings of the 54th American society for information science annual meeting*, Washington, DC. (pp. 162–169). Medford, NJ: Learned Information.

Borgman, C., Hirsh, S., Walter, V., & Gallagher, A. (1995). Children's searching behavior on browsing and keyword online catalogs: The science library catalog project. *Journal of the American Society for Information Science*, *46*(9), 663–684.

Broch, E. (2000). Children's search engines from an information search process perspective. *School Library Media Research*, *3*, 1–17. Retrieved from http://www.ala.org/ala/aasl/aaslpubsandjournals/slmrb/slmrcontents/volume32000/childrens.htm. Accessed on September 28, 2004.

Bruckman, A., & Bandlow, A. (2002). HCI for kids. In J. Jacko & A. Sears (Eds.), *The human-computer interaction handbook: Fundamentals, evolving technologies, and emerging applications* (pp. 2–39). Mahwah, NJ: Lawrence Erlbaum and Associates.

Busey, P., & Doerr, T. (1993). Kid's catalog: An information retrieval system for children. Youth Services in Libraries, *7*(1), 77–84.

Byrnes, J. P., & Bernacki, M. L. (2013). Cognitive development and information behavior. In J. Beheshti & A. Large (Eds.), *The information behavior of a new generation: Children and teens in the 21st century*. Lanham, MD: Scarecrow Press.

Chen, S. (2003). Searching the online catalog and the world wide web. *Journal of Educational Media & Library Sciences*, *41*(1), 29–43.

Cooper, L. (2002). A case study of information-seeking behavior in 7-year-old children in a semi-structured situation. *Journal of the American Society for Information Science and Technology*, *53*(11), 904–922.

Cooper, L. (2004). Children's information choices for inclusion in a hypothetical, child-constructed library. In M. Chelton & C. Cool (Eds.), *Youth information-seeking behavior: Theories, models, and issues* (pp. 181–210). Lanham, MD: Scarecrow Press.

Cooper, L. (2005). Developmentally appropriate digital environments for young children. *Library Trends*, *54*(2), 286–302.

Cunningham, S. (2011). Children in the physical collection: Implications for the digital library. In Proceedings *of the* ASIST, 2011, New Orleans, Louisiana.

David, P., Song, M., Hayes, A., & Fredin, E. (2007). A cyclic model of information seeking in hyperlinked environments: The role of goals, self-efficacy, and intrinsic motivation. *International Journal of Human-Computer Studies*, *65*(2), 170–182.

DeLoache, J. (1995). Early symbol understanding and use. *The Psychology of Learning and Motivation*, *33*, 65–114.

DeLoache, J. (2002). Early development of the understanding and use of symbolic artifacts. In U. Goswami (Ed.), *Blackwell handbook of childhood cognitive development* (pp. 206–226). Malden, MA: Blackwell Publishers.

DeLoache, J. (2004). Becoming symbol-minded. *TRENDS in Cognitive Sciences*, *8*(2), 66–70.

Dinosaur. (2007). *Britannica elementary encyclopedia.* Retrieved from Encyclopædia Britannica Online School Edition, http://archive.school.eb.com/. Accessed on February 12, 2007.

Drake, M. (Ed.). (2003). *Encyclopedia of library and information science* (2nd ed.). New York, NY: Marcel Dekker.

Dresang, E. (2005). Radical change. In K. Fisher, S. Erdelez, & McKechnie (Eds.), *Theories of information behavior* (pp. 298–302). Medford, NJ: Information Today.

Druin, A. (2005). What children can teach us: Developing digital libraries for children with children. *The Library Quarterly*, *75*(1), 20–41.

Druin, A., Bederson, B., Hourcade, J. Sherman, L., Revelle, G., Platner, M., … Weng, S. (2001, June 24–28). Designing a digital library for young children: An intergenerational partnership. In *Proceedings of the ACM/IEEE-CS joint conference on digital libraries*, Roanoke, Virginia (pp. 398–405).

Edmonds, L., Moore, P., & Balcom, K. (1990). The effectiveness of an online catalog. *School Library Journal*, *36*(10), 28–32.

Eisenberg, M., & Berkowitz, R. (1990). *Information problem-solving: The big six skills approach to library and information skills instruction.* Norwood, NJ: Ablex.

Everhart, N., & Hatcher, A. (2005). How relevant are standardized subject headings to school curricula? *Knowledge Quest*, *33*(4), 37–39.

File, T. (2013). *Computer and Internet use in the United States: Population characteristics.* Retrieved from http://www.census.gov/prod/2013pubs/p20-569.pdf

Garbarino, J., Stott, F., & Faculty of the Erikson Institute. (1992). *What children can tell us: Eliciting, interpreting, and evaluating critical information from children.* San Francisco, CA: Jossey-Bass.

Goonetilleke, R., Martins Shih, H., Kai On, H., & Fritsch, J. (2001). Effects of training and representational characteristics in icon design. *International Journal of Human-Computer Studies*, *55*, 741–760.

Gossen, T., & Nurnberger, A. (2013). Specifics of information retrieval for young users: A survey. *Information Processing and Management*, *49*, 739–756.

Greisdorf, H., & O'Connor, B. (2002). Modelling what users see when they look at images: A cognitive viewpoint. *Journal of Documentation*, *58*(1), 6–29.

Gross, M. (1995). The imposed query. *RQ*, *35*, 236–243.

Gross, M. (2006). *Studying children's questions: Imposed and self-generated information seeking at school.* Lanham, MD: Scarecrow Press.

Gross, M., & Saxton, M. (2001). Who wants to know?: Imposed queries in the public library. *Public Libraries*, *40*(3), 170–176.

Hirsh, S. (1996). *The effect of domain knowledge on elementary school children's information retrieval behavior on an automated library catalog.* Published dissertation, University of California, Los Angeles, CA.

Hirsh, S. (1997). How do children find information on different types of tasks? Children's use of the science library catalog. *Library Trends*, *45*(4), 725–746.

Hirsh, S. (2004). Domain knowledge and children's search behavior. In M. Chelton & C. Cool (Eds.), *Youth information-seeking behavior: Theories, models, and issues* (pp. 241–270). Lanham, MD: Scarecrow Press.

Hjorland, B. (2004). Domain analysis: A socio-cognitive orientation for information science research. *Bulletin of the American Society for Information Science and Technology*, *30*(3), 17–21.

Hjorland, B. (2005). The Socio-cognitive theory of users situated in specific contexts and domains. In K. Fisher, S. Erdelez, & McKechnie (Eds.), *Theories of information behavior* (pp. 339–343). Medford, NJ: Information Today.

Holmes, J., Robins, D., Zhang, Y., Salaba, A., & Byerly, G. (2006). *Report on the usability and effectiveness of Sirsidynix schoolrooms for students K-12*. Retrieved from http://stephenslighthouse.sirsidynix.com/archives/2007/02/public_library_1.html. Accessed on February 26, 2007.

Hooten, P. (1989). Online catalogs: Will they improve children's access? *Journal of Youth Services in Libraries*, *2*(3), 267–272.

Hourcade, J. P. (2008). Interaction design and children. *Foundations and Trends in Human-Computer Interaction*, *1*(4), 277–392.

Hutchinson, H., Bederson, B., & Druin, A. (2006). The evolution of the International Children's Digital Library searching and browsing interface. In P*roceedings of conference on interaction design and children*, Finland (pp. 105–112).

Hutchinson, H., Rose, A., Bederson, B., Weeks, A. & Druin, A. (2004). *The international children's digital library: A case study in designing for multi-lingual, multi-cultural, multi-generational audience*. Retrieved from http://hcil.cs.umd.edu/trs/2004-24/2004-24.html. Accessed on November 1, 2012.

Ingwersen, P. (1996). Cognitive perspectives of information retrieval interaction: Elements of a cognitive IR theory. *Journal of Documentation*, *52*(1), 3–50.

Ingwersen, P., & Jarvelin, K. (2005). *The turn: Integration of information seeking and retrieval in context*. Dordrecht, The Netherlands: Springer.

Jochmann-Mannak, H., Huibers, T., Lentz, L., & Sanders, T. (2010, July 23). Children searching information on the Internet: Performance on children's interfaces compared to Google. In *Towards accessible search systems — Workshop of the 33rd annual international ACM SIGIR conference on research and development in information retrieval*, Geneva, Switzerland (pp. 27–35).

Julien, C. A., Guastavino, C., & Bouthillier, F. (2012). Capitalizing on information organization and information visualization for a new-generation catalogue. *Library Trends*, *61*(1), 149–161.

KGBT 4. (2004). *Gulf of Mexico: Texas shark attacks common*. Retrieved from http://www.team4news.com/Global/story.asp?S=2136967. Accessed on February 9, 2007.

Kuhlthau, C. (1991). Inside the search process: Information seeking from the user's perspective. *Journal of the American Society for Information Science*, *42*(5), 361–371.

Kuiper, E., Volman, M., & Terwel, J. (2005). The web as an information resource in K-12 education: Strategies for supporting students in searching and processing information. *Review of Educational Research*, *75*(3), 285–328.

Large, A. (2005). Children, teenagers, and the web. *Annual Review of Information Science and Technology*, *39*(1), 347–392.

Large, A., Beheshti, J., & Rahman, T. (2002). Design criteria for children's web portals: The users speak out. *Journal of the American Society for Information Science and Technology*, *53*(2), 79–94.

Marchionini, G. (1995). *Information seeking in electronic environment*. New York, NY: Cambridge University Press.

Markman, E. (1989). *Categorization and naming in children: Problems of induction*. Cambridge, MA: MIT Press.

Martens, M. (2013). Considerations of how children think: Danish responses to the international children's digital library. *New Review of Children's Literature and Librarianship*, *19*, 139–156.

Moore, P., & St. George, A. (1991). Children as information seekers: The cognitive demands of books and library systems. *School Library Media Quarterly*, *19*, 161–168.

Ornager, S. (1997). Image retrieval: Theoretical and empirical user studies on accessing information in images. *Proceedings of the 60th American Society of Information Retrieval Annual Meeting*, *34*, 202–211.

Revelle, G., Druin, A., Platner, M., Bederson, B., Hourcade, J., & Sherman, L. (2002). A visual search tool for early elementary science students. *Journal of Science Education & Technology*, *11*(1), 49–57.

Rowlands, I., Nicholas, D., Williams, P., Huntington, P., Fieldhouse, M., Gunter, B., … Tenopir, C. (2008). The Google generation: The information behavior of the researcher of the future. *Aslib Proceedings: New Information Perspectives*, *60*(4), 290–310.

Scaife, M., & Rogers, Y. (1996). External cognition: How do graphical representations work? *International Journal of Human Computer Studies*, *45*(2), 182–213.

Schacter, J., Chung, G., & Dorr, A. (1998). Children's internet searching on complex problems: Performance and process analysis. *Journal of the American Society for Information Science*, *49*(9), 840–849.

Selwyn, N. (2009). The digital native — Myth and reality. *Aslib Proceedings*, *61*(4), 364–379.

Shaffer, D., & Kipp, K. (2010). *Developmental psychology: Childhood and adolescence*. Belmont, CA: Wadsworth Cengage Learning.

Shark. (2007). *Britannica elementary encyclopedia*. Retrieved from Encyclopædia Britannica Online School Edition, http://archive.school.eb.com/. Accessed on February 12, 2007.

Shneiderman, B., & Plaisant, C. (2004). *Designing the user interface: Strategies for effective human-computer interaction*. New York, NY: Pearson Education.

Singleton, R., Straits, B., & Straits, M. (1993). *Approaches to social research*. New York, NY: Oxford University Press.

Solomon, P. (1991). *Information systems for children: Explorations in information access and interface usability for an online catalog in an elementary school library*. Published dissertation, University of Maryland, College Park.

Solomon, P. (1993). Children's information retrieval behavior: A case analysis of an OPAC. *Journal of the American Society for Information Science*, *44*(5), 245–264.

Texas. (2007). *Britannica elementary encyclopedia*. Retrieved from Encyclopædia Britannica Online School Edition, http://archive.school.eb.com/. Accessed on February 12, 2007.

Walter, V., & Borgman, C. (1991). The science library catalog: A prototype information retrieval system for children. *Journal of Youth Services in Libraries*, *4*, 159–166.

Walter, V., Borgman, C., & Hirsh, S. (1996). The science library catalog: A springboard for information literacy. *School Library Media Quarterly*, *24*(2), 105–112. Retrieved from http://www.ala.org/ala/aasl/aaslpubsandjournals/slmrb/editorschoiceb/infopower/selectwalter.htm. Accessed on September 28, 2004.

Waxman, S., & Hatch, T. (1992). Beyond the basics: Preschool children label objects flexibly at multiple hierarchical levels. *Journal of Child Language*, *19*, 153–166.

Wyatt, R., & O'Connor, B. (2004). *Photo provocations: Thinking in, with, and about photographs*. Lanham, MD: Scarecrow Press.

Chapter 10

Designing an Intervention Tool for Students with Students

Jamshid Beheshti, Mohammed J. AlGhamdi, Charles Cole, Dhary Abuhimed and Isabelle Lamoureux

Abstract

Purpose – The chapter describes a four-year research project, the objective of which was to design and develop an intervention tool to assist middle school students in their information seeking when engaged in an inquiry-based learning project.

Methodology/approach – Bonded design method was used to design a proof-of-concept (POC) low-tech Guide, and focus group and Informant Design methods were utilized to develop a Web Guide.

Findings – In creating an intervention tool, whether low-tech paper-based or high-tech websites, different methodologies that relied heavily on the participation of students in the design process were successfully utilized.

Practical implications – The research shows that participation of children and adolescents in designing the content of technology for educational use is imperative.

Originality/value – This is a long-term research project, which is unparalleled and unique in its scope, duration, breadth, and depth. Having access to the grade eight classes in a single school over a four-year period has proven to be a remarkable research opportunity, seldom reported in the literature.

Keywords: Middle school students; information behavior; inquiry-based project; intervention tool; Bonded Design; ISP

New Directions in Children's and Adolescents' Information Behavior Research
Library and Information Science, Volume 10, 295–331

ISSN: 1876-0562/doi:10.1108/S1876-056220140000010050

10.1. Introduction

Today's children and teens have an insatiable appetite for information. Whether they are referred to as the digital natives (Prensky, 2001), the net savvy youth (Levin, Richardson, & Arafeh, 2002), digital children (Vandewater et al., 2007), the Google generation (Rowlands et al., 2008), generation M, for Media, Myspace, or the Millenials (Vie, 2008), or generation "V" (virtual) (Marshall, Dark, Goldman, Hacker, & Smith, 2009), they all have one thing in common — their information behavior is radically different from the generations before them.

Beheshti and Large (2013) categorize the information behavior of the new generation as skimming, multitasking, collaborating, and creating. Skimming comprises checking and viewing quickly, bouncing, and surfing of information (Rowlands et al., 2008). In the context of academic digital libraries, skimming is referred to as "*Horizontal information seeking*" where "people view just one or two pages from an academic site and then 'bounce' out, perhaps never to return" (Rowlands et al., 2008, p. 294). In one study, senior high school students believed that finding information for a school project was easy, and adopted a skimming behavior for reading long articles to find the required information (Chung & Neuman, 2007).

Multitasking is prevalent among the youth. The new generation or the "multitasking generation," depends on "digital juggling" for their daily information activities (Foehr, 2006; Wallis, 2006).

Bastian, a typical 14-year-old, sums up the new generation's information multitasking habits:

> My Dad always gets really annoyed at me when we watch TV together as he says that I should only do one thing at a time, rather than 100 things at a time. It is not that bad, yes I am on Facebook, texting my friends, chatting to people, gaming, browsing the Internet, looking at YouTube clips, but I am still watching the show. (Rasmussen, 2012)

This behavior is echoed by another teenager: "I like to be logged in to my laptop and iPad so I know when something happens, like someone writes on my wall or a photo or tags me. … I want to see it around me … way better than getting a text [message] or an email about it later … it keeps me up to date with everything going on" (Odom, Zimmerman, & Forlizzi, 2011, p. 1496). In fact, children as young as five years old have been observed to be engaged in multitasking (Spink, Danby, Mallan, & Butler, 2010).

The new generation is actively involved in creating and producing information. The success of commercial products such as Facebook, YouTube, and MySpace speaks volumes of the youth's desire to create and distribute information. Teens have embraced wholeheartedly the mobile technologies, which provide them with readily accessible means to produce digital contents in many formats, and distribute them on the social media. Content creation implies collaboration, an integral part of the new generation's information behavior, who shares freely their personal information on social networks. Collaboration and sharing are widespread among youth, both in their everyday life information activities and for their school work. Beheshti and Large (2013) conclude that a paradigm shift may be taking shape, where "brick and mortar libraries replaced gradually with virtual libraries, books with e-books, online public access catalogues (OPACs) with Google (and the like), and traditional reference materials with Wikipedia and similarly shared resources" (p. 240).

Yet, children and teens face obstacles and challenges ranging from determining appropriate terms and expressions for searching, and choosing suitable search results, to deciphering, organizing, and particularly synthesizing the retrieved information. A panel of experts, meeting to discuss the information behavior and needs of the new generation of users, concluded that a research agenda is *urgently* required to investigate the "characteristics and preferences of this tech savvy group that surprisingly lacks basic skills in information evaluation and retrieval" (Radford et al., 2008, p. 2). As information-seeking becomes more ubiquitous, the disconnect between the ever increasing sophistication and attractiveness of the devices or channels being developed to access information (via laptops and mobile phones, or social networks, etc.) and children's ability to actually retrieve information effectively becomes ever larger. Shenton (2008) investigating high school students' information-seeking behavior for academic projects, concluded that information skills "must be taught rigorously." Bilal (2012) suggests that "educating these young users in effective use of digital information tools, including web search engines, is vital for succeeding in the 21st century" (p. 1894).

While the current systems may include efficient search engines to help young people to overcome some of the obstacles, intervention mechanisms may have to be introduced in the future design of information systems developed for educational needs. In this chapter, the authors describe the type of intervention that might be helpful in an educational setting, the methodologies for building intervention tools and report on a long-term research for creating an intervention tool first as a low-tech paper-based prototype as a proof-of-concept (POC) and then designing a prototype web-based tool to help young people with their school projects.

10.2. Research Questions

In the educational environments, the challenges facing the children and adolescents when engaged in school projects may be daunting. In addition to overcoming their limited skills in searching and retrieving information, students may also be overwhelmed with decisions they have to make on relevancy of information to their assigned tasks, and on authentication, organization, and synthesis of that information. In a four-year research project, the authors explored and evaluated the effect of an intervention tool in the information seeking process of middle school students. The goal of the research was to design a tool to assist students overcome the potential challenges that they face in completing an assigned inquiry-based learning project.

The overarching research question of the project is: Can an intervention tool be designed and developed to assist middle school students in their inquiry-based school projects?

The specific research questions addressed in this chapter are:

1. What are the major challenges students face when they engage in an assigned inquiry-based project?
2. What type of tool may be designed and developed to assist students in their inquiry-based projects?

10.3. Literature Review

10.3.1. Current Systems

At the end of 2012, 6.8 billion mobile subscribers had registered with various telecommunication companies around the world. It is estimated that by 2016 there will be 8.5 billion subscribers of mobile technology (mobithinking, 2013a). Mobile technology is so ubiquitous that the US Federal Trade Commission (FTC) updated its guidelines for advertising to emphasis that websites must be mobile-friendly (mobithinking, 2013b). The digital advertising spending is now in excess of $100 billion (eMarketer, 2014). These devices are increasingly used for searching and retrieving information from the web. In the consumer market it is reported that 46 percent use mobile devices exclusively to perform online researching (Lee, 2013). In a study of 1611 participants, who logged nearly eight thousand hours of activity on their mobile devices, 65 percent of activities was for searching for information that began on a smartphone (Google, 2012). These devices have become so prevalent among the new generation that it is estimated that 40 percent of children younger than two years old and 80 percent of those between five and eight years old are using mobile devices, including smartphones and tablets (Kang, 2013). Some researchers argue that the mobile technologies offer a different learning experience from conventional technologies (Kukulska-Hulme & Traxler, 2005), and therefore design requirements cannot be simply transferred from one platform to another (Parsons, Ryu, & Cranshaw, 2006). Regardless of the application of the mobile technologies, whether for everyday life information seeking or for educational information needs, Google dominates the mobile searching with 91 percent of global market (Netmarketshare, 2014).

Studies show that children as young as five years old may be considered "technoliterate"; they are capable of and engage in information seeking activities on the web (Spink et al., 2010). While many systems have been designed for children and teens, Google is the primary retrieval engine for youth followed by a distant second- and third-placed Yahoo! and Bing, respectively (Bilal, 2012). Perhaps one reason that Google has been children's favorite system is its powerful search engine and ranking algorithm masked behind a simple interface. Many of the systems and interfaces designed for this age group do not take into account their searching and browsing skills, and preferences (Hutchinson, Bederson, & Druin, 2005), but a simple interface like Google perhaps at least does not pose additional barriers to an already complex procedure.

Bilal (2012), in comparing various search engines, concluded that each system has its own strengths and weaknesses, but that overall they may not effectively meet the youngsters' information seeking requirements. In an experimental study of five search engines most likely used by children and adolescents, Google, Yahoo!, Bing, Yahoo!Kids, and Ask Kids, she reported that while Google showed the best precision on natural language queries, overall, the precision ratio of relevant results among these search engines was less than 58 percent.

This number may be adequate if the notion that children can relatively easily distinguish relevant information from irrelevant ones is accepted (Shenton, 2008). However, some studies have demonstrated that young users may face some difficulty in choosing relevant information from a vast array of results produced by the search engines (Druin et al., 2009; Enochsson, 2005; Foss et al., 2012).

10.3.2. Intervention

The amount of digital content available for children and adolescents has increased significantly over the last decades. The web is a vast source of information, indispensable or superfluous, on which young users depend for their everyday life information needs as well as for their assigned school tasks (Shenton, 2007). Yet, children and adolescents face a myriad of challenges and obstacles in searching, selecting, retrieving, organizing, and synthesizing the digital information from the vast expanse of the web. In a comprehensive review of the literature, Large (2005) concluded that children encounter problems in selecting appropriate search terms, move too quickly through the web pages while spending little time reading the materials, and have difficulty judging the relevance of the retrieved pages. These observations have been confirmed by other researchers over the last decade (see, e.g., Bilal, 2000, 2002; Nicholas, Rowlands, Clark, & Williams, 2011), who have also pointed out other issues such as reading and comprehension difficulties (Cooper, 2002; Hultgren & Limberg, 2003), spelling problems when searching (Druin et al., 2009), too much or not enough information (Chung & Neuman, 2007), and a lack of understanding of searching options (Shenton & Dixon, 2004). Bilal (2013) also found that many children will find reading and comprehending retrieved results from search engines difficult for their cognitive levels. More broadly, the key challenges facing the youth have been identified to include complexity of information and information overload (Gasser, Cortesi, Malik, & Lee, 2012).

To contextualize the information seeking obstacles encountered by the young people particularly in an educational setting, the authors investigated a number of information seeking models. Many models have been proposed, for example, Wilson (1999), Bates (1989), Belkin, Oddy, and Brooks (1982), Ellis (1993), Marchionini (1995), Savolainen (1995), and Cole (2012) the core of which deals with: information need, searcher's characteristics, the environment, and the interaction of these three entities (Knight & Spink, 2008). Kuhlthau (1991, 2004) proposed one of the few empirical models based on actual field observations of high school students. Designed from the user's perspective, the original model, Information Search Process (ISP), consists of six stages (Kuhlthau, 2009, p. 2587):

- *Initiation*, when a person first becomes aware of a lack of knowledge or understanding, and feelings of uncertainty and apprehension are common.
- *Selection*, when a general area, topic, or problem is identified and initial uncertainty often gives way to a brief sense of optimism and a readiness to begin the search.
- *Exploration*, when inconsistent, incompatible information is encountered and uncertainty, confusion, and doubt frequently increase, and people find themselves "in the dip" of confidence.
- *Formulation*, when a focused perspective is formed and uncertainty diminishes as confidence begins to increase.
- *Collection*, when information pertinent to the focused perspective is gathered and uncertainty subsides as interest and involvement deepens.
- *Presentation*, when the search is completed with a new understanding enabling the person to explain his or her learning to others or in some way put the learning to use.

Kuhlthau's field observation is "an important point of departure for later work" (Rowley & Urquhart, 2007, p. 1163). The ISP model and subsequent studies based on the model are constructivist (Rowley & Urquhart, 2007), and as such their "approach provide perhaps the most sophisticated views on information use so far" (Savolainen, 2009, p. 188).

Kuhlthau introduced a number of new concepts in her information seeking model. She incorporated the concept of time and showed that people's conceptions of information change as they progress through the information problem. She emphasized the affective factor (feelings), and investigated its role on users as they moved through various stages of the ISP. Kuhlthau (1999) defined uncertainty as "a cognitive state that commonly causes affective symptoms of anxiety and lack of confidence" (p. 14). Uncertainty, however, is "natural and essential for constructing personal knowledge" in the ISP, which may require *intervention* that allows users to advance their knowledge.

Intervention in information seeking through various resources is supported by Vygotsky's theory (1978) of the Zone of Proximal Development (ZPD). ZPD "is the bandwidth of competence within which people learn" (Beheshti, Bowler, Large, & Nesset, 2006, p. 143). The lower limit of the zone consists of the tasks that can be accomplished independently, while the upper limit includes more complex tasks requiring interaction with "experts." Kuhlthau's notion of the *Zone of Intervention* is modeled upon the ZPD and is defined as "that area in which an information user can do with advice and assistance what he or she cannot do alone or can do only with great difficulty" (Kuhlthau, 2004, p. 129). Cooper (2002), in her study into the information seeking behavior of children, mentions both Vygotsky's ZPD and Kuhlthau's Zone of Intervention, suggesting that when searching in supportive contexts, children and young adults (Leide, Cole, Beheshti, Large, & Lin, 2007) are indeed capable of moving from non-specific browsing strategies to more focused searching strategies.

In sum, children and adolescents encounter challenges and obstacles in information seeking, particularly in educational environments. Kuhlthau's ISP Model and Zone of Intervention provide a conceptual framework that can inform research on the design and development of an intervention tool to assist the new generation in their information seeking.

10.3.3. Technology Design Methodologies

Designing an intervention tool is a complex task, which may require the choice of a relatively sophisticated methodology. In this section a few methodologies deemed appropriate for designing an intervention tool is reviewed.

In the 1980s, Norman and his colleagues coined the term "user-centered design" and popularized it with their book on *User centered system design: New perspectives on human-computer interaction* (Norman & Draper, 1986). User-centered design originated as a response to system-centered design prevalent in the preceding years. Up until then, technology was designed by specialists with limited feedback from the end-users. Since the 1980s, many design methodologies have been proposed and used in the field of human–computer interaction under the broad umbrella of user-centered design. In analyzing the literature, Nesset and Large (2004) and Large, Nesset, Beheshti, and Bowler (2006) extended the spectrum proposed by Carmel, Whitaker, and George (1993) to categorize the design methodologies, from the least to the most amount of end-user participation in the design process.

Contextual Design (Beyer & Holtzblatt, 1998) is placed on the far end of the participation spectrum indicating limited user involvement in the design process. The process relies mostly on ethnographic methods such as observation to investigate user behavior within their own naturalistic setting. While users may not be involved in all the phases of the process in the contextual design, their work habits are observed in their own environments under non-experimental and normal conditions. Low-tech prototyping, storyboards, and other visual techniques are employed to develop the user work model, which is subdivided into five processes: flow, sequence, artifact, cultural, and physical. Contextual Design has been used in automotive industry (Gellatly, Hansen, Highstrom, & Weiss, 2010), emergency management (Randall, Crebolder, Torenvliet, & Leal, 2013), and in the design of specialized software such as a web-based seismic monitor to observe earthquakes (Aktunc, Erol, & Garcia, 2012).

The end-users play a different role in Learner-Centered Design (Soloway, Guzdial, & Hay, 1994), which is based on the assumption that the target audience of technology may lack "work domain knowledge" (Quintana, Krajcik, Soloway, Fishman, & O'Connor-Divelbiss, 2000) and therefore are "learners." The Learner-Centered Design is informed by constructivist learning theories, using "scaffolding," where users learn by doing and are actively engaged in their work domain activities. Learners, therefore, are observed to ensure that the technology is adapted to their knowledge and learning styles. Participatory Design, first proposed by Floyd, Mehl, Reisin, Schmidt, and Wolf (1989) in the application of technology in the workplace in Sweden and later by Carmel et al. (1993) in a comparative analysis with the American Joint Application Design, requires the involvement of the user as the best qualified to determine the role of technology in improving their work. Low-tech prototypes are utilized in Participatory Design as tools to help participants to communicate with the designers.

The idea of partnering with children to design new technologies is a relatively new trend (Fails, Guha, & Druin, 2012). Traditionally, children's role in technological developments was limited to being end-users, who interacted with the technology after it was marketed. Gradually, children became involved as testers of the new technology such as LOGO, where their activities and reactions to the new software were observed by designers of the system. The use of children as test participants can be traced back to the work of Seymour Papert and his colleagues at the MIT research group in the late 1960s (Druin, 2002). Papert worked with children to develop a programming language that children tested and used for educational purposes. Alan C. Kay along with other researchers at Xerox PARC followed in Papert's footsteps and involved children as testers of Smalltalk, a programming language developed in the 1970s (Kay, 1996). However, the main discussions about involving children in the design teams began in the mid-1990s by Druin and Solomon (1996), Hanna, Risden, and Alexander (1997), and Scaife, Rogers, Aldrich, and Davies (1997). These researchers advocated that while in the past adult designers simply added "gratuitous animations and funny noises" in a vain attempt to make child-friendly systems (Hanna et al., 1997, p. 4), the application of user-centered design principles required the direct involvement of the target audience, the children. Druin and her design team (1997), which included children, developed KidPad as an authoring tool for children. Kafai and Bates (1997) recruited elementary school students to develop a children's website directory. Wilson (1988) relied on children as evaluators of an educational application throughout a formative research design process.

Gradually as more researchers began to involve children in the design teams, new conceptual methodologies were developed to accommodate a more systematic and methodical approach for participation of the young designers. Informant Design (Scaife et al., 1997) was proposed as a framework for maximizing children's input at various stages of the design process. Scaife and his colleagues used the Informant framework to solicit the views of children and teachers to develop multimedia software for teaching ecological concepts. It is noteworthy that the first instance of a child becoming involved in the technology design as an informant was reported by Solomon and Papert in 1976, when the researchers met on a regular basis with a grade one student over a two-year period to observe and discuss her use of LOGO (Solomon & Papert, 1976). During this long consultation period, the child would try to debug the software program, therefore informing the researchers of the shortcomings of the instructions written for young people.

Druin's earlier work with children led to the development of a new methodology, Cooperative Inquiry (Druin, 1999, 2002), which combines different techniques to involve children as equal partners in an intergenerational design team. Starting with simple low-tech design, the team uses contextual inquiry to capture users' ideas, roles, and tasks. Using Cooperative Inquiry, Druin and her team designed and developed the International

Children's Digital Library (ICDL), a multilingual digital library of children's books (Hutchinson, Bederson, & Druin, 2006). A derivative of Cooperative Inquiry, Bonded Design was conceived by Large et al. (2006) to design the bilingual History Trek portal on Canadian history for children. Similar to Cooperative Inquiry, an intergenerational team of adults and children forms the team in Bonded Design to develop new technologies. A mix of Informant and Participatory methodologies is utilized to inform the design, while children and adults bond together to work as equal partners. The primary difference between Cooperative Inquiry and Bonded Design is the length of time and the intensity with which children partner with adults. Whereas in the latter methodology children spend a relatively short time in the design process, in Cooperative Inquiry children may spend years as part of the design team. Several other methodologies for designing technology with children for children have been identified by Fails et al. (2012), including Bluebells where children participate during one stage of activities in a game-like design process, and Distributed Co-Design, where long-distance participation of children in the design teams from around the globe may be feasible through videoconferencing and other means of communication.

Which participatory methodologies to choose depends on several factors, including the goal and the purpose of the design, the type of technology for which the participatory design team is required, costs and efficiencies of the design process, and the age of the children. Regardless of the methodology, however, there is no doubt that children and adolescents have an important role to play in designing new technologies for the young generation, and should be included in the intergenerational design teams (Druin, 2002; Fails et al., 2012; Nesset & Large, 2004). As Nesset and Large (2004) state: "It has become obvious that as children's likes, dislikes, wants, and needs in relation to technology become more and more sophisticated, they must be involved in the design process in a meaningful way" (p. 159).

While developers have strived to create systems to alleviate some of the challenges facing children and adolescents, technologies designed for youngsters that are hardly used by them are a reflection of the designers' failure to grasp the new generation's basic needs and skills. Fails et al. (2012) state:

> When a team which is designing for children cannot work directly with children, there is a danger that they will incorrectly conceptualize who the child user is … This may result from many reasons including possibly a lack of interaction with children, or seeing children through adult eyes. Designers in this situation can fall into the trap of being self-referential and emotional in thinking of the child for whom they are designing. (Fails et al., 2012, p. 119)

10.4. Designing an Intervention Tool

10.4.1. Background

In 2010, a team of researchers (the authors) embarked on a four-year research project to explore the effect of an intervention tool on the information behavior of middle school students (grades 7–9, ages 12–15), when engaged in an assigned inquiry-based class project. The conceptual framework for the research is based on Kuhlthau's ISP model, which postulates that the information behavior of students is complex, consists of six stages, and involves thoughts, feelings, and actions in constructing new knowledge. Kuhlthau's ISP model is based on the constructivist learning theory, which claims that students construct new knowledge by internalizing newly found information using prior knowledge (Kuhlthau, 2004; Rowley & Urquhart, 2007). Kuhlthau proposes that students' information-seeking behavior evolves over the course of an inquiry-based school project. In Stages 1 and 2 of the ISP Model, students use their internal knowledge, past experience, interests, and hobbies and so on to initiate their search. In Stage 3, students search external resources on their topic in an iterative process, formulating basic questions that inform further information seeking (Kuhlthau, Heinström, & Todd, 2008). During this Stage, students attempt to make sense of the information they have collected by referring back to and adding to their internal knowledge base, resulting in construction of their own "worldview" on the project topic (Kuhlthau, Maniotes, & Caspari, 2007). However, this iterative process may also result in anxiety due to uncertainty. As more information is collected, students may feel more uncertain about their topic due to a variety of reasons such as information overload, or lack of relevant information on the topic. The basic principle behind the design of the intervention tool is based on Kuhlthau's Zone of Intervention, the central concept of which is to assist students when uncertainty increases. The intervention may be through professional intermediaries or through information systems.

The unparalleled research project, spanning over four years in one school, (from 2010 to 2013) is divided into three phases, as described in the next sections.

10.4.2. Phase I Study: Observations

In Phase I study, four of the authors studied the factors that drive middle school students engaged in an inquiry-based history project to seek information (Cole et al., 2013), and how these factors evolved over the time period of their school assignment (Beheshti, Cole, Abuhimed, & Lamoureux,

2014). Phase I study was designed to answer the first research question: *What are the major challenges students face when they engage in an assigned inquiry-based project?*

The information behavior of 44 grade eight students (13–14 years old) in a private school in Montreal was observed as their inquiry-based history project evolved during a twelve-week period, from initiation to completion. The students were required to complete the history project during the winter months, from late February to late May of 2011. The project consisted of three components: a thesis statement, the research process, and a final presentation, first in front of the class and about a week later in front of parents, teachers, and older students. Students had to choose a historical topic first, followed by a thesis statement or a research question. Teachers attempted to use the thesis statement as an opportunity to teach critical thinking skills grounded in inquiry-based learning. The structure of the historical thesis statement is a method of utilizing constructivist theory in teaching (Hernández-Ramos & De La Paz, 2009; Tobias & Duffy, 2009).

One of the objectives of Phase I was to investigate when and what type of intervention was required during the inquiry-based project. As per other ISP Model research, our study measured the evolution of the Feelings, Thoughts, and Actions of the study participants over the period of their class project.

The results of the first phase of the study showed that five factors defined the temporality of completing an inquiry-based assignment for these grade eight students:

I. *Goals*: About 80 percent of students had chosen their topics for their inquiry-based projects within 40 percent of the allotted time for the completion of the project. An intervention tool may decrease this decision time for choosing an appropriate topic, and may assist the remaining 20 percent of students, who had difficulty in focusing on a specific topic.
II. *Knowledge and Information Management*: Students were engaged in knowledge discovery, information seeking, and knowledge and information management during the course of their inquiry-based project. Students sensed that they should be more informed about their tasks, seek information, organize the information they had selected; and felt that they should be more focused on their topics. An intervention tool may assist students in broadening or narrowing their focus, guiding them to appropriate resources for their tasks and provide alternative sources of information.
III. *Consultation*: The results showed that students consulted their parents, siblings, and teachers consistently throughout the duration of the inquiry-based project. This finding suggests that students may have

attempted to reduce their uncertainty by using people as information resources. Although children's and adolescents' dependence on people for their everyday life information seeking has been investigated in the past (Agosto & Hughes-Hassell, 2006; Meyers, Fisher, & Marcoux, 2009; Shenton & Dixon, 2003), the act of consultation by students in completing an assigned school task has been seldom reported. Madden, Ford, and Miller (2007) conducted a general survey of students' impressions about the importance of various information resources, including people. They concluded that younger students between 11 and 14 years old rely on people as an information resource more than older students. Consultation is an important factor, which should be considered explicitly in the ISP model. While an intervention tool cannot replace people close to the students, it may provide sufficient guidance to reduce the need for consultation.

IV. *Positive Emotions*: Students expressed fairly positive attitudes throughout their inquiry-based project. It is possible that these students attending a private school had access to more resources, particularly to people such as informed parents and siblings, who could assist them in their projects, than students from lower socioeconomic status (SES).

V. *Negative Emotions*: Very few students in our study expressed negative feelings of anxiety and frustration during their projects. Contrary to the study by Kuhlthau et al. (2008), in this research, the *Negative Emotions* were not dominant. If students had encountered major problems and obstacles, they would have become confused and frustrated (Bilal, 2002; Branch, 2003; Holliday & Li, 2004; Kracker & Wang, 2002; Whitmire, 2003). This may be due to *Factor III: Consultation*, where students were constantly discussing their projects with teachers, parents and siblings, and other classmates. Students may be utilizing parents, teachers, and classmates to reduce uncertainty and therefore anxiety. This "consultation" factor is an important finding of the Phase I study.

A potential limitation of the research is the relatively high SES of the students attending a private school. These students may have had access to more resources, such as parents with university education, siblings in higher grades, and teachers in less populated classrooms, than students with lower SES attending public schools. Therefore, the results of some of the analysis regarding *Consultation*, *Positive Emotions*, and *Negative Emotions* may be slightly skewed. On the other hand, a few studies indicate that personality traits and individual characteristics of students may be correlated to their emotions and to their level of satisfaction with school work (Huebner & McCullough, 2000). In other words, while students' high SES may have had an impact on the results of the Phase I study, their individual characteristics, which were not investigated in this research project may play a greater role in determining their attitudes toward their school and their assigned projects, and perhaps their overall performance.

The results of Phase I study showed a need for an intervention tool: (a) to reduce the time required for choosing a topic; and (b) to reduce any uncertainty experienced during the first three Stages of ISP by attempting to substitute where possible consultations with parents, siblings, and teachers with the intervention tool.

10.4.3. Phase II Study: Low-Tech POC Intervention Tool

Phase II study was intended to answer the second research question: *What type of tool may be designed and developed to assist students in their inquiry-based projects?* Based on past experience, the authors decided to use a participatory design methodology to utilize prior knowledge of students and solicit their opinions in designing and developing an intervention tool.

There is a dearth of research on the methodologies for designing the content of the technology, rather than the technology to deliver the content. For example, in one study, authors described how they used Cooperative Inquiry to form an intergenerational design team with 9 to 11-year-old children to develop low-tech and high-tech prototype eBooks for children (Colombo & Landoni, 2013). The focus of the study, however, was not the content of the eBooks, but rather on its physical characteristics. Very few studies have reported designing contents with children and adolescents. Bilal and Wang (2005) recruited 11 middle school students to construct hierarchical science directories. Their findings showed that for concrete concepts, students' structures resembled those of Yahooligans! and KidsClick!, but for abstract concepts, the structures were very different from those in the directories/search engines. In a similar study, Bar-Ilan and Belous (2007) experimented with students in grades 4 and 5 and found that children were able to create hierarchical subject structures that were not significantly different from the structures of existing Web directories. The outcome of their research showed that even these young children could contribute to the design of subject hierarchies at the same level as the adult designers.

To design an intervention tool, the authors chose to employ the Bonded Design methodology, which compared to the other methodologies discussed earlier in this chapter, was deemed more suitable for the Phase II study. Reasons include:

- *Participation*: Children and adolescents fully participate in the process and are members of the design team. Like Cooperative Inquiry, Bonded Design relies on an intergenerational team, where a natural bond between adults as design experts and children as experts on being children is formed (Large et al., 2006).

- *Education environment*: Bonded Design adopts and adapts certain techniques borrowed from Learner-Centered Design (Scaife et al., 1997) by providing a learning environment for the participants. Considering that the main objective of this phase of the study was to create an intervention tool for an inquiry-based assigned class project, certain aspects of Learner-Centered Design were deemed appropriate to the design process.
- *Low-tech prototype*: The participants in the team (students in grade nine) do not need any special training to use paper and color markers to express their thoughts and feelings (Bilal, 2003). Like Contextual Design and Cooperative Inquiry, one of the initial outcomes of Bonded Design is a low-tech paper-based product, rather than highly developed technological solutions.
- *Feasibility and efficiency*: Unlike Cooperative Inquiry, Bonded Design was conceived to reduce the design time, decrease the cost of operation and expedite the process, while producing a high quality product (Large et al., 2006).
- *Familiarity with the methodology*: Over the last decade, researchers have successfully used Bonded Design to create a web portal for children (Large, Beheshti, Nesset, & Bowler, 2004), which was tested and has been accessed extensively from around the world (Beheshti, Large, & Tam, 2010).

10.4.4. Phase II Study: Method

For the purposes of Phase II study, the objective was to establish a POC outcome. POC is used to verify the viability and feasibility of the theories or concepts in real-world applications. In the field of information science, POC is used to characterize information and communication technology as reported in 20 percent of the literature (Sawyer & Huang, 2007). The POC was used to verify the application of Bonded Design methodology for creating content rather than the technology that delivers the content.

In September 2011, the same private school in Montreal that was the site of the Phase I study was contacted. Students who participated in the Phase I study (described earlier) were now in grade nine, and had successfully completed grade eight at the beginning of the summer. After obtaining the ethics certificates from the University, the students were contacted through the school's administration, consent forms were distributed to both parents and students, and volunteers were recruited to participate in this phase of the project. With the help of teachers, nine student volunteers were selected, who with six adults constituted the Bonded Design team.

The assumption in choosing these students for the design team was that since they had completed their inquiry-based history projects successfully five months earlier they could more readily contribute to the design of the content of the intervention tool.

The design sessions were held over 11 meetings (November 2011–February 2012). The number of students who participated in each meeting varied due to their commitment to other activities. However, the minimum number of participants was six students and four adults per session meeting. All the sessions were held in one of the school's classrooms during lunch periods, lasting between 40 and 50 minutes per session. As a token of appreciation for the students' participation, lunch and drinks were provided during each session. Guidelines set by the Bonded Design methodology were followed (Large et al., 2006):

1. Researchers met a few days before each session to identify the objectives of the session and plan the procedures to achieve these objectives.
2. Each session was led by one researcher, who outlined the objectives and procedures for that session, while other researchers observed and took notes. All sessions were audio recorded.
3. During the first three sessions, student members of the design team were asked to recall the first steps in starting their inquiry-based history projects. Following a modified version of the *Bags of Stuff* technique (Guha, Druin, & Fails, 2013) adapted for adolescents, each student member of the design team was provided with a large drawing sheet with color markers, and asked to represent by whichever technique they chose the entire process of conducting their history projects.
4. During the fourth session, one of the researchers introduced flowcharting as a technique for process design and presentation. For comparative analysis, the student members of the team were asked to use this technique to standardize their representations of the process.
5. These representations formed the basis of discussions in the following sessions. Consensus building is one of the most challenging tasks in participatory design, particularly among children. These challenges have led to the introduction of a new technique, *Mixing Ideas*, where each individual team member contributes to the final plan through a step-by-step process (Guha et al., 2004). A modified version of this technique was used to reach consensus among the team members on the process of topic selection for individual history projects, as well as subsequent steps in the process. Based on the consensus, a detailed flowchart was developed to guide and inform the design and development of the intervention tool.
6. During the sixth session, the flowchart was expanded and critical tasks were identified.

7. Students found formulating a thesis statement for their inquiry-based history project particularly challenging. Hence, during the seventh session exemplars of online thesis statement generators were studied to develop new ideas about the intervention tool.
8. During the eighth session, discussions continued around the students' requirements for an intervention tool.
9. Ideally, following the Bonded Design methodology, a low-tech paper-based intervention tool should have been designed by the team. However, due to severe time constraints, one of the researchers developed a draft tool and during the ninth session introduced it to the team. The team decided to name this tool, the Guide.
10. During the two remaining sessions, the team discussed in details the Guide, which was revised several times in order to incorporate all the team's suggestions and recommendations into the final design.

The Bonded Design team developed a detailed flowchart of the entire process for the completion of the inquiry-based history project after four sessions. For the sake of clarity, the flowchart has been divided into six figures, corresponding to six stages as designated by the Bonded Design team (Figures 10.1–10.6). The *Introduction and Brainstorming Stage* (Figure 10.1) is when students begin their projects by brainstorming and deciding to work alone or in groups. During the *Scope and Topic Stage* (Figure 10.2) students choose a tentative topic and begin preliminary research on that topic using the web, the library, or other resources such as YouTube. At this stage, they have to decide whether to broaden or narrow the scope of their research. Once they have focused on a specific topic, they will conduct a more in-depth research through a variety of resources in the *Research Stage* (Figure 10.3). In the *Thesis Stage 1* (Figure 10.4) students are ready to develop their thesis statement, which is presented to the teacher for approval. The teacher may approve the thesis statement with minor revisions, approve the thesis statement with major revisions, or may reject the thesis statement, during an iterative process. Once the thesis statement has been revised and approved, students conduct more research utilizing various information resources in the *Thesis Stage 2* (Figure 10.5). Finally, students have to decide on how to present their projects and practice their presentations in the *Presentation Stage* (Figure 10.6). The process identified independently by the Bonded Design team based on the participants' feedback has a remarkable resemblance to Kuhlthau's ISP model (Table 10.1).

Based on the flowchart, a draft Guide was designed and discussed during the Bonded Design sessions. The draft was later modified based on the participants' feedbacks and a final Guide (Figure 10.7) was produced in sufficient numbers to be distributed among all 100 students in five grade eight

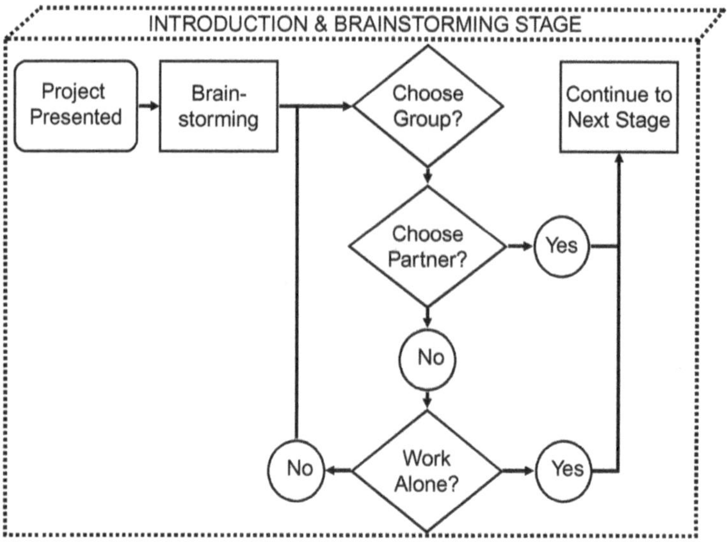

Figure 10.1: Introduction and brainstorming stage.

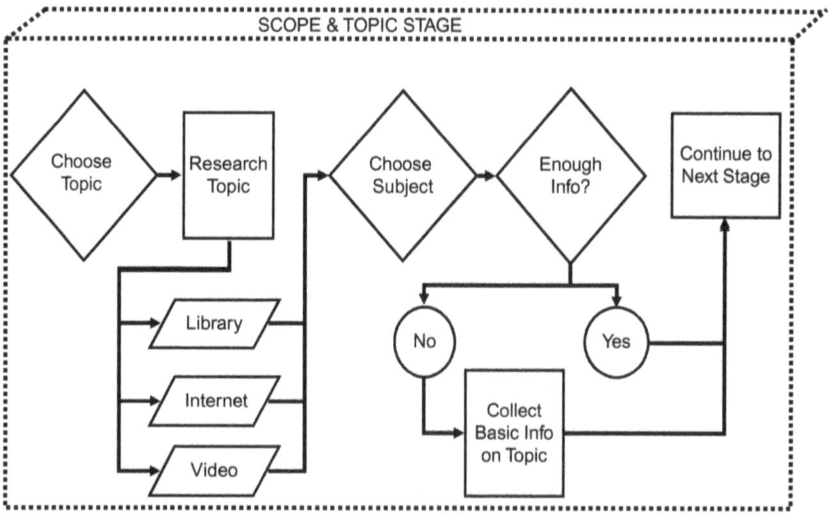

Figure 10.2: Scope and topic stage.

classes, who were just introduced to the inquiry-based history project in March 2012. A letter of consent accompanied the Guide informing students that they can volunteer to be part of the study.

As in the Phase I study weekly surveys, unobtrusive observations, and interview techniques were employed to collect data on students'

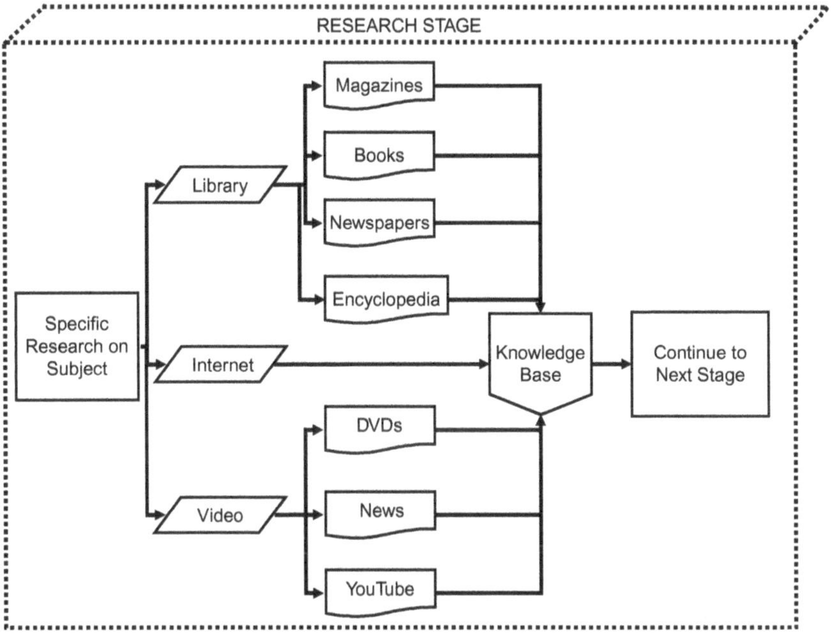

Figure 10.3: Research stage.

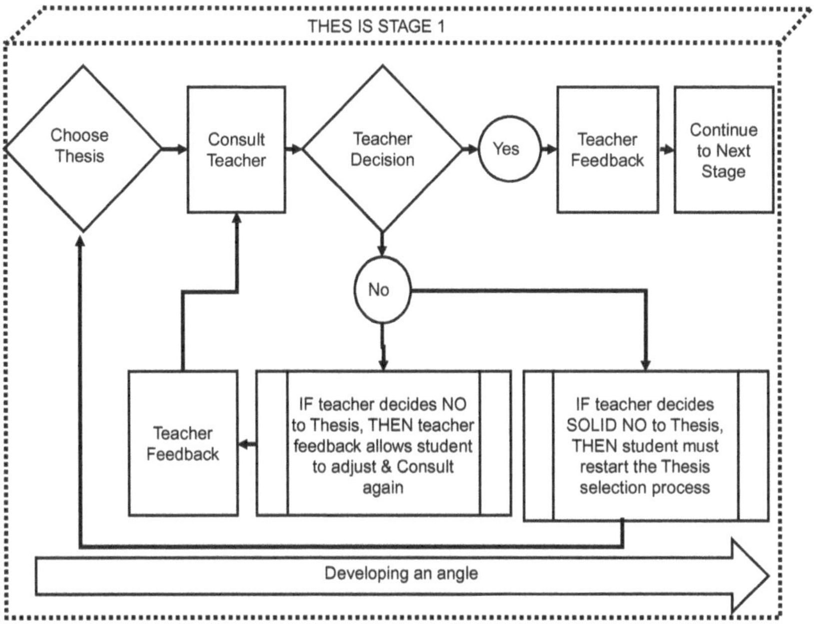

Figure 10.4: Thesis stage 1.

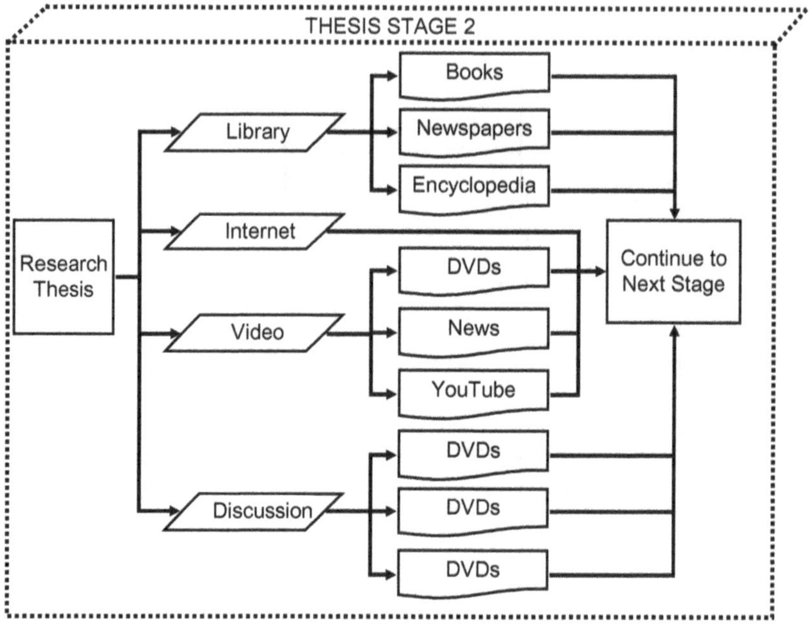

Figure 10.5: Thesis stage 2.

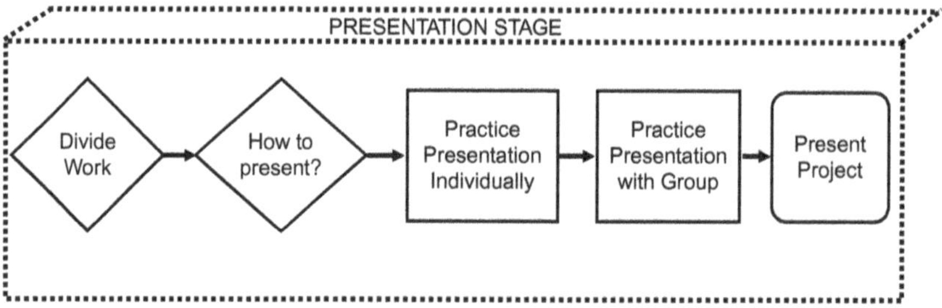

Figure 10.6: Presentation stage.

information behavior throughout the duration of the history project, the results of which will be reported in the forthcoming publications. At the end of the project (May 2012), a survey was distributed among all grade eight students about the Guide, consisting of specific questions about its features and usefulness. The survey was completed by 89 students.

10.4.5. Phase II Study: Results

The results of the survey conducted after the completion of the history project indicate that 12 percent of the students used the Guide in every class

Table 10.1: Comparing ISP model to stages identified by students.

ISP model					
Initiation	**Selection**	**Exploration**	**Formulation**	**Collection**	**Presentation**
Stages identified by students					
• Project introduced • Brainstorming • Individual/ group	• Select topic • Choose scope	• Research topic • Use various resources	• Formulate thesis statement • Obtain teacher's approval	• Research thesis statement • Collect specific information	• Decide on presentation style

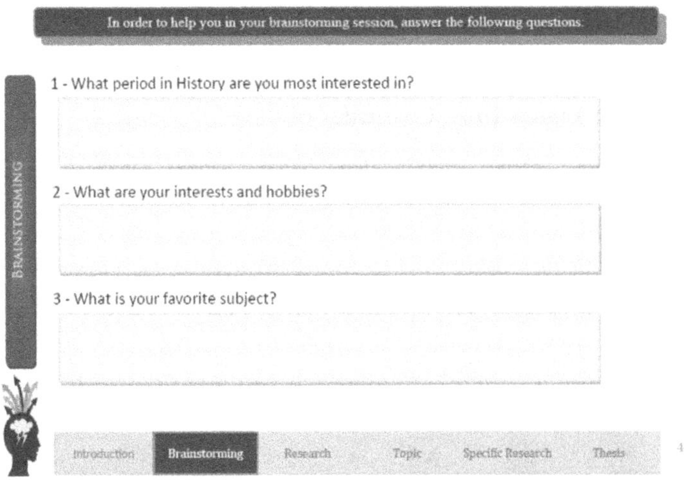

Figure 10.7: The guide: An example of a page on *Brainstorming*.

dedicated to the history project, 16 percent used it once a week, 38 percent used it "once in a while," 27 percent used it only once, and 7 percent reported that they did not use it at all (Figure 10.8). Many students (45%) found the "Brainstorming" section of the Guide most helpful for their projects, followed by the section on the "Thesis statement" (16%) (Figure 10.9). When asked how useful they viewed the Guide to be on a ten-point-scale, of those who had used the Guide, 44 percent ranked it above the mid-point mark. When asked if they would recommend the Guide to next year's grade eight students, 61 percent ranked it above the mid-point scale. Overall, 64 percent of students found the Guide enjoyable.

The responses to the open-ended question in the survey on how to improve the Guide were very informative, ranging from negative to constructive comments, providing some explanation for the usage data. With a few exceptions, many students in five grade eight classes used the Guide at

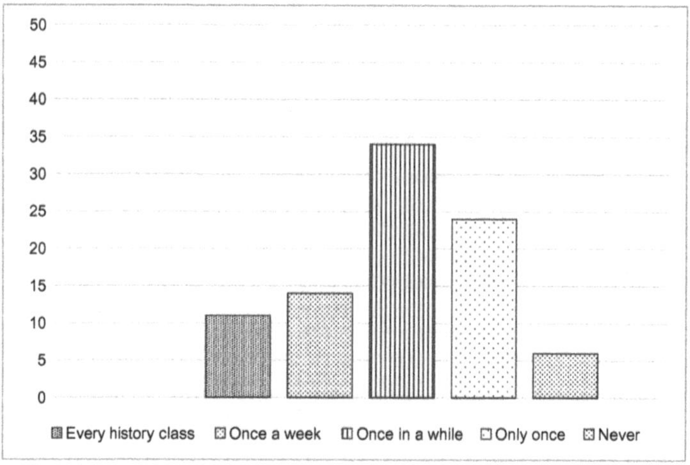

Figure 10.8: Frequency of use of the guide.

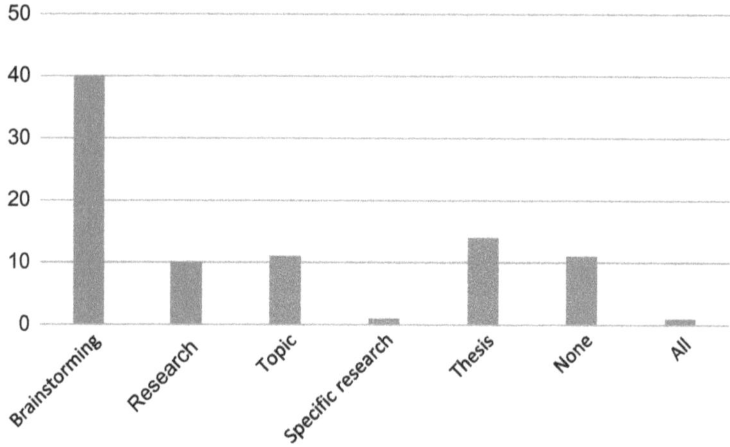

Figure 10.9: Guide was most helpful.

least once, most likely at the outset when the history project was first introduced to them by their teachers. Of the 61 comments made by the students who used the Guide, seven explicitly stated that they benefited from the Guide's section on "Brainstorming," which may have been a catalyst leading the students and setting them on the right track. One student commented "I like having a guide but once I am on the right track I don't really need it. This is how I felt after the brainstorming section of the Guide, it wasn't useful anymore." Another student stated "overall, it was a good jump start to organize my ideas. From then on, I didn't use it much." On the other hand, five students commented about reemphasizing certain parts of the process and playing down other parts. One student stated: "I would keep the thesis areas as a main focus since that is the most challenging part of the project, the research part and brainstorming I didn't find helpful because I already have my own ways of doing things that work for me."

Slightly more than half of respondents commented on more specificity, more details, and more examples that should have been incorporated in the Guide. For example, one student wrote: "It could use more details on pretty much every aspect though useful, it was somewhat vague," and several others echoed the same sentiment: "for the thesis statement section, use more examples of thesis statements of other subjects than the Romans. Overall, this guide quite helped me in this project." The Roman example to which this student referred was used to complement the handouts distributed to students by the teachers. Of course, there were a few negative comments as well: "I wouldn't use it, I would rather have a very detailed outline given to us and we would fill it out. I found that the guide kept repeating the same things." And, an equal number of positive comments: "Its great research guide, no need to improve [it]," while another student stated "make it mandatory for the students to use it, because not everyone used it."

Ideally, all the students should have used the Guide throughout their inquiry-based history project and found it useful. However, a number of student comments may provide insight about reasons for not using the Guide. One student stated: "make it [the Guide] a bit more aesthetically pleasing because it looked boring so I didn't want to use it." Another student wrote: "It was very well organized; however, the majority of the students including myself used their computers for all or most of the project. I didn't find it practical to bring it [the Guide] around with me all the time." And finally one student summed up the sentiments of many students: "I would make the Guide online." For these digital natives, many of whom have abandoned libraries for the Web, reference books for Wikipedia, and hardcopy textbooks for ebooks, the paper-based Guide may have seemed to be an old fashioned tool.

10.4.6. Phase III Study: A Web Guide

Once sufficient evidence about the appropriateness of the Guide as an intervention tool was obtained, the process of transforming the low-tech POC to a high-tech design began. In the Phase III study, a Web-based intervention tool, the Web Guide, was created. The online tool was designed and developed during late fall 2012 and early spring 2013. Based on the results of the Phase II study and students' feedbacks, the contents of the paper-based Guide were revised and transformed to a website. The Web Guide was designed keeping in mind guidelines by Loranger and Nielsen (2013) and the findings of the report by Rowlands et al. (2008) on the *Google Generation*. These and previous studies (e.g., Large, 2005; Large, Beheshti, Tabatabaei, & Nesset, 2009) have shown:

- Children and adolescents, while showing apparent technological skills, are generally overconfident of their abilities, particularly in using search engines.
- Children and adolescents often engage in skimming activities, bouncing from one page to the next, and exhibit impatient characteristics.
- Children and adolescents prefer to view rather than to read a lot of text on the web pages.
- Children and adolescents prefer aesthetically pleasing websites.

The design of the Web Guide was based on the proposed usability taxonomy by Alonso-Ríos, Vázquez-García, Mosqueira-Rey, and Moret-Bonillo (2009):

a) The website should be efficient in terms of physical and mental effort, and response time.
b) The website should be understandable: minimal amount of time and effort to understand the site.
c) All the elements, structures, and functions of the website should be consistent, clear, and memorable.
d) The website should be safe to ensure user confidentiality.
e) The website should be aesthetically appealing, and subjectively satisfying.

In view of the experience from Phase I and Phase II studies, a minimalist approach was adopted in designing the Web Guide, somewhat similar to Google's interface. One study shows that user perception of aesthetics of a webpage is negatively affected by the visual complexity of the page (Michailidou, Harper, & Bechhofer, 2008). To reduce the visual complexity, the use of background images and clutter was avoided, and instead attempts were made to use as much white space as possible. For the purposes of Phase III study, it was important that the interface did not distract the students from accessing the content. The website consisted of a modified version of the content of the paper-based Guide.

In February 2013, two focus group studies were conducted on the Web Guide. As in previous years, after obtaining the ethics certificates from the University, students in grade nine were contacted through the school's administration. Consent forms were distributed to both parents and students, and with the help of teachers eight student volunteers were selected.

Each focus group consisted of four grade nine students, who had completed the inquiry-based history project in previous year. Each student in the focus groups was provided a password to access the website and was asked to use the site for one week from the point of view of a grade eight student assigned the history project. Once the students had used the Web Guide, the focus groups met to discuss the online tool.

Four researchers were present during the group meetings, with one researcher taking the lead to pose questions and initiate the discussions. The methodology consisted of a mixture of focus group and Informant Design (Scaife et al., 1997), where students were treated as "native informants." A semi-structured questionnaire was designed to solicit information about the content, the interface, and the usability of the website. In order to gauge students' opinions and feelings, data on the following elements of the website were collected: visual clarity, navigation, content, control, feedback, errors, and consistency. These categories were based on the works of Lencastre and Chaves (2008) who developed a questionnaire to evaluate the usability of an educational website. The group meetings lasted approximately one hour during the students' lunch breaks. Procedure was as follows:

Session 1: The purpose of the project was described and the objectives of the focus group meetings were explained to students. The prototype Web Guide was demonstrated. Students were given a user name and password and were asked to use the website as eighth graders would to complete their history projects. They were encouraged to write their comments and recommendation prior to the next focus group session.

Session 2: Students were asked if they encountered any technical difficulties, and baring none, they were divided into two groups. Each group worked with two researchers; one facilitating the session and the other taking notes. In each group students discussed their problems, comments and suggestions regarding the Web Guide. The facilitator made sure all students participated in the discussion. After 20 minutes, the groups joined together to reach consensus on major issues and recommendations to improve the Web Guide.

Unlike in the Informant Design methodology, where mock-ups and rapid prototyping are co-constructed with children, in this study the Web Guide was already created. The mix method of focus group and Informant Design was employed for the following reasons:

- Students in this study were fairly tech savvy and had relatively extensive experience with the web, which allowed them to inform the design aspects of the website.
- Students had completed the history project about nine months earlier, which enabled them to inform the researchers about content, learning, and teaching practices.

– Due to time constraints for both the students and the researchers, focus group method was used as a vehicle to seek information about the design and the content of the Web Guide.

As a result of the focus groups meetings, the Web Guide was modified to reflect the suggestions, recommendations, and consensus reached by the students. A notebook for students to record their research results, reviews, findings, and thoughts for their projects, and a calendar for them to record deadlines and events were added to the website.

10.4.7. Phase III Study: Testing the Web Guide

The inquiry-based history project was assigned to grade eight students in March 2013. All grade eight students were provided with passwords to use the Web Guide. Once consent forms were signed by both parents and students, as in the first and second phases of the study described above, weekly surveys, unobtrusive observations, and interview techniques were employed to collect data on volunteer students' information behavior throughout the duration of the history project (the results of which will be reported in the forthcoming publications). At the end of the project a survey was distributed among all grade eight students about the Web Guide, consisting of specific questions about its features and its usefulness.

The survey, based on the work by Lencastre and Chaves (2008), and Zaharias and Poulymenakou (2009), was divided into three parts: questions about the content and its usefulness, questions regarding the usability of the site, and an open-ended question on how to improve the Web Guide. Specifically, the survey was focused on: Visual Clarity, Navigation, Content, Accessibility, Learning and Support, Self-assessment and Learnability, and Motivation to Learn. The 65 usable responses to five-point Likert scale questions have been summarized in Tables 10.2 and 10.3

Table 10.2: Web guide content.

Content	Agree	Neutral	Disagree	*N*
Links to outside resources are informative	68%	28%	5%	65
Concepts are clearly defined	77%	17%	6%	65
Site helped with the project	43%	34%	23%	65
Relied only on site for the project	12%	23%	65%	65
Site includes innovative features	57%	37%	6%	63
Site encourages further research	43%	34%	23%	65
Site is enjoyable	69%	22%	9%	65

Table 10.3: Web guide features.

Features	Agree	Neutral	Disagree	*n*
Ideal layout	78%	18%	3%	65
Ideal text size	87%	8%	5%	63
Ideal colors	84%	14%	2%	64
Navigation awareness	72%	22%	6%	65
Able to navigate between pages	83%	12%	5%	65
Able to exit the site at anytime	86%	12%	2%	65
Simple vocabulary	84%	11%	5%	64
Examples easy to understand	67%	20%	13%	61
Too much text	20%	25%	55%	65
Not enough text	14%	31%	55%	65
Site is free from technical problems	78%	17%	5%	65
Site is accessible from different browsers	78%	17%	5%	65
Error messages are easy to understand	66%	24%	10%	62
Note taking is easy	63%	29%	8%	65

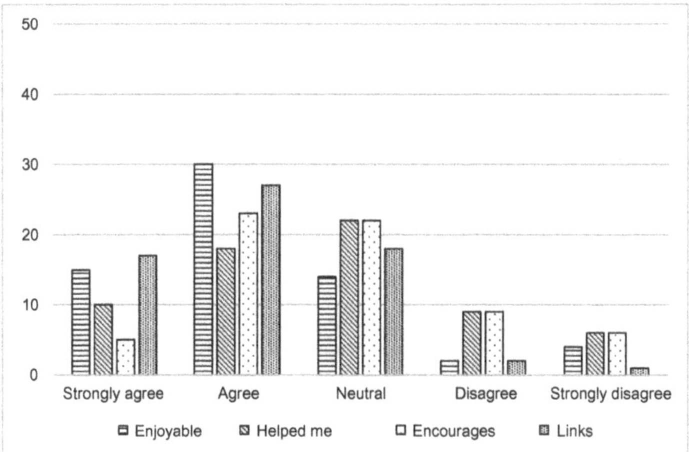

Figure 10.10: Web guide survey.

(Strongly Agree and Strongly Disagree categories have been combined with Agree and Disagree, respectively).

As Table 10.2 shows, naturally the majority of respondents did not rely solely on the Web Guide to complete their projects, but rather used many other resources including the web, and people such as their teachers, parents and siblings, as was observed in Phase I study (Beheshti et al., 2014).

As for the helpfulness of the Web Guide, 43 percent of students agreed, while 23 percent disagreed with this statement. As Figure 10.10 shows the distribution of responses are skewed in favor of agreement with the question of helpfulness. This result is encouraging and further indication of the original POC of the Guide. Responses to additional questions about the contents of the Web Guide show more promising results. As Table 10.2 indicates, 43 percent of students agreed that the website encouraged them to do further research on their topics, 69 percent enjoyed interacting with the site, and 57 percent thought the site offered innovative features. Table 10.3 summarizes students' perceptions of the website's features and its usability. Overall, from a usability perspective, the website was definitely a success, with the vast majority of students agreeing that most of its features are ideal and serve its intended purpose.

The open-ended comments on improving the Web Guide were equally enlightening. Of those students who used the site, 46 provided comments that can be divided into two broad categories: content, and the site's interface. Only 13 students out of 46 (28%) commented on the content, most of which dealt with the provision of more examples on the potential topics for the project, and more links to resources. One student commented: "add more ideas and topics and subjects we can include in our history project." Another stated: "include a research database, kind of like an online library." Finally, one student wrote a comment that, while very interesting and logical, was clearly beyond the scope of this research: "your website offers different resources but it would have been better if we type our topics and then you offer resources for that specific topic."

A wide range of comments regarding the interface of the site and its features were recorded, from the use of additional colors and background images, to suggestions about improving the notebook and the calendar. Four students commented that they wished the notebook would be visible all the time rather than only for specific stages of the research process. Five students commented on the appearance of the site: "add more colors," or "use pictures." Finally, several students praised the site, with comments ranging from "its good" to "personally I don't think the website needs improvement."

10.5. Discussion and Conclusion

This long-term research is unparalleled and unique in its scope, duration, breadth, and depth. Having access to the grade eight classes in a single school over a four-year period has proven to be a remarkable research opportunity, seldom reported in the literature. The setting is like a living laboratory, providing a real-life environment for observing and investigating the effect of intervention tools on information behavior of young students during an assigned inquiry-based learning project.

During the first phase of the study, we observed the students in grade eight classes as they embarked upon and completed their history projects. As a result of these observations, in the second phase of the study the guiding principles set by the Bonded Design methodology were followed to design a low-tech paper-based intervention tool to assist students engaged in the assigned inquiry-based learning project. The intergenerational Bonded Design team of nine students and five researchers met during 11 sessions over three months to design the Guide, a prototype low-tech intervention tool. The Guide consisted of the process as well as the content, including a few examples, which were deemed by the design team necessary and useful for grade eight students to complete their inquiry-based history projects. A survey at the completion of the project indicated that the majority of the students found the Guide beneficial, even though they felt that it lacked specificity and sufficient number of examples.

The Guide was a POC of the viability of the application of Bonded Design methodology to create content for technology for the new generation. The processes and stages identified in the Guide also resembled very closely to Kuhlthau's six stage ISP model, proving further that the application of the Bonded Design methodology to create content is feasible and worthwhile considering.

The lack of usage of the Guide and most of the criticisms recorded in the student comments may be attributed to its low-tech paper-based appearance. During the third phase of the research, the Guide was converted to a website, the Web Guide, with a minimalist interface design. A mixed methodology of focus group and Informant Design was then employed to solicit the opinions and suggestions of students for improving the Web Guide. As a result, the site was modified and new features were added. The Web Guide was made available to grade eight students as they were introduced to the inquiry-based history project. In this format, and with additional features, the Web Guide proved more successful than the paper-based Guide. In fact, the majority of students "enjoyed" the Web Guide.

In both cases, the low-tech paper-based Guide and the high-tech Web Guide, different methodologies that relied heavily on the participation of students in the design process were utilized. In this chapter, we examined the participation of students in designing the content of technology in an educational environment. The outcome was a successful POC low-tech intervention tool, and the transformation of this tool to a high-tech website, both of which were utilized by students for a real classroom inquiry-based assignment.

Today's generation expects to be engaged. Engagement means involvement, which can only be achieved through direct participation of the young users in the design process of new information systems. Many methodologies have been proposed to involve children and adolescents in the technology design process. While the degree of involvement may differ from one method to the next, the basic premise of including the young users in the design process is indisputable. We have had a unique opportunity to extend the limits of involving adolescents in the design process by using the Bonded Design methodology to create an intervention tool, the actual content, for the technology. Collaboration and content creation are two parameters of the shifting paradigm of information behavior of the new generation. In this time of change, methodologies that involve the young users to create content for technology seem to be a natural fit in the information behavior evolution.

Acknowledgments

The research reported in this chapter was facilitated by financial support from the Social Sciences and Humanities Research Council, Canada. We extend our gratitude to teachers and students who participated in this study.

References

Agosto, D. E., & Hughes-Hassell, S. (2006). Toward a model of the everyday life information needs of urban teenagers, part 1: Theoretical model. *Journal of the American Society for Information Science and Technology*, *57*(10), 1394–1403.

Aktunc, O., Erol, B. A., & Garcia, J. D. (2012). Redesign of a seismic monitor using contextual design. *International Journal of Software Engineering and Applications*, *3*(6), 1–18.

Alonso-Ríos, D., Vázquez-García, A., Mosqueira-Rey, E., & Moret-Bonillo, V. (2009). Usability: A critical analysis and a taxonomy. *International Journal of Human-Computer Interaction*, *26*(1), 53–74.

Bar-Ilan, J., & Belous, Y. (2007). Children as architects of web directories: An exploratory study. *Journal of the American Society for Information Science and Technology*, *58*(6), 895–907.

Bates, M. J. (1989). The design of browsing and berrypicking techniques for the online search interface. *Online Review*, *13*(5), 407–424.

Beheshti, J., Bowler, L., Large, A., & Nesset, V. (2006). Towards an alternative information retrieval system for children. In A. Spink & C. Cole (Eds.), *New directions in cognitive information retrieval* (Vol. 19, pp. 139–165). The Information Retrieval Series. Dordrecht, The Netherlands: Springer.

Beheshti, J., Cole, C., Abuhimed, D., & Lamoureux, I. (2014). Tracking middle school students' information behavior via Kuhlthau's ISP model: Temporality. *Journal of the Association for Information Science and Technology*. doi: 10.1002/asi.23230

Beheshti, J., & Large, A. (2013). The future. In J. Beheshti & A. Large (Eds.), *The information behavior of a new generation: Children and teens in the 21st century*. Lanham, MD: Scarecrow Press.

Beheshti, J., Large, A., & Tam, M. (2010). Transaction logs and search patterns on a children's portal. *Canadian Journal of Information and Library Science*, *34*(4), 391–402.

Belkin, N. J., Oddy, R. N., & Brooks, H. M. (1982). ASK for information retrieval: Part I. Background and theory. *Journal of Documentation*, *38*(2), 61–71.

Beyer, H., & Holtzblatt, K. (1998). *Contextual design: Defining customer-centered systems*. London: Academic Press.

Bilal, D. (2000). Children's use of the Yahooligans! Web search engine: I. Cognitive, physical, and affective behaviors on fact-based search tasks. *Journal of the American Society for Information Science and Technology*, *51*(7), 646–665.

Bilal, D. (2002). Children's use of the Yahooligans! Web search engine. III. Cognitive and physical behaviors on fully self-generated search tasks. *Journal of the American Society for Information Science and Technology*, *53*(13), 1170–1183.

Bilal, D. (2003). Draw and tell: Children as designers of Web interfaces. *Proceedings of the American Society for Information Science and Technology*, *40*(1), 135–141.

Bilal, D. (2012). Ranking, relevance judgment, and precision of information retrieval on children's queries: Evaluation of Google, Yahoo!, Bing, Yahoo!Kids, and ask Kids. *Journal of the American Society for Information Science and Technology*, *63*, 1879–1896.

Bilal, D. (2013). Comparing Google's readability of search results to the Flesch readability formulae: A preliminary analysis on children's search queries. In *Proceedings of the 76th American Society for information Science and Technology annual meeting (ASIS&T 2012)* (pp. 1–9). Medford, NJ: Information Today.

Bilal, D., & Wang, P. (2005). Children's conceptual structures of science categories and the design of Web directories. *Journal of the American Society for Information Science and Technology*, *56*(12), 1303–1313.

Branch, J. L. (2003). Instructional intervention is the key: Supporting adolescent information seeking. *School Libraries Worldwide*, *9*(2), 47–61.

Carmel, E., Whitaker, R. D., & George, J. F. (1993). PD and joint application design: A transatlantic comparison. *Communications of the ACM*, *36*(6), 40–48.

Chung, J. S., & Neuman, D. (2007). High school students' information seeking and use for class projects. *Journal of the American Society for Information Science and Technology*, *58*(10), 1503–1517.

Cole, C. (2012). *Information need: A theory connecting information search to knowledge formation*. Medford, NJ: Information Today.

Cole, C., Beheshti, J., Large, A., Lamoureux, I., Abuhimed, D. & Al-Ghamdi, M. (2013). Seeking information for a middle school history project: The concept of implicit knowledge in the students' transition from stage 3 to stage 4 in Kuhlthau's ISP Model. *Journal of the American Society for Information Science and Technology*, *64*(3), 558–573.

Colombo, L., & Landoni, M. (2013, June). Low-tech and high-tech prototyping for eBook co-design with children. In *Proceedings of the 12th international conference on interaction design and children* (pp. 289–292). ACM.

Cooper, L. Z. (2002). A case study of information-seeking behavior in 7-year-old children in a semistructured situation. *Journal of the American Society for Information Science and Technology*, *53*(11), 904–922.

Druin, A. (1999, May). Cooperative inquiry: Developing new technologies for children with children. In *Proceedings of the SIGCHI conference on human factors in computing systems* (pp. 592–599). ACM.

Druin, A. (2002). The role of children in the design of new technology. *Behavior and Information Technology (BIT)*, *21*, 1–25.

Druin, A., Foss, E., Hatley, L., Golub, E., Guha, M. L., Fails, J., & Hutchinson, H. (2009, June). How children search the internet with keyword interfaces. In *Proceedings of the 8th international conference on interaction design and children* (pp. 89–96). ACM.

Druin, A., & Solomon, C. (1996). *Designing multimedia environments for children.* New York, NY: Wiley.

Druin, A., Stewart, J., Proft, D., Bederson, B., & Hollan, J. (1997, March). KidPad: A design collaboration between children, technologists, and educators. In *Proceedings of the ACM SIGCHI conference on human factors in computing systems* (pp. 463–470). ACM.

Ellis, D. (1993). Modeling the information seeking patterns of academic researchers: A grounded theory approach. *Library Quarterly*, *63*(4), 469–486.

eMarketer. (2014). *Digital Ad spending worldwide to hit $137.53 billion in 2014.* Retrieved from http://www.emarketer.com/Article/Digital-Ad-Spending-Worldwide-Hit-3613753-Billion-2014/1010736

Enochsson, A. (2005). The development of children's Web searching skills — A non-linear model. *Information Research, 11*(1) paper 240. Retrieved from http://InformationR.net/ir/11-1/paper240.html]

Fails, J. A., Guha, M. L., & Druin, A. (2012). Methods and techniques for involving children in the design of new technology for children. *Foundations and Trends in Human-Computer Interaction*, *6*, 85–166.

Floyd, C., Mehl, W. M., Reisin, F. M., Schmidt, G., & Wolf, G. (1989). Out of Scandinavia: Alternative approaches to software design and system development. *Human-Computer Interaction*, *4*(4), 253–350.

Foehr, U. G. (2006). *Media multitasking among American youth: Prevalence, predictors and pairings.* Menlo Park, CA: Henry J. Kaiser Family Foundation. Retrieved from http://files.eric.ed.gov/fulltext/ED527858.pdf

Foss, E., Druin, A., Brewer, R., Lo, P., Sanchez, L., Golub, E., & Hutchinson, H. (2012). Children's search roles at home: Implications for designers, researchers, educators, and parents. *Journal of the American Society for Information Science and Technology*, *63*(3), 558–573.

Gasser, U., Cortesi, S., Malik, M., & Lee, A. (2012). *Youth and digital media: From credibility to information quality*. Cambridge, MA: Berkman Center for Internet & Society. Retrieved from http://ssrn.com/abstract=2005272

Gellatly, A. W., Hansen, C., Highstrom, M., & Weiss, J. P. (2010, November). Journey: General Motors' move to incorporate contextual design into its next generation of automotive HMI designs. In *Proceedings of the 2nd international conference on automotive user interfaces and interactive vehicular applications* (pp. 156–161). ACM.

Google. (2012). *The new multi-screen world: Understanding cross-platform consumer behavior*. Retrieved from http://ssl.gstatic.com/think/docs/the-new-multi-screen-world-study_research-studies.pdf

Guha, M. L., Druin, A., Chipman, G., Fails, J. A., Simms, S., & Farber, A. (2004, June). Mixing ideas: a new technique for working with young children as design partners. In *Proceedings of the 2004 conference on interaction design and children: Building a community* (pp. 35–42). ACM.

Guha, M. L., Druin, A., & Fails, J. A. (2013). Cooperative inquiry revisited: Reflections of the past and guidelines for the future of intergenerational co-design. *International Journal of Child-Computer Interaction*, *1*(1), 14–23.

Hanna, L., Risden, K., & Alexander, K. (1997). Guidelines for usability testing with children. *Interactions*, *4*(5), 9–14.

Hernández-Ramos, P., & De La Paz, S. (2009). Learning history in middle school by designing multimedia in a project-based learning experience. *Journal of Research on Technology in Education*, *42*(2), 151–173.

Holliday, W., & Li, Q. (2004). Understanding the millennials: Updating our knowledge about students. *Reference Services Review*, *32*(4), 356–366.

Huebner, E. S., & McCullough, G. (2000). Correlates of school satisfaction among adolescents. *The Journal of Educational Research*, *93*(5), 331–335.

Hultgren, F., & Limberg, L. (2003). A study of research on children's information behaviour in a school context. *The New Review of Information Behaviour Research*, *4*(1), 1–15.

Hutchinson, H. B., Bederson, B. B., & Druin, A. (2005). Interface design for children's searching and browsing. HCIL Technical Report, HCIL-2005-24, University of Maryland.

Hutchinson, H. B., Bederson, B. B., & Druin, A. (2006, June). The evolution of the international children's digital library searching and browsing interface. In *Proceedings of the 2006 conference on Interaction design and children* (pp. 105–112). ACM.

Kafai, Y., & Bates, M. (1997). Internet web-searching instruction in the elementary classroom: Building a foundation for information literacy. *School Library Media Quarterly*, *25*, 103–111.

Kang, C. (2013). Survey: For young children, mobile devices such as tablets, smartphones now a mainstay. The Washington Post, October 28. Retrieved from http://www.washingtonpost.com/business/technology/survey-for-young-children-mobile-devices-such-as-tablets-smartphones-now-a-mainstay/2013/10/27/7e386f3c-3f1f-11e3-a624-41d661b0bb78_story.html

Kay, A. C. (1996, January). The early history of Smalltalk. In *History of programming languages — II* (pp. 511–598). New York, NY: ACM.

Knight, S. A., & Spink, A. (2008). Toward a Web search information behavior model. In A. Spink & M. Zimmer (Eds.), *Web search* (Vol. 14, pp. 209–234). Springer Series in Information Science and Knowledge Management. Berlin: Springer-Verlag.

Kracker, J. & Wang, P. L. (2002). Research anxiety and students' perceptions of research: An experiment. Part II. Content analysis of their writings on two experiences. *Journal of the American Society for Information Science and Technology*, *53*(4), 295–307.

Kuhlthau, C. C. (1991). Inside the search process: Information seeking from the users' perspective. *Journal of the American Society for Information Science*, *42*(5), 361–371.

Kuhlthau, C. C. (1999). The role of experience in the information search process of an early career information worker: Perceptions of uncertainty, complexity construction, and sources. *Journal of the American Society for Information Science and Technology*, *50*(5), 399–412.

Kuhlthau, C. C. (2004). *Seeking meaning: A process approach to library and information processes*. Westport, CT: Libraries Unlimited.

Kuhlthau, C. C. (2009). Information Search Process (ISP) model. In *Encyclopedia of Library and Information Sciences* (3rd ed., pp. 2586–2591). New York, NY: Taylor and Francis. Published online: 09 Dec 2009.

Kuhlthau, C. C., Heinström, J., & Todd, R. J. (2008). The "information search process" revisited: Is the model still useful? *Information Research*, *13*(4) paper 355. Retrieved from http://InformationR.net/ir/13-4/paper355.html

Kuhlthau, C. C., Maniotes, L. K., & Caspari, A. K. (2007). *Guided inquiry: Learning in the 21st century*. Westport, CO: Libraries Unlimited.

Kukulska-Hulme, A. & Traxler, J. (2005). Mobile teaching and learning. In A. Kukulska-Hume, & J. Traxler (Eds.), *Mobile learning: A handbook for educators and trainers*. London: Routledge.

Large, A. (2005). Children, teenagers, and the web. *Annual Review of Information Science and Technology*, *39*(1), 347–392.

Large, A., Beheshti, J., Nesset, V., & Bowler, L. (2004). Designing web portals in intergenerational teams: Two prototype portals for elementary school students. *Journal of the American Society for Information Science and Technology*, *55*(13), 1140–1154.

Large, A., Beheshti, J., Tabatabaei, N., & Nesset, V. (2009). Developing a visual taxonomy: Children's views on aesthetics. *Journal of the American Society for Information Science and Technology*, *60*(9), 1808–1822.

Large, A., Nesset, V., Beheshti, J., & Bowler, L. (2006). "Bonded design": A novel approach to intergenerational information technology design. *Library & Information Science Research*, *28*(1), 64–82.

Lee, J. (2013). 46% of Searchers now use mobile exclusively to research [Study]. *Search Engine Watch*, May 1, 2013. Retrieved from http://searchenginewatch.com/article/2265547/46-of-Searchers-Now-Use-Mobile-Exclusively-to-Research-Study

Leide, J. E., Cole, C., Beheshti, J., Large, A., & Lin, Y. (2007). Task-based IR: Essay-types as query formulation devices for undergraduates researching a history essay. *Journal of the American Society for Information Science and Technology*, *58*(9), 1227–1241.

Lencastre, J. A., & Chaves, J. H. (2008). A usability evaluation of educational websites. *EADTU Conference 2008 — Online Proceedings*, Lifelong learning in higher education: Networked teaching and learning in a knowledge society. Retrieved from http://investigacao.ipiaget.org/edutec/ficheiros/14_NT_Usability%20evaluation%20of%20educational%20websites.pdf

Levin, D., Richardson, J., & Arafeh, S. (2002). Digital disconnect: Students' perceptions and experiences with the internet and education. In *Proceedings of the world conference on educational multimedia, hypermedia and telecommunications*, Chesapeake, VA (pp. 51–52).

Loranger, H. & Nielsen, J. (2013). *Teenage usability: Designing teen-targeted websites.* Retrieved from http://www.nngroup.com/articles/usability-of-websites-for-teenagers/. Accessed in December 2013.

Madden, A. D., Ford, N. J., & Miller, D. (2007). Information resources used by children at an English secondary school: Perceived and actual levels of usefulness. *Journal of Documentation*, *63*(3), 340–358.

Marchionini, G. (1995). *Information seeking in electronic environments.* Cambridge: Cambridge University Press.

Marshall, B., Dark, M., Goldman, J., Hacker, T., & Smith, A. (2009, March 18–20). Dark Web Patterns. In *Proceedings of the WebSci'09: Society On-Line*, Athens, Greece. Retrieved from http://journal.webscience.org/126/2/websci09_submission_28.pdf

Meyers, E. M., Fisher, K. E., & Marcoux, E. (2009). Making sense of an information world: The everyday-life information behavior of preteens. *Library Quarterly*, *79*(3), 301–341.

Michailidou, E., Harper, S., & Bechhofer, S. (2008, September). Visual complexity and aesthetic perception of web pages. In *Proceedings of the 26th annual ACM international conference on Design of communication* (pp. 215–224). ACM.

mobithinking. (2013a). *Global mobile statistics 2013 Part A: Mobile subscribers; handset market share; mobile operators.* Retrieved from http://mobithinking.com/mobile-marketing-tools/latest-mobile-stats/a

mobithinking. (2013b, April). *Websites must be mobile-friendly to comply with FTC's new digital advertising guidelines.* Retrieved from http://mobithinking.com/blog/mobile-friendly-ftc-compliance

Netmarketshare. (2014). Retrieved from https://www.netmarketshare.com/search-engine-market-share.aspx?qprid=4andqpcustomd=1

Nicholas, D., Rowlands, I., Clark, D., & Williams, P. (2011, January). Google generation II: Web behaviour experiments with the BBC. *Aslib Proceedings*, *63*(1), 28–45.

Norman, D. A., & Draper, S. W. (1986). *User centered system design; New perspectives on human-computer interaction.* Hillsdale, NJ: Lawrence Erlbaum Associates.

Odom, W., Zimmerman, J., & Forlizzi, J. (2011, May). Teenagers and their virtual possessions: design opportunities and issues. In *Proceedings of the SIGCHI conference on human factors in computing systems*, ACM (pp. 1491–1500).

Parsons, D., Ryu, H., & Cranshaw, M. (2006, July). A study of design requirements for mobile learning environments. In *Proceedings of the 6th IEEE international conference on advanced learning technologies*, Kerkrade, The Netherlands (pp. 96–100).

Prensky, M. (2001). Digital natives, digital immigrants. *On the Horizon*, *9*, 1–5.

Quintana, C., Krajcik, J., Soloway, E., Fishman, L. C. D. I. B., & O'Connor-Divelbiss, S. (2000). Exploring a structured definition for learner-centered design. In *Fourth international conference of the learning sciences*, University of Michigan, Ann Arbor (pp. 256–263).

Radford, M. L., Silipigni Connaway, L., Agosto, D. E., Cooper, L. Z., Reuter, K., & Zhou, N. (2008). Behaviors and preferences of digital natives: Information a research agenda. *Proceedings of the American Society for Information Science and Technology*, *44*(1), 1–15.

Randall, T., Crebolder, J., Torenvliet, G., & Leal, J. (2013). Applying contextual design to multiple teams in emergency management. In *Human-Computer interaction. Human-Centred design approaches, methods, tools, and environments* (pp. 109–118). Berlin: Springer.

Rasmussen, R. H. (2012). Quotes from children. *Kidsandmedia*. Retrieved from http://www.kidsandmedia.co.uk/quotes-from-children/

Rowlands, I., Nicholas, D., Williams, P., Huntington, P., Fieldhouse, M., Gunter, B. ... Tenopir, C. (2008, July). The Google generation: The information behaviour of the researcher of the future. *Aslib proceedings*, *60*(4), 290–310.

Rowley, J. & Urquhart, C. (2007). Understanding student information behavior in relation to electronic information services: Lessons from longitudinal monitoring and evaluation, part 1. *Journal of the American Society for Information Science and Technology*, *58*(8), 1162–1174.

Savolainen, R. (1995). Everyday life information seeking: Approaching information seeking in the context of "way of life". *Library and Information Science Research*, *17*(3), 259–294.

Savolainen, R. (2009). Information use and information processing: Comparison of conceptualizations. *Journal of Documentation*, *65*(2), 187–207.

Sawyer, S., & Huang, H. (2007). Conceptualizing information, technology, and people: Comparing information science and information systems literatures. *Journal of the American Society for Information Science and Technology*, *58*(10), 1436–1447.

Scaife, M., Rogers, Y., Aldrich, F., & Davies, M. (1997, March). Designing for or designing with? Informant design for interactive learning environments. In *Proceedings of the ACM SIGCHI conference on human factors in computing systems* (pp. 343–350). ACM.

Shenton, A. K. (2007). The information-seeking behaviour of teenagers in an English high school. *School Librarian*, *55*(3), 125–127.

Shenton, A. K. (2008). The information-seeking problems of English high schoolers responding to academic information need. *Library Review*, *57*(4), 276–288.

Shenton, A. K., & Dixon, P. (2003). Youngsters' use of other people as an information-seeking method. *Journal of Librarianship and Information Science*, *35*(4), 219–233.

Shenton, A. K., & Dixon, P. (2004). Issues arising from youngsters' information-seeking behavior. *Library and Information Science Research*, *26*(2), 177–200.

Solomon, C. J., & Papert, S. (1976, June). A case study of a young child doing Turtle Graphics in LOGO. In *Proceedings of the June 7–10, 1976, national computer conference and exposition* (pp. 1049–1056). ACM.

Soloway, E., Guzdial, M., & Hay, K. E. (1994). Learner-centered design: The challenge for HCI in the 21st century. *Interactions*, *1*(2), 36–48.

Spink, A., Danby, S., Mallan, K., & Butler, C. (2010). Exploring young children's web searching and technoliteracy. *Journal of Documentation*, *66*(2), 191–206.

Tobias, S., & Duffy, T. M. (Eds.). (2009). *Constructivist instruction: Success or failure?* New York, NY: Routledge.

Vandewater, E. A., Rideout, V. J., Wartella, E. A., Huang, X., Lee, J. H., & Shim, M. S. (2007). Digital childhood: Electronic media and technology use among infants, toddlers, and preschoolers. *Pediatrics*, *119*(5), e1006–e1015.

Vie, S. (2008). Digital divide 2.0: "Generation M" and online social networking sites in the composition classroom. *Computers and Composition*, *25*(1), 9–23.

Vygotsky, L. S. (1978). *Mind in society: The development of higher mental processes*. Cambridge, MA: Harvard University Press.

Wallis, C. (2006). The multitasking generation. *Time Magazine*, *167*(13), 48–55.

Whitmire, E. (2003). Epistemological beliefs and the information-seeking behavior of undergraduates. *Library and Information Science Research*, *25*(2), 127–142.

Wilson, K. S. (1988, May). Palenque: An interactive multimedia digital video interactive prototype for children. In *Proceedings of the SIGCHI conference on Human factors in computing systems* (pp. 275–279). ACM.

Wilson, T. D. (1999). Models in information behaviour research. *Journal of Documentation*, *55*(3), 249–270.

Zaharias, P., & Poulymenakou, A. (2009). Developing a usability evaluation method for e-learning applications: Beyond functional usability. *International Journal of Human-Computer Interaction*, *25*(1), 75–98.

Index